MARYLAND FREEDOM PAPERS

Volume 1

Anne Arundel County

Abstracted by
Jerry M. Hynson

HERITAGE BOOKS
2015

HERITAGE BOOKS
AN IMPRINT OF HERITAGE BOOKS, INC.

Books, CDs, and more—Worldwide

For our listing of thousands of titles see our website at
www.HeritageBooks.com

Published 2015 by
HERITAGE BOOKS, INC.
Publishing Division
5810 Ruatan Street
Berwyn Heights, Md. 20740

Copyright © 1996 Jerry M. Hynson

All rights reserved. No part of this book may be reproduced or transmitted in any form or by any means, electronic or mechanical, including photocopying, recording or by any information storage and retrieval system without written permission from the author, except for the inclusion of brief quotations in a review.

International Standard Book Numbers
Paperbound: 978-1-58549-333-3
Clothbound: 978-0-7884-6185-9

FOR LEMUEL

A teacher affects eternity; he can never tell where his influence stops.
--Henry Brooks Adams

ACKNOWLEDGEMENTS

It is not possible to explore a question or the past without the assistance of others.

I would like to extend my gratitude to the many scholars and teachers, who contributed to this work. Among them were; T. J. Lawrence, Pierre Davis, James Talbott, Ford K. Brown, Louis Sheppard, and Jacob Klein.

I am particularly grateful to the members of staff of the Maryland State Archives. The absence of their assistance and encouragement would have made this work impossible.

Finally, my gratitude extends to the members of my family for their encouragement, patience, and assistance.

Jerry M. Hynson

INTRODUCTION

In the course of studies in high school history classes I heard the phrase "...going to the courthouse to get my freedom papers." At that time the significance of the phrase made little or no impression upon me. However, it deposited a latent curiosity which provided the impetus for this work. What are Freedom Papers ? What do they look like ? What do you do with them ? These are the questions that I wanted answered.

During the era of slavery in the state of Maryland, the presence of both enslaved black persons and free black persons presented a quandary to the general population. Among the problems to be solved were;
1. How do we distinguish a free black from a slave ?
2. How do we control the free black population ?

Partial solutions to both of these problems were found in the use of the Deed of Manumission, and the Certificate of Freedom. Since slaves were regarded as personal property or chattel, the rights attached to their ownership could be transferred by legal instrument. Thus was created the Deed of Manumission, a legal document in which the owner renounced the traditional rights of ownership, granting them to the slave. This instrument was in effect, a transfer of title in the slave or slaves from the Master to the Slaves. It had to be in a specified legal form, signed by the Master, and two witnesses. It also had to be recorded with either the Register of Wills or in the Court System. The recording agents were required to keep accurate records of such deeds in the same way as deeds to land were kept. It is not clear what became of the originals of the deeds. Some have been found amongst court records. Others have been found in the family papers of the slave holding families, and others have been found among the possessions of former slaves.

In addition to the Deed of Manumission, the Certificate of Freedom was utilized. Manumitted slaves were required to obtain from the legal authorities, the court of county jurisdiction or the Register of Wills, a document known as a Certificate of Freedom. this document stated that the bearer had been freed, who granted the freedom, when it was granted, and carried the signature of the Court Clerk or the Register of Wills. To obtain it usually required an affidavit from a member of the community or local Justice of the Peace. It bore a cost of fifty cents. Thus providing a source of revenue for the state. Slaves were required to carry the certificate and present it to the authorities when requested.

Many such Certificates of Freedom and Deeds of Manumission have survived the passage of time and are found among the collections of the Maryland State Archives in Annapolis, Maryland. Microfilm copies are available for general research. The informationin these documents is helpful in genealogical research, since most of documents give dates, descriptions of slaves, conditions of freedom, and identification of owners. Many of the instruments give the location of the slave, and a brief statement of how ownership originated. In some of the instruments, parentage can be traced since the bearer is identified as the son or daughter of a former slave. e. g. Jenny the daughter of Mary, manumitted by Col. Rezin Hammond.

It is hoped that this book and subsequent volumes will provide assistance to those seeking family historical information about former slaves and slave owners.

The abstracts are self explanatory. However, to prevent confusion, I am giving a sample reading below.

Clarissa - Amelia Warfield - DOM 1 May, 1707; Raised in Anne Arundel County; Age 35, 5' 3", dark mulatto; TBF 5 June, 1808.

This entry should be interpeted as follows : " Clarissa was granted a Deed of Manumission by Amelia Warfield which was recorded May 1, 1707. Clarissa is age 35, 5' 3" tall, a dark mulatto (indicating mixed blood). She is to be free June 5, 1808. Clarissa was raised in Anne Arundel County."

I have also included a summary of laws related to manumission in the state of Maryland .

SOURCES

The abstractions contained in this work were derived from the following collections of the Maryland State Archives, Annapolis, Maryland :

ANNE ARUNDEL COUNTY
1806 - 1851(Cert. of Freedom)
MSA CR 47,242

ANNE ARUNDEL COUNTY
1851 - 1864 (Cert. of Freedom)
MSA CR 47,243

ANNE ARUNDEL COUNTY COURT
(Manumission Record)
1797 - 1807
A 1.
CR 47,242-1

ANNE ARUNDEL COUNTY COURT
(Certificates of Freedom)
1806 - 1807
A.1
CR 47,242 -1

Also helpful was William Kilty, *Laws of Maryland, Vol. 2.* Annapolis: Frederick Green, 1800. MCA 1310.

ABBREVIATIONS and TERMS

Certificate - Certificate of Freedom
DOM - Deed of Manumission
TBF - To be free

[1]Acts of the Maryland Assembly Related To Manumission

1715
Section 22.
All Negros imported past and present into the state and all children thereof are declared slaves for life. Baptism of a slave does not entitle that slave to manumission. Freedom may be granted by means of the last will and testament of the owner, provided that manumitted slaves are under the age of 45 and able to work.

1752
Chapter 1 of the Acts of the Maryland Assembly of 1752 represented the first attempt to establish a legal procedure for the granting of freedom to slaves. It required that deeds of manumission be executed by slave owners and recorded among the records of the county clerk. In most counties, such deeds were entered among the land records.

Laws of Md. 1796
Chap.LXVII
XIII. Manumission may be granted by will by any person or persons capable in law to make a valid will and testament, granting freedom or effecting the manumission of any slave or slaves belonging to said persons, provided that no manumission made by last will and testament shall be in prejudice of creditors, nor unless said slave or slaves shall be under the age of forty five years and able to work and gain a sufficient maintenance and livelihood at the time the freedom given shall commence.

XXIX AND BE IT ENACTED,
That where any person or persons possessed of any slave or slaves within this state, who are or shall be of healthy conditions, and sound in mind and body capable by labor to procure to him or them sufficient food and raiment, with other requisite necessities of life, and not exceeding forty-five years of age, and such person or persons possessing such slave or slaves as aforesaid, and being willing and desirous to set free or manumit such slave or slaves may, by writing under his, her, or their hand and seal, evidenced by two good and sufficient witnesses at least, grant to such slave or slaves his, her, or their freedom; and that any deed or writing, whereby freedom shall be given or granted to any such slave, which shall be intended to take place in the future shall be good to all intents, constructions, and purposes whatsoever from the time that such freedom or manumission is intended to commence by the said deed or writing, so that such deed or writing be not in prejudice of creditors, and that such slave, at the time of such freedom or manumission shall take place or commence, be not above the age aforesaid, and be able to work, and gain a sufficient livelihood and maintenance, according to the true intent and meaning of this act; which instrument of writing shall be acknowledged before one justice of the peace of the county wherein the person or persons granting such freedom shall reside, which justices shall endorse on the back of such instrument the time of the acknowledgment, and the party making the same, which he or they, or the parties concerned shall cause to be entered among the records of the county court where the person or persons granting such freedom shall reside, within six months after the date of such instrument of writing; and the clerk of the respective county courts within this state immediately upon the receipt of such instrument, endorse the time of his receiving the same, and shall well and truly enroll such deed or instrument in a good and sufficient book, in folio, to be regularly alphabeted in the names of both parties and to remain in the custody of said clerk for the time being among the records of the respective county courts; and that the said clerk shall, on the back of every such instrument, in a full legible hand, make an endorsement of such enrollment, and also of the folio of the book in which the same shall be enrolled, and to such endorsement set his hand, the person or persons requiring such entry paying the usual and legal fees for the same.

[1]Laws of Maryland, V.2, Revised & Collected by William Kilty, Annapolis, 1800, Printed by Frederick Green
MCA 1310

Acts of the Maryland Assembly Related to Manumission

XXX. AND BE IT ENACTED,

That a copy of such record, duly attested under the seal of such office shall at all times hereafter be deemed, to all intents and purposes, good evidence to prove such freedom.

1809 Chap. 171

If any Negro or mulatto female slave shall be declared to be free after any given period, etc., by will, or deed of, the manumission person making the same may determine the state and condition of the issue born during the time of service.

If not so determined the condition of the issue to be that of slave.

November, 1797

Chapter 15.
Reestablishes the right to import slaves into the state.

November, 1805

Chapter 66.
Certificates of freedom are to be granted only by the Clerks of the County Courts and Registrars of Wills. Both parties being required to maintain a registry of certificates issued.

Lost certificates may only be replaced upon oath of the loser or testimony of a disinterested and credible witness. Applicants for certificates must prove identity.

Free Negros, traveling out of the county in which they were born are required to obtain a certificate of freedom prior to such travel and carry it upon their person.

Certificates of freedom, issued to freeborn Negros traveling out of the state, are limited to those able to prove their identities and establish the manner in which freedom was obtained., or, prove the loss of a previously issued certificate.

The fee for a certificate of freedom is fifty cents.

November, 1809

Chapter 171.
If a female slave is granted freedom by means of deed of manumission or will, the grantor is empowered to determine the status of any issue. If the grantor fails to make such a determination, such issue are determined to be slaves.
A slave entitled to freedom by means of a deed of manumission or will, having such freedom conditioned upon the passage of a period of time, may not be sold out of state.

MARYLAND FREEDOM PAPERS

DEEDS OF MANUMISSION OF ANNE ARUNDEL COUNTY, MARYLAND
1797 - 1807

Name of slave (grantee) is given in bold; the name of the owner (grantor) is given at the the end of the entry.

Jocky. Henry Hall Dorsey - 27 Nov. 1797.
Jerry. Greenbury Hammond. Free upon the demise of Mr. Hammond.
Ruth. Free 5 Oct. 1797; **Daniel.** Free 8 Oct. 1798; **Levi.** Free 25 Dec. 1809; **Jim.** Free 25 Dec. 1811; **Hilliary.** Free 25 Dec. 1811: Jerningham Drury - 3 Feb. 1797.
Matthew. Free 1 Jan. 1796; **Frances.** Free 1 Jan. 1796; **Nell.** Free 1 Jan. 1811; **Sophia.** Free 1 Jan. 1806; **Hager.** Free 1 Jan. 1803; **Bet.** Free 1 Jan. 1810; **Sarah.** Free 1 Jan. 1798; **Fanny.** Free 1 Jan. 1810; **Rhode.** Free 1 Jan. 1813; Charles Drury - 3 Feb. 1797.
Grace. Free 17 March 1797; Samuel Peaco - 17 March 1797.
David. Free upon the demise of M's Gardner. Sarah Gardner - 12 April 1796.
Issac. Free 1 Jan. 1802. Abe Hill.
Jacob. Free 17 May 1797. John T. Shaff - 19 May 1797.
Libb. Free 1 Jan. 1796. Thomas Wilson - 4 May 1797.
Charles. Free 1 Jan. 1803. **Benjamin.** Free 1 Jan. 1806; **Henry.** Free 1 Jan. 1808 **Beck/Rebecca.** Free 27 May 1897; **Bett/Elizabeth.** Free 1 Jan. 1818; **Henrietta.** Free 1 Jan. 1808; **Sall/Sarah.** free 1 Jan. 1813. Thomas Wilson - 27 May 1797.
Jenn. Free 31 May 1897; Purchased at public sale from the estate of Captain John Stewart. John Shaw - 31 May 1897.
Poll. Free 4 July 1798; **Abraham.** Free 4 July 1808; **Beck.** Free 4 July 1811; **William.** Free 4 July 1816; **Patrick.** Free 4 July 1817; **Patience.** Free 4 July 1823; **Emanuel.** Free 4 July 1824; **Anna.** Free 4 July 1807; **Suck.** Free 4 July 1824. Elizabeth Dorsey - 28 Aug. 1797.
Dinah. Free 10 Oct. 1797. Helen Scott - 10 Oct. 1797.
Joseph, Will, Easter, Mary. All Free at age 21. William Weems - 9 Oct. 1797.
Jacob. 30 Oct. 1797. Free 30 Oct. 1797. Thomas Jennings.
Jeremiah. 23 Nov. 1797. Free 23 Nov. 1797. Nathan Williams.
Charity Folks. Free 7 Dec. 1797. Mary Rideout - 7 Dec. 1797.
Lydia. Free 1 July 1798; **Toby** - Free 1 Jan. 1806; **Nicholas** - Free 1 Jan. 1799; **Sylely.** Free 1 Jan. 1809; **Charles.** Free 1 Jan. 1820; **Artridge.** Free 1 Jan. 1818. Ebenezer Pumphrey - 16 Jan. 1797
Kesiah, John, Mary, Harriot, Nancy. Free 23 Jan. 1798. Jacob Forty - 23 Jan. 1798.
Charles. Free 27 Jan. 1798. John Weems - 27 Jan. 1798.
Charles. Free 15 Oct. 1800. John Weems - 1 Nov. 1798.
Dinah. Free 3 Jan. 1798; **Cezar** - Free 3 years hence; **Margaret** and any of her issue, Free at age 21. Thomas Whittingham - 3 Jan. 1798.
Grace, Sall, Sam, Grace, Beck, Judy, Milly, Ben. Free 10 March 1798. Eleanor Hall - 10 March 1798.
Ben. Purchased from the estate of Anna Wilkens, Free 8 May 1798. Randolph B. Latimer - 8 May 1798.
Joe, Titus, Bet, Issac, Vern. Free 1 Nov. 1800; **Sallie Joe.** Free 1 Nov. 1813; **Jannie.** Free 1 Nov. 1800; **Henry.** Free 1818; **Tim.** Free 10 Aug. 1805; **Bill.** Free 13 Jan. 1818; **John.** Free 1820. Charles Elder - 3 May 1798.
Ned Hill. Free 8 Nov. 1803. Samuel Rideout - 20 July 1798.
Mary/Poll. Free 1 June 1801; **Sarah.** Free 1 June 1808; **Ann** - Free 1 June 1820.
Matthew Robertson. Free 19 July 1798. Samuel Rideout & Richard Fossat - 19 July 1798.
Daniel Boston. Free 28 Sept. 1798.
Peerer. Free 3 Nov. 1815; **Andrew.** Free 3 Nov. 1818. Bryan Williams - 8 Oct. 1798.
Elizabeth, Mary. Free 29 Nov. 1798. John Phillips - 20 Nov. 1798.
Charles Bryan. Free 25 Dec. 1798. Jeremiah Chase - 25 Dec. 1798.
Robert. Free 17 Dec. 1813. Gerald Plummer - 17 Jan. 1799.
Mary Hicks. Free 4 Jan. 1799. John Gwinn - 24 Jan. 1799.
Nelly. Free 15 Feb. 1799. Jonathan Pinkney - 15 Feb. 1799.
Fanny. 12 Dec 1798. Anne Stinchcomb - 12 Dec. 1798.
Thomas. Free 12 April 1798; **Cassa.** Free 12 April 1799.

Valentine, Pompey, Ned, Sarah, Andrew, Nick. Free 13 April 1799. Poll. Free 2 years hence.; Bill. Free 2 years hence. Lucy Dorsey - 13 April 1799.
Polly. Free at age 18; Charles. Free at age 21. Richard Hopkins - 23 Feb. 1799.
Thomas Hall, George Whips Free 15 Feb. 1799. Richard Shipley - 15 Feb. 1799.
John Thomas. Free 15 Feb. 1799. Richard Shipley - 15 Feb. 1799.
Dinah. Free 12 March 1799. William Weems & Jacob Franklin - 7 April 1799.
Anne. Free 7 April 1804 Flora, Liely, Parkel, Charles, Solomon, Katie. Free 20 May 1799; Lemuel. Free 20 May 1808; Nacie. Free 20 May 1814; James. Free 20 May 1899; Sarah. Free 20 May 1811; Sukey. Free 20 May 1812; Henry. Free 20 May 1814; Mathias. Free 20 May 1816; William. Free 20 May 1824; Jeremiah. Free 20 May 1815; George. Free 20 May 1819; Berry. Free 20 May 1821; Thomas. Free 20 May 1815. Eleanor Franklin - 20 May 1799.
Nick, Caesar, Hannah, Sook, Jane. Free 25 June 1799. William Franklin - 25 June 1799.
Easter. Free at age 16; Shallop. Free at age 21. William Franklin - 25 June 1799.
Samuel. Free 9 July 1799. Rachael Watkins - 25 June 1799.
Jack, Rachael. Free 9 July 1799. Elizabeth Simmons - 9 July 1799.
William Coe. Free 26 July 1799 in consideration of payment of ten pounds. William Berbick - 26 July 1799.
Phillip. Free 20 Aug. 1799. Elizabeth Merriken - 20 Aug. 1799.
Peter Hawkins. Free 17 Aug. 1799. Benjamin Lane. 17 April 1799.
Joe. Free 25 Dec. 1801; Milly. Free 25 Dec. 1803; Moses. Free 25 Dec. 1810; Abraham. Free 25 Dec. 1810; Henry. Free 25 Dec. 1820. Eleanor Harrison - 11 Sept. 1799.
Sarah. Free 1 Jan. 1809. Ebenezer Pumphrey - 16 Sept. 1799.
Harriet Cheston, Sarah Cheston, her daughter. Free 25 Oct. 1799. Richard Hopkins - 25 Oct. 1799.
David, Dorkas, Ann. Free 12 Sept. 1799; James, Harriett, David, Sarah. Free at age 21. Mary Harrison - 12 Sept. 1799.
Harriett. Free 16 Nov. 1799. Allen Guynn - 16 Nov. 1799.
Rachel. Free 15 Dec. 1810; Rachael. Free 5 Dec. 1817; Nellie, Samuel. Free 15 Dec. 1799. Mary Norris - 16 Nov. 1799.
Hannah. Free 31 Dec. 1799 Richard Merriken - 31 Dec. 1799.
Mary. Free 25 Nov. 1799. Joshua Toogood - 25 Nov. 1799.
John. Free 17 Jan. 1800. Jeremiah P. Chase - 17 Jan. 1800.
Sarah. Free 20 Feb. 1800. James Wharsie, Eleanor Wharsie, Rachel Brewer - 20 Feb. 1800.
London Freeland. Free 4 March 1800. Benjamin Harrison, Philomon Spencer - 4 March 1800.
Jem. Free 20 Jan. 1800. Samuel Harrison - 20 Jan. 1800.
Lucy. Free 1 Jan. 1808. James Boone - 28 April 1800.
William Collins. Free 1 Jan. 1818. John Hurst - 2 July 1800.
Flora. Free 8 Jan. 1800. Elizabeth Mackubin - 8 Jan. 1800.
Arthur Rogers. Free 8 Oct. 1800. Samuel & Horatio Rideout - 8 Oct. 1800.
James Carter. Free 8 Oct. 1800. Samuel & Horatio Rideout - 8 Oct. 1800.
John. Free 15 ... , 1800. John P. Paca - 15 ... , 1800.
Rebecca. Free at age 29, any children to be free at age 21. Greenberry Ridgely - 7 April 1800.
Patty Butler, her son Bill. Free 23 June 1803. Walter Addison - 20 Oct. 1800.
Nicholas. Free 7 Nov. 1800. Mason Weems - 7 Nov. 1800.
Louther Bruce. Free 1 Oct. 1807. Walter D. Addison - 25 Oct. 1804.
Andrew Pembroke. Free 4 Nov. 1800. Walter D. Addison - 4 Nov. 1800.
Charles, Sukey, & Towerhill Pembrooke. Walter D. Addison - 25 Nov. 1800. Free 1 Oct. 1807.
Robert, Chloe. Free 7 Nov. 1800. Arminta Cummings - 7 Nov. 1800.
Nell. Free 1 Jan. 1801. Rachael Stansbury - 27 Oct. 1800.
Mary & Ellen. Free 1 Jan. 1813. Rachael Stansbury - 27 Oct. 1800.
Charles Stepney. Free 13 Dec. 1800. Samuel Rideout - 13 Dec. 1800.
Harry. Free 6 Feb. 1801. Vivian Pinkney - 6 Feb. 1801.
Packel. Free 11 May 1850. Anthony Nichols. Henry Maynadier - 11 May 1850.
Ruth. Free 2 May 1801; Jack. Free 1 March 1820. Benjamin Basford - 2 May 1801.
Jenny. Free 4 July 1801. James Usher - 4 July 1801.
Murrea. Free 4 Sept. 1801. Leonard Scott - 4 Sept. 1801 in consideration of payment of 5 shillings.

Harry. Free 4 Sept. 1801. Leonard Scott - 4 Sept. 1801 in consideration of payment of 5 shillings.
James. Free 4 Sept. 1801. Leonard Scott - 4 Sept. 1801 in consideration of payment of 5 shillings.
Nanny, Phillip, Adam, William. Free 7 Aug. 1801. Thomas Norman - 7 Aug. 1801.
George Doman. Free Sept. 1804. John Brown - 29 Aug. 1801.
Charles. Free 1 Sept. 1801. Anne Ogle - 24 Aug. 1801.
Doll/Dorothy. Free one year from the death of the mother of the grantor, at her (the mother) request. Grantor retains possession of numerous progeny of Dorothy. Walter Dulany - 5 Aug. 1802.
Sam, Nelly, All Issue. Free 7 April 1808. Samuel Rideout - 9 Sept. 1801; Grantor has power of attorney for Maria Emily Sainte Mayon La Landell, widow of Francis Maria La Landelle.
Jim. Free 14 Sept. 1801. Richard Weems - 14 Sept. 1801.
Jenny, Cornelious, Charles, Nick. All are free when they reach the age of 31. All are former slaves of Charles Carroll of Carrollton. William Hammond - 20 Oct. 1801.
Lucy Scott. Purchased from Joseph S. Poett of Montgomery County, Maryland. Free 21 Oct. 1801. Leonard Scott - 21 Oct. 1801.
Nanny Williams. Age 43, Free 21 Oct. 1801. Thomas Harris Junior - 21 Oct. 1801.
Benjamin. Free 1 Oct. 1809. Walter Dulany - 30 Oct. 1801.
Thomas Hanson, Sukey Hanson. Free 1 Oct. 1809. Walter Dulany - 30 Oct. 1801.
John Gold, His wife Jane Gold. Free 19 Nov. 1801. Joseph Stansbury - 19 Nov. 1801.
Sukey, Matilda, James. Free 5 Nov. 1801. William T. Yeldell - 5 Nov. 1801.
Margaret. Free 13 May 1801. William Kilty - 13 May 1801.
Lucy Scott. Free 27 Nov. 1801. Age 14 purchased from Joseph S. Belt. Leonard Scott - 27 Nov. 1801.
Sarah Green, her daughter Kitty. Free 19 Jan. 1802. Africa A. Green - 19 Jan. 1802.
Milly. Free 1 Feb. 1808, female issue to be free at age 21; males at age 25. John Gibson - 28 Jan. 1802.
Rachael, Lucy. Free 24 Dec. 1801 in consideration of $100. Mary Callahan - 24 Dec. 1801.
Willily, Rebeah, Eliza. Free upon the death of the grantor. Any issue to serve until the death of the grantor, or, if male until the age of 21; if female until the age of 16. Ann Howard - 1 Jan. 1802.
Caesar. Free 25 Dec. 1796. Richard Talbot - 4 Jan. 1802.
Ben. Free 20 Oct. 1812; Eliza. Free 16 March 1809.
Daniel, age 3; Edmund, age 1. Free at age 30. Elijah Gray - 19 Jan. 1802.
Anthony. Free 1 Jan. 1802. William Murray - 1 Jan. 1802.
Betty Stevens. Age 42, free 3 Feb. 1802. John Brewer - 3 Feb. 1802.
Lane, Joe. Lane is free 25 Dec. 1805; Joe is free 25 Dec. 1810. Philemon Spencer - 6 Feb. 1802.
Fannie Osborn, Christopher Osborn. Free 10 Feb. 1802. Thomas Hewitt - 10 Feb. 1802.
Betsy Jones. Free 25 Jan. 1802. Charles Hammond - 25 Jan. 1802.
Samuel Davis. Free 11 May 1802. John Stone - 11 May 1802.
Dinah, William, Nelly, George, Daniel, Phillip, John. Free 20 Feb. 1802. Joseph Court - 20 Feb. 1802.
Prince. Free 11 March 1802. Charles Wallace - 11 March 1802.
Charles. Free 8 March 1802. Nicholas Warfield, Thomas Mackbee, John Dorsey, William Hammond - 8 March 1802.
Ned. Free 15 Aug. 1806. William Ridgely - 15 Aug. 1806.
James, Ned, Fan, Rachael. Free 7 May 1802; Amos, Issac, Caleb, Nan. Free 20 Feb. 1805; Deb. Free 20 Feb. 1805; George. Free 1808; B—. Free 1803; Nick. Free 1817; Sarah. free 1807; Perry. Free 1822; Nace. Free 1824; Robert. Free 1823; Harry. Free 1811; Abraham. Free 1813; Ephriam. Free 1815; Ely. Free 1816; Zack. Free 1816. Charles Hammond - 7 May 1802.
Jacob. Age 41/42, purchased from Robert Goldsbourgh of Dorchester County, Free 3 June 1802. Horatio Rideout - 3 June 1802.
Jenny. Age 14, free 8 Jan. 1810. Rachael Stansbury - 11 Sept. 1802.
Jack. Free 1 Sept. 1805. Mary Records - 1 May 1802.
Hager. Purchased from the estate of the grantor's late husband, free 1 Dec. 1802. Eleanor Davidson - 27 Nov. 1802.
Sussanah, William, Phillip, Henry. Free 20 Nov. 1802. Darnell Bennett - 20 Nov. 1802.
John Joyce. Also called 'old shoemaker

John'; freedom purchased by Samuel Hopkins for $200, free 7 Dec. 1802. Charles Carroll of Carrollton - 7 Dec. 1802.
William Prout. 27 Sept. 1802. William is the son of Isabella, who was purchased from John Hepselius. Isabella having been set free after 12 years of service to McHenry. James McHenry - 27 Sept. 1802.
Peggy. Age 35; free in consideration of payment of 5 shillings. Jerome Plumme - 10 Jan. 1803.
Sussanah, William, Phillip, Henry. Free 17 Jan. 1803 William, Phillip, & Henry are sons of Sussanah. Darnell Bennett - 17 Jan. 1803.
Susanna Hawkins, Rachael Hawkins. Free 11 Feb. 1803 in consideration of payment of 20 pounds by Sussanna. Rachael is the child of Sussanna. John Welch - 11 Feb. 1803.
Frederick. Free 22 Feb. 1803. Leonard Gray - 22 Feb. 1803.
James Hall. Free 15 April 1803. Walter Harrison - 15 April 1803.
William Bush. Free 2 May 1803, purchased from John Addison of Prince Georges County Maryland. Samuel Rideout - 2 May 1803.
Elinor. Free 17 March 1803. Augustine Gambrill - 17 March 1803.
Priss. Free 6 April 1803, purchased from Elinor Bradford. Randolph B. Latimer - 6 April 1803.
Dinah, Sarah. Dinah is free 1 March 1817; Sarah is free 1 March 1820; male children are free at age 21, females at 25. Jerningham Drury - 20 April 1803.
Sam Shipley, Hannah Shipley. Catherine Shipley - 5 April 1803.
Charles, Sam, George, Jonathan, Lile, Peter, Ben, Luce, Esther, Moses, Bill. Free 1 March 1803, 1807, 1809, 1811, 1807, 1817, 1827, 1818, 1820, 1828, 1829 respectively. Male children to be free at the age of 25, females at 20. John Norwood - 1 March 1803.
Ned. Free at the end of six years; if he absconds he will serve double the time of his absence. Nathanial Chew - 6 June 1803.
Samuel. Free 28 Jan. 1803. Richard Chaney - 28 Jan. 1803.
Will Frost. Free 5 July 1803. John Brice - 5 July 1803.
Jane. Free 12 Jan. 1803. **Poll.** Free 1 Jan. 1807; **Anne.** Free 9 July 1803. John Weems - 9 July 1803.
Nick. A second instrument recorded to remove a cloud upon the original, which was recorded 30 May 1870. Thomas Bond - 10 July 1803.
Stephen Matthews. Age 23, TBF 8 Aug. 1803 Nicholas Matthews - 8 Aug. 1803.
Jeremiah Tannert. Jeremiah is the son of Peggy, a slave of Dr. Scott. TBF 30 Aug. 1803. Dr. Upton Scot.
Maria & her female child, age 1. TBF 1 Sept. 1808. Henry Johnson.
Aaron. TBF 1 Jan. 1814. William Weems - 23 Aug. 1803.
John Wilkes. TBF 9 March 1804. Arthur Shaff - 16 Sept. 1803.
Tom. TBF 30 Oct. 1803. Howard Duvall - 30 Oct. 1803.
Henny. TBF 25 Dec. 1804. **Ann**, age 5, TBF 25 Dec. 1816; **Mary**, age 3, TBF 25 Dec. 1818; **Sarah**, age 1 month, TBF 25 Dec. 1821 Francis Hancock - 9 Aug. 1803.
Frank, Jack, Dick, Cato, TBF 24 Sept. 1807; **Andrew, John, Cate, Cille, Henny**, TBF 24 Sept. 1810; **Moses, Solomon**, TBF 24 Sept. 1820; **Aggy**, TBF 24 Sept. 1809; **Henny**, TBF 24 Sept. 1811; **Charlotte**, TBF 24 Sept. 1824; **Bet**, TBF 24 March 1825. Nicholas Merriweather - 24 Sept. 1803.
Charles, Will. TBF 8 Sept. 1803; **Nead.** TBF 25 Dec., 1813; **Grace.** TBF 25 Dec. 1818; **Robert.** TBF 25 Dec. 1814; **Charety**, TBF 25 Dec. 1821; **Kitty**, TBF 25 Dec. 1817; **Anthony**, TBF 25 Dec. 1822; **Jack**, TBF 25 Dec. 1822, **Fanny.** TBF 25 Dec. 1822. David Weems - 8 Sept. 1803.
Grace & son Charles. TBF 3 Dec. 1803. Eilza Gassoway - 3 Dec. 1803.
Abraham Gaither, Lucy Gaither. Abraham TBF 1810, Lucy TBF 1813. Charles Dorsey - 1 Oct. 1803.
Harry. TBF 13 Dec. 1803. Niman Pinkney - 13 Dec. 1803.
Samuel Haywood. TBF 11 Jan. 1804. Thomas Folks - 11 Jan. 1804.
Polly Prout. TBF 19 Jan. 1804. William Prout - 19 Jan. 1804.
Beck. Recorded 27 Jan. 1804. TBF 29 July 1803. Margaret Sprigg - 29 July 1803.
Jacob. TBF 17 Jan. 1804. Elizabeth Merriken - 17 Jan. 1804.
Jenny. TBF 22 Feb. 1804. Rebecca Davidsson - 22 Feb. 1804.
Ned, Jason, Moses, Betty, Ruth, Valentine, Pol. TBF 13 April 1804. Rezin Hammond - 13 April 1804.
Rachel & child named Dinnah. TBF 10 April 1804. Rezin Hammond - 10 April 1804.
Charity. TBF 7 March 1804, Joseph Evans - 7 March 1804.

Poll & her child named Poll. recorded 21 March 1804. TBF 2 Nov. 1803. Phillip Hammond, 2 Nov. 1803.
William. TBF 17 April 1804. David Weems - 17 April 1804.
Joan. Free 2 May 1804. Richard Harwood - 2 May 1804.
Hariott. TBF 21 May 1804. Grace Hammens - 21 May 1804.
Henry. Free 1 Jan. 1815. William Weems - 7 May 1804.
Cassandra/ Milly. TBF 30 May 1804, William Brown - 30 April 1804.
Eleanor. TBF 17 March 1804. Gideon White - 17 March 1804.
Dick. TBF 15 June 1807. Seth Swetzer - 15 June 1807.
Nace. TBF 31 May 1804. John of Jones - 30 May 1804.
Richard Prout. TBF 31 May 1804. William Prout - 31 May 1804.
Nathanial Allen. TBF 6 June 1803. Purchased from Prince George's County Court. Richard Higgins - 6 June 1803.
Pender & his son John. TBF 17 April 1804; purchased from the estate of the late Charles Stewart. William Stewart - 17 April 1804.
Rachael Harris, David Harris, her son. TBF 4 April 1804. Robert Wallace - 4 April 1804.
Nace Snowden. TBF 3 Aug. 1804 provided grantor receive payment of $300 before release date. Mary Marshall - 3 Aug. 1804.
Subbro. TBF 17 July 1804. Thomas Lewis - 17 July 1804.
Priss. TBF 31 July 1804. Joseph Jenifer - 31 July 1804.
Lucy. TBF 23 Aug. 1804. Lucy & Charles Brewer as administrators for Charles MacCubbin - 23 Aug. 1804.
Charles & wife Sal or Sarah. TBF 3 June 1803. John Eager Howard - 3 June 1804.
Jenny, Kinoe, & Rosetta Drummer. TBF 18 Sept. John Hoskin Stone - 18 Sept. 1804.
Rachel & sons John, George. TBF 24 Aug. 1804. Archibald Golden - 24 Aug. 1804.
Benjamin Drummer, James Drummer, his son. Benjamin TBF 27 Sept. 1806, James TBF 27 Sept. 1810. John Hoskin Stone - 27 Sept. 1804.
Hannah. TBF 13 Nov. 1804. Margaret Sprigg - 13 Nov. 1804.
Nancy, Elizabeth, John, Alexander. TBF 13 Nov. 1804. William Reynolds - 17 Nov. 1804. Elizabeth & Nancy were purchased from Daniel of Saint Thomas Jenifer.

Reynolds subsequently married Elizabeth, acknowledging John and Alexander to be his children.
Easter, her children Anne & Betsy. TBF upon the death of the grantor. John Brown - 19 Nov. 1804.
Jack Richardson. TBF 30 Nov. 1804. Mary Rideout - 30 Nov. 1804.
Jack & his wife Nele. TBF 23 Jan. 1805. Thomas Worthington Howard - 23 Jan. 1805.
Mazey, Sukey, Rousby, Major, Levi, Tom. TBF 9 Feb. 1805. Leonard Scott - 9 Feb. 1805.
John Boone. Purchased from William Stockett, TBF 19 Feb. 1805. Joseph Court - 19 Feb. 1805.
Henny. TBF 25 Dec. 1805; Nace. TBF 25 Dec. 1807; Dinah & Sussanna. TBF 25 Dec. 1806; John. TBF 25 Dec. 1815; Thomas. TBF 25 Dec. 1820; James. TBF 25 Dec. 1823; Harny. TBF 25 Dec. 1825; Sarah. TBF 25 Dec. 1827; Henry. TBF 25 Dec. 1829; Ann. TBF 25 Dec. 1829; Mary. TBF 25 Dec. 1830; Harriett. TBF 25 Dec. 1831; Betsy. TBF 25 Dec. 1822; John. TBF 25 Dec. 1824; Samuel. TBF 25 Dec. 1826. Charles Pettibone - 26 Jan. 1805.
Nancy Mahoney, her children, Annie & Charles. TBF 1 March 1806; Nan, Caesar, Kunti, TBF 1 Feb. 1806; Chance age 10, TBF 1813; Lucy age 8, TBF 1815; Caesar age 6, TBF 1822; Betsy age 5, TBF 1817; Honor age 2 TBF 1819. Charles Carroll of Carrollton - 11 March 1800.
Eleanor Ross. TBF 14 March 1806. Sarah Edwards - 14 March 1806.
John Jones. TBF 8 April 1806. Charles Carroll of Carrollton - 8 April 1806.
Lib. TBF 15 April 1812; Letty Gray, TBF 19 April 1821; Eliza Gray, TBF 6 April 1806; Kitty Gray, TBF 6 April 1806. John Brice - 6 April 1806.
George Martin. Age 20. TBF 20 March 1815. Seth Sweetser - 20 March 1815.
Nacie. TBF 28 May 1806 in consideration of payment of seventy-five pounds. Sarah Marshall - 28 May 1806.
James. Sold to Peter Hagner of Washington, D. C. to serve from 10 April 1806 until 1 Oct. 1810. TBF 1 Oct. 1810. Elisha Harrison - 8 May 1806.
Sarah Harrison. TBF 27 June 1806. Issac Harrison - 27 June 1806.
Nanny. Age 26. TBF 26 July 1806 in consideration of payment of 5 shillings. Mary Wallace - 26 July 1806.
Nan. TBF 30 July 1806. Margaret Bulger, 30 April 1806.

Libby. Purchased from the estate of Thomas Wilson, TBF 9 July 1806. Thomas Monroe - 9 July 1806.
Henry Foote. TBF 19 Aug. 1806 in consideration of payment of 12 pounds, ten shillings, 3 pence. James Boothe - 19 Aug. 1806.
Tom Hall. TBF 20 July 1806. Edward & Mordica Hall - 20 July 1806.
James Richardson. Free 8 Jan. 1807. Horatio Rideout - 8 Jan. 1807.
Esther Wheeler. TBF 14 Jan. 1807. Jocky is the former slave of Henry Hall Dorsey. (See 1st. entry). Esther is identified as his daughter and former property of Aquila Pomphrey. Jocky Wheeler - 14 Jan. 1807.
Nacy. TBF 1 Oct. 1817. Thomas Morton - 3 Nov. 1806.
Issac Oliver, Lucy Oliver, Rachael Oliver, Elizabeth Oliver, Jacob Oliver. TBF 17 Nov. 1805. Elizabeth Oliver - 17 Nov. 1805.
Dick Burley, Daphne, Lewis, Lucy, William, Mary. Susanna Lane - 2 Nov. 1806.
Jenny. TBF 17 Oct. 1806. John Cord - 17 Oct. 1806.
Benjamin. Age 15. TBF 25 June 1820. Nicholas Merriweather - 6 Feb. 1807.
Cyrus. TBF 20 Nov. 1819. Nicholas Merriweather - 6 Feb. 1807.
Rachel Warfield. TBF 4 April 1807. Bani Warfield - 4 April 1807.
Moses Davis. Age 44. TBF 21 April 1807. William Brewer - 21 April 1807.
John Green. TBF 13 April 1807. John is the husband of Betty, "a black woman." Betty Green - 13 April 1807.
Sussanna Smith. age 20, TBF 15 May 1820. John Smith, 15 May 1807.
Jane. TBF 23 March 1807 in consideration of payment of $110 from Mr. John Donalson. Richard Merriken, 27 March 1807.
Lydia. TBF 9 May 1807. William Murray, 9 May 1807.
Nelly. age 16, TBF 5 May 1807. Sarah Edwards, 5 May 1807.
Jude/Juda. TBF 1 May 1807 in consideration of payment of $5. Richard Weedon, 1 May 1807.
Charles. age 35, TBF after the year 1823. Henry Duvall, 18 May 1807.
Samuel. age 38, TBF after the year 1822. John Merriken, 18 May 1807.
Bett, William, James, Sarah, Thomas. TBF 30 March 1807. John Chew Thomas, 30 March 1807.
Rachel & Rebecca Williams. TBF May 1816, male offspring of Rachel free at age 25, females at age 21. Thomas Elms, 15 June 1807.
Dinah. TBF 8 years from 1 Jan. 1805. William Weems, 10 June 1807.
Peter. TBF 29 Jan. 1807. Joshua Penn, Joseph Penn, Rachel Penn, Mary Penn, Sarah Danielson, Charles Danielson, 29 Jan. 1807.

CERTIFICATES OF FREEDOM
1810 - 1843

Dinah. Charles Pettibone. Certificate issued 22 Jan. 1811. Scar on left chin.
Fanny. No grantor is named. Certificate issued 27 Nov. 1810. Age about 22, 5', dark complexion, raised in AA Co. Freedom commenced 25 Dec. 1810.
Hilliary. DOM recorded by Abel Hills 5 Nov. 1810. Age about 24, 5' 6", dark complexion, small scar on forehead, raised in AA Co.
Samuel Hawkins. Born free and raised in AA Co. Certificate issued 22 Oct. 1810. Age about 16, 5' 3, brownish complexion.
Jack. No grantor named. Certificate issued 18 Feb. 1805. TBF 23 Jan. 1805. Age is about 35, 5' 7", small scar on right eyebrow, yellow complexion.
James Jackson. DOM recorded by Mary, Samuel, and Horatio Rideout 7 Aug. 1807. Certificate issued 19 Dec. 1807. Age about 26, 5' 6", bright mulatto."
Nicholas Matthews. Born free and raised in AA Co. Certificate issued 17 Dec. 1810. Age about 22, 5' 4", dark complexion.
Sussanna. DOM recorded by Charles Pettibone 22 Jan. 1811. Certificate issued 26 Jan. 1811. Certificate issued 26 Jan. 1805. Age about 28, 5' 8", dark complexion, raised in AA Co.
Wappion. DOM recorded by Francis Thekells 1 Feb. 1811. Certificate issued 10 Jan. 1811. Freedom began 1 Jan. 1811. Age about 40, 5' 5", brown complexion, raised in AA Co.
William. Born free and raised in AA Co. Certificate issued 10 Dec. 1807. Age 13, 5' mulatto.
Samuel Allen. DOM recorded by Richard

Cheney 8 Jan. 1803. Certificate issued 6 March 1811. Age about 33, 5' 10", full eyes, scar in the middle of forehead.
Peter. DOM recorded 26 March 1805 by William Weems. Certificate issued 20 March 1811. Dark complexion, 5' 7", age about 34, scars on left wrist & left forehead.
Henry Turner. Freeborn, raised in AA Co. Certificate issued 25 March 1811. mulatto, age 24, 5' 10", missing first joint little finger left hand.
Philis. DOM recorded by Eleanor Hall 10 March 1798. Certificate issued 27 March 1811. Dark complexion, 5' 1", small scar on left arm, age about 21, raised in AA Co.
Richard Savoy. DOM recorded by Daniel of St. Thomas Jennifer 13 April 1811. Certificate issued 14 April 1790; dark complexion, 5' '6", small scar on left-hand, age about 25.
Margaret Bladen. DOM recorded by Charles Wallace 12 Jan. 1811. Certificate issued 13 April 1811 mulatto, 5' 4", scar under right eye, lame in right leg, about 45 years old.
John Brown. Freeborn. Certificate issued 15 April 1811. Age about 21, 5' 5 1/2", dark complexion, crooked little finger on left hand, raised in AA Co.
James. DOM recorded by Jerningham Drury 3 Feb. 1797. Certificate issued 16 April 1811. 5' 7", about 26 dark complexion, small scar on left eyebrow, raised in AA Co.
Jerry Pepper. DOM recorded by David Robinson 25 Jan. 1791. Age about 73, 5' 3", dark complexion, pockmarked face, raised in AA Co.
Richard Kyer. Born free. Certificate issued 25 April 1811. About 17 years old, 5' 6", dark complexion, raised in AA Co.
Mary Folks. DOM recorded by Mary, Samuel, and Horatio Rideout 7 Aug. 1807. Certificate issued 29 April 1811. Age about 23, bright mulatto, 5' 3", raised in AA Co.
Charity Folks. DOM recorded by Mary, Samuel, and Horatio Rideout 7 Aug. 1807. Certificate issued 29 April 1811. Age about 52, 5'4", bright mulatto, raised in AA Co.
Harriet Calder. DOM recorded by Mary, Samuel, and Horatio Rideout 7 Aug. 1807. Certificate issued 29 April 1811. Age about 30, bright mulatto, 5' 1".
Nelly. Free born, raised in AA Co. Certificate issued 25 May 1811. Mulatto, age 23, 5' 1", scar over right eye.
Nelly. DOM recorded by Samuel Rideout 29 May 1811. Certificate issued 29 May 1811. Age about 48, dark complexion, 5' 1", thick lips, small scar on left side of mouth, raised in AA Co.
Catherine. DOM recorded by William Wilkins 3 March 1790. Certificate issued 31 May 1811. Age about 45, about 5' 2", freedom commenced 9 Feb. 1795, raised in AA Co.
Dinah. Freeborn. Certificate issued 1 June 1811 Age 23, 4' 10", scar on left arm, dark complexion, raised in AA Co.
Rachel Savoy. Free born, raised in AA Co. Certificate issued 27 June 1811, age about 14 years, dark complexion, 4' 8".
Priss. DOM recorded by Edward Timmins 21 May 1795. Certificate issued 24 June 1811, dark complexion, age about 22, 5' 3", small scar left arm, raised in AA Co.
Joe. DOM recorded by Philemon Spencer 6 Feb. 1802. Certificate issued 13 July 1811. Dark complexion, age about 32, 5' 7", small scar right cheek, and on side of left eye.
Polly. Freeborn. Certificate issued 23 July 1811, Dark complexion, 5' 5", scar on right arm, raised in AA Co.
James. Freeborn. Certificate issued 23 July 1811. Age 12, light complexion, 5', raised in AA Co.
Nelly. Freeborn and raised in AA Co. Certificate issued 23 July 1811. Age about 17, light complexion, 5' 1 1/2", small mole on nose.
Priscilla. Freeborn and raised in AA Co. Certificate issued 23 July 1811. Light complexion, 5' 3", small mole on her head.
Plina. Freeborn, raised in AA Co. Certificate issued 26 July 1811. Age about 30, dark complexion, 5', missing upper front tooth.
Joshua Toogood. Freeborn, raised in AA Co. Certificate issued Aug. 1811. About age 22, dark complexion, 5' 7."
Harry Mercer. DOM recorded by John Rideout 15 Nov. 1791. Certificate issued 2 Aug. 1811. Age about 27, 5 5 1/2", raised in AA Co.
Nancy Price. Certificate issued 7 Aug. 1811. Freeborn, raised in AA Co. Age about 17, 5' 4", dark complexion, small scar on left arm.
Thomas Fisher. Certificate issued 19 Aug. 1811. Freeborn and raised in AA Co. About 22, 5' 7 1/2", dark complexion, small scar above right eye.
Thomas Cook. Certificate issued 22 Aug.

1811. DOM recorded by Sarah Cord 18 Feb. 1811. Age about 42, 5' 6 1/2", black complexion.
Frederick Prout. Certificate issued 2 Sept. 1811. Freeborn, raised in AA Co. About 21, 5' 7 1/2", dark mulatto, stammers, small scar on right arm.
Grace. Certificate issued 10 Sept. 1811. DOM recorded by Elizabeth Gassoway 3 Dec. 1803. About 40, 5' 1", yellow complexion, freckles, mole on nose, raised in AA Co.
Charles. Certificate issued 10 Sept. 1811. DOM recorded by Elizabeth Gassoway 3 Dec. 1811. Age 10, 4' 3", light complexion, raised in AA Co.
Harriott. Certificate issued 10 Sept. 1811. DOM recorded by N. Pinkney 4 April 1809. About 21, 5', dark complexion, small mole on right of upper lip, raised in AA Co.
Stephen. Certificate issued 11 Sept. 1811,. DOM recorded by Zachariah Duvall 5 June 1792. About 35, 5' 9", scar on top of right foot & right arm, raised in AA Co.
Issac. Certificate issued 16 Sept. 1811. DOM recorded by Sarah Hopkins 12 Sept. 1811. Age unknown, light complexion, scar on right breast, about 5' 8."
William Jones. Certificate issued 17 Sept. 1811. Born free and raised in AA Co. 5' 11", yellow complexion.
Isabella. Certificate issued 21 Oct. 1811. Born Free and raised in AA Co. About 17, 5' 11 1/2", yellow complexion, scar on back of right hand.
Betsy Breenfoot. Certificate issued 25 Oct. 1811. Born free and raised in AA Co. About 23, 5' 8", yellow complexion, small scar left side of face.
Henry Organ. Born Free and raised in AA Co. Certificate issued 6 Nov. 1811. About 21, 5' 8", dark complexion, scar on right arm, face marked by smallpox.
James Wooten. DOM recorded by Richard Weems 14 Sept. 1801. Certificate issued 13 Nov. 1811 About 45, 5' 9", bright complexion, scar on left arm.
Nase Snowden. Born free and raised in AA Co. Certifciate issued 19 Nov. 1811. About 29, 5' 7", dark complexion, scar under right eye.
Sarah Savoy. Born free and raised in AA Co. Certificate issued 28 Nov. 1811. About 19, 5', dark complexion, scar on right cheek.
Charles. DOM recorded by John Pitts 17 June 1802. Certificate issued 24 Jan. 1812. About 27, 6', scar on right cheek, raised in AA Co.
William. DOM recorded by Thomas Norman 7 Aug. 1801. Certificate issued 22 Feb. 1812. About 40, 5' 4 1/2."
Phillip Boston. Freedom claimed by Petition in the "late" General Court against Richard Sprigg. Certificate issued 27 March 1812. About 40, 5' 11", small scar on left side of nose.
Bill Brister. DOM recorded by Daniel of St. Thomas Jennifer 14 April 1790. Freedom commenced 1 Jan. 1796. Certificate issued 1 April 1812 about 40, 5' 5 1/2" scars on right check and right eye, raised in Charles County.
Frank Matthews. DOM recorded by John Chew Thomas 3 Feb. 1810. Freedom commenced 1 Jan. 1812. Certificate issued 11 April 1812. About 30, 5' 6 1/2", brownish complexion, scar on left side of head, raised in AA Co.
Charles Parker. Born free and raised in AA Co. Certificate issued 20 April 1812. About 23, black complexion, 5' 6 1/2", scar over right eye.
Jacob. DOM recorded by Susanna Lane 23 April 1812. Certificate issued 23 April 1812. About 27, black complexion, 5' 8", small scar on right cheek.
Sophia. DOM recorded by Susanna Lane 23 April 1812. Certificate issued 23 April 1812. Age about 21, brown complexion, 5' 2", mole over right eyebrow, raised in AA Co.
Polly Castle. DOM recorded by Elizabeth ---. 25 Feb. 1810. Certificate issued 8 May 1812. Age about 29, 5' 5 1/2", light complexion, raised in AA Co.
Nicholas Duffin. DOM recorded by Mason Weems 7 Nov. 1800. Certificate issued 8 May 1812. Age about 38, brownish complexion, 5' 1/2", small scar on forehead.
William. Born free and raised in AA Co. Certificate issued 11 May 1812. Age about 15, 4' 7 1/2", dark brown complexion, small scar near left eyebrow.
Thomas. DOM recorded by Elizabeth Selby in the year 1801. Certificate issued 26 May 1812. Age about 20, 5' 4 1/2", brown complexion, marked in the face by smallpox.
Daphne. DOM recorded by Susanna Lane 3 June 1812. Certificate issued 3 June 1812. Age about 34, 5' 2", black complexion, small scars on right eye and wrist, raised in AA Co.
Francis Neale. DOM recorded by Samuel Rideout 4 June 1812. Certificate issued 5 June 1812. Age about 44, 5' 6 1/2", black

complexion, small scar on chin, raised in Prince George's County.
Murray Talbott. DOM recorded by Mary Rideout 19 March 1808. Certificate issued 5 June 1812. Age about 22, 5' 6", yellow complexion, three small scars on forehead, raised in AA Co.
James Turner. Born free and raised in AA Co. Certificate issued 1 Aug. 1812. Age about 22, 5' 7 1/2", light complexion, small scar on back of left leg.
Aaron. DOM recorded by Mordecai Stewart 5 Aug. 1790. Certificate issued 7 Aug. 1812. Age about 26, 5' 7", brown complexion, scar on first and second fingers of right hand, raised in AA Co.
Eleanor. DOM recorded by Gideon White 17 March 1804. Freedom commenced 7 June 1812. Certificate issued 13 Aug. 1812, Age about 43, 4' 11", dark brown complexion, raised in AA Co.
Rachael Dorsey. DOM recorded by Archibald Golden 4 Aug. 1804. Certificate issued 28 Aug. 1812. Age about 36, 5' 2 1/2", brown complexion, several small scars of right arm, raised in AA Co.
Robert Boston. Free born and raised in AA Co. Certificate issued 10 Sept. 1812. Age about 26, 5' 7", dark brown complexion, scars on left leg and back.
Jamina. DOM recorded by Susanna Lane 21 Sept. 1812. Cerificate issued 22 Sept. 1812. Age about 20, 5' 1 1/2", small scar over left eye, raised in AA Co.
John Parker. Free born and raised in AA Co. Certificate issued 12 Oct. 1812. Age about 22, 5' 11 3/4", yellowish complexion, scar on calf of left leg.
Ann Parker. Born free and raised in AA Co. Certificate issued 21 Oct. 1812. Age about 42, 5'3", brown complexion, raised in AA Co.
Charles Turner. Born free and raised in AA Co. Certificate issued 30 Dec. 1812. Age about 21, 5'9 3/4", light complexion, small scars on chin and left hand.
Thomas Burly. Born free and raised in AA Co. Certificate issued 31 Dec. 1812. Age about 25, 5' 7 3/4", light complexion.
John. DOM recorded by Susanna Lane 8 Jan. 1813. Certificate issued 8 Jan. 1813. Age about 22, 5' 10 1/2", scar on inner left leg, raised in AA Co.
James Titus. DOM recorded by John Merriken 14 Sept. 1811. Cerificate issued 14 Jan. 1813. Age about 40, 5' 6 1/2", dark complexion, blind in left eye, raised in AA Co.
Murrer. DOM recorded by John Merriken 14 Sept. 1811. Cerrificate issued 11 Jan. 1813. Age about 36, 5' 4", dark complexion, small scar on right cheek, raised in AA Co.
Archibald Hawkins. Born free and raised in AA Co. Certificate issued 11 Feb. 1813. Age about 21, 5' 5 1/2", dark complexion, scar on back of right hand.
Sarah Lucas. Certificate issued 15 March 1813. Born free and raised in AA Co. Age about 16, 5' 2 1/2", small scar on left side of nose.
William Watkins. Certificate issued 16 March 1813. Born free and raised in AA Co. Age about 21, 5' 5", dark brown complexion.
Dinah. Certificate issued 19 March 1813. DOM recorded by Phillip H. Watts 27, July 1808. Age about 20, brown complexion, 5' 4", small scar on back of left hand.
Sarah Organs. Certificate issued 20 March 1813. Born free and raised in AA Co. About 15 years of age, 5' 2 1/2", small scar on right arm.
James. Certificate issued 24 March 1813. DOM recorded by Lancelot Warfield and Thomas H. Dorsey 20 March 1813. Age about 50, brown complexion, 5' 9", mole under left eye, scar on top of forehead.
Judy Jiams. Certificate issued 3 April 1813. DOM recorded by Zachariah Duvall 6 April 1812. Age about 29, dark complexion, 5' 4 3/4", small scar on side of left eye. raised in Queen Anne's County.
Sall. Certificate issued 3 April 1813. DOM recorded by Zachariah Duvall 6 April 1812. Age about 21, dark complexion, 5' 2 3/4", raised in AA Co.
Rachel. Certificate issued 12 April 1813. DOM recorded by Joseph Cowman 22 March 1782. Age about 50, dark complexion, 5", small scar on right arm, raised in AA Co.
Rachel Wallace. Certificate issued 12 April 1813. Born Free and raised in AA Co. Age about 28, 5', small scar on right arm.
Benjamin Leigh. Certificate issued 3 May 1813. DOM recorded by George Watts 3 May 1813. Age about 25, 5' 2 1/2", dark complexion, small scars under lip, missing upper front tooth, raised in AA Co.
Mary Rogers. Certificate issued 21 July 1813. DOM recorded by Nicholas Brewer and Nicholas Baldwin 20 Aug. 1811. Age about 16, 5' 4", bright complexion, long dark hair, raised in AA Co.
Nancy Rogers. Cerrtificate issued 21 July 1813. DOM recorded by Nicholas Brewer and Nicholas Baldwin 20 Aug. 1811. Age

about 30, 5' 4", brown complexion, small scar under chin. Raised in AA Co.

William Williams. Certificate issued 28 July 1813,. DOM recorded by Eleanor Williams 3 Sept. 1811. Age complexion, raised in AA Co.

Rachael Harris. DOM recorded by Robert Wallace 4 April 1804. Age 27, dark complexion, raised in AA Co.

Rose Dorsey. Certificate issued 25 Nov. 1813. DOM recorded by Samuel Peaco 3 Aug. 1798. Freedom commenced 25 July 1802. Age about 40, 5' 3", scar on back of right hand, raised in Prince George's County.

Guy. Certificate issued 8 Jan. 1814. DOM recorded by Mordecai Stewart 5 Aug. 1791. Freedom commenced 1 Jan. 1814. Age about 24, 5' 6 1/2", dark complexion, small scar on right cheek, raised in AA Co.

Richard (a. k. a. "Dick"). Certificate issued 13 Jan. 1814. DOM recorded by Jeremiah Hughes 10 June 1811. Age about 25, 6', dark complexion, missing first joint left thumb, raised in AA Co.

Robert Johnson. Certificate issued 20 Jan. 1814. DOM recorded by James N. Weems 7 May 1808. Age about 34, complexion is black, small scar over left eye, raised in AA Co.

Lili/Luce. Certificate issued 17 March 1814. DOM recorded by Francis Cromwell 23 Aug. 1792. Age about 36, 5' 4 1/2", brown complexion, raised in AA Co.

Susannah Parker. Certificate issued 6 April 1814. Age about 38, 5' 1", brown complexion, small scar on right side of face, raised in AA Co.

Mint. Certificate issued 6 April 1814. DOM recorded by John O. L. Jones 23 Sept. 1805. Freedom commenced Jan. 1809, Age is about 40, 5' 1 1/2", brown complexion, raised in Prince George's County.

Rose. Certificate issued 13 April 1814. DOM recorded by Richard G. Halton 1 Feb. 1814, Age is about 40, 5' 3", dark complexion, raised in AA Co.

Jerry. Certificate issued 19 April 1814. DOM recorded 24 Nov. 1790, age about 27, brown complexion, 5' 9", raised in AA Co.

Peter Boston. Certificate issued 20 April 1814. Born free and raised in AA Co. age about 23, 5' 7 1/2", dark complexion, scar on left shin.

Thomas Sparrow. Certificate issued 27 April 1814. Born free and raised in AA Co. Age about 20, 5' 5 1/2", black complexion, small scar on left cheek.

Sall. Certificate issued 2 May 1814. DOM recorded by Susanna Lane 2 May 1814, 5' 1 1/2", two small scars on right cheek, lame in the right hip. raised in AA Co.

Patience. Certificate issued 20 May 1814. DOM recorded by Joseph Selby 5 Jan. 1792. Freedom commenced on 25 Dec. 1813, about 23, 5', brown complexion, scar on left shoulder, raised in AA Co.

Peggy Folks. Certificate issued 6 June 1814. Born free and raised in AA Co. Age about 20, 5' 4", yellowish complexion, small scar on left arm.

Bet. Certificate issued 6 June 1814. DOM recorded by Jeremiah Hughes 10 June 1811. Age about 22, dark complexion, 5' 5", raised in AA Co.

—ffy. Certificate issued 8 June 1814. DOM recorded by Johns Hopkins 21 July 1798, age about 38, 5' 3", brown complexion, 5' 3", several scars on both arms, raised in AA Co.

Hector. Certificate issued 21 June 1814. Born free and raised in AA Co., age about 24, 5' 7", dark complexion, scars on left arm and right shin.

Mary Ann Queen. Certificate issued 22 June 1814. Born free and raised in AA Co. Age about 15, 5' 5", brown complexion.

Nell. Certificate issued 28 June 1814. DOM recorded by Susannah Lane 28 June 1814. Age about 18, 5' 5", brown complexion, small scar on breast, raised in AA Co.

Jenny. Certificate issued 1 July 1814. DOM recorded by John and Lucy Smith 27 June 1814. Age about 30, 5' 2", brown complexion, small scar between the eyes, raised in AA Co.

Thomas alias Saucy. Certificate issued 5 July 1814. DOM recorded by Sarah Riggs 18 May 1814, age about 28, 5' 5", yellow complexion, straight black hair, raised in AA Co.

Henny Davis. Certificate issued 6 July 1814. DOM recorded by Johns Hopkins 15 Jan. 1800. Freedom commenced 15 June 1812, age about 46, 5' 6", brown complexion, scar on left cheek bone, raised in AA Co.

Pegg. Certificate issued 9 July 1814,. DOM recorded by Sussanna Lane 9 July 1814, Age about 16, 5', black complexion, small scar over right eye, raised in AA Co.

Henry Folks. 10 Jan. 1815. Born free and raised in AA Co. Age about 20, 5' 5", light complexion.

Thomas Caine. Certificate issued 7 March

1815. Born free and raised in AA Co. Age about 16, 5' 3 1/2" brown complexion, small scars on right eye and breast.
James Caine. Certificate issued 7 March 1815. Born free and raised in AA Co. Age 15, 5' 2 1/2", brown complexion, small scar on right arm.
Peter Goold. Certificate issued 11 March 1815. DOM recorded by Joseph Stansbury, 5 Jan. 1815. Age about 8 (?), 5' 11", small scar right ear, raised in AA Co.
James Meredith. Certificate issued 13 March 1815. Born free and raised in AA Co. Age about 26, 5' 10 1/2", bright complexion, face marked with smallpox, scar on corner of right eye.
George Martin. Certificate issued 20 March 1815. DOM recorded by Seth Sweetson 28 April 1806. Age about 31, 5' 10 1/2", brown complexion, scars on right hand and forehead, raised in AA Co.
Dick Mullen. Certificate issued 28 March 1815. DOM recorded by Nicholas Norman 12 Oct. 1810. Age about 41, 5' 11 1/2", scar on left foot, raised in AA Co.
Issac. Certificate issued 28 March 1815. DOM recorded by Thomas Norman 24 Nov. 1790. Age about 26, 5' 6 1/2", dark complexion, scar on left wrist, raised in AA Co.
Handy McCeoire. Certificate issued 28 March 1815. DOM recorded by William Alexander 29 March 1815. Age about 45, 5' 7 3/4", dark complexion, scar on chin, face marked by smallpox, raised in AA Co.
Davis, Fannie. Certificate issued 4 April 1815. DOM recorded by Bennett Harrison 24 March 1815. Age about 32, 5" 2 1/2", bright complexion, small scar on left arm.
Cassy. Certificate issued 5 April 1815. DOM recorded by Charles Pettibone 6 April 1815. Age about 30, 5' 1 3/4", dark complexion, scars on left cheek bone, and back of neck, raised in AA Co.
Lilvey. Certificate issued April 1815. DOM recorded by Charles Pettibone 6 April 1815. Age about 22, 5' 3", dark complexion, small scar on back of left hand, raised in AA Co.
Jacob. Certificate issued 8 April 1815. DOM recorded by Mary Robinson 8 March 1814. Age about 45, 5' 1", dark complexion, scars on right wrist and left hand, raised in AA Co.
Dick. Certificate issued 18 April 1815. DOM recorded by Thomas Norman 24 Nov. 1790. Age about 28, 5' 6", missing first joint second toe on left foot, raised in AA Co.

Gideon. Certificate issued 24 April 1815. Born free and raised in AA Co. Age about 23, 5' 8 1/4", brown complexion.
Ben. Certificate issued 24 April 1815. DOM recorded by Richard Talbott 4 Jan. 1802. Age about 28, 5' 5 1/2", black complexion, raised in AA Co.
Linda Jackson. Certificate issued 27 April 1815. DOM recorded by Richard Harwood (Hammond ?) of Thomas 26 April 1815. Age about 23, 5' 2", yellowish complexion, small scar on right elbow, raised in AA Co.
Abraham Brogden. Certificate issued 27 April 1815. Born free and raised in AA Co. Age about 24, 5' 6".
Charles. Certificate issued 27 April 1815. DOM recorded by Richard Harrison 23 July 1796. Freedom commenced 12 Sept. 1813. Age about 23, 5' 7", dark complexion, raised in AA Co.
Jacob. Certificate issued 18 May 1815. Born free and raised in AA Co. Age about 21, 5' 5", light complexion, black hair.
James Fisher. Certificate issued 23 May 1815. Born free and raised in AA Co. Age about 21, 5' 7 1/2", brown complexion, small scar over left eye.
Thomas Watkins. Certificate issued 24 May 1814. Born free and raised in AA Co. Age about 21, 5' 4 1/2", brown complexion, small scar on nose.
William Madison. Certificate issued 24 May 1814. Born free and raised in AA Co. Age about 25, 5' 10 1/2", dark complexion, scars on right hand and left wrist.
Benjamin Brown. Certificate issued 4 June 1815. Petitioned Anne Arundel Court against Samuel Maccubin Sept. 1813. About 21, 5' 7", brown complexion, small scar over left eye.
Thomas Harwood. Certificate issued 6 June 1815. DOM recorded by John and David Rowles 4 March 1815. Age about 31, 5' 4", scars on left hand and forehead, raised in AA Co.
Grace. Certificate issued 8 June 1815. DOM recorded by Eleanor Hall 10 March 1798. Age about 24, dark complexion, 5' 1 1/2", enlarged lobe on right ear, raised in AA Co.
Benjamin Dockier. Certificate issued 30 July 1815. Born free and raised in AA Co. 5', dark complexion, scar on brow.
Caleb. Certificate issued 1 July 1815. DOM recorded by William Franklin 25 June 1799. Age about 21, 5' 10", dark complexion, raised in AA Co.
Kitty Watkins. Certificate issued 4 July

1815. Born free and raised in AA Co. Age about 19, 5' 3 1/2", brown complexion, small scar on right hand.
Thomas Fisher. Certificate issued 18 July 1815. Born free and raised in AA Co. Age about 25, 5' 8 1/2", dark complexion, small scar above right eye.
William Watkins. Certificate issued 27 July 1815. Born free and raised in AA Co. Age out 24, 5' 6 1/2", brown complexion.
Elizabeth Mitchell. Certificate issued 5 Aug. 1815. DOM recorded by John Brice 25 July 1815. Age about 25, 5' 1", brown complexion. Raised in AA Co.
James Fisher. Certificate issued 7 Aug. 1815. Born free and raised in AA Co. About 25, 5' 5", brown complexion, scars over left eye and on right cheek. Old certificate recorded in Folio 55.
William Queen. Certificate issued 7 Aug. 1815. Born free and raised in AA Co. Age about 22, 5' 11", light complexion, small scar on left eyebrow.
Sam. Certificate issued 9 Aug. 1815. Born free and raised in AA Co., 5' 4", dark complexion, small scar on right cheek.
Issac. Certificate issued 9 Aug. 1815. Born free and raised in AA Co. Age about 19, 5' 4", dark complexion, large scar on right arm.
Samuel Wilson. Certificate issued 15 Aug. 1815. DOM recorded by Joseph Bowman 22 March 1782. Freedom commenced April 1802. Age about 34, 5' 5 1/2", dark complexion, large scar on left leg, raised in AA Co.
William Queen. Certificate issued 18 Aug. 1815 Born free and raised in AA Co. Mother is identified as Mary Queen. Age about 21, 5'8 1/2", dark complexion, scald scar on right arm near collarbone.
Issac Queen. Certificate issued 18 Aug. 1815. Born free and raised in AA Co. Mother is identified as Mary Queen. Age about 22, 5' 8", dark complexion, two small scars on left arm.
Rebecca. Certificate issued 24 Aug. 1815. DOM recorded by Greenbury Ridgely 28 April 1800. Age 20, 5' 4 1/2", dark complexion, scars on left jaw and cheekbone, raised in AA Co.
James Parker. Born free and raised in AA Co. Age about 25, 5' 10 1/2", dark complexion, scar top of right foot.
Charles Parker. Certificate issued 29 Aug. 1815. Born free and raised in AA Co. Age about 22, 6' 1", brown complexion, two scars on left arm.
Gabriel Queen. Certificate issued 9 Sept.

1815. Born free and raised in AA Co. Age about 19, 5' 8 1/2", dark complexion, small scar on forehead.
Solomon Brogden. Certificate issued 14 Sept. 1815. Born free and raised in AA Co. Age about 21, 5' 10", dark complexion, raised in AA Co.
Rachael. Certificate issued 18 Sept. 1815. DOM recorded by Richard Merriken 21 Dec. 1799 Age about 18, 5' 2", dark complexion, raised in AA Co.
Frances. Certificate issued 26 Sept. 1815. DOM recorded by Leonard --- 5 Oct. 1791. Age about 34, 5', dark complexion, raised in AA Co.
Abigail. Certificate issued 26 Sept. 1815. Born free and raised in AA Co. Age about 20, 5' 1", brown complexion.
Harry. Certificate issued 2 Oct. 1815. Born free and Raised in AA Co. Age about 23, 5' 1 1/2", dark complexion.
Daniel Boston. Certificate issued 3 Oct. 1815. Born free and raised in AA Co. Age about 22, 5' 4 1/2", dark complexion, small scar on right thumb.
Washington Parker. Certificate issued 4 Oct. 1815. Born free and raised in AA Co. Age about 13, 4' 4", light complexion.
Margaret Parker. Certificate issued 4 Oct. 1815. Born free and raised in AA Co. Age 7, 4', brown complexion.
Ellen Parker. Certificate issued 4 Oct. 1815. Born free and raised in AA Co. Age about 23, 5' 5", brown complexion.
Ann Parker. Certificate issued 4 Oct. 1815. Born free and raised in AA Co. Age about 21, 5' 3 1/2", light complexion, moles on right eye and left cheek.
Susan Parker. Certificate issued 4 Oct. 1815. Born free and raised in AA Co. Age about 19, 5' 4", dark complexion.
Margaret Parker. Certificate issued 4 Oct. 1815. Born free and raised in AA Co. Age about 20, 5' 2 1/2", dark complexion.
Patty Malinda Addison. Certificate issued 17 Oct. 1815. Born free and raised in Prince George's County. Age about 16, 5", bright complexion, long straight hair.
James Queen. Certificate issued 21 Oct. 1815. Born free and raised in AA Co. Age about 24, 5' 9 1/2", brown complexion, scar on right shoulder.
Cornelia. Certificate issued 28 Oct. 1815. DOM recorded by Zachariah Duvall 6 April 1812. Age about 49, 5' 2", brown complexion, small scars on left cheek and right arm.
Loudon. Certificate issued 23 Oct. 1815. DOM recorded by John Cowinan Junior 7

Jan. 1790. Freedom commenced 1805. Age about 30, 5' 5", dark complexion, small scar on right cheek.
Fanny. Certificate issued 25 Oct. 1815. DOM recorded by John Cowinan 20 July 1808. Age about 32, 5' 1", brown complexion.
Juba. Certificate issued 1 Nov. 1815. DOM recorded by Johnson Mayo 8 Aug. 1805. Freedom commenced 8 Aug. 1815. Age about 44, 5' 7", dark complexion.
Anne. Certificate issued 1 Nov. 1815. DOM recorded by John Weems of Richard 9 July 1803. Age is about 21, 5' 5", dark complexion, scar on left arm.
Poll. Certificate issued 1 Nov. 1815. DOM recorded by John Weems of Richard 9 July 1803. Age about 25, 5' 4 1/2", black complexion.
Priss. Certificate issued 1 Nov. 1815. DOM recorded by James Weems 29 May 1808. Age about 27, 5' 1", black complexion, scar on left elbow.
Fanny. Certificate issued 1 Nov. 1815. DOM recorded by James Weems 27 May 1808. Age about 22, 5' 3 1/2", light complexion, scar under right eye.
Ned Parker. Certificate issued 9 Nov. 1815. Born free and raised in AA Co. Age about 21, 6', brown complexion, large scar on back of right leg, speech impediment.
Henry Price. Certificate issued 14 Nov. 1815. Born free and raised in AA Co. Age about 23, 5' 4 1/2", brown complexion, scar on forehead.
Henrietta Price. Certificate issued 14 Nov. 1815. Born free and raised in AA Co. Age about 26, 5' 1", bright complexion.
Stephen. Certificate issued 20 Nov. 1815. DOM recorded by Joseph Selby 5 Jan. 1792. Freedom commenced 25 Dec. 1812. Age about 28, 5' 4 1/2", scar on upper lip, raised in AA Co.
Susan. Certificate issued 21 Nov. 1815. Born free and raised in AA Co. Age about 24, 5'1/2", dark complexion.
Sarah. Certificate issued 6 Dec. 1815. DOM recorded by Joseph Burneston 19 Jan. 1792. Age about 55, 5' 1 1/2", missing upper front teeth, scar on left thumb.
Dick. Certificate issued 5 Dec. 1815. DOM recorded by William Fisher 13 April 1790. Age about 30, 5' 9" brown complexion, small scar left forehead, raised in AA Co.
William Chambers 22 Dec. 1815. DOM recorded by Richard Hopkins of Gerard 12 July 1782. Age about 36, 5' 4", dark complexion, raised in AA Co.
William Winters. Certificate issued 20 Nov.

1815. DOM recorded by Joseph Selby 5 Jan. 1792. Original Certificate in Folio 27. Age about 21 6' 1 1/2", dark complexion, scar on back of right hand.
Elisha Parker. Certificate issued 8 Jan. 1816. Born free and raised in AA Co. Age about 23, 5' 8 1/2", brown complexion, small scar on upper lip.
Samuel Allen. Certificate issued 13 Jan. 1816. DOM recorded by Jane Woodward 13 Oct. 1814. Age about 39, 5' 7 1/2", brown complexion, five scars on breasts, raised in AA Co.
William Watkins. Certificate issued 19 Jan. 1816. DOM recorded by Zachariah Duvall 2 Sept. 1805. Age about 50, 5' 3", dark complexion, scar on upper lip, raised in AA Co.
Richard Bond. Certificate issued 22 Jan. 1816. Born free and raised in AA Co. Age about 22, 5' 10", dark complexion, small scar on breast.
Nathan Allen. Certificate issued 30 Jan. 1816. Born free and raised in AA Co. Age about 30, 5' 8", brown complexion.
John. Certificate issued 23 Jan. 1816. DOM recorded by Charles Pettibone 26 Jan. 1805. Age about 28, 5' 11", brown complexion, raised in AA Co.
William Ginges. Certificate issued 1 March 1816. DOM recorded by John, Dennis, and Abram Claude 8 Sept. 1813. Age about 29 years, 5' 8", bright complexion, scar on upper lip, straight black hair, raised in AA Co.
Viney. Certificate issued 7 March 1816. DOM recorded by Nicholas J. Watkins 7 March 1816. Age about 30, 4' 9", brown complexion, raised in AA Co.
Harriett. Certificate issued 11 March 1816. DOM recorded by John Thomas 7 Aug. 1804. Age about 30, 5' 4", brown complexion, long straight black hair, raised in AA Co.
Charles Baines. Certificate issued 16 March 1816. Born free and raised in AA Co. Age about 21, 5' 6", black complexion.
Edward Boothe. Certificate issued 20 March 1816. DOM recorded by Edward Boothe 19 March 1816. Age about 22, 5' 10", light complexion, raised in AA Co.
George. Certificate issued 26 March 1810. DOM recorded by John Norwood 7 March 1803. Age about 33, 5' 9 1/2", brown complexion, small scar above right eye, raised in AA Co.
Joshua. Certificate issued 1 April 1816. DOM recorded by Phillip W. Thomas 12 March. 1816. Age about 41, 5' 5 1/2",

black complexion, scar over right eye, raised in Prince George's County.

Jacob Oliver. Certificate issued 13 April 1816. DOM recorded by Elizabeth Oliver 17 Nov. 1800. Age about 24, 5' 11 1/2" bright complexion, raised in AA Co.

Poll. Certificate issued 16 April 1816. DOM recorded by Samuel Peaco 3 Aug. 1798. Age about 28, 5' 2 1/2", dark complexion, scar on left arm. Freedom commenced 25 Jan. 1814, raised in AA Co.

John Euices. Certificate issued 2 May 1816. DOM recorded by Margaret Callahan 31 Jan. 1811. Freedom commenced 1 Feb. 1816. Age about 26, 5' 6 1/2", light complexion.

Mary Richardson. Certificate issued 6 May 1816. Born free and raised in AA Co. Age about 21, 5'5", brown complexion, raised in AA Co.

Ann Mahoney. Certificate issued 7 May 1816. DOM recorded by Charles Mahoney 7 May 1816. Age about 18, 5' 3", bright complexion, scar under left arm, raised in AA Co.

Loney. Certificate issued 21 May 1816. DOM recorded by Abel Hill 26 July 1793. Age about 37, 5' 7 1/2", dark complexion, raised in AA Co.

Nina. Certificate issued 21 May 1816. DOM recorded by Abel Hill 26 July 1793. Age about 31, 5' 2", dark complexion, raised in AA Co.

Harry Parker. Certificate issued 25 May 1816. Born free and raised in AA Co. 5' 9 1/4", brown complexion, small scar on breast.

Philip Prout. Certificate issued 29 May 1816. Born free and raised in AA Co. Age about 23, 5' 9", brown complexion, scars on right eye and left forehead.

Thomas Harrison. Certificate issued 30 May 1816. Born free and raised in AA Co. Age about 28, 5' 11", brown complexion, scars on left shoulder and eyebrow.

Edward Harrison. Certificate issued 30 May 1816. Born free and raised in AA Co. Age about 19, 5' 7 1/2", brown complexion, scars on right jaw, forehead, and right ear.

George. Certificate issued 7 June 1816. DOM recorded by John Chew Thomas 12 Feb. 1812. Age about 22, 5' 5", dark complexion, raised in AA Co.

Sall. Certificate issued 7 June 1816. DOM recorded by Zachariah Duvall 5 June 1792. Freedom commenced 25 Dec. 1803. Age about 37, 5'3", black complexion, scar on right cheek, raised in AA Co.

Peerer. Certificate issued 11 June 1816. DOM recorded by Bryan Williams 9 Oct. 1798. Freedom commenced 3 Nov. 1815. Age about 33, 5' 7", black complexion, scar on right hand, raised in AA Co.

Delila Owings. Certificate issued 12 June 1816. Born free and raised in AA Co. Age about 23, 5' 5", yellow complexion, long straight hair, small scars on right eyebrow and left hand.

James Owings. Certificate issued 12 June 1816. Born free and raised in AA Co. Age about 30, 5' 7", bright complexion, large scar left leg.

John Easton. Certificate issued 12 June 1816. Born free and raised in AA Co. Age about 32, 5' 10", yellow complexion, face marked by smallpox, lumps on left arm.

Cassy. Certificate issued 29 June 1816. DOM recorded by John Merriken 21 May 1816. Age about 35, 5' 1 1/2", "high black complexion," scar on right ear.

John Packer. Certificate issued 25 July 1816. Born free and raised in AA Co. Age about 18, 5' 10 1/2", black complexion, small scars under left eye, and on forefinger of left hand.

Kass. Certificate issued 26 July 1816. DOM recorded by John Boone 26 July 1816. Age about 30, 5' 4", dark complexion, scar on left wrist, raised in AA Co.

Harry. Certificate issued 16 Aug. 1816. DOM recorded by Leonard Scott 4 Sept. 1801. Age about 24, 5' 6 1/2", dark complexion, raised in AA Co.

James. Certificate issued 16 Aug. 1816. DOM recorded by Leonard Scott 4 Sept. 1801. Age about 22, 5' 8 1/2", dark complexion, raised in AA Co.

Rachel Saunders. Certificate issued 17 Aug. 1816. Born free and raised in AA Co. Age about 34, 5' 5", dark complexion, scar on back of right hand, six fingers on left hand.

Patty. Certificate issued 17 Aug. 1816. DOM recorded by Horatio Gibson 11 Jan. 1811. Age about 40, 5' 3", dark complexion, raised in Talbot County.

William. Certificate issued 19 Aug. 1816. DOM recorded by William Cowman 4 Dec. 1813. Age about 21 8/12, 5' 8", dark complexion, small scar on right hand, raised in AA Co.

Sally. Cerrtificate issued 24 Aug. 1816. DOM recorded by Nicholas Brewer 19 Aug. 1816. Age about 35, 4' 11 1/2", dark complexion, small scar on forehead, raised in AA Co.

Robert Downs. Certificate issued 3 Sept.

1816. Born free and raised in AA Co. Age about 24, 5' 3 1/2", brown complexion, double great toe on both feet.
John Queen. Certificate issued 17 Sept. 1816. Born free and raised in AA Co. Age about 19, 5' 8", brown complexion, small scar on little finger left hand.
Jacob West. Certificate issued 17 Sept. 1816. DOM recorded by Amelia Gold 5 April 1816. Age about 44, 5' 9", yellowish complexion, raised in AA Co.
Amelia Gold. Certificate issued 17 Sept. 1816. DOM recorded by Joseph Stansbury 5 Dec. 1815. Age about 31, 5' 1 1/2", brown complexion, scar on right arm, raised in AA Co.
John Thomas. Certificate issued 5 Oct. 1816. Born free and raised in AA Co. Age about 26, 5' 7", black complexion, under lower lip.
Deborah. Certificate issued 5 Oct. 1816. DOM recorded by Bennett Darnall 29 April 1805. Age about 17, 5' 3", brown complexion, raised in AA Co.
Elizabeth. Certificate issued 21 Oct. 1816. DOM recorded by Bennett Darnall 29 April 1805. Age about 18, 5' 2", brown complexion, raised in AA Co.
Ann. Certificate issued 21 Oct. 1816. DOM recorded by Bennett Darnall 29 April 1805. Age about 14, 4' 11", brown complexion, small scar under right eye, raised in AA Co.
Dinah. Certificate issued 25 Oct. 1816. DOM recorded by William Weems 10 June 1807. Age about 28, 5' 1". Freedom commenced 1 Jan. 1813, raised in AA Co.
Mary Queen. Certificate issued 1 Nov. 1816. Born free and raised in AA Co. Age about 17, 4'10", light complexion.
Nancy Queen. Certificate issued 1 Nov. 1816. Born free and raised in AA Co. Age about 40, 5' 2", dark complexion, scars on left wrist and back.
Bellas. Certificate issued 9 Nov. 1816. DOM recorded by Sarah Lawton 6 Feb. 1795. Age about 41, 5' 1 1/2", dark complexion, small scar on left side of chin.
Shener. Certificate issued 18 Nov. 1816. DOM recorded by Stephen Boone 17 Nov. 1815. Freedom commenced 17 Nov. 1816. Age about 35, 5' 3", dark complexion, scar on chin, raised in AA Co.
Sarah Brown. Certificate issued 13 Nov. 1816. Born free and raised in AA Co. Age about 20, 5'1", black complexion, small scar under left eye.
Rachel Brown. Certificate issued 23 Nov. 1816. Born free and raised in AA Co. Age about 19, 5' 2", dark complexion.
Margaret Brown. Certificate issued 23 Nov. 1816. Born free and raised in AA Co. Age about 17, 5' 3", yellowish complexion, small scar in right eyebrow.
Ned Galloway. Certificate issued 19 Dec. 1816. DOM recorded by John Mackubin 11 Sept. 1816. Age about 39, 5' 7 1/2", brown complexion, scar on right of head.
Thomas Watkins. Certificate issued 8 Jan. 1817. Born free and raised in AA Co. Age about 22 1/2 years, 5' 4 1/2", brown complexion, small scar on nose.
William Queen. Certificate issued 11 March 1817. Born free and raised in AA Co. son of Nellie Queen. Age about 20, 5' 7 1/2", two small scars on right wrist.
Closy. Certificate issued 29 March 1817. DOM recorded by Oneal Cromwell 10 March 1786. Age about 58, 5'1 1/2", dark complexion, small scar on left eyebrow, raised in AA Co.
Milly. Certificate issued 29 March 1817. DOM recorded by Stephen Boone 22 March 1817. Age about 35, 5' 10", dark complexion, small scar on right chin, raised in AA Co.
Allen. Certificate issued 1 April 1817. DOM recorded by John Chew 29 March 1810. Age about 45, 5' 4 1/2", black complexion, raised in AA Co.
Phillip. Certificate issued 1 April 1817. DOM recorded by John Chew 29 March 1810. Age about 33, 5' 4", bright complexion, scar on left wrist, missing finger on right hand, raised in AA Co.
Abigail. Certificate issued 24 April 1817. Born free and raised in AA Co. Age about 30, 5' 5 1/2", brown complexion, small scar on left arm.
Robert Queen. Certificate issued 30 May 1817. Born free and raised in AA Co. Age about 38, 6' 1", brown complexion, small scars above left eye, scar on right arm.
Susan. Certificate issued 30 May 1817. Born free and raised in AA Co. Age about 15, 5' 1", dark complexion.
Ann. Certificate issued 30 May 1817. Born free and raised in AA Co. Age about 17, 5' 3 1/2", dark complexion, scar on right cheek.
John. Certificate issued 30 May 1817. Born free and raised in AA Co. Age about 12, 4' 9", dark complexion, scar on right foot.
P—sly. Certificate issued 2 June 1817. DOM recorded by Leonard Scott 9 Feb. 1805. Age about 21, 5' 7", dark complexion, small scar on left hand, raised in AA Co.

Sarah. Certificate issued 2 June 1817. Born free and raised in AA Co. Age about 15, 5' 1 1/4", dark complexion.
Caesar Boston. Certificate issued 7 June 1817. Born free and raised in AA Co. Age about 29, 5' 2", dark complexion, scar on right leg.
Lamer. Certificate issued 23 June 1817. DOM recorded by John Sewell 23 Nov. 1812. Freedom commenced 12 Dec. 1814. Age about 54, 5' 1", dark complexion, several scars on right arm, raised in AA Co.
Cate. Certificate issued 21 July 1817. DOM recorded by Mary Pearson 6 July 1789. Age about 57, 4' 10 1/2", dark complexion, small scar over left eye, raised in AA Co.
William Docker. Certificate issued 31 July 1817. Born free and raised in AA Co. Age about 22, 5' 8 1/2", brown complexion, small scars on left hand and both elbows.
Polly. Certificate issued 31 July 1817. DOM recorded by Francis Neale 5 Feb. 1816. Age about 44, 5' 4", dark complexion, raised in AA Co.
Samuel Garrett. Certificate issued 31 July 1817. Born free and raised in AA Co. Age about 21, 5' 3", dark complexion.
Milly. Certificate issued 5 Aug. 1817. DOM recorded by Henry Duvall 13 Jan. 1817. Age about 23, 5', brown complexion, small scar on left hand, raised in AA Co.
Cassandra Sparrow. Certificate issued 6 Aug. 1817. Born free and raised in AA Co. Age about 23, 5' 1, dark complexion.
David Queen. Certificate issued 14 Aug. 1817. Born free and raised in AA Co. Age about 22, 5' 6" brown complexion, scar on forehead above left eye, left hand, and right arm.
James Johnson. Certificate issued 15 Aug. 1817. Born free and raised in AA Co. Age about 27, 5' 6", brown complexion, scars on back of left hand and right leg.
Vachel Batson. Certificate issued 27 Aug. 1817. Born free and raised in AA Co. Age about 24, 5' 3", black complexion, small scar left nose.
Rhode. Certificate issued 12 Sept. 1817. DOM recorded by Charles Drury 3 Feb. 1797. Freedom commenced 1 Jan. 1813. Age about 22, 5' 5", brown complexion, "natural mark on left wrist and hand," raised in AA Co.
Phill. Certificate issued 12 Sept. 1817. DOM recorded by Williams Simmons (possibly Timmons) 11 Aug. 1790. Freedom commenced 28 April 1800. Age about 37, 5' 11 1/2", dark complexion, scar on neck, raised in AA Co.
Charles. Certificate issued 30 Sept. 1817. DOM recorded by Frances Cromwell 23 Aug. 1792. Freedom commenced 12 Sept. 1816. Age about 34, 5' 9", black complexion, nose marked by smallpox, raised in AA Co..
James Winters. Certificate issued 25 Oct. 1817. Born free and raised in AA Co. Age about 21, 5' 10", black complexion, missing third finger left hand, raised in AA Co.
Nacy. Certificate issued 11 Nov. 1817. DOM recorded by Thomas Morton 3 Nov. 1800. Freedom commenced 1 Oct. 1817. Age about 40, 5' 9 1/2". dark complexion, small scar on left arm, raised in AA Co.
Levy Hawkins. Certificate issued 14 Nov. 1817. Born free and raised in AA Co. Age about 21, 5' 7 1/2", dark complexion, scars on left hand and foot, raised in AA Co.
Henry Organ. Certificate issued 15 Nov. 1817. Born free and raised in AA Co. Age about 27, 5' 8", dark complexion, scar on right arm, face marked by smallpox.
Nanny. Certificate issued 18 Dec. 1817. Born free and raised in AA Co. Age about 45, 5', black complexion.
Samuel Hawkins. Certificate issued 26 Dec. 1817. Born free and raised in AA Co. Age about 23, 5' 8", brown complexion, scar on right shoulder.
Sukey. Certificate issued 10 Jan. 1818. DOM recorded by Leonard Scott 9 Feb. 1805. Age about 26, 5' 1", dark complexion, small scars on forehead and left wrist, raised in AA Co.
Robert Hall. Certificate issued 10 Jan. 1818. DOM recorded by Leonard Scott 14 June 1819. Freedom commenced 14 Dec. 1819. Age about 35, 5' 6 1/2", brown complexion, small scar under right eye, raised in AA Co.
Edward Bond. Cerificate issued 16 Jan. 1818. Born free and raised in AA Co. Age about 21, 5' 1", yellowish complexion.
Isaac. Certificate issued 21 Jan. 1818. DOM recorded by Nicholas J. Watkins. 29 Sept. 1808. Freedom commenced 1 Oct. 1817. Age about 30, 5' 7 1/2", yellow complexion, scars upper side of lip and right eyebrow, mole in corner of left eye, raised in A Co.
William Brookes. Certificate issued 23 Jan. 1818. DOM recorded by Susan Maccubin 14 June 1796. Freedom commenced 1 June 1805. Age about 46, 5' 8", yellow complexion, scar on left arm, raised in AA Co.

Charles. Certificate issued 5 Feb. 1818. DOM recorded by Mary Smith 5 March 1721. Age about 29, 5' 5 1/2", dark complexion, raised in AA Co.

Harry Martin. Certificate issued 27 Feb. 1818. DOM recorded by George Martin 24 Feb. 1818. Age about 23, 5' 8", brown complexion, raised in AA Co.

Dennis Queen. Certificate issued 10 March 1818. Born free and raised in AA Co. Age about 24, 5' 6", dark complexion, scar on left hand near thumb.

Anne Scoggle. Certificate issued 16 March 1818. Born free and raised in AA Co. Age about 17, 4' 11", dark complexion, small scar on right arm.

Hager Cook. Certificate issued 20 March 1818. DOM recorded by George Stinchcomb 21 Jan. 1818. Age about 42, 5' 2 1/2", light complexion, raised in AA Co.

Bet or Elizabeth. Certificate issued 31 March 1818. DOM recorded by Thomas Wilson 27 May 1797. Age about 25, 5', brown complexion, raised in AA Co.

Susan. Certificate issued 6 April 1818. DOM recorded by Robert Warfield 25 March 1818. Age 41, 5' 3", dark complexion.

Paul Queen. Certificate issued 7 April 1818. Born free and raised in AA Co. Age about 25, 5' 5 1/2", black complexion, small scar on right hand.

David Brown. Certificate issued 8 April 1818. DOM recorded by Charles S. Ridgely. 21 March 1818. Age about 40, 5'_", brown complexion, scars over right eye, left eye, across the nose, raised in AA Co.

Dick Haines. Certificate issued 21 April 1818. DOM recorded by Rachel Snowden 20 Nov. 1813. Age about 21, 5' 7", brown complexion, raised in AA Co.

Eleanor Boothe. Certificate issued 21 April 1818. DOM recorded by James Boothe 21 April 1818. Age about 45, 5' 3 1/2", brown complexion, lump under upper lip, raised in AA Co.

Maria. Certificate issued 22 April 1818. DOM recorded by Amelia Warfield 3 May 1808. Age about 27, 5' 3 1/2" yellowish complexion, raised in AA Co.

Thomas Mullen. Certificate issued 22 April 1818. DOM recorded by Joseph Franklin 2 April 1818. Age about 40, 5' 10 1/2", brown complexion, small scar near right eye, raised in AA Co.

Issac K. Certrificate issued 16 May 1818. Born free and raised in AA Co. Age about 22, 5' 5", dark complexion, scar on left arm.

James Turner. Certificate issued 22 May 1818. Born free and raised in AA Co. Age about 22, 6' 1", yellow complexion, small scar on right forehead.

George Brown. Certificate issued 25 May 1818. DOM recorded by George and John Bucher 25 May 1818. Age about 35, 6' 1", dark complexion, small scar left side of face, raised on Eastern Shore of Maryland.

Kitty Lee. Certificate issued 25 May 1818. Born free and raised in AA Co. Age about 14, 5' 2", black complexion, scars on inside of right wrist.

Fanny Davis. Certificate issued 25 May 1818. DOM recorded by Bennett Harrison 24 March 1815. Age about 35, bright complexion, small scar on left arm, raised in AA Co.

Benjamin Ennis. Certificate issued 17 June 1818. Born free and raised in AA Co. Age about 22, 5' 11", dark complexion, small scar on forehead.

William Snowden. Certificate issued 22 June 1818. Born free and raised in AA Co. Age about 28, 5" 8", dark complexion, scar on right cheek, missing toes on left foot.

Harriett Ennis. Certificate issued 8 July 1818. DOM recorded by Margaret Callahan 11 Jan. 1809. Age about 29, 5' 3", light complexion, scar on left shoulder, raised in AA Co.

Rose. Certificate issued 15 July 1818. DOM recorded by Frederick Green and Jonathon Pinkney 16 April 1807. Age about 38, 5' 5 12", dark complexion, raised in Calvert County.

Lucy Ward. Certificate issued 19 Aug. 1818. DOM recorded by Leonard Scott 21 Oct. 1801. Age about 31, 5' 3", dark complexion, raised in AA Co.

Sarah Boston. Certificate issued 20 Aug. 1818. Born free and raised in AA Co. Age about 30, 5' 4 1/2" small scar under left arm above the elbow.

May/Mary Boston. Certificate issued 20 Aug. 1818. Born free and raised in AA Co. Age about 58, 5' 3 1/2", black complexion.

Peter Boston. Certificate issued 22 Aug. 1818. Born free and raised in AA Co. Age about 35, 5' 6", black complexion, scar above left ankle, missing one front tooth.

Beveridge. Certificate issued 1 Sept. 1818. DOM recorded by Samuel Maccubbin 23 Feb. 1791. Age about 32, 5' 4", brown complexion, small scar on right cheek, lame in left leg, raised in AA Co.

— **Queen.** Certificate issued 8 Sept. 1818. Born free and raised in AA Co. Age about 18, 5' 10 1/2", dark complexion, small scar on right arm.

Eleanor Queen. Certificate issued 8 Sept. 1818. Born free and raised in AA Co. Age about 39, 45', dark complexion, small scar on forehead.

Chastity Queen. Certificate issued 8 Sept. 1818. Born free and raised in AA Co. Age about 41, 5' 1", dark complexion, small scar on right arm.

Elizabeth Speaks. 8 Sept. 1818. Born free and raised in AA Co. Age about 22; 5' 5", light complexion.

Matthias. 18 Sept. 1818. DOM recorded by Eleanor Yieldhall. 12 May 1799. Age about 27, 5' 6 1/2", black complexion, scars on right hand and in corner of left eye, raised in AA Co.

Samuel Johnson. Certificate issued 6 Oct. 1818. DOM recorded by Rachael Snowden 20 Nov. 1813. Age about 45, 6', bright complexion, scar between thumb and forefinger of right hand. Raised in AA Co.

Fanny. Certificate issued 6 Oct. 1818. DOM recorded by Ann Morrison 29 July 1818. Age about 37, 5' 2", brown complexion, small scar over left eye, right thumb injured. Raised in AA Co.

Liley. Certificate issued 18 Oct. 1818. DOM recorded by Mary Israel 7 Sept. 1818. Age about 30, 5' 3 1/2", bright complexion, scars on breast and right arm, raised in AA Co.

Darky Boston. Certificate issued 26 Oct. 1818. Born free and raised in AA Co. Age about 32, 4' 11", dark complexion, small scar on right cheek, mole on right side of chin.

Sally Turner. Certificate issued 27 Oct. 1818. Born free and raised in AA Co. Age about 26, 5' 1", yellowish complexion, slightly deaf, scar on left elbow.

Dennis. Certificate issued 12 Nov. 1818. DOM recorded by Mary Steele 11 Nov. 1818. Age about 43, 5' 10", light complexion, mole under left nostril, raised in AA Co.

Harriet Prout. Certificate issued 18 Nov. 1818. Born free and raised in AA Co. 5' 9 1/2", 20 Aug. 1813. Freedom commenced 1 Jan. 1818. Age about 22, 5' 4", black complexion, small scars over left eye.

Thomas Chambers. Certificate issued 21 Jan. 1819. DOM recorded by Eleanor Yieldhall Thomas 28 May 1799. age about 21, 5' 5", dark complexion.

Richard Savoy Garrett. Certificate issued 25 Jan. 1819. Born free and raised in AA Co. Age about 27, 5' 4 1/2", brown complexion.

Abigail. Certificate issued 27 Jan. 1819. DOM recorded by Mary Arminger and Richard Hutton 24 Oct. 1817. Age about 40, 5' 1", black complexion, small mole left side of nose, raised in AA Co.

Clarissa Boston. Certificate issued 5 Feb. 1819. Born free and raised in AA Co. Age about 35, 5' 3", yellowish complexion, two large scars on right arm.

Peggy Garrett. Certificate issued 6 Feb. 1819. Born free and raised in AA Co. Age about 19, 5' 1 1/2", brown complexion.

John Queen. Certificate issued 9 Feb. 1819. Born free and raised in AA Co. Age about 28, 5' 8", black complexion.

George Chager. Certificate issued 28 Feb. 1819. Born free and raised in AA Co. Age about 22, 5' 10", yellowish complexion, scar on right jaw.

Susanna Parker. Certificate issued 4 March 1819. Born free and raised in AA Co. Age about 35, 5' 5", brown complexion, small scar on forehead.

Margaret Hackney. Certificate issued 13 March 1819. Born free and raised in AA Co. Age about 50, 5' 5 1/2", dark complexion, scar on left shoulder.

Ignacious (Nace) Hanson. Certificate issued. 8 April 1819. DOM recorded by Mary Merriken 7 April 1819. Age about 44, 6' 1", black complexion, small scar on left wrist, raised in AA Co.

Sarah Parker. Certificate issued 8 April 1819. Born free and raised in AA Co. Age about 40, 5' 4 1/2", dark complexion, scars on left wrist and cheek.

Tom. Certificate issued 19 April 1819. DOM recorded by Charles M. Dorsey 10 April 1819. Age about 35, 5' 7", black complexion, raised in AA Co.

Rezin. Certificate issued 19 April 1819. DOM recorded by George Dorsey 23 May 1810. Age about 27, 5' 11", dark complexion, scar on left arm, raised in AA Co.

Issac. Certificate issued 10 April 1819. DOM recorded by Charles Dorsey 10 April 1819. Age about 39, 5' 5", brown complexion, two scars left arm, raised in AA Co.

Daniel. Certificate issued 21 April 1819. DOM recorded by John Harriman 23 Feb. 1813. Age about 54, 5' 5 1/2", dark complexion, crooked finger of right hand, raised in AA Co.

Henry Parker. Certificate issued 22 April 1819. Born free and raised in AA Co. Age

about 20, 5' 9", black complexion.
Harriott Carter. Certificate issued 24 April 1819 Born free and raised in AA Co. Age about 23, 5' 2", dark complexion.
Abraham. Certificate issued 26 April 1819 Born free and raised in AA Co. Age about 22, 5' 7", black complexion, small scar over left eye.
Issac. Certificate issued 26 April 1819 Born free and raised in AA Co. Age about 22, 5' 7", black complexion, two scars on left cheek.
Jane. Certificate issued 27 April 1819. DOM recorded by Daniel of St. Thomas Jennifer 14 April 1793. Freedom commenced 1 Jan. 1796. Sometimes called "Little Jane." Age about 44, 5' 1 1/2", brown complexion, mole on right eyelid, raised in AA Co.
Letty. Certificate issued 27 April 1819. Born free and raised in AA Co. Age about 22, 5' 1 1/2", small scars above right elbow, brown complexion.
Nancy. Certificate issued 28 April 1819. Born free and raised in AA Co. Age about 18, 5' 1/2", brown complexion, small scar above left elbow.
Milly. Certificate issued 28 April 1819. Born free and raised in AA Co. Age about 20, 5', brown complexion, small scar on right arm.
Bell. Certificate issued 11 May 1819. DOM recorded by James McCulloch 13 July 1805. Age about 46, 5' 4", brown complexion, scar on left arm, face slightly marked by smallpox, raised in AA Co.
Dinah. Certificate issued 17 May 1819. DOM recorded by Anne Jennifer 14 May 1819. Age about 36, 5' 1 1/2", black complexion, small scar near left eye, raised in Anne Arundel County.
Ragis Queen. Certificate issued 22 May 1819. Born free and raised in AA Co. Age about 21, 5' 4", dark complexion, scars back of left hand.
Charles. Certificate issued 22 May 1819. DOM recorded by Anne Jennifer 21 May 1819. Age about 42, 5' 6 1/2", black complexion, Raised in AA Co.
Susan Parker. Certificate issued 27 May 1819. Born free and raised in AA Co. Age about 20, 5', black complexion, scar on back of left shoulder.
Benjamin Alfred. Certificate issued 27 May 1819. DOM recorded by Thomas, Mary and Sarah Norris 15 Nov. 1799. Age about 23, 5' 5 1/2", black complexion, small scar on. back of left hand, raised in AA Co.

Stacey. Certificate issued 29 May 1819. DOM recorded by Sussanah W--- 30 Nov. 1813. Age about 32, 4' 9 1/2". black complexion, several scars about the right elbow, raised in AA Co.
Charles. Certificate issued 30 May 1819. DOM recorded by John Hall 18 July 1791. Age about 32, 5' 8", bright complexion, scar on top of head, raised in Anne Arundel County.
Esther. Certificate issued 31 May 1819. DOM recorded by John Hall 18 July 1791. Age about 30, 5' 3 1/2", brown complexion, small scar on left side of nose, raised in AA Co.
Harry. Certificate issued 1 June 1819. DOM. recorded by Anne Jennifer 21 May 1819. Age about 37, 5' 7 1/2", brown complexion, small scar back of left hand, raised in Anne. Arundel County.
Kitty Prout. Certificate issued 15 June 1819. Born free and raised in AA Co. Age about 30, 5' 2", brown complexion, small scars on right jaw and left arm.
George. Certificate issued 5 July 1819. DOM recorded by Thomas, Sarah, and Mary Norris 15 Nov. 1799. Age about 27, 5' 2", black complexion, several scars on left arm, raised in AA Co.
Joseph Thomas. Certificate issued 29 July 1819. Born free and raised in AA Co. Age about 22, 6', black complexion, raised in AA Co.
Daniel. Certificate issued 31 July 1819. DOM recorded by Anne Jennifer 14 May 1819. Age about 22, 5' 8", black complexion, scars. on left hand and right shoulder, raised in AA Co.
Fliva. Certificate issued 21 Aug. 1819. DOM recorded by Jerningham Drury 9 Nov. 1805. Freedom commenced 1 Sept. 1815. Age about 45, 5' 5 1/2", brown complexion, scar on left arm, missing first joint of the forefinger of the right hand, raised in AA Co.
Thomas Parker. Certificate issued 21 Aug. 1819. Born free and raised in AA Co. Age about 26, 5' 10", mulatto, scars across the nose and left side of face.
William Parker. Certificate issued 21 Aug. 1819. Born free and raised in AA Co. Age about 36, 5' 8", dark complexion, small. scar on left arm.
Mary Brown. Certificate issued 21 Aug. 1819. Born free and raised in AA Co. Age about 30, 5' 2 1/2", dark complexion, several scars on right wrist and left hand.
Fanny Queen. Certificate issued 30 Aug. 1819. Born free and raised in AA Co. Age

about 18, 5' 3 1/2", brown complexion, small scars over right eye and under left eye. (Name may be Fancy not Fanny).
Sussanna Campbell. Certificate issued 31 Aug. 1819. DOM recorded by Margaret Hopkins 6 Aug. 1811. a. k. a "Sukey." Age about 35, 5' 10 3/4", black. complexion, raised in AA Co.
Nacky. Certificate issued 31 Aug. 1819. DOM recorded by Rachel Snowden 20 Nov. 1813. Age about 28, 5' 5 1/2", brown complexion, small scar on cheek near the right eye, raised in AA Co.
Joe Matthews. Certificate issued 31 Aug. 1819. DOM recorded by Rachel Snowden 20 Nov. 1813. Age about 22, 5' 10", dark complexion, scar on right underjaw, raised in AA Co.
Ned. Certificate issued 31 Aug. 1819. DOM recorded by Margaret Hopkins 20 Aug. 1813. Freedom commenced 1 Jan. 1814. Age about 45, 5' 6", bright complexion, small scar back of left hand, raised in Montgomery County.
Ruth. Certificate issued 31 Aug. 1819. DOM recorded by Margaret Hopkins 20 Aug. 1813. Freedom commenced 1 Jan. 1814. Age about 32, 5' 4", brown complexion, scar right lower neck, raised in Montgomery County.
Beck. Certificate issued 31 Aug. 1819. DOM recorded by Margaret Hopkins 20 Aug. 1813. Freedom commenced 1 Jan. 1814. Age about 29, 5' 1 1/2", dark complexion, scar on right arm, raised in Montgomery County.
Rachel. Certificate issued 31 Aug. 1819. DOM recorded by Margaret Hopkins 20 Aug. 1813. Freedom commenced 1 Jan. 1814. Age about 26, 5' 6", scar on left underarm, raised in Montgomery County.
Lucy. Certificate issued 31 Aug. 1819. DOM recorded by Margaret Hopkins 20 Aug. 1813. Freedom commenced 1 Jan. 1814. Age about 39, 5' 3 1/2", raised in AA Co.
Lucy. Certificate issued 2 Sept. 1819. DOM recorded by David Robinson 25 Jan. 1791. Freedom commenced 1 Jan. 1811. Age about 34, dark complexion, two small scars on neck, raised in AA Co.
George. Certificate issued 3 Sept. 1891. DOM recorded by Ann Jennifer 21 May 1819. Age about 45, 5' 7 1/2", black complexion, scar. on left corner of upper lip, raised in AA Co.
Elisha Brogden. Certificate issued 4 Sept. 1891. Born free and raised in AA Co. Age about 21, 5' 6 1/2", black complexion, scar on left thigh.
Charity. Certificate issued 7 Sept. 1819. DOM recorded by Joseph Evans 7 March 1804. Original Certificate of Freedom issued 27 Aug. 1813, proven to be stolen. Age about 26, 5' 2 1/2", brown complexion, raised in AA Co.
George. Certificate issued 10 Sept. 1819. DOM recorded by Eleanor Yieldhall 28 May 799. Freedom commenced 28 May 1819. Age about 27, 5' 2 1/2" complexion, scar on back of right hand, raised in AA Co.
Daniel. Certificate issued 10 Sept. 1819. DOM recorded by Margaret Hopkins 20 Aug. 1813. Freedom commenced 1 Jan. 1814. Age about 31, 5' 2 1/2", yellow complexion, scar or knot on back of head, raised in Montgomery County.
Priss. Certificate issued 10 Sept. 1819. DOM recorded by Margaret Hopkins 20 Aug. 1813. Freedom commenced 1 Jan. 1814. Age about 25, 5' 1", brown complexion, large scar on outside of left leg. raised in Montgomery County.
Nan. Certificate issued 10 Sept. 1819. DOM recorded by Margaret Hopkins 20 Aug. 1813. Freedom commenced 1 Jan. 1814. Age about 34, 5' 4 1/4", black complexion, small scar on left forearm, raised in Montgomery County.
Kessy. Certificate issued 10 Sept. 1819. DOM recorded by Margaret Hopkins 20 Aug. 1813. Freedom commenced 1 Jan. 1819. Age about 19, 5' 3 1/2", brown complexion, large scar on left knee, raised in Montgomery County.
Anthony. Certificate issued 27 Sept. 1819. DOM recorded by Margaret Hopkins 20 Aug. 1813. Freedom commenced 1 Jan. 1819. Age about 24, 5' 11", two scars on right foot, raised in Montgomery County.
Benjamin Bacon. Certificate issued 28 Sept. 1819. DOM recorded by Joseph R, Hopkins 25 Sept. 1819. Age about 30, 5' 3 1/2", black complexion, scar on little finger.
Peter Parker. Certificate issued 30 Oct. 1819. Born free and raised in AA Co. Age about 21, 5' 6", brown complexion, three scars on right arm, one on back of head.
Cadioallades Brooks. Certificate issued 5 Nov. 1819. Born free and raised in AA Co. Age about 25, 5' 7", black complexion, scars on thumb and wrist.
Susannah Parker. Certificate issued 9 Nov. 1819. Born free and raised in AA Co. Age about 22, 5' 2", brown complexion, left hand crippled by burn.

Thomas Brown. Certificate issued 11 Nov. 1819. Born free and raised in AA Co. Age about 26, 5' 3 1/2", dark complexion, black mark on right calf, three scars below right knee.

Shaddrach Issac. Certificate issued 15 Sept. 1819. Born free and raised in AA Co. Age about 25, 5' 10", black complexion, scar near left eye. small piece of upper lip missing.

Fanny. Certificate issued 16 Nov. 1819. DOM recorded by--- Harrison 31 Aug. 1816. Age about 43, 5' 3 1/2", yellowish complexion, small scar on right side over nose, raised in AA Co.

Charles Matthews. Certificate issued 19 Nov. 1819. Born free and raised in AA Co. Age about 24, 5' 7 1/2", brown complexion, scar on left arm above the wrist.

Bill Matthews. Certificate issued 19 Nov. 1819. Born free and raised in AA Co. Age about 21, 5' 5 1/2", mulatto.

Nince Hemmings. Certificate issued 29 Nov. 1819. DOM recorded by Louis Gassoway 16 Nov. 1819. Age about 31, 5' 2", bright complexion, small scars right side of nose, and back of right hand. raised in AA Co.

William Johnson. Certificate issued 7 Dec. 1819. Born free and raised in AA Co. Age about 22, 5" 10", black complexion, scar on top of right foot.

Will. Certificate issued 20 Dec. 1819. DOM recorded by Jeremiah Gaither 16 Dec. 1819. Age about 42, 6' 1", brown complexion, small scars near right nostril and on left thumb, raised in AA Co.

John. Certificate issued 5 Jan. 1820. DOM recorded by William Stewart 17 April 1804. Age 22, 5' 7 1/2", dark complexion, small scars over and under left eye, raised in AA Co.

Ellen Young (Nel). Certificate issued 25 Jan. 1820. DOM recorded by Elijah Pennington 25 Jan. 1820. Age about 41, 5' 5", dark complexion, scar on under left arm above the elbow, raised in AA Co.

Abram Smith. Certificate issued 28 Jan. 1819. Born free and raised in AA Co. Age about 24, 5' 7 1/2", light complexion.

James Price. Certificate issued 21 Feb. 1820. Born free and raised in AA Co. Age about 17, 5' 4 1/2", brown complexion, "J D" and "E P" tattooed on right arm.

James Cain. Certificate issued 21 Feb. 1820. Born free and raised in AA Co. Age about 20, 5' 5 1/2", brown complexion, small scar above right wrist.

James Green. Certificate issued 29 Feb.

1820. Born free and raised in AA Co. Age about 21, 5' 8", black complexion, small scars over left eye, on right cheek, end of fourth finger right hand.

Dinah Brown. Certificate issued 12 April 1820. Born free and raised in AA Co. Age about 17, 5', black complexion, scar on left arm above the elbow.

Rachel Lee. Certificate issued 27 April 1820. Born free and raised in AA Co. Age about 16, 5' 3", black complexion, small scar on nose.

Dick Williams. Certificate issued 16 May 1820. DOM recorded by John Chew Thomas 12 Feb. 1812. Age about 30, 5' 7" brown complexion, marked in face by smallpox. raised in AA Co.

John. Certificate issued 25 May 1820. DOM recorded by John Chew Thomas 12 Feb. 1812. Age about 32, 5' 5", black complexion, small scar on nose, raised in AA Co.

Peter. Certificate issued 25 May 1820. DOM recorded by John Chew Thomas 12 Feb. 1812. Age about 30, 5' 10", black complexion, small scar under left eye, raised in AA Co.

Jim. Certificate issued 25 May 1820. DOM recorded by John Chew Thomas 12 Feb. 1812. Age about 21, 5' 8", brown complexion, scar near right eye, Freedom commenced 1 Jan. 1820, raised in AA Co.

Vache. Certificate issued 25 May 1820. DOM recorded by John Chew Thomas 12 Feb. 1812. Age about 45, 5' 8", brown complexion, small scar on nose. Freedom commenced 1 Jan. 1817, raised in AA Co.

Polly. Certificate issued 25 May 1820. DOM recorded by John Chew Thomas 12 Feb. 1812. Age about 43, 5' 5", black complexion, scar on top of head, raised in AA Co.

Peter. Certificate issued xion [?], small scar under left eye, raised in AA Co.

Jim. Certificate issued 25 May 1890. DOM recorded by John Chew Thomas 12 Feb. 1812. Age about 21, 5' 8", brown complexion, scar near right eye, freedom commenced 1 Jan. 1800, raised in. AA Co.

Catherine Hackney. Certificate issued 5 June 1820 Born free and raised in AA Co. Age about 19, 5' 2 1/2", brown complexion, small scar on left forehead.

Tom Sands. Certificate issued 17 July 1820. DOM recorded by William H--- 15 May 1818. Age about 45, 5" 7", bright complexion, small scars on chin, right temple, and under each eye, raised in AA Co.

Deborah Clarke. Certificate issued 21 Aug. 1820. DOM recorded by Eleanor Clarke 22 June 1820. Age about 24, 5' 5", bright complexion, raised in AA Co.

John Cooke. Certificate issued 8 Sept. 1820. DOM recorded by Richard Stringer 24 Dec. 1811. Age about 30, 5' 10", black complexion, scar on back of left hand, raised in Montgomery County.

Dick. Certificate issued 26 Sept. 1820. DOM recorded by Sarah Merriweather 25 March 1809. Age 28, 5' 8 1/2", black complexion, scars over nose, on right eye, and chest, raised in AA Co.

Charles Parker. Certificate issued 29 Sept. 1820. Born free and raised in AA Co. Age about 23, 5' 4", brown complexion, small scar on left side of nose.

Milly Parker. Certificate issued 29 Sept. 1820. Born free and raised in AA Co. Age about 18, 5' 11", black complexion, small scar on forehead.

Richard Williams. Certificate issued 11 Nov. 1820. Born free and raised in AA Co. Age about 19, 5' 11", light complexion, small. scars on left cheek and third finger left hand.

Charles. Certificate issued 18 Nov. 1820. DOM recorded by Ann Jennifer 14 May 1819. Age 43, 5' 9", brown complexion, two small scars on left side of neck, raised in AA Co.

Charity Prout. Certificate issued 30 Nov. 1820. Born free and raised in AA Co. Age about 19, 5' 1", bright complexion, scar on left cheek.

James Johnson. Certificate issued 9 Dec. 1820. DOM recorded by George Johnson 14 April 1812. Age about 20, 5' 9", dark complexion, small scar on little finger left hand, raised in AA Co.

Ely. Certificate issued 22 Dec. 1820. DOM recorded by Charles Hammond of Charles 7 May 1802. Age 23, 5' 7", dark complexion, raised in AA Co.

Zack. Certificate issued 22 Dec. 1820. DOM recorded by Charles Hammond of Charles May 1802. Freedom commenced 1816. Age 23, 5' 7", yellowish complexion, small scar on forehead raised in AA Co.

Jacob Boston. Certificate issued 1 Jan. 1821. Born free and raised in AA Co. Age about 19, 5' 8", dark complexion, small scar over right eye.

William. Certificate issued 22 Feb. 1821. DOM recorded by Sussanna Lane 21 Nov. 1806. Age about 22, 5' 8", brown complexion, raised in AA Co.

Benjamin Brown. Certificate issued 13 March 1821. DOM recorded by John Hooper 13 March 1821. Age about 35, 5' 10 1/2", brown complexion, small scar left side of face, raised in AA Co.

Samson Frazier. Certificate issued 14 March 1821. DOM recorded by Hester Hood 10 March 1821. Age 38, 5' 8", black complexion, scars on chest, right nostril, and right eye; raised in AA Co.

William —. Certificate issued 24 March 1821. Born free and raised in AA Co. Age about 21. 5' 8 1/2", black complexion, small scars under right eye, in corner of both eyes, and back of right hand.

Nicholas Scott. Certificate issued 26 March 1821. DOM recorded by Eliza Hammond 7 March 1821. Age about 35 5' 9 1/2", brown complexion, raised in AA Co.

Nace Williams. Certificate issued 18 April 1819. DOM recorded by Rezin H. Snowden 16 April 1821. Age about 40, 5' 4 1/2", brown complexion, small scar in right eyebrow; raised in AA Co.

Peter. Certificate issued 23 April 1821. DOM recorded by Sarah Merriweather 25 March 1908. Freedom commenced 1820. Age 26, 5' 9", black complexion, small scar on forehead, raised in AA Co.

Mary Thomas. Certificate issued 22 May 1821. DOM recorded by John Franklin 13 March 1821. Age about 35, 5', light complexion, scar in corner of left eye and on both cheeks, raised in AA Co.

Minta (Mista ?). Certificate issued 13 June 1821. DOM recorded by Mary Wy--- Jan. 1810. Age about 22, 5' 6", black complexion, scar on left check. Freedom commenced 29 Jan. 1821, raised in AA Co.

Daniel L—. Certificate issued 18 June 1821. Born free and raised in AA Co. Age about 23, 5' 7", brown complexion, small scars on right cheek and upper lip.

Louisa Fr—. Certificate issued 26 June 1821. DOM recorded by John Price 4 March 1806. Age about 19, 5' 3 1/2", yellow complexion, two small scars on back of neck, raised in AA Co.

James Price. Certificate issued 2 July 1821. Born free and raised in AA Co. Age about 18, 5' 8", brown complexion, small. scar on left arm.

John Queen. Certificate issued 24 July 1821. Born free and raised in AA Co. Age 22, 5' 7", dark complexion, two scars on. right leg below the knee, small scar on back of. left hand.

Jasper Jenkins. Certificate issued 21 Aug. 1821. DOM recorded by George Wills 25 July 1821. Age about 40, 5' 8", black complexion, small scar on left arm, raised in AA Co.

Ben. Certificate issued 27 Aug. 1821. DOM recorded by Joseph Prout 20 Feb. 1802. Age about 26, 5' 9 1/2", black complexion, small scar arm, raised in AA Co.

Cate. Certificate issued 1 Sept. 1821. DOM recorded by Leonard Mallonee (Malony ?) 20 May 1821. Age about 35, 5' 6", dark complexion, small scar on left wrist, raised in. AA Co.

Minta. Certificate issued 28 Sept. 1821. DOM recorded by Richard Conner 13 June 1821. Age about 42, 5' 5", black complexion, scar on back of right hand, raised in AA Co.

Elvira. Certificate issued 28 Sept. 1821. DOM recorded by Richard Conner 13 June 1821. Age about 15, 5' 1 1/2", brown complexion, small scar corner of right eye, raised in AA Co.

Maria Boston. Certificate issued 4 Oct. 1821. DOM recorded by Sarah Galloway and Virgil--- 2 Oct. 1821. Age about 57, 5' 3 1/2", black complexion, raised in AA Co.

Arminta Chew. Certificate issued 21 Nov. 1821. Freedom obtained by judgment in AA Co. Court Oct. 1821 upon petition filed against Nicholas Brewer, trustee of George---, an insolvent debtor. Age about 42, 5' 5", brown complexion, small scar on inside of left arm, raised in AA Co.

Dilly Taylor. Certificate issued 3 Oct. 1821. Born free and raised in AA Co. Age about 19, 5' 6", yellow complexion, scar on neck.

Dinah Hall. Certificate issued 6 Dec. 1821. DOM recorded by Richard B. Watts 5 Dec. 1821. Age about 22, 5' 2", black complexion, scar on left arm, raised in AA Co.

Thomas Phelps. Certificate issued 26 Dec. 1821. Born free and raised in AA Co. Age about 21, 5' 9", bright complexion, two small marks on each arm, small scar on right arm.

Saul. Certificate issued 27 Dec. 1821. DOM recorded by Francis Hancock 6 March 1819. Age 35, 5' 4 1/2", black complexion, two small scars on breast, raised in AA Co.

William Carter (Bill). Certificate issued 28 Dec. 1821. DOM recorded by Sarah Riggs 18 May 1814. Age about 31, 5 1/2"; brown complexion; small scar on left eyebrow; raised in AA Co.

Rezin. Certificate issued 10 Jan. 1822. DOM recorded by Sarah Riggs 1814. Age about 20; 5' 6"; bright complexion; sharp face; small scar on chin; mullatto; raised in AA Co.

Nack. Certificate issued 10 Jan. 1822. DOM recorded by Sarah Riggs 18 May 1814. Age about 28; 5' 4 1/2"; brown complexion; small scar on right arm; mulatto; raised in AA Co.

Airry. Certificate issued 10 Jan. 1822. DOM recorded by Sarah Riggs 18 May 1814. Age about 26; 5' 1 1/2"; bright complexion; long black hair; scar under right jawbone; mullatto; raised in AA Co.

Cordelia (Delia). Certificate issued 10 Jan. 1822. DOM recorded by Sarah Riggs 18 May 1814. Age about 24; 5' 5 1/2"; bright complexion; small mole near right ear; mulatto; raised in AA Co.

Maria. Certificate issued 10 Jan. 1822. DOM recorded by Sarah Riggs 18 May 1814. Age about 18; 5' 1 1/2"; bright complexion; scar on back of right hand; raised in AA Co.

Caroline. Certificate issued 10 Jan. 1822. DOM recorded by Sarah Riggs 18 May 1814. Mulatto, raised in AA Co. age about 16; 5' 11 1/2", bright complexion, small scars on both cheeks and right wrist.

Caleb (Cale). Certificate issued 4 Feb. 1822. DOM recorded by Nicholas L--- 7 Nov. 1809. Age about 40; 5'---"; scar on right side of upper lip; Freedom commenced 1 Jan. 1822; raised in AA Co.

Mary Anne Howard. Certificate issued 6 Feb. 1822. DOM recorded by Issac and Nicey P---, Rachel Brown, and Phillip Hammond 29 June 1818. Age about 23; 5' 2"; bright complexion; long straight hair; raised in AA Co.

Ruth Howard. Certificate issued 6 Feb. 1822. DOM recorded by Phillip Howard Feb. 1822. Age about 23; 5' 2"; bright complexion; long straight hair; raised in AA Co.

Thomas Brashears. Certificate issued 7 Feb. 1822. Born free and raised in AA Co. Age about 22; 5' 7 1/2"; light complexion; small scar over left eye.

George Mayers (Meyers). Certificate issued 12 Feb. 1822. DOM recorded by John O. L. Jones 26 March 1816. Age about 36; 5' 7"; light complexion; small scar over left eye; mole in left whiskers; raised in Prince George's County.

Frank Howard. Certificate issued 26 March 1822. DOM recorded by John Franklin 26 March 1822. Age about 48; 5' 5 1/2"; dark complexion; scar on inside of left arm; raised in AA Co.

Nance. Certificate issued 16 April 1822. DOM recorded by James Williams 23 June 1821. Age about 44; 5' 1"; dark com-

plexion; small scar on forehead; raised in AA Co.
Eleais Queen. Certificate issued 31 May 1822. Born free and raised in AA Co. Age about 21; 5' 6"; black complexion; small scars on face.
William Issac. Certificate issued 8 June 1822. Born free and raised in AA Co. Age About 30; 5' 10"; dark complexion; scars on inside of left wrist and under lip.
Samuel Hackman Junior. Certificate issued 16 June 1822. Born free and raised in AA Co. Age about 21; 5' 4"; dark complexion.
George Boston. Certificate issued 16 July 1822. DOM recorded by Joseph Count 20 Feb. 1802. Age about 29; 6' 1"; dark complexion; raised in AA Co.
Jim. Certificate issued 7 Aug. 1822. DOM recorded by Sarah Riggs 18 May 1814. Age about 28; 5' 9"; black complexion; scar on right wrist; raised in AA Co.
Sampson. Certificate issued 7 Aug. 1822. DOM recorded by Sarah Riggs 18 May 1814. Age about 23; 5' 10"; brown complexion; scar on forefinger of left hand; raised in AA Co.
Hannah. Certificate issued 7 Aug. 1822. DOM recorded by Henry Hammond 23 Feb. 1811. Age about 38; 5' 4"; dark complexion; scars on right corner of mouth, left eye corner, and back of right hand; raised in AA Co.
Laphea Kelly. Certificate issued 21 Aug. 1822. Born free and raised in AA Co. Age about 21; 5' 5"; dark complexion; scar on right ear.
Bill. Certificate issued 10 Dec. 1822. DOM recorded by Sarah Merriweather 25 March 1809. Age about 27; 5' 5"; black complexion; scar on breast; raised in AA Co.
Moses. Certificate issued 10 Dec. 1822. DOM recorded by Nicholas Merriweather 24 Sept. 1803. Freedom commenced 1820. Age about 28; 5' 8 1/2"; black complexion; scars near left nostril and back of left hand; raised in AA Co.
Charles. Certificate issued 10 Dec. 1822. DOM recorded by Wesley Linthicum 16 Dec. 1822. Age about 39; 5' 4 1/2"; brown complexion; scars between left eye and ear and near the right ear; raised in AA Co.
Cate. Certificate issued 10 Jan. 1823. DOM recorded by Francis Cromwell 23 Aug. 1792. Freedom commenced 19 Dec. 1822. Age about 34; 5' 2"; brown complexion; scar on right cheek; raised in AA Co.
Sophia. Certificate issued 22 Jan. 1823.

DOM recorded by Richard Conner 13 June 1821. Age about 17; 5' 1 1/2"; brown complexion; raised in AA Co.
Richard. Certificate issued 22 Jan. 1823. DOM recorded by Richard Conner 13 June 1821. Age about 25; 6' 3 1/2"; black complexion; scar on outside of left---, raised in AA Co.
John Cromwell. Certificate issued 13 Feb. 1823. Born free and raised in AA Co. Age about 21; 5' 4"; black complexion; scar on right wrist.
Matthew. Certificate issued 8 March 1823. DOM recorded by Charles Drury 3 Feb. 1797. Age about 28; 5' 8"; dark complexion; small scars on forehead and second finger of left hand; Freedom commenced 1 Jan. 1816; raised in AA Co.
John Johnson. Certificate issued 17 March 1823. DOM recorded by Hester and Elizabeth Hood 2 Dec. 1822. Age about 40; 5' 8 1/4"; black complexion; scar on the---; raised in AA Co.
Sarah Johnson. Certificate issued 17 March 1823. DOM recorded by Hester and Elizabeth Hood 2 Dec. 1822. Age about 44; 5' 1/2"; brown complexion; lost first joint of forefinger of left hand; raised in AA Co.
Cassandra Frazier. Certificate issued 17 March 1823. DOM recorded by Hester and Elizabeth Hood 2 Dec. 1822. Age about 35; 5' 5 1/4"; dark complexion; scar on back of left hand; raised in AA Co.
Anne Taylor. Certificate issued 17 March 1823. DOM recorded by Hester and Elizabeth Hood 2 Dec. 1822. Age about 23; 5' 4 1/2"; black complexion; scar on left side of face; raised in AA Co.
Norry Harrison. Certificate issued 17 March 1823. DOM recorded by Hester and Elizabeth Hood 2 Dec. 1822. Age about 25; 5' 8 1/2"; black complexion; scar upon upper lip and over left eyebrow; raised in AA Co.
Jerry Spriggs. Certificate issued 17 March 1823. DOM recorded by Hester and Elizabeth Hood 2 Dec. 1822. Age about 44; 5' 1/2"; brown complexion; missing first joint of forefinger left hand; raised in AA Co.
Charity Parker. Certificate issued 19 March 1823. Born Free and raised in AA Co. Age about 37; 5' 4"; brown complexion; raised in AA Co.
Kitty Prout. Certificate issued 20 March 1823. DOM recorded by Elizabeth Hood 19 March 1823. Age about 33; 5' 2"; black complexion, small scar near right thumb; raised in AA Co.

Hester Aleen (Allen ?). Certificate issued 20 March 1823. DOM recorded by Hester and Elizabeth Hood 2 Dec. 1822. Age about 31; 5' 5"; black complexion; scars on right wrist and under the left eye; raised in AA Co.

Darkey Young. Certificate issued 20 March 1823. DOM recorded by Hester and Elizabeth Hood 2 Dec. 1822. Age about 23; 5' 3"; black complexion; small scar on bend of right arm; raised in AA Co.

Eliza Brown. Certificate issued 26 March 1823. DOM recorded by Hester and Elizabeth Hood 2 Dec. 1822. Age about 25; 5' 4"; black complexion; scars on right elbow and back of right hand; raised in AA Co.

Louisa Parker. Certificate issued 28 March 1823. DOM recorded by Hester and Elizabeth Hood 2 Dec. 1823. Age about 25; 5' 2 1/2"; black complexion; small scar on back of left hand; raised in AA Co.

John Smith. Certificate issued 1 April 1823. Born Free and raised in AA Co. Age about 26; 5' 9"; dark complexion; scar over left eye; raised in AA Co.

Nancy Mahand (Nanny). Certificate issued 22 May 1823. DOM recorded by Charles Carroll of Carrollton 11 March 1806. Age about 57; 4' 11"; brown complexion; scar over left eye.

Charles Mahand. Certificate issued 22 May 1823. DOM recorded by Charles Carroll of Carrollton 11 March 1806. Age about 21; 5' 6 1/2"; bright complexion; raised in AA Co.

Elizabeth Beicley (Beasley ?). Certificate issued 15 July 1823. Born free and raised in AA Co. Age about 29; 5' 4"; brown complexion; small scar on left corner of mouth.

Tom Haywood. Certificate issued 16 July 1823. DOM recorded by Bill Haywood 14 March 1812. Age about 25; 5' 3"; dark complexion; scars on left knee, right foot, and left leg; raised in AA Co.

Lule. Certificate issued 26 July 1823. DOM recorded by John Price 19 June 1806. Freedom commenced 15 April 1812. Age about 34; 5'; yellow complexion; small scar between fingers of right hand; raised in AA Co.

Edward Parker. Certificate issued 18 Aug. 1823. Born free and raised in AA Co. Age about 20; 5' 4 1/2"; light complexion; scar on left hand. Raised in AA Co.

Richard. Certificate issued 19 Aug. 1823. DOM recorded by Eleanor Yieldhall 8 May 1799. Freedom commenced in 1804. Age about 47; 5' 3 1/2"; black complexion; scar on belly and face marked by smallpox; raised in AA Co.

Charity. Certificate issued 29 Aug. 1823. DOM recorded by Joseph Evans 7 March 1804. Freedom commenced 27 Aug. 1818. Age about 30, 5' 2 1/2"; brown complexion; raised in AA Co.

Jane Charles (Shorter ?). Certificate issued 29 Aug. 1823. DOM recorded by Peter Shorter (Charles ?) 20 July 1820. Age about 27; 5'; brown complexion; small scar on forehead; raised in AA Co.

Sarah Shorter. Certificate issued 29 July 1823. DOM recorded by Peter Shorter 20 July 1820. Age about 21; 4' 10"; brown complexion; scar on right hand; raised in AA Co.

Peter. Certificate issued 7 Sept. 1823. DOM recorded by Ann Jenifer, executor of Joseph Jennifer 21 May 1819. Age about 21; 5' 6"; black complexion; raised in AA Co.

Joseph. Certificate issued 10 Sept. 1823. DOM recorded by Charles Hammond of Charles, Esq. 7 May 1802. Age about 24; 5' 8"; brown complexion; Freedom commenced in 1818. Raised in AA Co.

Haricot. Certificate issued 17 Sept. 1823. DOM recorded by Alle--- 16 Nov. 1799. Age about 25; 5' 3 1/2"; black complexion; raised in AA Co.

Sukey. Certificate issued 18 Sept. 1823. DOM recorded by Nathanial Chew 13 Sept. 1823. Age about 40; 5' 3" dark complexion; scar on breast; raised in AA Co.

Charles Calvert. Certificate issued 17 Oct. 1823. DOM recorded by Joseph McCurry (?) 23 Aug. 1816. Age 43; 5' 4"; dark complexion; raised in AA Co.

Robert Brown. Certificate issued 14 Nov. 1823. Born free and raised in AA Co. Age about 27; 5' 4"; black complexion; scars on right arm and left hand.

Fanny. Certificate issued 22 Dec. 1823. DOM recorded by Ann Jennifer 6 Aug. 1819. Age about 24; 5' 1"; brown complexion; scar on back of left hand; raised in AA Co.

Samuel Cheers. Certificate issued 16 Jan. 1824. Born free and raised in AA Co. Age about 21; 5' 4"; black complexion; small scars on upper lip and forehead.

William. Certificate issued 22 Jan. 1824. DOM recorded by Eleanor Yieldhall 28 May 1799. Age about 25; 5' 6"; yellow complexion; small scar over right eye; raised in AA Co.

Benjamin. Certificate issued 24 Jan. 1824. DOM recorded by Eleanor Yieldhall 28

May 1799. Age about 27; 5' 4"; dark complexion; small scars on left thumb and under left eye; raised in AA Co.
George. Certificate issued 26 Jan. 1824. DOM recorded by Eleanor Yieldhall 28 May 1799. Age about 31; 5' 2 1/2"; black complexion; thick lips; raised in AA Co.
Tom. Certificate issued 28 Jan. 1824. DOM recorded by George Stinchcomb 28 Jan. 1824. Age 42; 5' 7"; dark complexion; scar over left eye; another on right cheek; raised in AA Co.
Samuel Prout. Certificate issued 7 Feb. 1824. Born free and raised in AA Co. Age about 21; 5' 8"; dark complexion; scar on end of middle finger of right hand.
Benjamin Troy. Certificate issued 7 Feb. 1824. Born free and raised in AA Co.; age about 27; 5' 5"; dark complexion; small scar under left eye.
Gustavus. Certificate issued 10 March 1824. Born free and raised in AA Co. Age about 25; 5' 8"; black complexion; small scar on left cheek.
McCall Queen. Certificate issued 17 March 1824. Born free and raised in AA Co. Age about 22; 5' 3"; brown complexion; small scar on left wrist.
Charles Phillips. Certificate issued 19 March 1824. DOM recorded by Henry Duvall 18 May 1809. Freedom commenced 1 Jan. 1824. Age 36; 5' 10"; dark complexion; scar on left cheek; raised in AA Co.
William Hicks. Certificate issued 29 March 1824. DOM recorded by A. H. Plummer 26 March 1824. Age about 21; 5' 6"; brown complexion; small scar corner of right eye; raised in AA Co.
Charity Brown. Certificate issued 6 April 1824. DOM recorded by Henry (Harry ?) Hooper 9 April 1824. Age 27; 5' 3"; black complexion; raised in AA Co.
Ben. Certificate issued 19 April 1824. DOM recorded by John Norwood 7 March 1803. Freedom commenced during 1823. Age 28; 5' 9"; dark complexion; several small scars over left eye; raised in AA Co.
Thomas Price. Certificate issued 26 April 1824. Born free and raised in AA Co. Age about 19; 5' 6"; brown complexion; scars near right ear and corner of right eye.
Harriet Gale (Yale?). Certificate issued 18 May 1826. DOM recorded by Jeremiah T. Chase 18 May 1824. Age 21; 5' 4 1/2"; bright complexion; scars on left arm and back of right hand; raised in AA Co.
Henry Troy. Certificate issued 16 June 1824. Born free and raised in AA Co. Age about 37; 5' 1"; black complexion; scar on little finger of left hand.
John. Certificate issued 21 June 1824. DOM recorded by Jonathan N. Loughlin 9 May 1808. Age about 24; 5' 9"; dark complexion; scar below left eye; several scars on back of left hand; raised in AA Co.
Maria. Certificate issued 21 June 1824. DOM recorded by Jonathan N. Loughlin 9 May 1808. Age about 22; 5' 1 1/2"; dark complexion; scar near right ear; raised in AA Co.
Tom Haywood. Certificate issued 9 July 1824. DOM recorded by Bill Haywood 19 March 1812. Age about 21; 5' 3"; dark complexion; scar over left knee, another on left leg; raised in AA Co.
Washington. Certificate issued 18 July 1824. Born free and raised in AA Co. Age about 23; 5' 11"; black complexion; scar under right eye.
Benjamin Brown. Certificate issued 31 July 1824. Freedom recovered by petition in the AA Co. Court against Samuel Maccubbin Sept. 7, 1813. Age about 30; 5' 6 1/2"; brown complexion; small scar over left eye; raised in AA Co.
Kitty Joice. Certificate issued 16 Aug. 1824. Born free and raised in AA Co. Age about 19; 5' 6 1/2"; black complexion.
Edmond Brewer. Certificate issued 27 Aug. 1824. Born free and raised in AA Co. Age about 20; 5' 7"; dark complexion; scar on left calf.
Nancy. Certificate issued 2 Sept. 1824. DOM recorded by Samuel ? Hopkins March 1824. Age 24; 5' 3 1/2"; black complexion; raised in AA Co.
Amelia Hackman. Certificate issued 2 Sept. 1824. Born free and raised in AA Co. Age about 19; 5' 6 1/2"; brown complexion; small scar on right arm; another on left arm.
James Matthews. Certificate issued 7 Sept. 1824. DOM recorded by Charles Pettibone 26 Jan. 1805. Age about 30; 5' 8 1/2"; black complexion; scars on right wrist; right thumb; back of right hand and inside of left arm; raised in AA Co.
Nancy Bayley. Certificate issued 20 Sept. 1824. Born free and raised in AA Co. Age about 26; 5'; brown complexion.
Kitty. Certificate issued 2 Oct. 1824. DOM recorded by John --- 14 March 1811. Age about 22; 5' 4 1/2"; black complexion; raised in AA Co.
Henry ---. Certificate issued 29 Oct. 1824. Born free and raised in AA Co. Age about 16; 5' 4"; black complexion; small scar on forefinger of left hand.

Rezin Proud. Certificate issued 29 Oct. 1824. Born free and raised in AA Co. Age about 18; 5' 7 1/2" dark complexion; small scar right side of face near the mouth.
Molly. Certificate issued 15 March 1825. DOM recorded by A. Stinchcomb 2 March 1808. Age 25; 5' 1 1/2"; Black complexion; scar over left eye; raised in AA Co.
Flora. Certificate issued 25 March 1825. Born free and raised in AA Co. Age about 20; 5"; black complexion; scars on right elbow and left arm.
George Hackney. Certificate issued 25 March 1825. Born free and raised in AA Co. Age about 21; 5' 8"; dark complexion.
Frederick Parker. Certificate issued 13 April 1825. Born free and raised in AA Co. Age about 22; 5' 5"; black complexion; scar over right eye.
Anthony. Certificate issued 21 April 1825. DOM recorded by David Weems 8 Sept. 1803 Age about 39; 5' 8 1/2"; brown complexion; small scars on upper lip and under lip; raised in AA Co.
Jacob. Certificate issued 2 May 1825. DOM recorded by Annie Kelly 4 May 1820. Age about 35; 5' 9"; dark complexion; small scars under lip, on left cheek; has lost part of left ear; raised in AA Co.
Adeau (Andrew ?) Brown. Certificate issued 7 May 1825. DOM recorded by Mary Callahan 10 April 1821. Age about 25; 5' 2 1/2"; light complexion; raised in AA Co.
Mary Queen. Certificate issued 22 May 1825. Born free and raised in AA Co. Age about 25; 5' 5"; dark complexion; scar in right corner of mouth.
Sally Queen. Certificate issued 22 May 1825. Born free and raised in AA Co. Age about 23; 5' 3 1/4"; dark complexion; small scar over left eye; small mole under lip.
William Hicks. Certificate issued 21 May 1825. DOM recorded by Ann H. Plummer 26 March 1824. Age about 22; 5' 6"; dark complexion; small scar near corner of right eye; raised in AA Co.
Edward (Emmanuel, Edmund ?) Prout. Certificate issued 23 May 1825. Born free and raised in AA Co. Age about 27; 5' 6"; dark complexion; small scar between eyes, another in the right eye.
Henny. Certificate issued 26 May 1825. Obtained freedom by petition to the AA Co. against William Woodfield Oct. 1824. Age about 31; 4' 9 1/2"; brown complexion; small scar on right arm; raised in AA Co.
Charlotte. Certificate issued 26 May 1825. Born free and raised in AA Co. Age about 19; 5' 4"; dark complexion; small scars on left cheek and jaw.
James Price. Certificate issued 26 May 1825. Born free and raised in AA Co. Age about 22; 5' 9"; brown complexion; small scar on left arm; tattoo on right arm with female figure with letters JP and ED.
Priscilla. Certificate issued 27 May 1825. DOM recorded by David Robinson 7 March 1818. Age about 30; 5' 4"; dark complexion; small scar over left cheekbone; another in left eyebrow; mole on the throat; raised in AA Co.
Peggy Parker. Certificate issued 7 June 1825. Born free and raised in AA Co. Age about 20; 5' 1"; dark complexion; small scar on right cheek.
Sarah Phelps (Phillips ?). Certificate issued 19 July 1825. Born free and raised in AA Co. Age about 21; yellow complexion; two small scars on back of each hand.
Orange. Certificate issued 20 Aug. 1825. DOM recorded by Mary --- 29 Jan. 1810. Age about 30; 5' 4 1/2"; light complexion; scar on left knee; raised in AA Co.
Charlotte. Certificate issued 19 Sept. 1825. DOM recorded by Jonathan Loughlin 2 June 1805. Age about 45; 4' 11 1/2"; dark complexion; raised in AA Co.
Mary. Certificate issued 27 Sept. 1825. DOM recorded by Phillip H. Hopkins 24 June 1815. Age about 44; 5' 8"; brown complexion; two small scars on right arm; raised in AA Co.
Sarah Butler. Certificate issued 13 Oct. 1825. DOM recorded by John and Dennis Claude 14 April 1823. Age about 28; 5'; bright complexion; raised in AA Co.
Susan Smith ("now Susan Stewart"). 13 Oct. 1825. DOM recorded by J--- Fowler 18 Nov. 1815. Age about 29; 5"; light complexion; scar on right side of neck; raised in AA Co.
Suck. Certificate issued 17 Oct. 1825. DOM recorded by Marry Merriweather 11 Nov. 1811. Age about 31; 5' 5"; black complexion; small scar on back of left hand; raised in AA Co.
Hannah. Certificate issued 17 Oct. 1825. DOM recorded by William Osgood 6 April 1820. Age about 35; 5' 2"; dark complexion; small scar near corner of left eye; raised in AA Co.
Matilda Davis. Certificate issued 5 Nov. 1825. Born free and raised in AA Co. Age about 16; 5' 1"; light complexion; small scar near corner of right eye.
Rachael Hinsman. Certificate issued 12 Nov. 1825. Born free and raised in AA Co.

Age about 28; 5' 1" brown complexion; no scars or marks.

Levi Miles. Certificate issued 12 Nov. 1825. Born free and raised in AA Co. Age about 24; 5' 4 1/2"; black complexion; small scar on nose.

Benjamin Nelson. Certificate issued 22 Nov. 1825. DOM recorded by Huel W--- 13 Nov. 1813. Freedom commenced 25 Dec. 1819. Age about 30; 5' 7"; bright complexion; dark spot on each cheek; right arm dislocated; raised in AA Co.

Nathan. Certificate issued 26 Nov. 1825. Born free and raised in AA Co. Age about 28; 5' 7"; black complexion; face marked by smallpox.

Daniel. Certificate issued 29 Nov. 1825. DOM recorded by George G. Br--- 28 Nov. 1825. Age about 21; 5' 3"; light complexion; large scar on left ear; raised in AA Co.

Nicholas Parker. Certificate issued 29 Nov. 1825. Born free and raised in AA Co. Age about 23; 5' 4"; brown complexion; no scars or marks.

Viney Jennings. Certificate issued 1 Dec. 1825. Born free and raised in AA Co. Age about 25; 5' 1"; brown complexion; missing two upper front teeth.

James Henson (Newson ?). 6 Dec. 1825. DOM recorded by Mary L. Web---? 3 Dec. 1825. Age about 40; 5' 5"; black complexion; small scar on left cheek; raised on the Eastern Shore of Maryland.

Mary Prout. Certificate issued 15 Dec. 1825. Born free and raised in AA Co. Age about 17, 5' 10"; black complexion; no marks or scars.

John Garrett. Certificate issued 16 Dec. 1825. Born free and raised in AA Co. 5' 5 1/2"; brown complexion; small scars on left nostril and hand.

Solomon. Certificate issued 16 Dec. 1825. DOM recorded by John O. L. Jones 23 Sept. 1805. Freedom commenced 8 Nov. 1820. Age about 28; 5' 8 1/2"; black complexion; raised in AA Co.

Josephine (?) Boone. Certificate issued 9 Dec. 1825. Born free and raised in AA Co. Age about 21; 5' 7"; brown complexion; small scar near corner of right eye.

John Boone. Certificate issued 9 Dec. 1825. Born free and raised in AA Co. Age about 22; 5' 3 1/2"; yellow complexion; small scar on right side of chin.

Jacob Parker. Certificate issued 3 Jan. 1826. Born free and raised in AA Co. Age about 21; 5' 6"; brown complexion; small scar over left eye.

— Sprigg. Certificate issued 11 Jan. 1826. Born free and raised in AA Co. Age about 22; 5' 3"; brown complexion; no scars or marks.

John Toogood. Certificate issued 12 Jan. 1826. Born free and raised in AA Co. Age about 22; 5' 7"; black complexion; small mole over right eye.

Solomon Allen. Certificate issued 12 Jan. 1826. Born free and raised in AA Co. Age about 21; 5' 2 1/2"; dark complexion; small scar under the left eye.

Thomas Garrett. Certificate issued 13 Jan. 1826. Born free and raised in AA Co. Age about 21; 5' 5"; brown complexion; small scar on left wrist.

Richard. Born free and raised in AA Co. Age about 22; 5' 4"; yellow complexion; no scars or marks.

Daniel Troy. Certificate issued 28 Jan. 1826. DOM recorded by William and Mary Glover 7 Jan. 1825. Age about 41; 5' 5"; black complexion; no perceptible marks; raised in AA Co.

James Bowser. Certificate issued 11 March 1826. DOM recorded by Phillip Boston Key 7 Jan. 1814. Age about 24; 5' 3"; black complexion; two scars on left leg; raised in AA Co.

Harry. Certificate issued 21 March 1826. DOM recorded by Charles Pettibone 29 Jan. 1805. Freedom commenced 25 Dec. 1825. Age 28; 5' 6"; dark complexion; no perceptible scars.

Betty. Certificate issued 1 April 1826. DOM recorded by Samuel McCubbin 3 Feb. 1791. Freedom commenced at age 21. Age about 41, 5' 2"; black complexion; lightly marked by smallpox; raised in AA Co.

David. Certificate issued 18 April 1826. DOM recorded by Sarah Merriweather 25 March 1809. Freedom commenced in 1824. Age about 27; 5' 5"; black complexion; small scar on nose; raised in AA Co.

Andrew. Certificate issued 2 May 1826. DOM recorded by Martha P. Childs 15 June 1822. Age about 36; 5' 7"; black complexion; no perceptible marks or scars; raised in AA Co. Freedom commenced 5 Jan. 1826.

Rhoda. Certificate issued 2 May 1826. DOM recorded by Martha P. Childs 15 June 1822. Freedom commenced 1 Jan. 1826. Age about 33; 5'; brown complexion; large scar on right of face; raised in AA Co.

Joe Queen. Certificate issued 11 May 1826. Born free and raised in AA Co. Age about

21; 6"; black complexion; no marks or scars.
Kitty. Certificate issued 25 May 1826. DOM recorded by Leonard Scott 1 May 1816. Freedom commenced 25 May 1826. Age about 21; 5' 4"; black complexion; small scar near corner of left eye; raised in AA Co.
Mary Parker. Certificate issued 25 May 1826. Born free and raised in AA Co. Age about 23; 5'; black complexion; scar on left cheek.
Andrew Queen. Certificate issued 2 June 1826. Born free and raised in AA Co. Age about 21; 5' 1"; black complexion; large scar on right elbow.
Kinsey Griffin. Certificate issued 17 June 1826. Born free and raised in AA Co. Age about 24; 5' 6 1/2"; black complexion; small scar on back of right hand.
Kitty Green. Certificate issued 26 June 1826. DOM recorded by Africa Green 11 Jan. 1802. Age 29; 5' 3"; brown complexion; no marks or scars; raised in AA Co.
William Castle. Certificate issued 3 Aug. 1826. DOM recorded by Elizabeth C--- 21 Feb. 1810. Age about 18; 5' 5 1/2"; bright complexion; no scars or marks; raised in AA Co.
Charlotte. Certificate issued 8 Aug. 1826. Born free and raised in AA Co. Age about 18; 5'; dark complexion; no marks or scars.
Will— Brown. Certificate issued 16 Aug. 1826. Born free and raised in AA Co. Age about 30; 5' 9"; yellow complexion; scar on side of right foot.
Sarah Toppin. Certificate issued 22 Aug. 1826. Born free and raised in AA Co. Age about 29; 5' 4 1/2"; black complexion; scar on back of each hand.
James Johnson. Certificate issued 26 Aug. 1826. Born free and raised in AA Co. Age about 21; 5' 5 1/2"; dark complexion; small scar on each hand.
Acksah — Badys(Brayer?). Certificate issued 28 Aug. 1826. Born free and raised in AA Co. Age about 36; 5; 2"; black complexion; small scar on right eyebrow.
Eliza Badys (Brayer ?). Certificate issued 28 Aug. 1826. Born free and raised in AA Co. Age about 25; 5' 5 1/2"; yellow complexion; small scar on back of right arm.
Nace Badys (Brayer ?). Certificate issued 28 Aug. 1826. Born free and raised in AA Co. Age about 23; 5' 8 1/4"; yellow complexion; small scar in left eyebrow; two small scars over left eye.
John Ross. Certificate issued 29 Aug. 1826 Born free and raised in AA Co. Age about 21; 5' 5"; yellow complexion; two small scars.
Andrew Parker. Certificate issued 31 Aug. 1826. Born free and raised in AA Co. Age about 22; 5' 7"; dark complexion; small scar over right eye, another on right hand.
Flora. Certificate issued 31 Aug. 1826. DOM recorded by John Chew Thomas 3 Feb. 1810. Age about 38; 5' 3"; black complexion; small scars on right thumb and wrist; raised in AA Co.
John Watkins. Certificate issued 2 Sept. 1826. Born free and raised in AA Co. Age about 28; 5' 1"; black complexion; small scars over right eye and on left wrist.
Mary Parker. Certificate issued 6 Sept. 1826. Born free and raised in AA Co. Age about 38; 5' 1 1/2"; black complexion; small scar on left cheekbone.
Richard Elliott. Certificate issued 9 Sept. 1826. DOM recorded by Frederick Wills 9 Sept. 1826. Age about 42; 5' 5"; black complexion; small scars on forehead and right calf; raised in AA Co.
Andrew. Certificate issued 27 Sept. 1826. DOM recorded by Elizabeth Hood 6 April 1810. Age about 44; 5' 4 1/2"; black complexion; scar over the right eye; raised in AA Co.
Henny Fr—. Certificate issued 4 Oct. 1826. DOM recorded by John Brice 10 Sept. 1813. Age about 23; 5' 2 1/2"; light complexion; three scars on left arm; raised in AA Co.
William Gibson. Certificate issued 16 Oct. 1826. DOM recorded by Geneva S--- 22 Sept. 1826. Age about 35; 5' 8"; brown complexion; small scars on right thumb and left leg; raised in AA Co.
Betty. Certificate issued 28 Oct. 1826. DOM recorded by James Allison 28 Oct. 1826. Age about 26; 5' 1 1/2"; light complexion; scar on each side of mouth; raised in AA Co.
John. Certificate issued 8 Nov. 1826. DOM recorded by Mary Elson, deceased 13 March 1824. Age about 44; 5' 8"; black complexion; lame in left hip; crooked third finger of left hand; raised in AA Co.
Cloe. Certificate issued 8 Nov. 1826. DOM recorded by Mary Elson, deceased 13 March 1824. Age about thirty three years; 5' 3 1/2"; black complexion; small scar over right eye; raised in AA Co.
Parker. Certificate issued 9 Nov. 1826. DOM recorded by Martha P. Childs 15 June 1822. Age about 41; 5' 3"; dark com-

plexion; small scar on forehead; raised in AA Co.
Vachel. Certificate issued 16 Nov. 1826. DOM recorded by Rachel Snowden 20 Nov. 1813. Age about 23; 5' 5"; yellow complexion; scar over breast; raised in AA Co.
Dick Matthews. Certificate issued 16 Nov. 1826. DOM recorded by Rachel Snowden 20 Nov. 1813. Age about 23; 5' 2"; black complexion; raised in AA Co.
Fanny. Certificate issued 16 Nov. 1826. DOM recorded by Rachel Snowden 20 Nov. 1813. Age about 41; 5'; yellow complexion; two scars on right leg; raised in AA Co.
Hannah. Certificate issued 16 Nov. 1826. DOM recorded by Rachel Snowden 20 Nov. 1813. Age about 25; 5' 2 1/2"; brown complexion; small scar on left arm; raised in AA Co.
A. Brower (Brown ?). Certificate issued 14 Nov. 1826. Born free and raised in AA Co. 5' 8"; black complexion; speech impediment.
Mary Parker. Certificate issued 18 Nov. 1826. Born free and raised in AA Co. Age about 24; 5' 4"; black complexion.
Rebecca Turner. Certificate issued 25 Nov. 1826. Born free and raised in AA Co. Age about 22; 5' 5"; brown complexion; mole on left corner of mouth; raised in AA Co.
Stephen Watkins. Certificate issued 28 Nov. 1826. DOM recorded by Lucy Harwood 17 March 1823. Age about 26; 5' 6"; yellow complexion; small scar on forehead; raised in AA Co.
Polly Matthews. Certificate issued 12 Dec. 1826. Born free and raised in AA Co. Age about 19; 5' 2"; bright complexion; small scar on forehead.
Nelly Matthews. Certificate issued 12 Dec. 1826. Born free and raised in AA Co. Age about 42; 5'; brown complexion; small scar near corner of right eye.
Rachel Matthews. Certificate issued 12 Dec. 1826. Born free and raised in AA Co. Age about 22; 5' 6 1/2"; black complexion; small scar left side of face.
Kitty Matthews. Certificate issued 12 Dec. 1826. Born free and raised in AA Co. Age about 46; 5' 5"; brown complexion; small scar near left nostril.
Vachel Matthews. Certificate issued 12 Dec. 1826. Born free and raised in AA Co. Age about 27; 4' 10"; brown complexion; scar on right hand and over left eye.
Hannah Matthews. Certificate issued 12 Dec. 1826. Born free and raised in AA Co.

Age about 19; 4' 10 1/2"; dark complexion.
Henry Parker. Certificate issued 13 Dec. 1826. Born free and raised in AA Co. Age about 26; 5' 10; black complexion; small scar on middle finger left hand.
Maria Adams. Certificate issued 3 Jan. 1827. DOM recorded by Charles Carroll of Carrollton. 19 Sept. 1823. Freedom commenced 3 June 1826. Age about 26; 5' 2 1/2" dark complexion; scar on left arm. Raised in AA Co.
Joseph. Certificate issued 11 Jan. 1827. DOM recorded by Phillip Hammond Hopkins 5 Jan. 1827. Age 42; 5' 2 1/2"; light complexion; scar under left eye; raised in AA Co.
William Johnson. Certificate issued 13 Jan. 1827. Born free and raised in AA Co. Age about 21; 5' 3 1/2"; yellow complexion; two scars on forehead over left eye.
Lloyd Parker. Certificate issued 13 Jan. 1827. DOM recorded by Margaret Hopkins 20 Aug. 1813. Age 23; 5' 4"; black complexion; two scars over right eye; raised in AA Co.
Lewis Hawkins. Certificate issued 24 Jan. 1827. Born free and raised in AA Co. Age about 22; 5' 6 3/4"; dark complexion; small scars under right eye and on cheek.
Charles Stewart. Certificate issued 6 Feb. 1827. DOM recorded by Catherine Kelly 6 Feb. 1827. (Side notation refers to possible cancellation of this deed 20 Oct. 1829). Age 34; 5' 7"; yellow complexion; scar on right wrist; raised in AA Co.
Peter. Certificate issued 12 Feb. 1827. DOM recorded by Richard Cromwell 1826. Age about 36; 5' 7"; brown complexion; small scar on left wrist; raised in AA Co.
Thomas Freeland. Certificate issued 15 Feb. 1827. Born free and raised in AA Co. Age about 22; 5' 6"; black complexion; small scar under left eye.
Stephen Fisher. Certificate issued 28 Feb. 1827. DOM recorded by Richard Weems 8 Feb. 1827. Age about 44; 5' 4 1/2"; yellow complexion; large scar on right leg; small scar on right cheek; raised in AA Co.
Gilbert Brasheaws (Bradshaw, Brashears ?). Certificate issued 7 March 1827. Born free and raised in AA Co. Age about 24; 5' 5 1/2"; black complexion; small scar on left wrist.
James Cagis. Certificate issued 8 March 1827. Born free and raised in AA Co. Age about 22; 5' 7 1/2"; dark complexion; large scar under left jawbone; small scar under left eye; another on left wrist.

Mary Anderson. Certificate issued 8 March 1827. Born free and raised in AA Co. Age about 22; 5' 3 1/2"; brown complexion; small scar near corner of right eye.
Rosetta Kent. Certificate issued 10 March 1827. Born free and raised in AA Co. Age about 26; 5' 4 1/2"; black complexion; no perceptible scars or marks.
Simon. Certificate issued 12 March 1827. DOM recorded by John W. Lonsdale 12 March 1827. Age about 40; 5' 7"; black complexion; scars on left cheek, nose, and wrist; raised in Montgomery County.
Hannah. Certificate issued 17 March 1827. DOM recorded by John Reece 5 Jan. 1793. Freedom commenced 4 Jan. 1802. Age about 46; 5' 6 1/2"; black complexion; scars on left elbow and forehead; raised in AA Co.
Maria. Certificate issued 17 March 1827. Born free and raised in AA Co. Age about 20; 5' 5"; black complexion; no marks or scars.
Anna. Certificate issued 17 March 1827. DOM recorded by Stephen Boone 17 May 1815. Age about 22; 4' 10"; brown complexion; scar above right elbow. Freedom commenced 9 Feb. 1824; raised in AA Co.
Maria Jones. Certificate issued 24 March 1827. DOM recorded by Thomas J--- 22 May 1821. Age about 22; 5' 2"; black complexion; small scar on corner of right eye;another back of left hand; raised in AA Co.
William. Certificate issued 27 March 1827. DOM recorded by John Chew Thomas 12 Feb. 1812. Freedom commenced 1 Jan. 1827. Age about 22; 5' 5"; black complexion. Freedom commenced 1 Jan. 1827. Raised in AA Co.
Jeremiah. Certificate issued 28 March 1827. DOM recorded by Eleanor Yieldhall 28 May 1799. Freedom commenced in 1814. Age about 40; 5' 5"; black complexion; scars in each eyebrow; raised in AA Co.
Benjamin Parker. Certificate issued 28 March 1827. Born free and raised in AA Co. Age about 26; 5' 2 1/2"; black complexion; small scar over each eye.
Dinah. Certificate issued 27 March 1827. DOM recorded by Charles Griffith 9 Sept. 1818. Freedom commenced in 1827. Age about 32; 5' 1 1/2"; scars on left elbow, over left eye; raised in AA Co.
John Brown. Certificate issued 2 April 1827. Black complexion; scar on right side of neck.
Thos. E. Brown. Certificate issued 20 April 1827. Born free and raised in AA Co. Age about 17; 5' 1 1/2"; black complexion; deformed right hand.
Nancy Warren (Warner ?). Certificate issued 4 April 1827. Born free and raised in AA Co. Age about 38; 5' 1"; light complexion; long straight hair.
William B—. Certificate issued 9 April 1827. Born free and raised in AA Co. Age about 28; 5' 7"; small scar over corner of left eye.
Charlotte Bond. Certificate issued 10 April 1827. Born free and raised in AA Co. Age about 30; 5' 1 1/2"; brown complexion; scars on forehead between the eyes and on left cheek.
Sarah Darkins. Certificate issued 11 April 1827. Born free and raised in AA Co. Age about 33; 5' 2"; brown complexion; scar on left hand.
Nancy Smith. Certificate issued 13 April 1827. DOM recorded by Jacob Fowler 18 Nov. 1815. Age about 42; 5'; yellow complexion; small moles on the face; raised in AA Co.
Nancy Brown. Certificate issued 14 April 1827. Born free and raised in AA Co. Age about 38; 5' 4 1/2"; black complexion; missing two front teeth.
Selena Brown. Certificate issued 14 April 1827. Born free and raised in AA Co. Age about 27; 5' 3"; dark complexion; scar on right side of neck.
Sarah Brown. Certificate issued 14 April 1827 Born free and raised in AA Co. Age about 23; 5' 1"; dark complexion; scar under right jaw.
Vachel. Certificate issued 16 April 1827. DOM recorded by Charles Greenbury Griffith 2 Dec. 1822. Age about 27; 5' 9"; light complexion; scar over left eye; raised in AA Co.
Andrew. Certificate issued 17 April 1827. DOM recorded by Bryan Williams 9 Oct. 1898. Freedom commenced 3 Nov. 1818. Age about 42; 5' 4"; black complexion; large scar on right side of face; small scar on forehead; raised in AA Co.
Daniel Parker. Certificate issued 18 April 1827. Born free and raised in AA Co. Age about 23; 5' 6"; brown complexion; scars on breast, forehead, and right hand.
George. Certificate issued 21 April 1827. DOM recorded by Mary Smith (South ?) 5 March 1791. Age about 43; 5' 6"; black complexion; scar on left hand; raised in AA Co.
William Minor. Certificate issued 28 April 1827. Born free and raised in AA Co. Age

about 26; 5' 5"; black complexion; crooked little finger on left hand.

Jacob Johnson. Certificate issued 30 April 1827. Born free and raised in AA Co. Age about 28; 5' 5"; dark complexion; scar on forehead.

Issac. Certificate issued 1 May 1827. Born free and raised in AA Co. Age about 25; 5' 4 1/2"; black complexion; "vacancy in lower front teeth"; small scars on right hand.

Landy. Certificate issued 1 May 1827 Born free and raised in AA Co. Age about 23; 5' 4"; black complexion; small scar on right hand.

N. Scott. Certificate issued 1 May 1827. Born Free and raised in AA Co. Age about 23; 5'; black complexion; no marks or scars.

James Deivies. Certificate issued 1 May 1827. DOM recorded by Sarah Norris (Morris ?) 2 Aug. 1824. Freedom commenced 5 April 1827. Age about 25; 5' 1"; dark mulatto complexion; two small scars over right eye; raised in AA Co.

Eleanor. Certificate issued 1 May 1827 Born free and raised in AA Co. Age about 31; 5' 4"; black complexion; two small scars on right arm.

Jenny. Certificate issued 1 May 1827 Born free and raised in AA Co. Age about 29; 5' 4"; black complexion; small scar on back of right hand.

Hamial. Certificate issued 2 May 1827. DOM recorded by Richard G--- 6 Dec. 1826. Age about 40; 5' 2 1/2"; dark complexion; small scar on left hand.

Henry Matthews. Certificate issued 2 May 1827. DOM recorded by Richard Lockett 23 March 1826. Age about 38; yellow complexion; 5' 7 1/2"; two small scars on left wrist; raised in AA Co.

Lemuel. Certificate issued 3 May 1827. DOM recorded by N--- Cross 3 Sept. 1807. Age about 34; 5' 7"; black complexion; small scar on left eyebrow; raised in AA Co.

Sarah Forty. Certificate issued 2 June 1827. DOM recorded by Jacob Forty 3 Jan. 1798. Age about 42; 4' 11"; black complexion; two small scars on forehead; raised in AA Co.

Mary Forty. Certificate issued 2 June 1827. DOM recorded by Jacob Forty 3 Jan. 1798. Age about 30; 5' 1"; black complexion; scar on forehead; raised in AA Co.

Harriett Forty. Certificate issued 2 June 1827. DOM recorded by Jacob Forty 3 Jan. 1798. Age about 38; 4' 9"; black complexion; no scars or marks; raised in AA Co.

— Wright. Certificate issued 2 June 1827 Born free and raised in AA Co. Age about 27; 5' 6 1/2"; black complexion; scar on under lip.

Benjamin Wright. Certificate issued 2 June 1827. Born free and raised in AA Co. Age about 24; 5' 8 1/2"; black complexion; large scar on right foot.

Joseph Robinson. Certificate issued 2 June 1827. Born free and raised in AA Co. Age about 21; 5' 10"; black complexion; scar on left cheek.

Caroline Robinson. Certificate issued 2 June 1827. Born free and raised in AA Co. Age about 22; 5' 5 1/2"; black complexion; no scars or marks.

Hester Robinson. 2 June 1827. Born free and raised in AA Co. Age about 17; 5' 4"; black complexion; no marks or scars.

John Queen. Certificate issued 5 June 1827. Born free and raised in AA Co. Age about 23; 5' 1 1/2"; yellow complexion; scars on forehead and near corner of left eye.

Charles Shorter. Certificate issued 16 July 1827. DOM recorded by Peter Shorter 10 July 1823. Age about 34; 5' 3 1/2"; yellow complexion; small scar on right hand; raised in AA Co.

David. Certificate issued 2 Aug. 1829. DOM recorded by Margaret Hopkins 20 Aug. 1813. Age about 21; 5' 3"; bright complexion; scar on left wrist; raised in AA Co.

Nachey. Certificate issued 2 Aug. 1827. DOM recorded by Margaret Hopkins 20 Aug. 1813. Age about 18; 5'; bright complexion; scars on wrist and right hand; raised in AA Co.

Bob. Certificate issued 2 Aug. 1827. DOM recorded by Margaret Hopkins 20 Aug. 1813. Age about 21; 5' 10 3/4"; dark complexion; scar on right cheek bone; scar on left nostril; raised in AA Co.

Daniel. Certificate issued 2 Aug. 1827. DOM recorded by Margaret Hopkins 20 Aug. 1813. Age about 27; 5' 6"; black complexion; large scar on right cheek; raised in AA Co.

Gustavies. Certificate issued 2 Aug. 1827. DOM recorded by Margaret Hopkins 20 Aug. 1813. Age about 21; 5' 8"; dark complexion; scar on right arm, another on left knee; raised in AA Co.

Samuel Queen. Certificate issued 25 Aug. 1827. Born free and raised in AA Co. Age

about 26; 5' 9 1/2"; black complexion; small scars on forehead.
Betty N—. 29 Aug. 1827. DOM recorded by Frederick --- 5 July 1816. Age about 41; 4' 10 1/2"; brown complexion; raised in AA Co.
Hannah Braafoot (Bradford ?). Certificate issued 6 Sept. 1827 Born free and raised in AA Co. Age about 23; 5' 4 /2"; dark complexion; small scar in corner of left eye.
Nancy Queen. Certificate issued 6 Sept. 1827 Born free and raised in AA Co. Age about 16; 5' 2 1/2"; light complexion; long straight hair.
Sophia Sulivan. Certificate issued 30 Sept. 1827. DOM recorded by John B. Bordley 5 Dec. 1785. Age about 40; 5' 1 1/2"; dark complexion; small scar on forehead: raised in AA Co.
Nanny. Certificate issued 21 Sept. 1827. DOM recorded by Joseph Evans 22 Aug. 1819. Age about 49; 5' 1"; small scar on left cheek; raised in AA Co.
Nancy Davis. Certificate issued 22 Sept. 1827 Born free and raised in AA Co. Age about 17; 5' 6"; dark complexion;small scar near corner of right eye; raised in AA Co.
Cassy L— Certificate issued 22 Sept. 1827 Born free and raised in AA Co. Age about 26; 5' 1/2"; black complexion; scar on left thumb.
Polly Davis. Certificate issued 22 Sept. 1827. DOM recorded by Phillip I. Thomas 17 Dec. 1808. Age about 29; 5' 4 1/2"; brown complexion; no scars or marks; raised in AA Co.
Betsy. Certificate issued 28 Sept. 1827. DOM recorded by John S. Maccubbin 5 Sept. 1827. Age about 26; 5' 5 1/2"; brown complexion; mole near corner of left eye; raised in AA Co.
Richard. Certificate issued 17 Oct. 1827. DOM recorded by Julia Ann Dorsey Feb. 1821. Age about 45; 5' 6"; dark complexion; scars on upper lip and forehead; raised in AA Co.
Phillis Oss—. Certificate issued 18 Oct. 1827. DOM recorded by Samuel Douglass 7 Sept. 1796. Age about 42; 5' 1 1/2"; light complexion; long hair; raised in AA Co.
Eleanor Gaithers. Certificate issued 2 Oct. 1827. Born free and raised in AA Co. Age about 31; 5' 6 1/2"; yellow complexion; no scars or marks.
Rachael Gaithers. Certificate issued 2 Oct. 1827. Born free and raised in AA Co. Age about 50; 5' 2 1/2"; dark complexion; scar on chin.
Richard Gaither. Certificate issued 2 Oct. 1827. Born free and raised in AA Co. Age about 35; 5' 9"; dark complexion; scar on left side of neck.
William T—. 13 Oct. 1827. Born free and raised in AA Co. Age about 27; 5' 5 1/4"; dark complexion; scar on right lower ... .
Davies Green. Certificate issued 1 Dec. 1827. Born free and raised in AA Co. Age about 45; 5' 8 1/2"; brown complexion; scar on back of right hand.
John Green. Certificate issued 1 Dec. 1827. Born free and raised in AA Co. Age about 25; 5' 2 1/2"; yellow complexion; scar on back of right hand.
Nancy Green. Certificate issued 1 Dec. 1827. Born free and raised in AA Co. Age about 27; 5' 1 1/2"; brown complexion; small mole on nose.
Ned. Certificate issued 22 Dec. 1827. DOM recorded by John W. Duvale 22 Dec. 1827. Age about 21; 5' 6"; black complexion; small scar on forehead; raised in AA Co.
Nacy Ba—es. Certificate issued 28 Dec. 1827. DOM recorded by Ann Boone 28 Dec. 1827. Age about 38; 5' 7 1/2"; black complexion; small scar on back of right hand; raised in AA Co.
John Nicechull (Nichols ?). 3 Jan. 1828. DOM recorded by Joseph Chancy (Chaney ?) 3 Jan. 1827. Age about 40; 5' 4 1/2"; black complexion;small scar over left cheek bone; raised in AA Co.
Dow Madison Robinson. Certificate issued 5 Jan. 1828. DOM recorded by Ann Jackson 5 Jan. 1828. Age about 20; 5' 4 1/2"; black complexion; large issued scar on right wrist; small scar over left eye; raised in AA Co.
Kitty. Certificate issued 19 Jan. 1828. DOM recorded by William Gover 15 Dec. 1827. Age about 24; 5' 1"; dark complexion; small scar under left eye; raised in AA Co.
Bessie Smith. Certificate issued 21 Jan. 1828. DOM recorded by Sarah Ann H--- 10 Sept. 1817. Age about 42; 5' 8"; dark complexion; scar on left foot; raised in AA Co.
Gabriel Queen. Certificate issued 21 Jan. 1828. Born free and raised in AA Co. Certificate issued Age about 21; 5' 8 1/2"; black complexion; scar on back of right hand.
Henry Crowner. Certificate issued 2 Feb. 1828. Born free and raised in AA Co. Age about 18; 5' 7 1/2"; dark complexion; small

mole on upper lip.
Theodore T. Stewart. Certificate issued 11 Feb. 1828. DOM recorded by Ann Stewart 2 March 1808. Age about 27; 5' 9 1/2"; light complexion; small scar on right cheekbone; raised in AA Co.
Henry Boston. Certificate issued 1 March 1828. Born free and raised in AA Co. Age about 25; 5' 1"; dark complexion; small scar over right eye, another on back of right hand.
Lydia Waters. Certificate issued 3 March 1828. Born free and raised in AA Co. Age about 22; 5' 7 1/2"; black complexion; scar issued on each wrist.
Issac Philips. Certificate issued 10 March 1828. Born free and raised in AA Co. Age about 23; 5' 10'; Yellow complexion; issued small scar near corner of left eye; scar near right temple.
Deborah. Certificate issued 2 April 1828. DOM recorded by---. 31 March 1828. Age about 34; 5' 2 1/2"; dark complexion; no scars or marks; raised in AA Co.
Sarah. Certificate issued 8 April 1828. Born free and raised in AA Co. Age about 34; 5' 5 1/2"; black complexion; no marks or scars.
Rezin Boone. Certificate issued 12 April 1828. Born free and raised in AA Co. Age about 21; 5' 2 1/2"; yellow complexion; small scar on chin.
Eleanor (Elsinore?) Norris. 18 April 1828. Born free and raised in AA Co. Age about 17; 5' 2"; brown complexion; scar on neck near right collarbone.
Jacob. Certificate issued 21 April 1828. DOM recorded by--- Hobbs 12 April 1811. 5' 5"; black complexion; scar ... right eye; raised in AA Co.
Nathan Nelson. Certificate issued 23 April 1828. DOM recorded by Philemon D. Ridgely 20 Feb. 1828. Age about 42; 5'"7"; black complexion; scar on upper lip; missing fingers on right hand; raised in AA Co.
Henry Gibson. Certificate issued 8 May 1828. DOM recorded by G--- H. Snowden 2 Sept. 1825. Age about 23; 5' 1"; yellow complexion; small scar between eyes; raised in AA Co.
Hercules Gibson. Certificate issued 8 May 1828. DOM recorded by G. H. Snowden 8 Sept. 1825. Age about 22; 5" ? "; yellow complexion; small scar on each side of right hand; raised in AA Co.
William Harrison. Certificate issued 20 May 1828. DOM recorded by Benjamin Gaither 10 Feb. 1816. Age about 47; 5' 3 1/2." black complexion; small scar over left eye; raised in AA Co.
William Prout. Certificate issued 21 May 1828. Born free and raised in AA Co. Age about 21; 5' 4"; dark complexion; scar on neck near left collarbone; scar on each little finger.
John Henry Cooke. Certificate issued 21 May 1828. Born free and raised in AA Co. Age about 22; 5'; dark complexion; large scar on right wrist.
Kitty Thompson. Certificate issued 2 June 1828. DOM recorded by Lewis Duvall 18 Feb. 1801. Age about 30; 5' 2 1/2"; dark complexion; no scars or marks; raised in AA Co.
Thomas Parker. Certificate issued 4 June 1828. Born free and raised in AA Co. Age about 19; 5' 7"; black complexion; small scar on chin.
Nelly Nicholson. Certificate issued 10 June 1828. DOM recorded by Joseph Count 20 Feb. 1802. Age about 37; 5' 2 1/2"; dark complexion; small scar on left wrist; raised in AA Co.
Edward Johnson. Certificate issued 12 June 1828. Born free and raised in AA Co. Age about 26; 5' 8 1/2"; black complexion; scar on left arm.
Henry Wilson. Certificate issued 10 July 1828. DOM recorded by Thomas Wilson 10 July 1828. Age about 23; 5' 8 1/2"; dark complexion; scar on right cheek; raised in AA Co.
Minty Powell. Certificate issued 10 July 1828. DOM recorded by Thomas Joice 15 July 1823. Age about 40; 5' 1"; light complexion; scar on right hand; raised in AA Co.
Phillip Jacobs. Certificate issued 15 July 1828. DOM recorded by Eleanor Maccubbin 15 July 1828. Age about 45; 5' 1"; dark complexion; scar on left side of forehead; raised in AA Co.
Kitty Merreet. Certificate issued 1 Aug. 1828. Born free and raised in AA Co. Age about 25; 5' 6 1/2"; black complexion; scar on right cheek.
Priscilla Brooks. The balance of this document, as well as pages 296, and 297 are missing from the document. Hence, no other information can be derived.
Daniel. Certificate issued 22 Oct. 1828. DOM recorded by Elijah Gray 19 Jan. 1802. Age about 30; 5' 8 1/2"; black complexion; raised in AA Co.
Joshua Burgess. Certificate issued 29 Oct. 1828. DOM recorded by Solomon Grooves 25 May 1826. Age about 34; 5' 3 1/2";

black complexion; scar in left eyebrow; raised in AA Co.
Fanny. Certificate issued 27 Nov. 1828. DOM recorded by John Wood 1 July 1790. Age about 57; 5'; dark complexion; small scars on left cheek and left foot; raised in AA Co.
Nace Brown. Certificate issued 2 Dec. 1828. DOM recorded by Rachael Snowden 13 April 1827. Age about 35; 5' 4"; black complexion; small scars over right eye and between the eyes; raised in AA Co.
William Savoy. Certificate issued 10 Dec. 1828. Born free and raised in AA Co. Age about 25; 5' 5"; black complexion; no scars or marks; raised in AA Co.
Moses Savoy. Certificate issued 18 Dec. 1828. Born free and raised in AA Co. Age about 22; 5' 5"; black complexion; no marks or scars.
John Thomas. Certificate issued 19 Feb. 1829. DOM recorded by Henry Lyon Davis 1 Sept. 1828. Age about 34; 5' 6 1/2"; black complexion; small scar near corner of right eye and on back of right hand; raised in AA Co.
Thomas Adams. Certificate issued 13 March 1829. DOM recorded by Richard Brown 27 April 1825. Age about 45; 5' 7"; dark complexion; first and second fingers of left hand are crooked.
Stephen Johnson. Certificate issued 14 March 1829. DOM recorded by Lucy Harwood 19 March 1823. Age about 42; 5' 1/2"; dark complexion; scar on left arm; raised in AA Co.
Charles. Certificate issued 30 March 1829. Born free and raised in AA Co. Age about 22; 5' 3"; dark complexion; small scars under left ear and breast.
James Parker. Certificate issued 6 April 1829. Born free and raised in AA Co. Age about 23; 5' 11"; black complexion; scar on left arm.
Nicholas. Certificate issued 18 April 1829. DOM recorded by Eliza Hood 7 March 1817. Age about 40; 5' 8"; black complexion; scar over each eye; raised in AA Co.
Abraham Jones. Certificate issued 31 April 1829. DOM recorded by James Pryor 26 Jan. 1825. Age about 48; 5' 8"; black complexion; raised in AA Co.
John Cain. Certificate issued 14 May 1829. Born free and raised in AA Co. Age about 23; 5' 6 1/2"; light complexion; scar on right throat.
Thomas Phillips. Certificate issued 2 June 1829. Born free and raised in AA Co. Age about 29; 5' 8 1/2"; yellow complexion.

Patience Taylor. Certificate issued 19 June 1829. DOM recorded by Susanna Nyville 13 Nov. 1813. Age about 26; 5' 3 1/2"; dark complexion; scar on back of neck; raised in AA Co.
Joseph Parker. Certificate issued 9 July 1829. Born free and raised in AA Co. Age about 21; 5' 7 1/2"; black complexion; scars over left eye and near left nostril.
Charles William Willigman. 11 July 1829. DOM recorded by Thomas Harris 26 Dec. 1821. Age about 22; 5' 7"; light complexion; small scar on back of right hand.
Henny Hey. Certificate issued 19 Aug. 1829. Born free and raised in AA Co. Age about 17; 4' 10 1/2"; black complexion; scar on left arm.
John Queen. Certificate issued 21 Sept. 1829. Born free and raised in AA Co. Age about 20; 5' 8 1/2"; dark complexion; scar on forehead.
Sarah Queen. Certificate issued 21 Sept. 1829. Born free and raised in AA Co. Age about 13; 5' 1"; dark complexion.
Charles Stewart. Certificate issued 2 Oct. 1829. DOM recorded by Catherine Thelty 6 Feb. 1829. Age about 36; 5' 7"; yellow complexion; scar on right wrist; raised in AA Co.
Anne Carroll. Certificate issued 13 Oct. 1829. DOM recorded by Rachael Deale 7 Oct. 1819. Age about 27; 4' 11 1/2"; light complexion; large scar on right arm; raised in AA Co.
Kizzey Queen. Certificate issued 22 Oct. 1829. Born free and raised in AA Co. Age about 40; 5' 11 1/2"; dark complexion; small scar near right nostril.
Nelly Cheri (Cherry ?). Certificate issued 23 Oct. 1829. DOM recorded by Richard Brown Junior 20. Jan. 1794. Age about 36; 5' 1/2"; dark complexion; small scar on left arm; raised in AA Co.
Mary Pritchard. Certificate issued 23 Oct. 1829. Born free and raised in AA Co. Age about 26; 5' 5 1/2"; bright complexion; scar on back of left hand.
Elizabeth Green. Certificate issued 3 Nov. 1829. Born free and raised in AA Co. Age about 18; 5'; dark complexion; small scar under left eye; small scar on left cheek.
Rachael Ann Green. Certificate issued 3 Nov. 1829. Born free and raised in AA Co. Age about 20; 4' 11"; dark complexion; small scar on right arm.
Hannah Green. Certificate issued 3 Nov. 1829. Born free and raised in AA Co. Age about 16; 4' 11 1/2"; dark complexion; scar over left eye.

William Turner. Certificate issued 7 Nov. 1829. Born free and raised in AA Co. Age about 23; 5' 7 1/2"; brown complexion; small scar on breast.

Rachael Hammond. Certificate issued 9 Nov. 1829. DOM recorded by John Sewell 15 Aug. 1808. Age about 34; 5'; dark complexion; welt on back of left hand; raised in AA Co.

Charles Allen. Certificate issued 24 Nov. 1829. Born free and raised in AA Co. Age about 26; 5' 4 1/2"; brown complexion; scar on back of neck and forefinger of left hand.

William Williams. Certificate issued 10 Dec. 1829. DOM recorded by John O. L. Jones 23 Sept. 1805. Age about 29; 5' 4"; black complexion; small scar on right wrist; raised in AA Co.

Benjamin Brown. Certificate issued 22 Dec. 1829. DOM recorded by Dennis H. Battee 1 April 1824. Age 26; 5' 4 1/2"; dark complexion; small scar on back of left hand; raised in AA Co.

Kitty Goodin. Certificate issued 24 Dec. 1829. DOM recorded by Anne Boone 24 Dec. 1879. Age about 38; 5' 5 1/2"; dark complexion; small scar on left wrist; raised in AA Co.

William King. Certificate issued 31 Dec. 1829. DOM recorded by Arminta Harrison 31 Aug. 1816. Age about 20; 5' 7"; black complexion; small scar on forehead; raised in AA Co.

Edward Ennis. Certificate issued 6 Jan. 1830. DOM recorded by Margaret Callahan 11 Jan. 1809. Age about 22; 5' 3"; bright complexion; small scar on left thumb; raised in AA Co.

Darius Green. Certificate issued 10 Jan. 1830. Born free and raised in AA Co. Age about 23; 5' 9 1/2"; black complexion.

Issac Parker. Certificate issued 26 Jan. 1830. Born free and raised in AA Co. Age about 21; 5' 7"; black complexion; small scar between the eyes.

William Jones. Certificate issued 1 March 1830. DOM recorded by Aaron Jones 1 March 1830. Age about 21; 5' 4 1/2"; dark complexion; small scars over right eye and on left cheek bone; raised in AA Co.

Thomas Thomas. Certificate issued 4 March 1830. DOM recorded by George Wills 17 Feb. 1813. Age about 36; 5' 8"; black complexion; small scar on upper lip and left wrist; raised in AA Co.

Dennis Edwards. Certificate issued 30 March 1830. Born free and raised in AA Co. Age about 28; 5' 4"; black complexion; small scar near corner of right eye and one on the nose; raised in AA Co.

Noah Hawkins. Certificate issued 21 April 1830. Born free and raised in AA Co. Age about 31; 5' 10"; black complexion; small scar on forehead.

John Edwards. Certificate issued 21 April 1830. Born free and raised in AA Co. Age about 24; 5' 9"; black complexion; no perceptible marks.

Bob Urquhart. Certificate issued 21 April 1830. DOM recorded by Robert Welch (of Ben). 18 July 1826. Age about 47; 5' 7 1/2"; dark complexion; raised in AA Co.

Hess. Certificate issued 8 May 1830. DOM recorded by Robert Welch (of Ben). 18 July 1826. Age about 17; 5' 5"; dark complexion; no perceptible marks; raised in AA Co.

Jim Urgahart. Certificate issued 8 May 1830. DOM recorded by Robert Welch (of Ben). 18 July 1826. Age about 13; 4' 10"; black complexion; small scar on forehead; raised in AA Co.

Sam Wallace. Certificate issued 8 May 1830. DOM recorded by Robert Welch (of Ben). 18 July 1826. Age about 33; 5' 7 1/2"; brown complexion; no perceptible marks; raised in AA Co.

Sam Hall. Certificate issued 8 May 1830. DOM recorded by Robert Welch (of Ben). 18 July 1826. Age about 18; 5' 6 1/2"; black complexion; no perceptible marks; raised in AA Co.

Jerry Hall. Certificate issued 8 May 1830. DOM recorded by Robert Welch (of Ben) 18 July 1826. Age about 17; 5' 5"; black complexion; small scar on forehead; raised in AA Co.

Charles Hodge. Certificate issued 8 May 1830. DOM recorded by Robert Welch (of Ben) 18 July 1826. Age about 47; 5' 9"; black complexion; scar on right side of neck; raised in AA Co.

Bill Urgahart. Certificate issued 8 May 1830. DOM recorded by Robert Welch (of Ben) 18 July 1826. Age about 18; 5' 6"; brown complexion; scar on right eye; raised in AA Co.

Ned Rawlings. Certificate issued 8 May 1830. DOM recorded by Robert Welch (of Ben) 18 July 1826. Age about 47; 5' 5"; brown complexion; several scars on face; raised in AA Co.

John Davis. Certificate issued 8 May 1830. DOM recorded by Robert Welch (of Ben) 18 July 1826. Age about 25; 5' 10"; dark complexion; scar on left cheek; raised in AA Co.

Suck Davis. Certificate issued 8 May 1830. DOM recorded by Robert Welch (of Ben) 18 July 1826. Age about 22; 4' 11 1/2"; brown complexion; scar on right wrist; raised in AA Co.

Samuel Cromwell. Certificate issued. 8 May 1830. Born free and raised in AA Co. Age about 22; 5' 5 1/2"; black complexion; scar on back of left hand; raised in AA Co.

Nancy Ross. Certificate issued 8 May 1830. Born free and raised in AA Co. Age about 21; 5' 4"; dark complexion; small scar on face; another on right arm.

Abigail Cromwell. Certificate issued 8 May 1830. Born free and raised in AA Co. Age about 19; 5' 4"; dark complexion; small scar on forehead.

Susan Cromwell. Certificate issued 8 May 1830. Born free and raised in AA Co. Age about 24; 5' 2 1/2"; dark complexion; small scar on upper lip.

Sophia Stevens. Certificate issued 22 May 1830. DOM recorded by Ruth Needon 22 Dec. 1812. Age about 40; 5' 1"; black complexion; no marks; raised in AA Co.

Maria Stevens. Certificate issued 22 May 1830. Born free and raised in AA Co. Age about 17; 5' 2"; brown complexion; two scars on left arm.

Eliza Hull. Certificate issued 27 May 1830. Born free and raised in AA Co. Age about 19; 5' 2 1/2"; yellow complexion; no marks or scars.

Emory Tilghman. Certificate issued. 3 July 1830 Born free and raised in AA Co. Age about 24; 5' 9"; dark complexion; scar on forehead.

John Brogden. Certificate issued 13 July 1830 Born free and raised in AA Co. Age about 21; 5' 9 1/2"; yellow complexion; "contraction of chin occasioned by a burn."

Nicholas Christmas. Certificate issued 19 July 1830. DOM recorded by Susan Franklin 9 Nov. 1816. Age about 23; 5' 8 1/2"; black complexion; scar on right leg; raised in AA Co.

Priscilla Richards. Certificate issued 28 July 1830. DOM recorded by Solomon Clarridge 18 June 1830. Age about 42; 5' 1"; black complexion; scar on left arm; raised in AA Co.

Charlotte Shaaff. Certificate issued. 31 Aug. 1830. DOM recorded by George Brewer 29 Dec. 1824. Age about 21; 5'; bright complexion; scar on middle finger of left hand; raised in AA Co.

Ellen Lewis. Certificate issued 11 Sept. 1830. Born free and raised in AA Co. Age about 22; 5' 5 1/4"; bright complexion; scar across upper lip; scar on left wrist.

Ginny Lewis. Certificate issued 11 Sept. 1830. Born free and raised in AA Co. Age about 24; 5' 3 1/4"; brown complexion; scar on left eyebrow.

Anne. Certificate issued 14 Sept. 1830. DOM recorded by Charles Pettibone 26 Jan. 1805. Age about 29; 5' 2 1/2"; dark complexion; no marks or scars; raised in AA Co.

Henry Brown. Certificate issued 29 Sept. 1830. Born free and raised in AA Co. Age about 30; 5' 5 1/2"; dark complexion; small scar on right hand.

Henry. Certificate issued 6 Oct. 1830. DOM recorded by Charles Pettibone 26 Jan. 1805. Age about 28; 5'; black complexion; scar on right hand; raised in AA Co.

Gustava Dorsey. Certificate issued. 26 Oct. 1830. DOM recorded by Amey Howard 30 Sept. 1830. Age about 29; 5' 5 1/2"; brown complexion; scars on forehead and across left eyebrow; raised in AA Co.

William. Certificate issued 26 Oct. 1830. DOM recorded by Robert Warfield 6 April 1830. Age about 24; 5' 5 1/2"; bright complexion; no marks or scars; raised in AA Co.

Edward. Certificate issued 26 Oct. 1830. DOM recorded by Mary Ann Warfield 18 Oct. 1828. Age about 30; 5' 7 1/2"; brown complexion; no marks or scars; raised in AA Co.

John. Certificate issued 26 Oct. 1830. DOM recorded by Ephraim Hobb 18 Oct. 1828. Age about 27; 5' 6 1/2"; bright complexion; no marks or scars; raised in AA Co.

Charlotte. Certificate issued 5 Nov. 1830. DOM recorded by Alexander Magruder 30 July 1830. Age about 35; 5' 2"; black complexion; scar on right elbow; raised in AA Co.

Horace Bishop. Certificate issued 8 Dec. 1830. DOM recorded by Mary Callahan 15 May 1821. Age about 21; 5' 5 1/2"; yellow complexion; scar on right side of face; raised in AA Co.

Samuel Green. Certificate issued 16 Dec. 1830. Born free and raised in AA Co. Age about 24; 5' 8 1/2"; black complexion; scar on left wrist.

William. Certificate issued 30 Dec. 1830. DOM recorded by Robert Welch of Ben 18 July 1826. Age about 23; 5' 8 1/4"; dark complexion; no marks or scars; raised in AA Co.

Iannetta Clark. Certificate issued 5 Jan. 1831. Born free and raised in AA Co. Age about 22; 5' 3"; light complexion; long black hair.

James Richardson. Certificate issued. 6 Jan. 1831. Born free and raised in AA Co. Age about 35; 5' 5"; dark complexion; scar on right cheek; scar near corner of right eye.

John Green. Certificate issued 13 Jan. 1831. Born free and raised in AA Co. Age about 25; 5' 7 1/2"; black complexion; face scarred by smallpox.

John Hanson. Certificate issued 28 Feb. 1831. Born free and raised in AA Co. Age about 20; 5' 8"; yellow complexion; scar on third finger left hand.

Ann Kent. Certificate issued 3 March 1831. Born free and raised in AA Co. Age about 15; 4' 11"; black complexion; no scars or marks.

John Harrison. Certificate issued 12 March 1831. DOM recorded by Stephen Prei. 26 Jan. 1826. Age about 35; 5' 3"; black complexion; no marks or scars; raised in AA Co.

Ben Bowlas. Certificate issued 30 March 1831. Born free and raised in AA Co. Age about 26; 5' 5 3/4"; black complexion; scars on left side of lower lip and neck.

William Bedlam (Bedham ?). Certificate issued 7 April 1831. Born free and raised in AA Co. Age about 22; 5' 6"; dark complexion; scar under right eye.

Daniel Boston. Certificate issued 19 April 1831. DOM recorded by Richard Foggett 28 Sept. 1798. Age about 32; 5' 8 1/2"; light complexion; scar on right big toe; raised in AA Co.

Robert Ross. Certificate issued 9 May 1831. Born free and raised in AA Co. About 22; 5' 7 1/2"; black complexion; small scar near left eye.

John Brown. Certificate issued 23 May 1831. Born free and raised in AA Co. Age about 22; 5' 5 1/2"; black complexion; small scar over left eye.

James Gaither. Certificate issued 23 May 1831. Born free and raised in AA Co. Age about 32; 5' 8"; brown complexion; small scar on left cheek.

Elizabeth Gaither. 23 May 1831. Born free and raised in AA Co. Age about 20; 5' 2"; brown complexion; large scar over right side of neck, another near corner of left eye.

Mary Gaither. Certificate issued 23 May 1831. Born free and raised in AA Co. Age about 16; 5' 2"; brown complexion; no marks or scars.

Samuel Gaither. Certificate issued 23 May 1831. Born free and raised in AA Co. Age about 22; 5' 7"; brown complexion; no marks or scars.

Sarah Gaither. Certificate issued 23 May 1831. Born free and raised in AA Co. Age about 19; 5' 6"; brown complexion; no marks or scars.

Jeremiah Gaither. Certificate issued 23 May 1831. Born free and raised in AA Co. Age about 24; 5' 6 1/4"; brown complexion; small scars right corner of mouth and under jawbone.

Martha Ann Williams. Certificate issued. 13 June 1831 Born free and raised in AA Co. Age about 21; 5'; bright complexion; small scar on forehead.

Charlotte Boston. 21 June 1831. DOM recorded by John Boston 27 June 1831. Age about 28; 5' 3"; brown complexion; small scar over left eye; raised in AA Co.

Susan Brown. Certificate issued 30 June 1831. Born free and raised in AA Co. Age about 39; 5'; yellow complexion; small scar near right ear.

Henrietta Parker. Certificate issued 2 July 1831. Born free and raised in AA Co. Age about 17; 4' 11"; brown complexion; no marks or scars.

Rachael Johnson. Certificate issued 13 July 1831. DOM recorded by Dicius H. Bottee 28 Feb. 1826. Age about 31; 5' 1"; scar on right arm; raised in AA Co.

Harriett Boston. Certificate issued 19 July 1831. Born free and raised in AA Co. Age about 23; 5' 4"; dark complexion; small scar on left cheekbone.

Charity Bishop. Certificate issued 20 July 1831. DOM recorded by Mary Ann Rideout 7 Aug. 1807. Age about 38; 5' 1 1/2"; yellow complexion; mole on right side of chin; raised in AA Co.

Watt Gassaway. Certificate issued 23 July 1831. DOM recorded by William Brewer 16 May 1820. Age about 31; 5' 10"; bright complexion; no marks or scars; raised in AA Co.

John Smith. Certificate issued 6 Aug. 1831. DOM recorded by Stephen Lee 29 March 1831. Age about 40; 5' 2 1/2"; yellow complexion; no marks or scars; raised in AA Co.

John H—. Certificate issued 6 Aug. 1831. DOM recorded by Lucy Harwood 7 March 1823. Age about 45; 5' 7"; dark complexion; scar on forefinger of right hand; raised in AA Co.

William Dorsey. Certificate issued 10 Aug.

1831. DOM recorded by Orlando --- 11 March 1826. Age about 47; 5' 6 1/2"; black complexion; small scar on left cheek; another over right eye; raised in AA Co.
Gustavious Scott. Certificate issued 20 Aug. 1831. DOM recorded by Mary Stuvell (Stovewall ?) 12 April 1810. Age about 25; 5' 8 1/2"; brown complexion scars on right hand and left arm; raised in AA Co.
L. Price. Certificate issued 17 Sept. 1831. Born free and raised in AA Co. Age about 30; 5' 10 1/2"; light complexion; scar over left eye.
Nacina Lucas. Certificate issued 26 Sept. 1831. Born free and raised in AA Co. Age about 23; 5' 1 1/2"; light complexion; scar over right eye; another on finger of right hand.
Henry Merrikin. Certificate issued 1 Oct. 1831. Born free and raised in AA Co. Age about 23; 5' 8 1/2"; black complexion; small scar on forehead; scar under right eye.
Abraham Franklin. Certificate issued 1 Oct. 1831. Born free and raised in AA Co. Age about 21; 5' 6"; black complexion; scar under left eye.
David Johnson. Certificate issued 3 Oct. 1831. Born free and raised in AA Co. Age about 26; 5' 5 1/2"; dark complexion; small scars on right cheek and top of head.
Issac Johnson. Certificate issued 3 Oct. 1831. Born free and raised in AA Co. Age about 24; 5' 8 1/2"; dark complexion; small scars over left eye, two on right wrist.
Richard Johnson. Certificate issued 3 Oct. 1831. Born free and raised in AA Co. Age about 25; 5' 5 1/2"; brown complexion; small scar over left eye, another on right arm.
John Merrikin. Certificate issued 8 Oct. 1831. Born free and raised in AA Co. Age about 21; 5' 11"; black complexion; scar over right eye.
Mary Anderson. Certificate issued 14 Oct. 1831. Born free and raised in AA Co. Age about 12; 4' 4"; brown complexion; no scars or marks.
John Anderson. Certificate issued 14 Oct. 1831. Born free and raised in AA Co. Age about 17; 5' 7"; brown complexion; no marks or scars.
Ann Anderson. Certificate issued 14 Oct. 1831. Born free and raised in AA Co. Age about 19; 5' 4"; brown complexion; small tissued scar near left eye.
Joseph Anderson. Certificate issued 14 Oct. 1831. Born free and raised in AA Co. Age about 16; 5' 3 1/2"; brown complexion; no marks or scars.
Vachel Waters. Certificate issued 15 Oct. 1831. Born free and raised in AA Co. Age about 22; 5' 10"; brown complexion; small scar under left jawbone; another on left arm.
Noah Waters. Certificate issued 15 Oct. 1831. Born free and raised in AA Co. Age about 32; 6' 1"; brown complexion; scars on right leg and forefinger of right hand.
John Maynard. Certificate issued 17 Oct. 1831. Born free and raised in AA Co. Age about 21; 5' 5 1/2"; dark complexion; small scar over left eye.
David Brown. Certificate issued 18 Oct. 1831. DOM recorded by Sarah --- 30 Dec. 1830. Age about 40; 5' 4"; black complexion; scar on right knee and middle finger of right hand; raised in AA Co.
Margaret Queen. Certificate issued 22 Oct. 1831. Born free and raised in AA Co. Age about 24; 5' 2 1/2"; dark complexion; small scar near right corner of mouth.
Richard Garrett. Certificate issued 28 Oct. 1831. Born free and raised in AA Co. Age about 25; 5' 7 1/2"; brown complexion; scar on forehead and under right eye.
Bea Snowden. Certificate issued 5 Nov. 1831. Born free and raised in AA Co. Age about 22; 5' 3 1/2"; black complexion; scar on upper lip; scars on left cheek; scar near left temple.
Emanuel Queen. 8 Nov. 1831. Born free and raised in AA Co. Age about 27; 5' 10"; black complexion; small scar on left eyebrow.
George Toogood. 9 Nov. 1831. DOM recorded by John Sewell 15 Aug. 1808. Age about 42; 5' 10 1/2"; black complexion large scar on breast.
Ellen Toogood. Certificate issued 9 Nov. 1831. Born free and raised in AA Co. Age about 21; 5' 10 1/2"; black complexion; no marks or scars.
Nelly Parker. Certificate issued 11 Nov. 1831. DOM recorded by Davis Hawk 31 Oct. 1830. Age about 35; 5' 4"; brown complexion; raised in AA Co.
Richard H. Cain. Certificate issued 16 Nov. 1831. Born free and raised in AA Co. Age about 25; 5' 6 1/2"; brown complexion; scar on left side of head.
Rebecca Bishop. Certificate issued 16 Nov. 1831. DOM recorded by Mary Callahan 15 May 1820. Age about 23; 5' 4 1/2"; bright complexion; raised in AA Co.
Robert Walker. Certificate issued 16 Nov. 1831. DOM recorded by Elijah Williams 6

March 1821. Age about 29; 5' 9"; brown complexion; small mole under left eye; raised in AA Co.

William Brown. Certificate issued 27 Nov. 1831. Born free and raised in AA Co. Age about 35; 5' 10"; yellow complexion; scar on right foot.

John Matthews. Certificate issued 26 Nov. 1831. DOM recorded by William Matthews 8 March 1817. Age about 26; 5' 11"; brown complexion; second and third fingers of both hands are joined; raised in AA Co.

Milly Matthews. Certificate issued 26 Nov. 1831. DOM recorded by William Matthews 8 March 1817. Age about 22; 5' 3"; brown complexion; several small scars on right wrist; raised in AA Co.

Darky or **Dorcas Boston.** Certificate issued 26 Nov. 1831. DOM recorded by William Matthews 8 March 1817. Age about 35; 5' 1"; brown complexion; small scar on back of right hand; raised in AA Co.

Anna Matthews. Certificate issued 26 Nov. 1831. DOM recorded by John Chew Thomas 3 Feb. 1810. Age about 26; 5' 1 1/2"; dark complexion; scar on back of left hand; raised in AA Co.

Ezekiel Hooper. Certificate issued 12 Dec. 1831. DOM recorded by Henry Hooper 15 April 1815. Age about 28; 5' 5"; black complexion; small scar on throat; raised in AA Co.

Elizabeth Beas. Certificate issued 12 Dec. 1831. Born free and raised in AA Co. Age about 20; 5' 2"; yellow complexion; no scars or marks.

Tom Thomas. Certificate issued 30 Dec. 1831. DOM recorded by John Price 2 Jan. 1817. Age about 32; 5' 5"; dark complexion; scar on right calf; raised in AA Co.

Libby Boston. Certificate issued 2 Jan. 1832. Born free and raised in AA Co. Age about 18; 5' 2"; yellow complexion; small scar on right cheek.

Annie Boston. Certificate issued 2 Jan. 1832. Born free and raised in AA Co. Age about 16; 5' 3 1/2"; dark complexion small scar between the eyes.

George Howard. Certificate issued 13 Jan. 1832. DOM recorded by John G. Brown 7 Jan. 1819. Age about 38; 5' 8"; bright complexion; scars on forehead and upper lip; raised in AA Co.

Thomas Watkins. Certificate issued 18 Jan. 1832. Born free and raised in AA Co. Age about 22; dark complexion; scars on forehead and neck; has speech impediment.

Henry Brunfoot. Certificate issued 20 Jan. 1832. Born free and raised in AA Co. Age about 23; 5' 4"; brown complexion; scar on breast.

John Brunfoot. Certificate issued 20 Jan. 1832. Born free and raised in AA Co. Age about 23; 5' 7 1/2"; yellow complexion; no marks or scars.

Roannah Cager. Certificate issued 15 Feb. 1832. Born free and raised in AA Co. Age about 22; 5' 1"; yellow complexion; two moles on right side of face.

David Pratt. Certificate issued 22 Feb. 1832. Born free and raised in AA Co. Age about 22; 5' 9 1/2"; dark complexion; scars on right cheek and right side of neck.

William Hawkins. Certificate issued 27 Feb. 1832. DOM recorded by Jerningham Drury 9 Dec. 1805. Age about 27; 5' 8 1/2"; dark complexion; two small scars right wrist, small scar on left wrist, small scar on top of left foot; raised in AA Co.

John Cager. Certificate issued 29 Feb. 1832. Born free and raised in AA Co. Age about 26; 5' 9 1/2"; brown complexion; two small scars below left eye; small scar on back of right hand.

Mary Sylvester. Certificate issued 29 Feb. 1832. DOM recorded by Gerard Hobbs 6 July 1824. Age about 37; 4' 10 1/2"; yellow complexion; no marks or scars; raised in AA Co..

James Sylvester. Certificate issued 29 Feb. 1832. DOM recorded by Henry Hobbs 12 April 1811. Age about 39; 5' 6 1/2"; black complexion; small scar on forehead; raised in AA Co.

Abraham Thomas. Certificate issued 29 Feb. 1832. DOM recorded by Henry Hobbs 12 April 1811. Age is omitted; 5' 6"; black complexion; scars near left temple and on back of head; raised in AA Co.

Daniel Boston. Certificate issued 3 March 1832. Born free and raised in AA Co. Certificate issued. Age about 23; 5' 7"; yellow complexion; scar near corner of left eye.

Charles Watkins. Certificate issued 3 March 1832. Born free and raised in AA Co. Age about 31; 5' 5"; yellow complexion; scar under right eye.

Samuel Watkins. Certificate issued 3 March 1832. Born free and raised in AA Co. Age about 29; 5' 4"; dark complexion; scars on left side of forehead and on breast.

Robert Allen. Certificate issued 5 March 1832. Born free and raised in AA Co. Age about 19; 5' 7"; dark complexion; scar on forehead.

George. Certificate issued 9 March 1832. DOM recorded by Richard G. Hutton 9 Nov. 1819. Age about 38; 5' 2"; dark complexion;scar on right cheek; raised in AA Co.

James. Certificate issued 9 March 1832. DOM recorded by Richard G. Hutton 9 Nov. 1819. Age about 36; 5' 2"; dark complexion; scar in right eyebrow; raised in AA Co.

Little (Lillie ?)James. Certificate issued 9 March 1832. DOM recorded by Richard G. Hutton 9 Nov. 1819. Age about 33; 5' 3"; dark complexion; scar over right eye; raised in AA Co.

Phillip Darnall. Certificate issued 13 March 1832. DOM recorded by Bennet Darnall 6 May 1805. Age about 32; 5' 9 1/2"; yellow complexion; scar on left arm; raised in AA Co.

Kiziah Davis. Certificate issued 13 March 1832. Born free and raised in AA Co. Age about 25; 5' 3"; dark complexion; small scar near corner of left eye.

Deborah Stewart. Certificate issued 13 March 1832. Born free and raised in AA Co. Age about 19; 5' 3 1/2"; dark complexion; scar over right eye.

Juliet. Certificate issued 14 March 1832. DOM recorded by Catherine Hutton 5 Jan. 1831. Age about 25; 5' 5"; dark complexion; scar on forehead; raised in AA Co.

Nancy. Certificate issued 16 March 1832. DOM recorded by Richard G. Hutton 9 Nov. 1819. Age about 32; 4' 10"; dark complexion; small mole on right arm; raised in AA Co.

Alinta. Certificate issued 14 March 1832. DOM recorded by Richard D. Hutton 9 Nov. 1819. Age about 30; 5' 3 1/2"; brown complexion; scar on left wrist; two on arm; raised in AA Co.

Ann Toogood. Certificate issued 14 March 1832. Born free and raised in AA Co. Age about 16; 5' 3"; yellow complexion; scar on back of left hand.

William Wilkes. Certificate issued 14 March 1832. DOM recorded by Henry Price 14 March 1832. Age about 40; 5' 8 1/2"; bright complexion; small scar on nose; raised on Eastern shore of Maryland.

Rebecca Frost. Certificate issued 16 March 1832. DOM recorded by John Brice 4 March 1806. Age about 40; 5' 3"; light complexion; freckled face; raised in AA Co.

Charles Thomas. Certificate issued 21 March 1832. Born free and raised in AA Co. Age about 22; 5' 7 1/2"; black complexion; small scars corner of left eye and near left nostril.

Caesar Williams. Certificate issued 21 March 1832. DOM recorded by William Kilty, Chancellor. 5 March 1806. Age about 41; 5' 8"; dark complexion; scars on nose, between the eyes, and on forehead.

William Williams. Certificate issued 21 March 1832. DOM recorded by William Kilty, Chancellor 5 March 1806. Age about 39; 5' 6 1/2: dark complexion; small scar in right eyebrow small moles on nose and right cheek.

William Turner. Certificate issued 29 March 1832. Born free and raised in AA Co. Age about 25; 5' 9"; yellow complexion; small scars on left eyebrow and left thumb.

Nancy Parker. Certificate issued 31 March 1832. Born free and raised in AA Co. Age about 25; 5' 2"; dark complexion; small scar on back of left hand.

Susan Parker. Certificate issued 31 March 1832. Born free and raised in AA Co. Age about 17; 5' 5"; black complexion; small scar in corner of right eye.

Ruchel Barnes. Certificate issued 5 April 1832. Born free and raised in AA Co. Age about 22; 5' 11 1/2"; dark complexion; scar on forehead.

Dinah Barnes. Certificate issued 5 April 1832. Born free and raised in AA Co. Age about 22; 5' 3"; dark complexion; scar on left arm.

Charlotte Barnes. Certificate issued 5 April 1832. Born free and raised in AA Co. Age about 19; 5' 3"; dark complexion; scar on right arm.

Nancy Anderson. Certificate issued 6 April 1832. Born free and raised in AA Co. Age about 42; 5' 1/2"; dark complexion; small mole near left eye; small scars on right hand and right nostril.

Eliza Parker. Certificate issued 10 April 1832. Born free and raised in AA Co. Age about 30; 5' 2"; yellow complexion; scar on nose; long black hair.

Susane Parker. Certificate issued 10 April 1832. Born free and raised in AA Co. Age about 24; 5'; black complexion; scar on right wrist.

Mary Ann Parker. Certificate issued 10 April 1832. Born free and raised in AA Co. Age about 20; 4' 11"; dark complexion; scar on left eyebrow.

Eleanor Wright. Certificate issued 14 April 1832. DOM recorded by Joseph Selby 5

Jan. 1792. Age about 35; 5' 10"; dark complexion; lost second finger of left hand; small scar on forehead; raised in AA Co.
Patience Morrison. Certificate issued 14 April 1832. DOM recorded by Joseph Selby 5 Jan. 1792. Age about 31; 4' 11"; dark complexion; scar on left shoulder.
Jerry Anderson. Certificate issued 14 April 1832. Born free and raised in AA Co. Age about 23; 5' 6 1/2"; black complexion; small scars between eyes and on right cheek.
Rachael Matthews. Certificate issued 16 April 1832. Born free and raised in AA Co. Age about 20; 5' 1/2"; dark complexion; no marks or scars.
Ned Dorsey. Certificate issued 16 April 1832. DOM recorded by Nicholas Merriweather 4 Sept. 1803. Age about 30; 5' 10"; dark complexion; face marked by smallpox; raised in AA Co.
Cyrus Johnson. Certificate issued 16 April 1832. DOM recorded by Nicholas Merriweather 10 Jan. 1807. Age about 40; 5' 5 1/2"; black complexion; 2 scars on right hand; missing upper front teeth; raised in AA Co.
Ephraim Janson. Certificate issued 17 April 1832. DOM recorded by Julia Ann Dorsey 19 Feb. 1821. Age about 42; 5' 8 1/2"; dark complexion; no marks or scars; raised in AA Co.
Dennis Powell. Certificate issued 17 April 1832. DOM recorded by Julia Ann Dorsey 19 Feb. 1821. Age about 31; 5' 9 1/2"; black complexion; small scar on forehead; raised in AA Co.
Agnes Hardy. Certificate issued 17 April 1832. DOM recorded by Nicholas Merriweather 24 Sept. 1803. Age about 43; 5' 3", dark complexion; small scars corner of left eye, between the eyes, and left wrist; raised in AA Co.
Peter Dorsey. Certificate issued 17 April 1832. DOM recorded by George Dorsey 3 May 1810. Age about 62; 5' 3"; black complexion; small scar on nose; raised in AA Co.
Rachel Carroll. Certificate issued 17 April 1832. DOM recorded by Mary Merriweather 11 Nov. 1811. Age about 32; 5', yellow complexion; no marks or scars; raised in AA Co.
Benjamin Smith. Certificate issued 17 April 1832. DOM recorded by Thomas W. Turner 9 Dec. 1826. Age about 50; 5' 6 1/2"; brown complexion; no marks or scars; raised in AA Co.

Rebecca Matthews. Certificate issued 18 April 1832. Born free and raised in AA Co. Age about 22; 5' 5 1/2"; yellow complexion; scar under left eye.
Julia Ann Harwood. Certificate issued 18 April 1832. Born free and raised in AA Co. Age about 16; 4' 11"; dark complexion; small scar on back of right hand.
Beky Wallace. Certificate issued 18 April 1832. Born free and raised in AA Co. Age about 35; 5' 6"; yellow complexion; lump on back of left hand.
Charlotte Williams. Certificate issued 18 April 1832. Born free and raised in AA Co. Age about 40; 5' 3 1/2"; yellow complexion; no marks or scars.
Milly Jackson. Certificate issued 18 April 1832. Born free and raised in AA Co. Age about 45; 5' 5 1/4"; yellow complexion; no marks or scars.
Mary Queen. Certificate issued 20 April 1832. Born free and raised in AA Co. Age about 22; 5' 1/2"; dark complexion; small scar on wrist.
Nancy Queen. Certificate issued 20 April 1832. Born free and raised in AA Co. Age about 18; 4' 10 1/2"; brown complexion; wart on back of right hand.
Ann Queen. Certificate issued 20 April 1832. Born free and raised in AA Co. Age about 31; 4' 11"; dark complexion; scar over left eye and under right eye.
Henry Boston. Certificate issued 20 April 1832. Born free and raised in AA Co. Age about 25; 5' 5"; dark complexion; scar on left hand.
Thomas Anderson. Certificate issued 21 April 1832. Born free and raised in AA Co. Age bout 29; 5' 3 1/2"; black complexion; no marks or scars.
Maria Watkins. Certificate issued 21 April 1832. DOM recorded by Lucy Harwood 10 April 1827. Age about 30; 5' 1/2"; black complexion; small scar on back of right hand; raised in AA Co.
Rachel Boston. Certificate issued 21 April 1832. Born free and raised in AA Co. Age about 16; 5' 3"; brown complexion; no marks or scars.
Sophia Watkins. Certificate issued 21 April 1832. Born free and raised in AA Co. Age about 27; 4' 3/4"; yellow complexion; no marks or scars.
Catherine Boston. Certificate issued 21 April 1832. Born free and raised in AA Co. Age about 18; 5' 3 1/2"; dark complexion; no marks or scars.
John Brown. Certificate issued 21 April 1832. Born free and raised in AA Co. Age

about 21; 5' 6"; yellow complexion; small scar on forefinger of right hand.
Anna Frazier. Certificate issued 23 April 1832. DOM recorded by Margaret Hopkins 21 Aug. 1813. Age about 26; 5' 4"; yellow complexion; small scar on left wrist; raised in AA Co.
Erasmus Hopkins. Certificate issued 23 April 1832. DOM recorded by Margaret Hopkins 21 Aug. 1813. Age about 24; 5' 3 1/4"; dark complexion; small scar in right eyebrow; raised in AA Co.
Tom Lyles. Certificate issued 23 April 1832. DOM recorded by Margaret Hopkins 21 Aug. 1813. Age about 24; 5' 5 1/2"; yellow complexion; no marks or scars; raised in AA Co.
Joe Lyles. Certificate issued 23 April 1832. DOM recorded by Margaret Hopkins 21 Aug. 1813. Age about 23; 5' 4"; dark complexion; mole near left eye; scar on back of left hand; raised in AA Co.
Polly Mitchell. Certificate issued 23 April 1832. Born free and raised in AA Co. Age about 37; 5' 1 1/4"; dark complexion; scar on neck.
Anna Brown. Certificate issued 23 April 1832. Born free and raised in AA Co. Age about 39; 4' 8 1/2"; brown complexion; small scar on left breast.
Milly Young. Certificate issued 24 April 1832. DOM recorded by Margaret Mercer 18 Sept. 1830. Age about 32; 5' 4 1/2"; black complexion; no marks or scars; raised in AA Co.
John Young. Certificate issued 24 April 1832. DOM recorded by Margaret Mercer 18 Sept. 1830. Age about 38; 5' 4 1/2"; black complexion; small scar near right eye; raised in AA Co.
Forrester Young. Certificate issued 24 April 1832. DOM recorded by Margaret Mercer 18 Sept. 1830. Age about 14; 4' 6 1/4"; black complexion; scars under. eye, on chin and forehead; raised in AA Co.
Julia Ann Isaacs. Certificate issued 24 April 1832. Born free and raised in AA Co. Age about 21; 5' 2 3/4"; yellow complexion; no marks or scars.
Thomas Matthews. Certificate issued 24 April 1832. Born free and raised in AA Co. Age about 22; 5' 6 3/4"; black complexion; scar on nose.
Susan Ann Isaacs. Certificate issued 24 April 1832. Born free and raised in AA Co. Age about 17; 5' 5 1/2"; yellow complexion; scar on right arm.
Richard Harris. Certificate issued 24 April 1832. Born free and raised in AA Co. Age

about 21; 5' 11"; brown complexion; scar on left side of face.
Sarah Queen. Certificate issued 24 April 1832. Born free and raised in AA Co. Age about 30; 5' 1/4"; dark complexion. Certificate issued missing forefinger of right hand.
Polly Toogood. Certificate issued 24 April 1832. Born free and raised in AA Co. Age about 19; 5' 1 1/4"; dark complexion; scar under right eye.
Nancy Toogood. Certificate issued 24 April 1832. Born free and raised in AA Co. Age about 17; 5' 3 3/4"; brown complexion; large scar on back of head.
Polly Warfield. Certificate issued 24 April 1832. Born free and raised in AA Co. Age about 22; 5' 2"; yellow complexion; scar on right arm.
John Lunks. Certificate issued 25 April 1832. DOM recorded by Charles Pettibone 26 Jan. 1805. Age about 36; 5' 5 1/4"; yellow complexion; scar on forehead and left side of face; raised in AA Co.
Sarah Lunks. Certificate issued 25 April 1832. DOM recorded by Charles Pettibone 26 Jan. 1805. Age about 32; 5' 3"; black complexion; no marks or scars; raised in AA Co.
Luther Crowner. Certificate issued 26 April 1832. Born free and raised in AA Co. Age about 23; 5' 5 1/2"; black complexion; large scar on left elbow; scar over right eye.
Julia Anne Jones. Certificate issued 26 April 1832. Born free and raised in AA Co. Age about 25; 5' 3"; yellow complexion; long hair; no marks or scars.
Daniel Matthews. Certificate issued 26 April 1832. DOM recorded by Richard Hopkins 16 April 1796. Age about 45; 5' 7"; light complexion; scars on right arm and between the eyes; raised in AA Co.
Lydia Matthews. Certificate issued 26 April 1832. DOM recorded by Richard Hopkins 16 April 1796. Age about 42; 5' 3"; yellow complexion; two small moles on upper lip; raised in AA Co.
Eliza Matthews. Certificate issued 26 April 1832. Born free and raised in AA Co. Age about 20; 4' 11"; light complexion; long straight hair.
Delilah Johnson. Certificate issued 28 April 1832. Born free and raised in AA Co. Age about 20; 5' 11"; black complexion; two scars on back of right hand; missing end of second toe of right foot.
Kitty Spencer. Certificate issued 28 April 1832. Born free and raised in AA Co. Age

about 16; 5' 2"; dark complexion; small scars on right wrist and cheek.
Henry Franklin. Certificate issued 28 April 1832. Born free and raised in AA Co. Age about 31; 5'; black complexion; scar on right arm; small web inside of left thumb.
Abraham Franklin. Certificate issued 28 April 1832. Born free and raised in AA Co. Age about 21; 5' 2 1/2"; black complexion; small scar on back of right hand.
William Queen. Certificate issued 28 April 1832. Born free and raised in AA Co. Age about 22; 5' 3 1/2"; black complexion; scar in corner of right eye, on the nose, another on forehead.
Eleanor Burley. Certificate issued 28 April 1832. Born free and raised in AA Co. Age about 31; 5' 4"; light complexion; scar on left side of neck.
Crissy Queen. Certificate issued 28 April 1832. Born free and raised in AA Co. Age about 19; 5' 3 1/2"; yellow complexion; small scar on left cheek.
Eliza Queen. Certificate issued 28 April 1832. Born free and raised in AA Co. Age about 17; 5' 2 1/2"; dark complexion; scars on left cheek, right arm, and left hand or wrist.
Winny Queen. Certificate issued 28 April 1832. Born free and raised in AA Co. Age about 55; 5' 2"; brown complexion; small scar on forehead.
Monaco Queen. Certificate issued 28 April 1832. Born free and raised in AA Co. Age about 52; 5' 1"; yellow complexion; scar near corner of right eye.
Milly Queen. Certificate issued 28 April 1832. Born free and raised in AA Co. Age about 35; 5' 1"; yellow complexion; small lump on left ear.
Matilda Boone. Certificate issued 28 April 1832. Born free and raised in AA Co. Age about 21; 5' 1"; dark complexion; scar on left cheek.
Phillip Buckingham. Certificate issued 30 April 1832. DOM recorded by George Scott 25 April 1832. Age about 32; 5' 5"; scars under right eye and over lip; raised in AA Co.
Betsy Johnson. Certificate issued 30 April 1832. Born free and raised in AA Co. Age about 17; 4' 11"; black complexion; two small scars on right hand.
Priscilla Cager. Certificate issued 30 April 1832. Born free and raised in AA Co. Age about 20; 5' 1"; black complexion; scar on right arm; mole on upper lip.
Liley Walker. Certificate issued 1 May 1832. DOM recorded by Ebenezer Pumphrey 16 Jan. 1798. Age about 44; 5' 1/2"; black complexion; several small moles on left side of face; raised in AA Co.
Artridge Johnson. Certificate issued 1 May 1832. DOM recorded by Ebenezer Pumprey 16 Jan. 1798. Age about 35, 4' 10 1/2"; black complexion; small scar on middle finger of right hand; raised in AA Co.
Polly Ringgold. Certificate issued 1 May 1832. DOM recorded by Phillip Hammond 2 Nov. 1803. Age about 35; 5' 3 1/2"; brown complexion; scars on left wrist and forehead; raised in AA Co.
Sally Cager. Certificate issued 1 May 1832. Born free and raised in AA Co. Age about 18; 5' 1"; brown complexion; small scars on back of right hand and end of right thumb; raised in AA Co.
Harriett Queen. Certificate issued 1 May 1832. Born free and raised in AA Co. Age about 21; 4' 5 1/2"; brown complexion; small scar on right cheek.
Mary Queen. Certificate issued 1 May 1832. Born free and raised in AA Co. Age about 23; 5' 1/2"; dark complexion; no marks or scars.
Delia Queen. Certificate issued 1 May 1832. Born free and raised in AA Co. Age about 25; 5' 3 1/2"; brown complexion; no marks or scars.
Lucretia Brown. Certificate issued 1 May 1832. Born free and raised in AA Co. Age about 27; 5' 1/2"; brown complexion; small scar over right eye; small mole on left cheek.
Louisa Crowner. Certificate issued 2 May 1832. Born free and raised in AA Co. Age about 21; 5' 5"; black complexion.
Fannie Brookes. Certificate issued 2 May 1832. Born free and raised in AA Co. Age about 21; 5' 1/2"; light complexion; small scar over right eye; long straight hair.
Tom Calvert. Certificate issued 2 May 1832. Born free and raised in AA Co. Age about 22; 5' 4 1/2"; brown complexion; small scars on left wrist and right arm.
Suddy Calvert. Certificate issued 2 May 1832. Born free and raised in AA Co. Age about 19; 5' 5 1/2"; dark complexion; scars on back, front of head and left wrist.
William Calvert. Certificate issued 2 May 1832. Born free and raised in AA Co. Age about 18; 5' 4" dark complexion; scars in left eyebrow and on left arm.
Samuel Brogden. Certificate issued 2 May 1832. DOM recorded by Augustine L--- 17 July 1808. Age about 33; 5' 8 1/2"; dark complexion; scars over right eye and between the eyes; raised in AA Co.

Basil Edwards. Certificate issued 3 May 1832. Born free and raised in AA Co. Age about 22; 5' 5 1/2"; black complexion; no marks or scars.
Mary Edwards. Certificate issued 3 May 1832. Born free and raised in AA Co. Age about 17; 5' 1/2"; black complexion; scar on nose.
Sarah Johnson. Certificate issued 3 May 1832. DOM recorded by Benjamin Stansbury 13 April 1813. Age about 39; 5' 5 1/2"; dark complexion; scars on right and left sides of neck and breast; raised in AA Co.
Matilda. Certificate issued 3 May 1832. Born free and raised in AA Co. Age about 16; 5' 1"; brown complexion; scar. under chin.
Mary. Certificate issued 3 May 1832. Born free and raised in AA Co. Age about 35; 5' 1 1/2"; brown complexion; scar on little finger of right hand.
Harriott. Certificate issued 3 May 1832. Born free and raised in AA Co. Age 25; 5' 5 1/2"; dark complexion; scar on left cheek.
Hagar. Certificate issued 3 May 1832. Born free and raised in AA Co. Age about 27; 5' 2 1/2"; black complexion; small scar on back of right hand and left wrist.
Sibby. Certificate issued 3 May 1832. DOM recorded by John Brice 19 April 1806. Age about 40; 5' 2"; dark complexion; several scars in neck and breast; raised in AA Co.
Michael Hunt. Certificate issued 5 May 1832. DOM recorded by John Brice 4 March 1806. Age about 50; 5' 5"; black complexion; several scars on forehead; raised in AA Co.
George Powell. Certificate issued 5 May 1832. DOM recorded by John Brice 4 March 1806. Age about 45; 5' 5"; black complexion; several scars on left wrist; raised in AA Co.
Debby Prout. Certificate issued 5 May 1832. Born free and raised in AA Co. Age about 24; 5' 3"; yellow complexion; small scar on left eyebrow.
Mary Prout. Certificate issued 5 May 1832. Born free and raised in AA Co. Age about 21; 4' 3"; dark complexion; several scars on forehead; scar over left eyebrow.
Robert Boston. Certificate issued 5 May 1832. Born free and raised in AA Co. Age about 32; 5' 7"; black complexion; large scar on left cheek.
Isaac Williams. Certificate issued 5 May 1832. Born free and raised in AA Co. Age about 26; 5' 5"; black complexion; scar on upper lip.
Mary Brown. Certificate issued 7 May 1832. DOM recorded by Greenbury Ridgely 26 April 1830. Age about 30; 5' 1 1/2"; dark complexion; scars on left shoulder and right leg; raised in AA Co.
Sarah Jackson. Certificate issued 7 May 1832. DOM recorded by John Brice 17 Sept. 1805. Age about 45; 5' 1"; black complexion; small scar on forehead and third finger of left hand; raised in AA Co.
Thomas Young. Certificate issued 7 May 1832. Born free and raised in AA Co. Age about 21; 5' 7"; brown complexion; small mole on right wrist.
Louisa Edwards. Certificate issued 7 May 1832. Born free and raised in AA Co. Age about 18; 5' 2 1/2"; black complexion; small mole on right eye.
Aquila Boston. Certificate issued 7 May 1832. Born free and raised in AA Co. Age about 25; 5' 8 1/2"; dark complexion; small scars on forehead, left wrist, and corner of left eye.
Priscilla Pea. Certificate issued 7 May 1832. Born free and raised in AA Co. Age about 20; 5' 1/2"; dark complexion; small scars on right cheek, over right eye and back of right hand.
Nancy Boston. Certificate issued 7 May 1832. Born free and raised in AA Co. Age about 30; 5' 3 1/2"; black complexion; small scar on right wrist.
John Crowner. Certificate issued 7 May 1832. Born free and raised in AA Co. Age about 22; 5' 7"; black complexion; scar near corner of right eye.
William Maynard. Certificate issued 7 May 1832. Born free and raised in AA Co. Age about 21; 5' 4"; brown complexion; small scar on forehead and corner of left eye.
Isaac Hawkins. Certificate issued 8 May 1832. Born free and raised in AA Co. Age about 24; 5' 8"; black complexion; scar on back of left hand.
Saul Green. Certificate issued 8 May 1832. DOM recorded by Elijah Williams 6 March 1821. Age about 37; 5' 2"; black complexion; scars on breast and right arm; raised in AA Co.
Mary Walker. Certificate issued 8 May 1832. DOM recorded by Elijah Williams 6 March 1821. Age about 24; 5' 1/2"; yellow complexion; scar on back of right hand.
Sall. Certificate issued 8 May 1832. DOM recorded by Zachariah Duvall 5 June 1792. Age about 53; 5' 3"; black complexion; scars on right cheek and back of right

hand; raised in AA Co.
Julia. Certificate issued 8 May 1832. Born free and raised in AA Co. Age about 27; 5' 2 1/2"; black complexion; small scars over right eye and on left wrist.
Nancy Queen. Certificate issued 8 May 1832. Born free and raised in AA Co. Age about 32; 5' 2 1/2"; yellow complexion; scar on left arm.
Eliza Queen. Certificate issued 8 May 1832. Born free and raised in AA Co. Age about 22; 4' 11"; dark complexion; small scar under left eye; large scar on right arm.
Isaac Holliday. Certificate issued 8 May 1832. DOM recorded by Sarah Mundy 1 Feb. 1828. Age about 27; 5' 7"; brown complexion; scars on forehead and right arm; raised in AA Co.
Odessa Crowner. Certificate issued 8 May 1832. DOM recorded by John Brice 25 Sept. 1805. Age about 28; 5' 4"; black complexion; scar over left eye; raised in AA Co.
Peter Montgomery. Certificate issued 8 May 1832. Born free and raised in AA Co. Age 22; 5' 11"; dark complexion; two small scars near corner of left eye.
Julia Ross. Certificate issued 10 May 1832. Born free and raised in AA Co. Age about 19; 5' 3 1/2"; black complexion, small scar on left arm.
Susan Wright. Certificate issued 10 May 1832. Born free and raised in AA Co. Age about 20; 5' 3 1/2"; black complexion; no marks or scars.
Alexander Garrett. Certificate issued 10 May 1832. Born free and raised in AA Co. Age about 22; 5' 6 1/2"; black complexion; scars on lip and back of right hand.
Thomas Garrett. Certificate issued 10 May 1832. Born free and raised in AA Co. Age about 15; 4' 11 1/2"; black complexion; small scars near left eye and over right eye.
Samuel Wilson. Certificate issued 10 May 1832. Born free and raised in AA Co. Age 24; 5' 5 1/2"; yellow complexion; small scars over right eye and on left wrist; third finger of right hand crooked.
Robert Boston. Certificate issued 10 May 1832. DOM recorded by --- Hackett 9 May 1829. Age about 30; 5' 5"; black complexion; scars between the eyes, over the right eyebrow, on back of right eye; raised in AA Co.
Matilda Hawkins. Certificate issued 11 May 1832. DOM recorded by Jerningham Drury 26 Dec. 1810. Daughter of Flava; Age about 24; 5' 2"; yellow complexion; scar over left eye; raised in AA Co.
Susan Hawkins. Certificate issued 11 May 1832. DOM recorded by Jerningham Drury 26 Dec. 1810. Daughter of Flava; Age about 26; 4' 10 1/2"; dark complexion; large scar right side of forehead; raised in AA Co.
Mary Stewart (Poll). Certificate issued 11 May 1832. DOM recorded by --- Wood 24 July 1824. Age about 26 5' 2 1/2"; dark complexion; scar on right arm; raised in AA Co.
Sarah E. Watkins. Certificate issued 11 May 1832. DOM recorded by Joseph Harwood 4 Jan. 1813. Age about 25; 4' 10"; brown complexion; raised in AA Co.
Jane Watkins. Certificate issued 11 May 1832. Born free and raised in AA Co. Age about 23; 4' 9"; brown complexion; scar on right side of forehead.
Henrietta Watkins. Certificate issued 11 May 1832. Born free and raised in AA Co. Age about 20; 4' 8"; brown complexion; small mark on left side of neck.
Polly Todd. Certificate issued 11 May 1832. DOM recorded by Nicholas P--- 10 Aug. 1816. Age about 17; 5' 1"; dark complexion; small scar back of left hand; raised in Anne Arundel. County.
Any (Annie ?). Certificate issued 12 May 1832. DOM recorded by Sarah E. Murray 13 Dec. 1830. Age about 53; 5' ; dark complexion; raised in AA Co.
Anthony. Certificate issued 12 May 1832. DOM recorded by Sarah E. Murray 13 Dec. 1830. Age about 16; 4' 10 1/2"; dark complexion; small scars corner of left eye and on right wrist; raised in AA Co.
Edward Ford. Certificate issued 12 May 1832. Born free and raised in AA Co. Age about 25; 5' 4"; dark complexion; small scars over and under the right eye.
Charlotte Ford. Certificate issued 12 May 1832. Born free and raised in AA Co. Age about 23; 5' 1/2"; dark complexion; small scar over right eye.
Jeremiah Tanner. Certificate issued 12 May 1832. Born free and raised in AA Co. Age about 24; 5' 4 1/2"; yellow complexion; small scar over left eye.
Sarah Davis. Certificate issued 12 May 1832. Born free and raised in AA Co. Age about 41; 5' 1 1/2"; yellow complexion; several small moles on the face.
John Davis. Certificate issued 12 May 1832. Born free and raised in AA Co. Age about 21; 5' 3"; yellow complexion; small mole between the eyes; small scar inside

of left hand.
Ceasar Wallas. Certificate issued 12 May 1832. DOM recorded by Aquila Edwards 24 June 1786. Age about 53; 5' 6"; black complexion; small scars over right eye and back of head; raised in AA Co.
Sarah Johnson. Certificate issued 12 May 1832. Born free and raised in AA Co. Age about 35; 5' 3 1/2"; dark complexion; scars near corner of left eye and on left thumb.
Sophia Johnson. Certificate issued 12 May 1832. Born free and raised in AA Co. Age about 17; 5' 1 1/2"; light complexion; small mole on left side of neck.
Jenny. Certificate issued. Certificate issued 12 May 1832. DOM recorded by William Weems 20 Jan. 1814. Age about 37; 5' 3 1/2"; black complexion; small scar left side of neck; raised in AA Co.
Hannah. Certificate issued. Certificate issued 12 May 1832. DOM recorded by John Brice 4 Nov. 1806. Age about 36; 4' 11"; black complexion; raised in AA Co.
Rachael. Certificate issued 12 May 1832. DOM recorded by John Brice 4 Nov. 1806. Age about 55; 5' 11"; black complexion; raised in AA Co.
Phillip Boston. Certificate issued 5 May 1832. Born free and raised in AA Co. Age about 29; 5' 5"; brown complexion; Tattoo on right arm "P. B---.".
Jenny Green. Certificate issued 5 May 1832. DOM recorded by Henry Hammond 10 April 1818. Age about 34; 5' 3"; black complexion; small scars on nose and right wrist; raised in AA Co.
Ann Spencer. Certificate issued 5 May 1832. Born free and raised in AA Co. Age about 20; 5' 3"; yellow complexion; small scar on left side of face.
Adam Dove. Certificate issued 5 May 1832. Born free and raised in AA Co. Age about 42; 5' 1 1/2"; brown complexion; small scar back of right hand; small mole under right eye.
Rachel Bias. Certificate issued 5 May 1832. Born free and raised in AA Co. Age about 13; 5' 1 1/2"; black complexion; scar near corner of left eye.
Henny Bias. Certificate issued 5 May 1832. Born free and raised in AA Co. Age about 27; 5' 4"; brown complexion; scar near left eye, another on left cheek.
Sarah Hill. Certificate issued 5 May 1832. Born free and raised in AA Co. Age about 17; 5' 1"; dark complexion; small scar on right eyebrow.
Edmond Pitts. Certificate issued 5 May 1832. DOM recorded by Elijah Gray 19 Jan. 1802. Age about 30; 5' 7 1/2"; black complexion; small scar on chin; raised in Anne County.
Elizabeth Sunder. Certificate issued 16 May 1832. Born free and raised in AA Co. Age about 15; 5' 10 1/2'; black complexion; small scars on right side of neck and on right shoulder.
Priscilla Baldwin. Certificate issued 16 May 1832. Born free and raised in AA Co. Age about 30; 5'; dark complexion; small scar back of left hand.
John Baldwin. Certificate issued 16 May 1932. Born free and raised in AA Co. Age about 18; 5' 5"; yellow complexion; small scar near right corner of mouth.
Eliza Snowden. Certificate issued 16 May 1932. Born free and raised in AA Co. Age about 24; 5' 1"; black complexion; small scar on right arm and over left eye.
Sarah Snowden. Certificate issued 16 May 1932. DOM recorded by Francis Hancock 29 Aug. 1803. Age about 29; 4' 11"; black complexion; scar on back of neck; face marked by smallpox; raised in AA Co.
Mary Thomas. Certificate issued 16 May 1932. DOM recorded by Francis Hancock 29 Aug. 1803. Age about 32; 5' 1/2"; yellow complexion; scars on right cheek, back of right hand; raised in AA Co.
Hannah Hawkins. Certificate issued 16 May 1932. Born free and raised in AA Co. Age about 45; 5' 3 1/2"; dark complexion; several scars about face.
Flavilly Jones. Certificate issued 16 May 1932. Born free and raised in AA Co. Age about 15; 5' 3"; brown complexion; no marks or scars.
Eliza Hawkins. Certificate issued 16 May 1932. Born free and raised in AA Co. Age about 17; 5' 3"; yellow complexion; small mole near left temple.
Margaret Hawkins. Certificate issued 16 May 1932. Born free and raised in AA Co. Age about 35; 5' 2"; black complexion; scars on left cheek and right ear.
Priscilla Hawkins. Certificate issued 16 May 1932. Born free and raised in AA Co. Age about 37; 5' 2 1/2"; yellow complexion; no marks or scars.
Rhoda Edwards. Certificate issued 16 May 1932. Born free and raised in AA Co. Age about 30; 4' 1"; black complexion; scars on nose and under left eye.
Charity Edwards. Certificate issued 16 May 1932. Born free and raised in AA Co. Age about 22; 5' 1 1/2"; black complexion; scar on left thumb.
Samuel Jones. Certificate issued 16 May

1932. Born free and raised in AA Co. Age about 40; 5' 8 1/2"; yellow complexion; scars on nose between the eyes, left thumb, and forefinger of left hand.
Peter Davidge. Certificate issued 7 May 1832. Born free and raised in AA Co. Age about 30; 5' 5 1/2"; yellow complexion; scar in left eyebrow.
Henry Lee. Certificate issued 7 May 1832. DOM recorded by Hercules L. Gibson 24 Jan 1811. Age about 21; 5' 3 1/2", yellow complexion; large scar over right forehead; raised in AA Co.
Maria. Certificate issued 7 May 1832. DOM recorded by Jemima Duvall 8 Jan. 1825. Age 24; 5' 3"; black complexion; small scar on back of left hand; raised in AA Co.
Martha Lee. Certificate issued 7 May 1832. Born free and raised in AA Co. Age about 16; 5' 1 1/2"; yellow complexion; scar on back of right hand.
Nancy Lee. Certificate issued 7 May 1832. Born free and raised in AA Co. Age about 18; 5' 4"; yellow complexion; scar on breast.
Betty Lee. Certificate issued 7 May 1832. Born free and raised in AA Co. Age about 19; 5' 4"; dark complexion; small mole near right corner of mouth.
Lewis Lee. Certificate issued 7 May 1832. Born free and raised in AA Co. Age about 22; 5' 6"; yellow complexion; scar on nose and breasts.
Washington Ijams. Certificate issued 7 May 1832. Born free and raised in AA Co. Age about 25; 5' 5 1/2"; black complexion; several scars on forehead; scar on right arm.
William Queen. Certificate issued 8 May 1832. Born free and raised in AA Co. Age about 21; 6' 1"; yellow complexion; small scar under left eye; crooked middle finger left hand.
Noah Queen. Certificate issued 8 May 1832. Born free and raised in AA Co. Age about 26; 5' 2 1/2"; dark complexion; scar on forefinger of left hand.
Edward Queen. Certificate issued 8 May 1832. Born free and raised in AA Co. 5' 5 1/2"; black complexion; scars near right corner of mouth and back of hand.
Thomas Queen. Certificate issued 8 May 1832. Born free and raised in AA Co. Age about 23; 5' 2 1/2"; dark complexion; scar on left wrist.
Robert Queen. Certificate issued 8, May 1832. Born free and raised in AA Co. Age about 20; 5' 6 1/2"; small scar over left eye.

John Queen. Certificate issued 8 May 1832. Born free and raised in AA Co. Age about 22; 5' 3"; black complexion; scar under right eye.
Joseph Queen. Certificate issued 8 May 1932. Born free and raised in AA Co. Age about 23; 5' 6"; black complexion; two scars on chin; scar on forehead.
Elizabeth Savoy. Certificate issued 8 May 1932. Born free and raised in AA Co. Age about 19; 5' 1"; yellow complexion; small mole near corner of right eye; moles on right arm.
Richard Savoy. Certificate issued 8 May 1832. Born free and raised in AA Co. Age about 21; 5' 8 1/2"; brown complexion; no marks or scars.
James Harrison. Certificate issued 18 May 1832. DOM recorded by Richard Harrison 23 July 1796. Age about 43; 5; 6 1/2"; dark complexion; face marked by smallpox; raised in AA Co.
James Scrivner. Certificate issued 18 May 1832. Born free and raised in AA Co. Age about 33; 5' 11"; dark complexion; scar on little finger of left hand.
William Scrivener. Certificate issued 18 May 1832. Born free and raised in AA Co. Age about 28; 5' 11 1/2"; dark complexion; no marks or scars.
Elizabeth Harrison. Certificate issued 18 May 1832. Born free and raised in AA Co. Age about 20; 5' 2"; black complexion; scar on ball of left thumb.
Charles Williams. Certificate issued 18 May 1832. Born free and raised in AA Co. Age about 21; 5' 3"; black complexion; scars on upper lip and over corner of left eye.
Benjamin Toogood. Certificate issued 19 May 1832. DOM recorded by Nicholas Toogood 5 Jan. 1792. Age about 45; 5' 7"; yellow complexion; scar on nose between the eyes; two small scars on breasts; raised in AA Co.
Mary Toogood. Certificate issued 19 May 1832. Born free and raised in AA Co. Age about 20; 5' 1 1/2"; brown complexion; small scar on back of each hand.
Henry Dodson. Certificate issued 19 May 1832. DOM recorded by Mary Gross 3 Sept. 1807. Age about 39; 5' 7"; black complexion; scars on forehead; scars on back of right hand; raised in AA Co.
Harriett Queen. Certificate issued 19 May 1832. Born free and raised in AA Co. Age about 18; 5' 4 1/2"; dark complexion no marks or scars.
Harriett Turner. Certificate issued 21 May 1832. Born free and raised in AA Co. Age

about 20; 5' 6"; yellow complexion; no marks or scars.
Eleanor Turner. Certificate issued 21 May 1832. Born free and raised in AA Co. Age about 42; 5' 3 1/2"; yellow complexion; small mole near left nostril.
Allen Turner. Certificate issued 21 May 1832. Born free and raised in AA Co. Age about 18; 5' 3 1/2"; yellow complexion; small scars on forehead and on left eyebrow.
James Barnet. Certificate issued 21 May 1832. Born free and raised in AA Co. Age about 25; 5' 4"; black complexion; scars on forefinger of each hand and on right knee.
Thomas Turner. Certificate issued 21 May 1832. Born free and raised in AA Co. Age about 24; 5' 11 1/2"; brown complexion; scars on left foot and back of left hand.
Thomas Turner. Certificate issued 21 May 1832. Born free and raised in AA Co. Brown complexion; two scars on right ankle.
Samuel B. Barnett. Certificate issued 21 May 1832. Born free and raised in AA Co. Age about 23; 5' 9 1/2"; dark complexion; small scars on forehead and left knee.
Charles Hayes. Certificate issued 21 May 1832. Born free and raised in AA Co. Age about 36; 5' 5"; black complexion; two small scars on forehead.
Frederick Samuel. Certificate issued 21 May 1832. Born free and raised in AA Co. Age about 26; 5' 8 1/2"; brown complexion; small scar on left ankle.
Bennett Hayes. Certificate issued 21 May 1832. Born free and raised in AA Co. Age about 38; 5' 9"; black complexion; large scar on right leg; lame in right leg.
Sarah Ann Pur—. Certificate issued 21 May 1832. Born free and raised in AA Co. Age about 17;5' 1 1/2"; dark complexion; number of scars about the face; large scar on back of right shoulder.
Jacob Queen. Certificate issued 21 May 1832. Born free and raised in AA Co. Age about 28; 5' 5 1/2"; dark complexion;scar in forehead over right eye.
Michael Queen. Certificate issued 21 May 1832. Born free and raised in AA Co. Age about 23; 5' 5"; black complexion; scar on forehead over left eye.
John Queen. Certificate issued 21 May 1832. Born free and raised in AA Co. Age about 22; 5' 2"; black complexion; scars in left eyebrow, over right eye, and on right cheek.
Ann Key. Certificate issued 21 May 1832. Born free and raised in AA Co. Age about 18; 4' 11"; black complexion; small scars between the eyes, and on forefinger of right hand.
Jonny Bias. Certificate issued 21 May 1832. Born free and raised in AA Co. Age about 18; 5' 2"; black complexion; small scar on back of right hand.
Henny Chew. Certificate issued 21 May 1832. Born free and raised in AA Co. Age about 23; 4' 11"; brown complexion; small scar on back of right hand.
John Carroll. Certificate issued 21 May 1832. Born free and raised in AA Co. Age about 23; 5' 7 1/2"; dark complexion; small scar near left eye.
James Blackeston. Certificate issued 21 May 1832. DOM recorded by Richard M. Chase 9 Sept. 1830. Age about 44; 5' 5"; black complexion; scar on back of right hand; raised in AA Co.
Eliza A. Wilson. Certificate issued 22 May 1832. Born free and raised in AA Co. Age about 15; 5' 1"; brown complexion; scar on forehead.
William Wilson. Certificate issued 22 May 1832. Born free and raised in AA Co. Age about 21; 5' 2 1/2"; brown complexion; scar on back of left hand.
Dennis Digges. Certificate issued 22 May 1832. DOM recorded by Robert Welch of Ben 4 Dec. 1830. Age about 40; 5' 9"; dark complexion; scar on back of right hand; raised in AA Co.
Harriott Wilson. Certificate issued 22 May 1832. DOM recorded by Richard Weems 9 July 1803. Age about 30; 5' 1/2"; black complexion; small scar on breast; raised in AA Co.
Eleanor Wilson. Certificate issued 22 May 1832. DOM recorded by Richard Weems 9 July 1803. Age about 27; 4' 11"; dark complexion; scar on right arm; raised in AA Co.
John Boston. Certificate issued 22 May 1832. Born free and raised in AA Co. Age about 21; 5' 10"; dark complexion; small scars on forehead; name is marked on left arm.
Charity Step. Certificate issued 22 May 1832. DOM recorded by Stephen Boone 17 Nov. 1815. Age about 37; 4' 9 1/2"; black complexion; small scar on left; raised in AA Co.
Hannah Ijiams. Certificate issued 22 May 1832. DOM recorded by Martha Robinson 4 June 1815. Age about 28; 4' 10 1/2"; black complexion; no marks or scars; raised in AA Co.
Julia Wilson. Certificate issued 22 May

1832. Born free and raised in AA Co. Age about 14; 5' 4"; brown complexion; no marks or scars.
Joshua Ennis. Certificate issued 22 May 1832. Born free and raised in AA Co. Age about 24; 5' 5 1/2"; dark complexion.
Elizabeth Stevens. 22 May 1832. Born free and raised in AA Co. Age not discernible; 5' 5"; dark complexion; large scar on forehead.
Titus Blunt. Certificate issued 22 May 1832. Born free and raised in AA Co. Age about 23; 5' 1/2"; black complexion.
Richard Blunt. Certificate issued 22 May 1832. Born free and raised in AA Co. Age about 21; 5' 7 1/2"; dark complexion; scar on left wrist.
Princees Thompson. 22 May 1832. Born free and raised in AA Co. Age about 23; 5' 8"; brown complexion; scars on each arm just above wrist.
Harriott Jacobs. 23 May 1832. Born free and raised in AA Co. Age about 22; 5' 2"; yellow complexion; scars on right side of neck and face; small scar on back of right hand.
Nancy Brown. 23 May 1832. Born free and raised in AA Co. Age about 30; 5' 2"; dark complexion; scar on right corner of mouth.
Betsy Hayes. 23 May 1832. Born free and raised in AA Co. Age about 27; 5' 1/2"; black complexion; small scar on left arm.
Priscilla Mullen. 23 May 1832. Born free and raised in AA Co. Age about 16; 5' 4"; brown complexion; small scar on left wrist.
Elizabeth Mullen. 23 May 1832. DOM recorded by Richard Mullen 2 Oct. 1819. Age about 19; 5' 4 1/2"; brown complexion; small moles left corner of mouth and left cheek; raised in AA Co.
Sarah Turner. 23 May 1832. Born free and raised in AA Co. Age about 28; 5'; brown complexion; small mole under left eye.
Richard Turner. 23 May 1832. Born free and raised in AA Co. Age about 24; 5' 11 1/2"; light complexion; small scar near corner of left eye; large scar on back of left hand.
Molly Parker. 23 May 1832. Born free and raised in AA Co. Age about 18; 5' 5"; black complexion; no marks or scars.
Mahaila Powell. 23 May 1832. Born free and raised in AA Co. Age about 19; 5' 3"; black complexion; small mole near left nostril; small scar on each arm.
Rachel Powell. 23 May 1832. Born free and raised in AA Co. Age about 14; 5' 1 1/2"; black complexion; small scar under right eye.
Fanny Queen. 23 May 1832. Born free and raised in AA Co. Age about 22; 4' 10"; black complexion small scars on chin and back of right hand.
William Queen. 23 May 1832. Born free and raised in AA Co. Age about 30; 5' 3"; brown complexion; small scar on each leg.
Benjamin Moore. 23 May 1832. DOM recorded by Tolly Moore 22 May 1815. Age about 27; 5' 11"; brown complexion; small scars on forehead and back of left hand; raised in AA Co.
Frank Moore. 23 May 1832. DOM recorded by Tolly Moore 22 May 1815. Age about 26; 4' 5"; brown complexion; no marks or scars; raised in AA Co.
Charles Brookes. 23 May 1832. Born free and raised in AA Co. Age about 19; 5' 5"; light complexion; small scar on forehead.
Richard Wallace. 23 May 1832. Born free and raised in AA Co. Age about 22; 5' 5"; Dark complexion; small scar near corner of left eye.
Jane Barrett. 23 May 1832. Born free and raised in AA Co. Age about 17; 5' 1"; brown complexion; no marks or scars.
Nancy Alsop. 23 April 1832. Born free and raised in AA Co. Age about 16; 4' 11 1/2"; dark complexion; small scar on forehead; two small scars on left hand.
Richard Ennis. 23 May 1832. Born free and raised in AA Co. Age about 21; 5' 4 1/2"; black complexion; scars on left wrist and each arm.
Sarah Ennis. 23 May 1832. DOM recorded by William Fisher 13 April 1790. Age about 53; 5' 2 1/2"; dark complexion; small scar on forehead; raised in AA Co.
Nancy Holland. 23 May 1832. Born free and raised in AA Co. Age about 18; 5' 4"; yellow complexion; small scar near corner of left eye.
Sally Batson. 23 May 1832. Born free and raised in AA Co. Age about 26; 4' 11".
Fanny Queen. 23 May 1832. Born free and raised in AA Co. Age about 30; 5' 1"; black complexion; small scar on forehead.
John Harris. 24 May 1832 Born free and raised in AA Co. Age about 24; 5' 7"; dark complexion; small. scar on forehead, another on left wrist.
Samuel Green. 24 May 1832. DOM recorded by John Merriken 18 May 1807. Age about 52; 5' 7 1/2"; black complexion; scars on right thumb and forefinger of left hand; raised in AA Co.
John Counts. 25 May 1832. DOM recorded

by Samuel (Lemuel ?) H. Beale 2 May 1826. Age about 34; 5' 7 1/2"; yellow complexion; raised in AA Co.
Harriet Smith. 25 May 1832. DOM recorded by Daniel Smith 6 July 1831. Age about 24; 5' 2 1/2"; dark complexion; small scars on forehead and right wrist; raised in AA Co.
William Easton. 25 May 1832. Born free and raised in AA Co. Age about 27; 5' 5"; yellow complexion; small scar on ball of right thumb.
Charles Hobbs. 25 May 1832. Born free and raised in AA Co. Age about 21; 5' 11"; brown complexion; small scar near corner of left eye.
Thomas Johnson. 25 May 1832. Born free and raised in AA Co. Age about 21; 5' 8"; dark complexion; scar on forehead over right eye.
Nanny Wells. 25 May 1832. Born free and raised in AA Co. Age about 19; 5' 5 1/2"; black complexion; scar on right cheek below eye.
William Jones. 25 May 1832. DOM recorded by Mary Pearson 5 June 1789. Age about 48; 5' 3"; dark complexion; raised in AA Co.
Polly Countee. 25 May 1832. Born free and raised in AA Co. Age about 20; 5' 1"; black complexion; small scar on forehead.
Rebecca Turner. 25 May 1832. Born free and raised in AA Co. Age about 25; 5' 5 1/2"; black complexion; no marks or scars.
George Countee. 25 May 1832. Born free and raised in AA Co. Age about 21; 5' 7 1/2"; black complexion; no marks or scars.
Kitty. 25 May 1832. Born free and raised in AA Co. Age about 22; 5' 1 1/2"; black complexion; scar on right wrist.
Mary Williams. 25 May 1832. DOM recorded by Charles Pettibone 26 Jan. 1805. Age about 29; 5' 6"; black complexion; scars on right wrist and ball of thumb; raised in AA Co.
Lucy Johnson. 25 May 1832. Born free and raised in AA Co. Age about 23; 5' 4"; black complexion; small scar on left wrist.
John Johnson. 25 May 1832. Born free and raised in AA Co. Age about 28; 5' 9"; black complexion; scar over left eye.
Janet Johnson. 25 May 1832. Born free and raised in AA Co. Age about 20; 5' 2"; black complexion; small scar over left eye.
Samuel Watkins. 26 May 1832. DOM recorded by John Norwood 7 March 1803. Age about 54; 5' 6"; dark complexion; lame in left leg; raised in AA Co.
Willy Digges. 26 May 1832. Born free and raised in AA Co. Age about 13; 5' 3"; dark complexion; two small scars on right thumb.
Edward Brown. 26 May 1832. Born free and raised in AA Co. Age about 28; 5' 3 1/2"; dark complexion; no marks or scars.
Henry Matthews. 26 May 1832. DOM recorded by Samuel Pearson 18 Jan. 1808. Age about 32;; 5' 8"; black complexion; small scar near corner of left eye; raised in AA Co.
Rachel Hammond. 26 May 1832. Born free and raised in AA Co. Age about 16; 4' 10 1/2"; dark complexion; no marks or scars.
Charlotte Cromwell. 26 May 1832. Born free and raised in AA Co. Age about 16; 5' 1"; black complexion; no marks or scars.
Ann Shuaff. 26 May 1832. Born free and raised in AA Co. Age about 15; 5' ; dark complexion; no marks or scars.
Delilah Hill. 26 May 1832. Born free and raised in AA Co. Age about 19; 5' 2 1/2"; dark complexion; small scar on nose; another on left hand.
Stephen Johnson. 26 May 1832. Born free and raised in AA Co. Age about 19; 5' 6"; black complexion; small scar on left side of nose.
John Ross. 26 May 1832. Born free and raised in AA Co. Age about 19; 5' 7"; black complexion; scar over right eye.
Charles Duppin. 26 May 1832. Born free and raised in AA Co. Age about 30;5' 7"; dark complexion; scar on inside of left arm.
John Burgess. 26 May 1832. Born free and raised in AA Co. Age about 25; 5' 1/2"; brown complexion; small scar on right wrist.
Lucretia Bruce. 26 May 1832. Born free and raised in AA Co. Age about 19. 5' 3 1/2"; black complexion; small scars on right wrists and back of neck.
James Nash. 26 May 1832. Born free and raised in AA Co. Age about 28; 5' 5"; dark complexion; small scar on forehead.
Charlotte Williams. 26 May 1832. Born free and raised in AA Co. Age about 23; 5' 3 1/2"; dark complexion; small scar over left eye.
Louisa Myers. 28 May 1832. DOM 13 Jan. 1816. (Grantor not identified) Age about 19; 5' 6 1/2"; yellow complexion; two small marks on face; raised in AA Co.
George Allen. 28 May 1832. Born free and raised in AA Co. Age about 32; 5' 6 1/2"; dark complexion; scars on back of neck and right leg.

Dick Johnson. 28 May 1832. DOM recorded by Lucy Howard 24 May 1830. Age about 45; 6' 2"; dark complexion; small scar on right hand; raised in AA Co.

Matilda Queens. 28 May 1832. DOM recorded by Mary Howard 24 May 1832. Age about 23; 5' 4"; dark complexion; small scar back of left hand; raised in AA Co.

Thomas Key. 28 May 1832. Born free and raised in AA Co. Age about 22; 5' 5 1/2"; black complexion; small scar on forehead near left eye.

Mary Thomas. 28 May 1828. Born free and raised in AA Co. Age about 17; 5' 1 1/2"; black complexion; scar on left shoulder.

Cassy Merriken. 28 May 1832. Born free and raised in AA Co. Age about 24; 5' 5"; yellow complexion; large scar on left arm.

James Boothe. 28 May 1832. Born free and raised in AA Co. Age about 54; 5' 5"; dark complexion; no marks or scars.

Minta. 28 May 1832. DOM recorded by Joseph Hopkins 25 May 1832. Age about 43; 5'; brown complexion; no marks or scars; raised in AA Co.

Hagar. 28 May 1832. Born free and raised in AA Co. Age about 29; 5' 1 1/2"; black complexion large scar on right arm; burn on breast.

Kitty. 28 May 1832. No statement as to origination of freedom. Age 26; 5' 3"; dark complexion; mole on left ear; scar on right elbow; raised in AA Co.

Lavina. 28 May 1832. Born free and raised in AA Co. Age 35; 5' 3 1/2"; dark complexion; scar on little finger left hand.

William Creek. 28 May 1832. DOM recorded by Gilbert Howell 6 July 1790. Age about 55; 5' 7"; black complexion; blind in left eye; raised in AA Co.

Julianna West. 28 May 1832. Born free and raised in AA Co. Age about 16; 5' 1/2"; bright complexion; no marks or scars.

Nancy. 28 May 1832. Born free and raised in AA Co. Age about 20; 5' 4 1/2"; small scar on right wrist.

Dinah Jackson. 28 May 1832. Born free and raised in AA Co. Age about 17; 4' 11 1/2"; black complexion; small scar on back of left hand.

George Thomas. May 1832. DOM recorded by John Merriken 14 Sept. 1811. Age about 60; 5' 6"; dark complexion; blind in left eye; raised in AA Co.

Jack Powell. 28 May 1832. DOM recorded by Henry Owens 18 April 1827. Age about 33; 5' 3 1/2"; dark complexion; small scar on back of left hand; raised in AA Co.

Isaac Harrod. 28 May 1832. Born free and raised in AA Co. Age about 30; 5' 5"; dark complexion; scar on forehead; scar over left eye; mole on right side of neck.

Nancy Boston. 28 May 1832. DOM recorded by Nicholas Swormstedt 22 Oct. 1810. Age about 40; 5' 1 1/2"; black complexion; no marks or scars; raised in AA Co.

Sarah Clarke. 28 May 1832. Born free and raised in AA Co. Age about 23; 5' 2 1/2"; black complexion; small scar near corner of right eye.

Eliza Isaacs. 28 May 1832. Born free and raised in AA Co. Age about 33; 5' 4"; black complexion; small scar on breast.

Matilda Williams. 28 May 1832. Born free and raised in AA Co. Age about 22; 5'"; black complexion; small scars on forehead and back of right hand.

Sarah Williams. 28 May 1832. Born free and raised in AA Co. Age about 18; 5' 2 1/2"; dark complexion; small scar near right eye.

Dinah Sanders. 28 May 1832. Born free and raised in AA Co. Age about 20; 5' 1"; black complexion; no marks or scars.

Caroline Isaacs. 28 May 1832. Born free and raised in AA Co. Age about 20; 5' 4"; black complexion; small scar near corner of right eye, another on left wrist.

Betsy Williams. 28 May 1832. Born free and raised in AA Co. Age about 20; 5' 2"; dark complexion; small scar on left cheek.

Samuel Williams. 28 May 1832. Born free and raised in AA Co. Age about 22; 5' 9"; black complexion; small scars near corner of left eye and second finger of left hand.

Richard Chew. 28 May 1832. Born free and raised in AA Co. Age about 21; 5' 9"; dark complexion; small scar on back of right hand.

Barbara Matthews. 28 May 1832. DOM recorded by John Chew Thomas 12 Feb. 1812. Age about 35; 5'; brown complexion; two small scars on nose; small scar on second finger of right hand; raised in AA Co.

Mary Williams. 28 May 1832. Born free and raised in AA Co. Age about 23; 5' 3 1/2"; dark complexion; small scar on lower lip.

Elizabeth Sanders. 28 May 1832. Born free and raised in AA Co. Age about 25; 5' 8"; dark complexion; scar on forehead and each little finger.

Mary Matthews. 28 May 1832. Born free and raised in AA Co. Age about 17; 5' 2"; brown complexion; no marks or scars.

Hazel Haynes. 28 May 1832. Born free and raised in AA Co. Age about 26; 5' 3"; brown complexion; small scars on forehead and each foot.
Richard Saunders. 28 May 1832. Born free and raised in AA Co. Age about 39; 5' 7 1/2"; black complexion; scars on upper lip and little fingers.
Mary Hammond. 28 May 1832. Born free and raised in AA Co. Age about 23; 5' 1/2"; yellow complexion; small scar on left cheek.
Nancy Barnett. 28 May 1832. Born free and raised in AA Co. Age about 48; 5' 1"; dark complexion; small scar on right side of face.
Charlotte Myers. 28 May 1832. Born free and raised in AA Co. Age about 25; 5' 2"; brown complexion; scar over right eye.
Nace Hammond. 28 May 1832. Born free and raised in AA Co. Age about 18; 5' 5; yellow complexion; small scar on forehead.
Richard Hammond. 28 May 1832. Born free and raised in AA Co. Age about 23; 5' 7"; brown complexion; small scars on forehead and back of left hand.
Frances Barnett. 28 May 1832. DOM recorded by William Fisher 13 April 1790. Age about 47; 5' 6 1/2"; black complexion; blind in right eye.
Charles Hammond. 28 May 1832. Born free and raised in AA Co. Age about 27; 5' 5"; yellow complexion; no marks or scars.
Lot Prout. 28 May 1832. Born free and raised in AA Co. Age about 29; 5' 10 1/2"; dark complexion; scars on upper lip, chin, and right wrist.
Polly Henson. 28 May 1832. DOM recorded by William Wilson 20 Jan. 1814. Age about 43; 5' 0"; yellow complexion; no marks or scars.
Anne Queen. 28 May 1832. Born free and raised in AA Co. Age about 27; 5' 3"; black complexion; no marks or scars.
Solomon Barnett. 28 May 1832. Born free and raised in AA Co. Age about 41; 5' 8 1/2"; black complexion; two scars on right arm.
Wappen (Wassen ?) Davis. 28 May 1832. Born free and raised in AA Co. Age about 37; 5' 11 1/2"; black complexion; large scar on throat, another on back of both hands.
John Queen. 28 May 1832. Born free and raised in AA Co. Age about 30; 5' 7 1/2"; yellow complexion; enlarged lower right ear.
Nancy Ann Allen. 28 May 1832. Born free and raised in AA Co. Age about 22; 5' 2 1/2"; brown complexion; no marks or scars.
Mary Allen. 28 May 1832. Born free and raised in AA Co. Age about 18; 4' 11 1/2"; yellow complexion; many freckles on face.
Patsy Allen. 28 May 1832. Born free and raised in AA Co. Age about 17; 5' 6"; black complexion; small scar on right wrist.
William Allen. 28 May 1832. Born free and raised in AA Co. Age about 22; 5' 5"; black complexion; no marks or scars.
Sarah Harris. 28 May 1832. DOM recorded by Joseph R. Hopkins 24 July 1826. Age about 47; 5' 1 1/2"; dark complexion; two small moles under left eye. Raised in AA Co.
Betsy Harrison. 28 May 1832. DOM recorded by Joseph R. Hopkins 24 July 1826. Age about 26; 5' 4"; brown complexion; small scar under left eye. Raised in AA Co.
Sally Rutland. 28 May 1832. DOM recorded by Rachel Snowden 20 Nov. 1813. Age about 22; 5' 3"; dark complexion; small scar on right side of chin. Raised in AA Co.
Sam Herbert. 28 May 1832. DOM recorded by Rachel Snowden 20 Nov. 1813. Age about. 23; 5' 6"; black complexion; small scars on forehead. Raised in AA Co.
Jacob Matthews. 28 May 1832. DOM recorded by Rachel Snowden 20 Nov. 1813. Age about 22; 5' 3"; dark complexion; small scars on forehead and left thumb. Raised in AA Co.
Harriet Rutland. 28 May 1832. DOM recorded by Rachel Snowden 20 Nov. 1813. Age about 25; 4' 11 1/2"; dark complexion; no marks. or scars; raised in AA Co.
Mary Bull. 28 May 1832. DOM recorded by Rachel Snowden 20 Nov. 1813. Raised in AA Co. Age about 25; 5' 6"; light complexion; no marks or scars.
Patsy Bull. 28 May 1832. DOM recorded by Rachel Snowden 20 Nov. 1813. Raised in AA Co. Age about 23. 5' 6 1/2"; light complexion; moles on back of neck and behind left ear.
Louisa Bull. 28 May 1832. DOM recorded by Rachel Snowden 20 Nov. 1813. Raised in AA Co. Age about 27; 5' 2 1/2"; light complexion; mole on left side. of neck.
Nancy Berry. 28 May 1832. DOM recorded by Rachel Snowden 20 Nov. 1813. Raised in AA Co. Age about 27; 5' 1"; black complexion; mole on nose.
Nicholas Matthews. 28 May 1832. DOM recorded by Anna Maria Snowden 2 Nov. 1814. Raised in AA Co. Age about 31; 6'

1"; black complexion; small scar over each eye.
Maria Scott. 28 May 1832. DOM recorded by Anna Maria Snowden 2 Nov. 1814. Raised in AA Co. Age about 34; 4' 11"; dark complexion; 2 moles on back of neck.
Kate Brookes. 28 May 1832. DOM recorded by Anna Maria Snowden 2 Nov. 1814. Raised in AA Co. Age about 35; 5'; brown complexion; several moles on face.
Kitty Matthews. 28 May 1832. Born free and raised in AA Co. Age about 16; 5' 1 1/2"; dark complexion; no marks or scars.
Charlotte Watson. 28 May 1832. DOM recorded by Elizabeth and Hestor Hood 2 Dec. 1820. Age about 16; 5' 5 1/2"; black complexion; small scar under chin.
Nelly Gardner. 28 May 1832. Born free and raised in AA Co. Age about 18; 5' 8"; dark complexion; several scars on right sided of face.
Frances Scott. 28 May 1832. Born free and raised in AA Co. Age about 39; 5' 4 1/2"; black complexion; scar on head.
David Ennis. 28 May 1832. Born free and raised in AA Co. Age about 27; 4' 1"; dark complexion; scars on forehead and upper lip.
Sarah Ennis. 29 May 1832. DOM recorded by Lewis Neth 30 July 1829. Age about 31; 5' 2:' yellow complexion; no marks or scars. Raised in AA Co.
Ann Johnson. 29 May 1832. DOM recorded by Edward Williams 4 Oct. 1828. Age about 42; 5' 3"; brown complexion; small scar on right arm, very corpulent; raised in AA Co.
Henry Hanson. 29 May 1832. Born free and raised in AA Co. Age about 19; 5' 4 1/2"; yellow complexion; scar on right hand; has speech impediment.
Sarah Jones. 29 May 1832. Born free and raised in AA Co. Age about 35; 5' 3"; yellow complexion; no marks or scars.
Herring Parker. 29 May 1832. Born free and raised in AA Co. Age about 23; 5' 2 1/2"; yellow complexion; scar between the eyes.
Harriett Parker. 29 May 1832. Born free and raised in AA Co. Age about 24; 5' 5 1/2"; dark complexion; scar on forehead.
Betsy Parker. 29 May 1832. Born free and raised in AA Co. Age about 32; 5' 5 1/2"; dark complexion; small scars on forehead and left cheek.
Margaret Parker. 29 May 1832. Born free and raised in AA Co. Age about 39; 5' 3"; dark complexion; scar on left arm.
Nancy Parker. 29 May 1832. Born free and raised in AA Co. Age about 49; 5' 4 1/2"; yellow complexion; small scar on left breast.
Kitty Ann Parker. 29 May 1832. Born free and raised in AA Co. Age about 18; 5' 5"; yellow complexion; few facial freckles.
Lydia Parker. 29 May 1832. Born free and raised in AA Co. Age about 16; 5' 2 1/2"; dark complexion; scar on breast.
Mary Branfoot. 29 May 1832. Born free and raised in AA Co. Age about 23; 5' ; dark complexion; scar on right arm.
Mary Thomas. 29 May 1832. Born free and raised in AA Co. Age about 18; 5' 4"; yellow complexion; small scar on middle finger of right hand; another on right side of neck.
Caroline Parker. 29 May 1832. Born free and raised in AA Co. Age about 17; 5' 4"; black complexion; small scars on forehead and back of right hand.
Richard Garrett. 29 May 1832. Born free and raised in AA Co. Age about 17; 5' 4"; dark complexion; small scars back of left hand. and right arm.
Rachel Byas. 29 May 1832. Born free and raised in AA Co. Age about 18; 5' 1 1/2"; dark complexion; no marks or scars.
Nancy Brasheers. 29 May 1832. Born free and raised in AA Co. Age about 24; 5' 3 1/2"; yellow complexion; no marks or scars.
William Parker. 29 May 1832. Born free and raised in AA Co. Age about 25; 5' 9; brown complexion; small scar on forehead and right hand.
Flora Gantt. 29 May 1832. Born free and raised in AA Co. Age about 30; 5' 2 1/2; brown complexion; no marks or scars.
Jane Johnson. 29 May 1832. Born free and raised in AA Co. Age about 36; 5' 1/2"; brown complexion; scar on left arm.
Rachel Queen. 29 May 1832. Born free and raised in AA Co. Age about 29; 5'; dark complexion; no scars or marks.
Levi Gray. 29 May 1832. Born free and raised in AA Co. Age about 26; 5' 6"; brown complexion; scar on back of right hand.
Otho Gray. 29 May 1832. Born free and raised in AA Co. Age about 30; 5' 5"; brown complexion; small scar on middle finger of left hand.
Susan Queen. 29 May 1832. Born free and raised in AA Co. Age about 17; 4' 11"; dark complexion; scar on back of left hand.
Elizabeth Queen. 29 May 1832. Born free and raised in AA Co. Age about 23; 5'

1/2"; dark complexion; scar on inside of left wrist; another on back of left wrist.
Betsy Davis. 29 May 1832. Born free and raised in AA Co. Age about 16; 4' 11 1/2"; yellow complexion; no marks or scars.
Cornelious Emerson. 9 May 1832. Born free and raised in AA Co. Age about 18; 5' 5 1/2"; black complexion; small scar on forehead.
John Emerson. 29 May 1832. Born free and raised in AA Co. Age about 21; 5' 8"; black complexion; scars on right arm, left hand, and left leg.
Jerry Allen. 29 May 1832. DOM recorded by Elizabeth Glester Hood 2 Dec. 1822. Raised in AA Co. Age about 24; 5' 10"; black complexion; small scars on left ear and left thumb.
John Augustus. 29 May 1832. DOM recorded by Richard Conner 10 June 1821. Age about 24; 5' 9 1/2"; yellow complexion; wart on right corner of mouth; raised in AA Co.
Peter Wilkins. 29 May 1832. DOM recorded by Jonathan Laughlin 2 June 1810. Age about 25; 5' 4"; black complexion; scar on back of head; has speech impediment; raised in AA Co.
Eliza Booth. 29 May 1832. Born free and raised in AA Co. Age about 32; 5' 3"; dark complexion; no marks or scars.
Phillip Cook. 29 May 1832. Born free and raised in AA Co. Age about 47; 5' 2"; yellow complexion; scar on chin; small lump on forehead.
Eliza Ann Nichols. 29 May 1832. Born free and raised in AA Co. Age about 21' 4' 9"; black complexion; no marks or scars.
Rachel Jones. 29 May 1832. DOM recorded by William Weems 26 March 1805. Age about 28; 5' 1/2"; dark complexion; small scar on left wrist, several on back of right hand. Raised in AA Co.
Betsy Jones. 29 May 1832. DOM recorded by Mary Pearson 6 July 1789. Age about 43; 4' 11"; dark complexion; large scar on right wrist and hand; raised in AA Co.
Nancy Green. 29 May 1832. DOM recorded by George Whipps 22 March 1807. Age about 50; 4' 6"; yellow complexion; two small scars on right arm; raised in AA Co.
Ann Savoy. 30 May 1832. Born free and raised in AA Co. Age about 19; 4' 11 1/2"; dark complexion; small scar on right side of upper lip.
Harriot Green. 30 May 1832. Born free and raised in AA Co. Age about 18; 5' 4"; brown complexion; scar on right arm.
Rachel Hardy. 30 May 1832. Born free and raised in AA Co. Age about 21; 5' 0"; brown complexion; scar on right arm.
James Gray. 30 May 1832. DOM recorded by John Pitts 25 Jan. 1811. Age about 31; 5' 4 1/2"; brown complexion; scar on each arm; white spot on pupil of left eye; raised in AA Co.
Mary Howard. 30 May 1832. Born free and raised in AA Co. Age about 25; 5' 3"; bright complexion; scar on end of right thumb.
Milly Turner. 30 May 1832. DOM recorded by Mary Shipley 14 March 1821. Age about 28; 5' 4 1/2"; dark complexion; cataract on right eye; scar on forefinger of right hand; raised in AA Co.
Priscilla Creek. 1 June 1832. Born free and raised in AA Co. Age about 26; 5' 2 1/2"; dark complexion; no marks or scars.
Samuel Matthews. 1 June 1832. DOM recorded by Henry Matthews 7 July 1827. Age about 56; 5' 6"; brown complexion. Raised in AA Co
Aaron Necessities. 1 June 1832. Born free and raised in AA Co. Age about 21; 5' 2"; dark complexion;. scar on left instep.
George Dorsey. 1 June 1832. DOM recorded by Rezin Snowden 23 May, 1810. Age about 40; 5' 10 1/2'; dark complexion; small scars over left eye, on forehead, and on left arm. Raised in AA Co.
Benjamin Stewart. 1 June 1832. DOM recorded by Nicholas Merriwether 6 February, 1807. Age about 40; 5' 5 1/2"; black complexion; scars in corner of left eye, another on right ...; raised in Anne Arundel County.
— Walker. 1 June 1832. DOM recorded by Nicholas and Mary Ridgely 5 Oct. 1831. Age about 20; 5' 4 1/2"; black complexion; scar on left arm; raised in AA Co.
Henry Swann. 1 June 1832. Born free and raised in AA Co. Age about 48; 5' 7"; dark complexion' scars on left arm & right leg.
Fancy Urquahart. 1 June 1832. DOM recorded by David Weem 8 December, 1803. Age about 35; 5' 1 1/2"; brown complexion; small scar on right cheek; raised in AA Co.
Susan Brown. 1 June 1832. Born free and raised in AA Co. Age about 20; 5' 7"; two scars on right arm, another on forehead.
Mary Brown. 1 June 1832. Born free and raised in AA Co. Age about 16; 4' 11 1/2"; black complexion; small scar on forehead.
A— Oliver. 2 June 1832. DOM recorded by Frances Oliver 1 Oct. 1827. Age about 22; 5' 7"; yellow complexion; no marks or

scars; raised in AA Co.

Margaret Gray. 2 June 1832. Born free and raised in AA Co. Age about 31; 5' 1/2"; brown complexion; small scar on left arm; has lost upper front teeth.

Beck Gray. 2 June 1832. Born free and raised in AA Co. Age about 32; 5' 1"; yellow complexion;. large scar on left wrist.

James Ross. 4 June 1832. DOM recorded by Samuel Rideout 22 Sept., 1807. Age about 27; 5' 4 1/2"; dark complexion; scar on left breast; raised in AA Co.

Hannah Gaana. 5 May 1832. DOM recorded by Archibald Mason 14 Dec. 1821. Age about 41; 5' 4"; black complexion; scar under right eye, another in left eye brow; raised in AA Co.

Polly Brown. 6 June 1832. Born free and raised in AA Co. Age about 35; 5' 1 1/2"; black complexion; scars on left arm and over left eye.

Sally Matthews. 6 June 1832. Born free and raised in AA Co. Age about 18; 4' 11 1/2"; brown complexion; small scar on right cheek.

Rachel Cooper. 6 June 1832. Born free and raised in AA Co. Age about 19; 5' 3"; brown complexion; small scar on each wrist.

Joseph Harris. 6 June 1832. Born free and raised in AA Co. Age about 23; 5' 8"; small scar across right eye; another on back of right hand.

Daniel Queen. 7 June 1832. Born free and raised in AA Co. Age about 45; 5' 3 `/2"; dark complexion; small scar on back of right hand.

Sarah Williams. 7 June 1832. Born free and raised in AA Co. Age about 16; 5' 3"; yellow complexion; small scar on forehead.

Sarah Matthews 7 June 1832. Born free and raised in AA Co. Age about 35; 5' 3 1/2"; black complexion; no scars or marks.

Darky Williams. 7 June 1832. Born free and raised in AA Co. Age about 39; 5' 3 1/2"; black complexion; scar on forehead.

Peter Brown. 9 June 1832. Born free and raised in AA Co. Age about 31; 5' 3/12"; small scar on lower lip; two scars over corner of left eye.

Augustine Hawkins. 9 June, 1832. Born free and raised in AA Co. Age about 22; 5' 5 1/2"; black complexion; small scar on left cheek; another near corner of left eye; another on forehead.

L........ Queen. 9 June, 1832. Born free and raised in AA Co. Age about 34; 5' 6 1/2"; yellow complexion; dark spot on forehead; scar on left eyebrow; two dark spots in left eye.

Harriiot Boone. 11 June 1832. DOM recorded by Sarah Riggs 18 May, 1814. Age about 34; 4' 10 1/2"; small scar on left arm. Raised in AA Co.

Mary Hall. 11 June 1832. Born free and raised in AA Co. Age about 17: 4' 11"; black complexion; scar on right wrist.

John Hanson. 11 June 1832. DOM recorded by Zachariah Duvall 6 April 1812. Age about 21; 5' 8"; yellow complexion; scar over left eye; raised in AA Co.

Chloe Rhodes. 14 June 1832. DOM recorded by John Roads 8 April, 1826. Age about 50; 5' 4"; dark complexion; scar on breast, little finger of left hand is crooked. Raised in AA Co.

John Rhodes. 14 June 1832. DOM recorded by Nicholas Merriweather 24 Sept. 1803. Age about 62; 5' 4 1/2"; yellow complexion; little finger of left hand is crooked. Raised in AA Co.

Hager Muellin. 16 June 1832. DOM recorded by Richard Muellin 22 Oct. 1817. Age about 16; 5' 4"; yellow complexion; small scar on back of right hand. Raised in AA Co.

Henry Hull. 16 June 1832. DOM recorded by Joseph Phelps 6 Aug. 1817. Age about 35; 5' 9 1/2"; black complexion; scar on back of left hand. Raised in AA Co.

Susan Brown. 21 June 1832. Born free and raised in AA Co. Age about 36; 5"; black complexion; scars under lip and on chin.

William Turner. 29 June 1832. Born free and raised in AA Co. Age about 29; 5' 7"; yellow complexion; small scar in left eyebrow.

Patience Snowden. 10 July 1832. DOM recorded by William Hammond 20 April 182?. Age about 34; 4' 11"; brown complexion; scar over left eye; scar on right arm. Raised in AA Co.

Nace Bacon. 11 July 1832. DOM recorded by Rachel Howard 10 April, 1827. Age about 40; 5' 3 1/2"; black complexion; scar over right eye, another back of left hand. Raised in AA Co.

Flora Thomas. 16 July 1832. Born free and raised in AA Co. Age about 23; 5' 6"; black complexion; scar on left cheek.

Priscilla Thomas. 16 July 1832. Born free and raised in AA Co. Age about 32; 5" 6'; black complexion; three scars on left arm.

Daniel Thomas. 17 July 1832. Born free and raised in AA Co. Age about 22: 5' 5"; dark complexion; small scar on left cheek;

another on back of left hand.
Charles Counts. 21 July 1832. Born free and raised in AA Co. Age about 20: 6'; yellow complexion; small scar on forefinger of left hand.
Stacey Jackson. 21 July 1832. DOM recorded by Sussanna Wyrell 30 Nov. 1813. Age about 46; 4' 9"; black complexion; several scars on right arm; raised in AA Co.
Fanny Lowry. 31 July 1832. DOM recorded by Adam Miller, John Miller, James Hunter & William Parsons 17 May 1832. Age about 38; 5' 5"; black complexion; several small scars on forehead. Raised in AA Co.
Mary Dodson. 31 July 1832. DOM recorded by Adam Miller, John Miller, James Hunter & William Parsons 17 May 1832. Age about 32; 5' 2"; black complexion; small scars on left cheek, left wrist, back of head. Raised in AA Co.
James Anderson 8 Aug., 1832. Born free and raised in AA Co. Age about 19; 5' 1"; brown complexion; number of scars about right knee; scar near right ear.
Luce Taylor. 9 Aug. 1832. Born free and raised in AA Co. Age about 20; 5' 5 1/2"; brown complexion; face heavily scarred from burns; mouth is contracted.
Lucy Lucas. 23 August, 1832. DOM recorded by Ruth Davis 14 Sept. 1831. Age about 39; 5' 2 1/2"; dark complexion; scar on right arm; weal on elbow; raised in AA Co.
Elizabeth Dulany. 28 Aug., 1832. Born free and raised in AA Co. Age about 19; 5'; yellow complexion; small scars in right eyebrow & near left thumb.
Sarah Ann Dulany 28 Aug. 1832. Born free and raised in AA Co. Age about 17; 5' 2"; brown complexion; scar on left cheek.
John Green. 1 Sept. 1832. DOM recorded by Betty Green 13 April 1807. Age about 70; 4' 10" black complexion; scars on forehead and right wrist; raised in AA Co.
Jane Queen. 29 Sept. 1832. Born free and raised in AA Co. Age about 19; 5' 4"; yellow complexion; scar on forefinger of right hand.
Sarah Thomas. 24 Oct. 1832. DOM recorded by Nicholas Owens 29 Sept., 1824. Age about 40; 5' 2 1/4"; dark complexion; no marks or scars. Raised in AA Co.
Pomphrey Williams 29 Oct., 1832. DOM recorded by John Brice 26 Aug., 1831. Age about 36; 5' 6 1/2"; black complexion; small scars on right cheek, left temple.

Raised in AA Co.
Elizabeth Ann Smith 13 Nov., 1832. Born free and raised in AA Co. Age about 14; 5' 1/2"; light complexion; scar over left eye.
Nancy Philips. 14 Nov., 1832. Born free and raised in AA Co. Age about 13; 4' 8 1/2" light complexion; two small moles over left eye.
Henry H. Price. 28 Nov. 1832. Born free and raised in AA Co. Age about 15; 5' 7 1/2"; light complexion; small scar on forehead.
Samuel Gambrill. 17 Dec. 1832. DOM recorded by Andrew Sheen 23 June 1820. Age about 33; 5' 5"; dark complexion; small scar in right eyebrow. Raised in AA Co.
Julianna Queen. 22 Dec. 1832. Born free and raised in AA Co. Age about 23; 5' 4"; brown complexion; two small moles on left side of nose; small scar on left cheek.
John Allen. 5 Jan. 1833. Born free and raised in AA Co. Age about 42; 5' 5 1/2"; dark complexion; scars on breast and right side of cheek.
Stephen Blacke. 18 Jan. 1833. DOM recorded by Thomas T--- 8 January, 1831. Age about 45; 5' 9"; dark complexion; small scar on left wrist. Raised in AA Co.
Alfred Parkes (Parker ?) 5 Feb. 1833 Born free and raised in AA Co. Age about 21; 5' 4 1/2"; brown complexion; large scar from right to left eye.
Sarah Green. 16 Feb. 1833. Born free and raised in AA Co. Age about 18; 5'; black complexion; scar under left eye.
Dinah Brown. 26 Feb. 1833. Born free and raised in AA Co. Age about 30; 4' 11 1/2"; dark complexion; small scar on left eye.
Henry Ennis. 9 March 1833. Born free and raised in AA Co. Age about 27; 5' 5"; black complexion; no marks or scars.
Jack Thomas. 11 March 1833. DOM recorded by John Brice 2 Jan. 1817. Age about 30; 5' 5"; dark complexion; scar near left corner of mouth. Raised in AA Co.
Nelson Love. 13 March 1833. Born free and raised in AA Co. Age about 21; 5' 10"; dark complexion; scar on left cheek.
Milly Jenkins. 15 March 1833. DOM recorded by Elijah Moore 6 Dec. 1830. Age about 34; 5'; brown complexion; small lump on left wrist. raised in AA Co.
Betsy Dunkins. 27 March 1833. DOM recorded by Aaron Welch 7 June, 1821. Age about 23; 5' 3"; yellow complexion; scars on right forefingers and back of left

hand; raised in AA Co.
Rezin. 2 April 1833. DOM recorded by Charles Drury 3 Feb. 1797. Age about 22; 5' 8"; brown complexion; small scar under left eye. Raised in AA Co.
William Queen. 4 April 1833 Born free and raised in AA Co. Age about 21; 5' 7 1/2"; dark complexion; scar on back of left hand.
Phillis Scott. 15 April 1833. Born free and raised in AA Co. Age about 17; 5' 4 1/2"; brown complexion; three small scars on right arm.
Cate Jackson. 23 April 1833. DOM recorded by Charles G. Luthia--- 3 April 1813. Age about 48; 5'; dark complexion; no marks or scars. Raised in AA Co.
Sussanna Jackson 23 April 1833. DOM recorded by Charles G. Luthia--- 3 April 1813. Age about 21; 4' 11"; dark complexion; no marks or scars.
Mary Ann Jackson 23 April 1833. Born free and raised in AA Co. Age about 16; 4' 11"; dark complexion; no marks or scars.
David Neale. 23 April 1833. Born free and raised in AA Co. Age about 21; 5' 8"; black complexion; small scar over each eye.
Henry Shephard 15 May, 1833. DOM recorded by George Walls 14 May 1818. Age about 30; 5' 4"; yellow complexion; small mole near left corner of mouth, Raised in AA Co.
Francis Jones. 18 May 1833 DOM recorded by Aaron Jones 1 March 1830. Age about 20; 5' 8"; yellow complexion; small scar over corner of right eye. Raised in AA Co.
Rachel Harris. 17 June 1833 DOM recorded by Robert Wallace 4 April 1804. Age about 40; 5' 2 1/4"; black complexion; no marks or scars; raised in AA Co.
Polly Boston. 22 June 1833 DOM recorded by Lucy Harwood 17 March 1823. Age about 32; 5' 3"; black complexion; no marks or scars. Raised in AA Co.
Chloe Phillips. 24 June 1833. DOM recorded by Elizabeth Macubin 14 Jan. 1833. Age about 40; 5' 2 1/2"; light complexion; small scar on left cheek. Raised in AA Co.
Ezekiel Brown. 5 July, 1833. Born free and raised in AA Co. Age about 21; 6' 1/2"; dark complexion. Longitudinal scar on forehead.
William Hall. 27 July 1833. Born free and raised in AA Co. Age about 14; 4' 10"; brown complexion; scar on back of left hand.
Samuel Harrison 23 Aug. 1833. DOM recorded by Charles Slater, John South, and Henry Matthews 14 June 1833. Age about 39; 5' 10 1/2"; black complexion. Raised in AA Co.
Washington Bowies. 26 Aug. 1833. Born free and raised in AA Co. Age about 21; 5' 6"; brown complexion; small scar on forehead. Raised in AA Co.
Sophey Tydings. 17 Sept. 1833 DOM recorded by Ann Franklin 14 Sept. 1833. Age about 43; 4' 3 1/2"; bright complexion; no marks or scars. Raised in AA Co.
Mary Young. 19 Sept. 1833. Born free and raised in AA Co. Age about 18; 5' 10 1/2"; brown complexion; no marks or scars.
William Queen. 28 Sept. 1833. Born free and raised in AA Co. Age not given; 5' 1"; dark complexion; scars on forehead and upper lip.
Harriett Harrison. 10 Oct. 1833 DOM recorded by John Merriken 25 May 1816. Age about 30; 5' 1/2"; dark complexion; no marks or scars.
Nelly Spencer. 26 Oct. 1833 DOM recorded by Margaret --- 26 Oct. 1833. Age about 31; 5' 4 1/2"; dark complexion; scar on left arm. Raised in AA Co.
Jim Lynn. 28 Oct. 1833. DOM recorded by Amy Howard 24 May 1830. Age about 44; 5' 10"; dark complexion; no marks or scars. Raised in AA Co.
Jacob Williams. 4 Nov. 1833. DOM recorded by Thomas Cross 1 Nov. 1833. Age 47; 5' 5"; dark complexion; large scar across the forehead. Raised in AA Co.
Linny Williams. 4 Nov. 1833. DOM recorded by Thomas Cross 1 Nov. 1833. Age about 41; 5'; brown complexion; no marks or scars. Raised in AA Co.
William Williams. 4 Nov. 1833. DOM recorded by Thomas Cross 1 Nov. 1833. Age about 21; 5' 5 1/2"; dark complexion; scar on forehead. Raised in AA Co.
Elizabeth Williams. 4 Nov. 1833. DOM recorded by Thomas Cross 1 Nov. 1833. Age about 15; 5' 3 1/2"; dark complexion; no marks or scars. Raised in AA Co.
Harriet Williams. 4 Nov. 1833. DOM recorded by Thomas Cross 1 Nov. 1833. Age about 14; 5' 3 1/2"; scar above right eyebrow. Raised in AA Co.
Richard Williams. 4 Nov. 1833. DOM recorded by Thomas Cross 1 Nov. 1833. Age about 10; 4' 6"; dark complexion; no marks or scars. Raised in AA Co.
Ariana Williams. 4 Nov. 1833 DOM recorded by Thomas Cross 1 Nov. 1833.

Age about 9' 4' 10; dark complexion; no marks or scars; raised in AA Co.
John Williams. 4 Nov. 1833. DOM recorded by Thomas Cross 1 Nov. 1833. Age about 8; 4' 3"; black complexion; small scar on forehead. Raised in AA Co.
Joseph Williams. 4 Nov. 1833. DOM recorded by Thomas Cross 1 Nov. 1833. Age about 6; 3' 6"; black complexion; no marks or scars. Raised in AA Co.
Sally Williams. 4 Nov. 1833. DOM recorded by Thomas Cross 1 Nov. 1833. Age about 24; 5' 4"; yellow complexion; scar on both sides of face. Raised in AA Co.
Adeline Ward. 23 Nov. 1833. DOM recorded by Lucy Harwood 17 March 1823. Age about 30; 5' 1/2"; yellow complexion; mole in corner of right eye; another in left corner of mouth. Raised in AA Co.
Jacob Denniss. 4 Dec. 1833. DOM recorded by Sarah Norris 2 Aug. 1824. Age about 24; 5' 6"; yellow complexion; small moles on right cheek and arm. Raised in AA Co.
Harry. 3 Jan. 1834. DOM recorded by Aaron Welch 7 June 1820. Age about 25; 5' 7"; yellow complexion; speech impediment; small scar on upper lip. Raised in AA Co.
Richard Browne. 31 March 1834. Born free and raised in AA Co. Age about 21; 6' 2"; black complexion; small scar in corner of left eye.
Rebecca Davis. 31 March 1834. DOM recorded by Emanuel Dodds 14 July 1827. Age about 43; 5' 4 1/2"; brown complexion; mole over right eye. Raised in AA Co.
Nicholas Green. 3 April 1834 DOM recorded by Sarah Warfield 8 Dec. 1823. Age about 35; 5' 5"; dark complexion; scar on left arm. Raised in AA Co.
Susan Freeland. 17 April 1834. Born free and raised in AA Co. Age about 20; 5' 2 1/2"; yellow complexion; small scar on left arm.
Mary Matthews. 19 April 1834. Freedom recovered by petition against Elias P. Legg in AA Co. Court in the October term of 1833. Age about 25; 5' 5"; brown complexion; small scar on right cheek. Raised in AA Co.
Dinah Diggs. 23 May 1834. DOM recorded by Jerningham Drury 21 April 1803. Age about 45; 5' 5"; black complexion; small scar near left ear; small moles on left hand and wrist. Raised in AA Co.
Maria Johnson (daughter of Dinah) 23 April 1834. DOM recorded by Jerningham Drury 21 April 1803. Age about 26; 5' 1"; black complexion; scar near left wrist; mole on inside of left hand. Raised in AA Co.
Bill Toogood. 20 May 1834. DOM recorded by Benjamin L--- 2 Aug. 1810. Age about 26; 5' 4 1/2"; black complexion small scar near corner of left eye; another on corner of mouth; lost finger of left hand.
George W. Barry. 22 May 1834. DOM recorded by Hester & Elizabeth Hood 2 Dec. 1823. Age about 21; 5' 4"; black complexion; small scars on right cheek, left temple, & left leg. Raised in AA Co.
Tye Murdock. 22 May 1834. DOM recorded by Sussanah --- 10 Nov. 1813. Age about 25; 5' 2"; black complexion; small scar on nose: fingers of left hand are crooked; raised in AA Co.
James Cain. 23 May 1834. Born free and raised in AA Co. Age about 30; 5' 5"; brown complexion; small scar on right arm.
Henrietta Frost. 2 June 1834. Born free and raised in AA Co. Age about 17; 5'; yellow complexion; no marks or scars.
Henry Ennis. 23 July 1834. DOM recorded by Lewis Neth 13 July 1829. Age about 19; 5' 5 1/4"; yellow complexion; scar on right arm. Raised in AA Co.
Benjamin Brown. 2 Aug. 1834. DOM recorded by Joseph Cowman 16 Nov. 1805. Age about 33; 5' 9 1/2"; dark complexion; small scar on right cheek. Raised in AA Co.
Maria Burgess. 23 Aug. 1834. DOM recorded by Lucy Harwood 17 March, 1823. Age about 45; 4' 11"; black complexion; no marks or scars. Raised in AA Co.
Reuben. 25 Aug. 1834. DOM recorded by Amos Clark 21 April 1834. Age about 26; 5' 11 1/2"; black complexion; scar on left thumb. Raised in AA Co.
John Forty. 6 Sept. 1834. DOM recorded by Jacob Forty 23 Jan. 1798. Age about 50; 5' 5"; black complexion; no marks or scars. Raised in AA Co.
Susan Butler. 20 Sept. 1834. DOM recorded by Henry Magruder 14 June, 1826. Age about 33; 4' 10"; brown complexion: small scar under left ear. raised in AA Co.
Matilda Matthews. 30 Sept. 1834. Freedom recovered by judgment in AA Co. Court against Elias R. Legg and Richard Williams October, 1832. Age about 23; 5' 3"; brown complexion; small mole on forefinger of right hand. Raised in AA Co.

Davey Dorsey. 13 Dec. 1834. DOM recorded by Eleanor Shipley 14 March, 1820. Age about 37; 5' 4 1/2"; black complexion; scar under left eye; middle finger of right hand is crooked. Raised in AA Co.

Stephen Dorsey. 13 Dec. 1834. DOM recorded by Eleanor Shipley 14 March 1820. Age about 32; 5' 4 1/2"; black complexion; scars in right eyebrow, and forehead. Raised in AA Co.

Emanuel Parker. 2_ Dec. 1834. Born free and raised in AA Co. Age about 19; 5' 6"; yellow complexion; no marks or scars.

Robert Th—. 28 Jan. 1835. DOM recorded by Michael Dorsey et. al. 31 Oct. 1817. Age about 40; 5' 7"; light complexion; scar on left cheek. Raised in AA Co.

Charles Dorsey. 3 Feb. 1835. Born free and raised in AA Co. Age about 24; 5'6"; brown complexion; large scar of back of left hand.

Sarah Jacobs. 5 March 1835. Born free and raised in AA Co. Age about 17; 4'; black complexion; scar on forehead above right eye; scar on right cheek.

Harriet Jacobs. 5 March 1835. Born free and raised in AA Co. Age about 17; 5' black complexion; scar on forehead over right eye; scar on right cheek.

Catherine Hammond. 4 June 1835. DOM recorded by Philip H. Wootts 13 Sept. 1808. Age about 25; 4' 10"; black complexion; scar on left shoulder. Raised in AA Co.

James Brown. 22 June 1835. DOM recorded by William Brewer 21 June 1820. Age about 30; 5' 4 1/4"; brown complexion; small mole on upper part of chin. Raised in AA Co.

Amos Garrett. 16 July 1835. Born free and raised in AA Co. Age about 23; 5' 7"; dark complexion; small scars over right eye & on right leg.

Hiriam Richards. 9 Sept. 1835. DOM recorded by Benjamin Thomas 18 May 1822. Age about 34; 5' 9"; dark complexion; scars on left arm & wrist. Raised in AA Co.

Susan Green. 26 Oct. 1835. Born free and raised in AA Co. Age about 17; 5' 2"; bright complexion; no marks or scars.

Judy Price. 28 Oct. 1835. DOM recorded by Stephen Beard 26 Jan. 1820. Age about 30; 5'; black complexion; no marks or scars. Raised in AA Co.

Matilda Boardley. 5 Nov. 1835. Born free and raised in AA Co. Age about 17; 5' 4 1/2"; brown complexion; two scars on left side of neck.

Washington Gray. 6 Nov. 1835. Born free and raised in AA Co. Age about 22; 5' 4 1/4"; dark complexion; small scar on back of right hand.

Sacou Green. 21 Nov. 1835. DOM recorded by George Whi--- 22 March 1807. Age about 30; 5' 7"; light complexion; small scars on left hand; raised in AA Co.

Harriett Garrett. 18 Dec. 1835. Born free and raised in AA Co. Age about 20; 5' 1"; brown complexion; no marks or scars.

Margaret Queen. 13 Jan. 1836. Born free and raised in AA Co. Age about 18; 4' 11"; brown complexion; scar on left side of face.

Henry Offer. 13 Jan. 1836. Born free and raised in AA Co. Age about 22; 5' 9 1/2"; brown complexion; two scars on back of left hand.

Henny Boardley. 14 Jan. 1836. Born free and raised in AA Co. Age about 22; 5' 9 1/2"; black complexion. Small scar over left eye.

Ann Ringgold. 14 Jan. 1836. DOM recorded by Thomas James 17 Sept. 1827. Age about 37; 5'; brown complexion; scars on right arm and hand. Raised in AA Co.

Owen Green. 23 Jan. 1836. DOM recorded by George Whi. 22 March 1807. Age about 28; 5' 7"; light complexion; large scar on right thigh. Raised in AA Co.

Flora. 15 March 1836. DOM recorded by Lydia Greenwell 15 Aug. 1835. Age about 37; 5' 3 1/2"; yellow complexion. Raised in AA Co.

James Queen. 26 March 1836. Born free and raised in AA Co. Age about 25; 5' 3 1/2"; brown complexion; small scar over right eye.

William Bowser. 29 March 1836. Born free and raised in AA Co. Age about 21; 5' 1 1/2"; black complexion. Several scars on left knee.

William Henry Smith. 26 April 1836. DOM recorded by Susannah Wyorill 20 Nov. 1813. Age about 25; 5' 6 1/4"; brown complexion; small scars corner of left eye, forehead, and back of left hand. Raised in AA Co.

Harriett Green. 29 April 1836. Born free and raised in AA Co. Age about 17; 5' 2"; dark complexion; small scars on left cheek and hand.

William Collins. 18 May 1836. Born free and raised in AA Co. Age about 22; 5' 1"; light complexion; small scar on nose between the eyes.

Mary Hanson. 18 May 1836. Born free and

raised in AA Co. Age about 19; 5' 2 3/4"; light complexion. No marks or scars.
William Hanson. 18 May 1836. Born free and raised in AA Co. Age about 17; 5' 7 3/4'; dark complexion; mole on left arm.
Mary Ann Brice. 21 May 1836. Born free and raised in AA Co. Age about 17; 5' 1"; black complexion; no marks or scars.
Bob Osborn. 23 May 1836. DOM recorded by John Merriken 21, 1817. Age about 35; 5' 5 1/2"; dark complexion; scar on nose and under left eye.
Susan —. 23 May 1836. DOM recorded by Charles Pettibone 15 Jan. 1815. Age about 30; 4' 11 1/2"; brown complexion; small scar on back of left hand. Raised in AA Co.
Richard Gantt. 24 May 1836. Born free and raised in AA Co. Age about 22: 5' 4 1/2"; black complexion; no marks or scars.
Ann Brooks. 26 May 1836. DOM recorded by Nelson--- 5 Jan. 1814. Age about 38; 5' 1 1/2"; yellow complexion; no marks or scars. Raised in AA Co.
Rosetta Hindsman. 3 June 1836. Born free and raised in AA Co. Age about 18; 4' 11"; dark complexion; small scar near corner of left eye.
William Jackson. 6 June 1836. Born free and raised in AA Co. Age about 21; 5' 3 1/2"; dark complexion; small scars on forehead and back of left hand.
Jacob Johnson. 2 July 1836. DOM recorded by Elijah. --- 25, 1825. Age about 40, 5' 6"; black complexion. Raised in AA Co.
Elizabeth Harris. 8 July 1836. Born free and raised in AA Co. Age about 16; 4' 10 1/4"; light complexion, Small moles on nose and left eyebrow.
James Matthews. 11 July 1836. Born free and raised in AA Co. Age about 21; 5' 3 1/2"; black complexion; large scar on right side of neck.
Thomas Mitchell. 16 July 1836. Born free and raised in AA Co. Age about 40; 5' 3"; brown complexion; small scar on forehead over right eye.
Benjamin J. Culdess. 22 July 1836. Born free and raised in AA Co. Age about 24; 5' 3 1/2"; very bright complexion; no marks or scars.
Sarah Queen. 23 July 1836. Born free and raised in AA Co. Age about 18; 5' 1"; dark complexion; no marks or scars.
Ann Queen. 2 Aug. 1836. Born free and raised in AA Co. Age about 17; 4' 11"; dark complexion; small scar over right eye.
Maria Garrett. 3 Aug. 1836. DOM recorded by Elizabeth Robinson 13 June 1829. Age about 30; 5' 10 1/2"; small scar on left arm near the wrist. Raised in AA Co.
Eliza Queen. 6 Aug. 1836. Born free and raised in AA Co. Age. about 30; 5' 2 1/2"; brown complexion; small scar on forehead over left eye.
Susan Ray. 13 Sept. 1836. Born free and raised in AA Co. Age about 26; 5' 2"; dark complexion; scar on inside of right arm.
Henrietta Barnette. 4 Oct. 1836. Born free and raised in AA Co. Age about 18; 5' 3"; brown complexion; no marks or scars.
Mary Ann Barnette. 4 Oct. 1836. Born free and raised in AA Co. Age about 21; 5' 3"; dark complexion; no marks or scars.
Issac Parker. 17 Oct. 1836. Born free and raised in AA Co. Age about 22; 5' 5 1/2"; brown complexion; long scar on right arm.
Violetta Boston. 26 Oct. 1836. Declared free by Act of the General Assembly of Maryland in Dec. Session 1835, Chapter 266. Age about 23; 5' 5 1/2"; dark complexion; no marks or scars.
Kitty Ross. 28 Oct. 1836. DOM recorded by Stephen Bean 26 Jan. 1820. Age about 30; 5' 1 1/2"; brown complexion; no marks or scars. Raised in AA Co..
Elizabeth Ward. 1 Nov. 1836. Born free and raised in AA Co. Age about 20; 5' 9"; brown complexion.
Henry Brown. 11 Nov. 1836. DOM recorded by William Brown 24 March 1813. Age about 24; 5' 11"; dark complexion; scar on left wrist. Raised in AA Co.
Samuel Scroggins. 21 Nov. 1836. DOM recorded by Jeremiah Jones 9 June 1836. Age about 55; 5' 8"; black complexion; small scar on left eyebrow. Raised in AA Co.
Levi Pack. 22 Nov. 1836. DOM recorded by Jacob Williams 22 April 1820. Age about 36; 5' 3 1/2"; black complexion; small scar near corner of right eye. Raised in AA Co.
Nicholas. 29 Nov. 1836. DOM recorded by 22 Sept. 1831. Age about 33. The balance of this entry is illegible.
Sophia Ward. 21 Dec. 1836. Born free and raised in AA Co. Age about 17; 5' 10"; bright complexion; no. marks or scars.
Susan Boston. 6 Jan. 1837. Declared free by act of the Maryland General Assembly in the December Session of 1835. Chapter 266. Age about 19; 5' 6"; dark complexion; no marks or scars; raised in AA Co.
Mary Boston. 6 Jan. 1837. Declared free by act of the Maryland General Assembly in the Dec. Session of 1835, Chapter 266. Age about 21; 5' 1"; dark complexion; scar

on right arm and mole on right corner of mouth. Raised in AA Co.

Jane Boston. Declared free by act of the Maryland General. Assembly in the Dec. Session of 1835, Chapter 266. Age about 16; 5' 4 1/2"; dark complexion; scar on right side of chin. Raised in AA Co.

William Lomax. 17 Jan. 1837. DOM recorded by John Childs 3 Aug. 1836. Age about 42; 5' 10 1/2"; bright complexion; small mole under left eye; scar on inside of lower lip. Raised in AA Co.

Joseph Carrot. 15 Feb. 1837. Born free and raised in AA Co. Age about 20; 5' 2"; light complexion; scars on left cheek and corner of left eye.

James Henry. 20 Feb. 1837. DOM recorded by Henry Matthews 26 June 1827. Age about 25; 5' 5 1/2"; light complexion. No scars or marks. Raised in AA Co.

Richard Joyce. 7 March 1837. Born free and raised in AA Co. Age about 22; 5' 8"; dark complexion; small scars in left eyebrow, nose, and left thumb.

Hillary Wilson. 21 March 1837. DOM recorded by Charlotte Hutton 20 Jan. 1830. Age about 34; 5' 7 3/4"; dark complexion; small scars on left side of nose and left wrist. Raised in AA Co.

Charity Parker. 21 March 1837. DOM recorded by Hestor Cromwell 15 July 1819. Age not given. 5' 1 1/2"; yellow complexion; small scar on left eyebrow; has long hair. Raised in Anne Arundel. County.

Rosetta Brown. 24 March 1837. DOM recorded by Hester and Elizabeth Hood 2 Dec. 1822. Age about 20; 5' 4 1/2"; black complexion; scar on each shoulder; another on chin. Raised in AA Co.

Ann Snowden. 10 April 1837. DOM recorded by Henry Hammond 23 Feb. 1811. Age about 37; 5' 2"; yellow complexion; scar on right arm; small mole in left ear. Raised in AA Co.

Maria Williams. 17 April 1837. Born free and raised in AA Co. Age about 24; 5' 4 1/2"; dark complexion; scars under corner of right eye and back of right hand.

Samuel Hopkins. 17 April 1837. DOM recorded by Mary Israel 9 Sept. 1837. Age about 27; 5' 10 1/4; black complexion; scar on back of head. Raised in AA Co.

William Hall. 20 April 1837. DOM recorded by Thomas Hall 27 Nov. 1816. Age about 23; 5' 6 1/2"; black complexion; scars in right eyebrow and above the right eye. Raised in AA Co.

Richard Hall. 20 April 1837. DOM recorded by Thomas Hall 27 Nov. 1816. Age about 21; 5' 5 3/4"; dark complexion; large scar on breast. Raised in AA Co.

Edward Hall. 26 April 1837. Born free and raised in AA Co. Age about 20; 5' 7 1/4"; dark complexion; black mark on forefinger of right hand.

Eliza Severness. 15 May 1837. DOM recorded by Isacc Severness 10 Nov. 1813. Age about 30; 5' 2 1/2"; black complexion; no marks or scars. Raised in AA Co.

Romina Booth. 15 May 1837. Born free and raised in AA Co. Age about 18; 5' 2 1/2'; brown complexion; small mole on left side of nose.

Eliza Lucas. 15 May 1837. DOM recorded by Thomas --- 10 Oct. 1829. Age about 33; 5' 1 3/4"; light complexion; scars on corner of right eyebrow and nose. Raised in AA Co.

Susan Pack (Park ?). 6 June 1837. DOM recorded by Jacob Williams 22 April 1820. Age about 40; 5' 4 1/2" black complexion; small scar on left side of forehead. Raised in AA Co.

Polly Burgess. 20 June 1837. DOM recorded by Phillip Clayton 18 Feb. 1831. Age about 43; 5' 2 1/2"; dark complexion; scar on right arm. Raised in AA Co.

Doll Scott. 28 June 1837. DOM recorded by Lydia Gambrill 28 June 1837. Age about 38; 5' 3"; yellow complexion; lost two front teeth, raised in AA Co.

John Smith. 8 July 1837. Freedom obtained by judgment in the AA Co. Court in the Oct. term 1835 against Joliet. Burke. Age about 23; 5' 3 1/2"; brown complexion; raised in AA Co.

Nancy E— 10 July 1837. Freedom obtained by judgment in the AA Co. Court in the Oct. term 1835 against Thomas Allen. Age about 37. (Balance. of this document is unreadable.)

Jim Sharp. 5 Aug. 1837. Freedom obtained by judgment in the AA Co. Court in the Oct. term 1835 against Thomas Allen. Age about 41; 5' ! 1/2"; dark complexion; small scar in right eyebrow; raised in AA Co.

Mary Ann Queen. 26 Aug. 1837. Born free and raised in AA Co. Age about 17; 5' 1 1/2"; brown complexion; scar in corner of left eyebrow.

Jack Adams. 26 Aug. 1837. DOM recorded by Butch Shephard 27 July 1816. Age about 27; 5' 7 1/2" black complexion; scar over right eye. Raised in AA Co.

Eliza Scott. 1 Sept. 1837. Born free and raised in AA Co. Age about 20; 5' 5"; yellow complexion; scar on right wrist.

Julia Ann Brown. 9 Sept. 1837. DOM recorded by Joseph --- 4 March 1804. Age about 23; 5' 1 1/2"; bright complexion; no marks or scars; raised in AA Co.
Pheles Green. 15 Sept. 1837. DOM recorded by Benjamin Sewell 3 Aug. 1810. Age about 45; 5' 2"; brown complexion; scar under right eye; raised in AA Co.
Daniel Boston. 29 Sept. 1837. DOM recorded by William Pritchard 29 Sept. 1822. Age about 26; 5' 9"; dark complexion; no marks or scars; raised in AA Co.
Robert Queene. 9 Oct. 1837. Born free and raised in AA Co. Age about 21; 5' 4 1/2"; brown complexion; scar in left eyebrow.
James Price. 11 Oct. 1837. Born free and raised in AA Co. Age about 34; 5' 9"; yellow complexion; small scars near corner of right eye and on left thumb.
Lloyd Gough. 23 Oct. 1837. DOM recorded by William Bateman 13 June 1810. Age about 31; 5' 8"; dark complexion; no marks or scars; raised in AA Co.
Issac Vanhorn. 24 Oct. 1837. DOM recorded by Beowulf Hobbs 11 April 1811. Age about 30; 5' 4"; black complexion; missing part of left hand; raised in AA Co.
Edward Dowell. 24 Oct. 1837. DOM recorded by Thomas Price 19 Aug. 1831. Age about 34; 5' 7"; brown complexion; small scars on forehead and forefinger of left hand; raised in AA Co.
Jenny Johnson. 24 Oct. 1837. DOM recorded by Benjamin Willsby 4 May 1820. Age about 28; 4' 11 1/2"; dark complexion; no marks or scars; raised in AA Co.
Samuel Howard. 3 Nov. 1837. Born free and raised in AA Co. Age about 22; 5' 7"; brown complexion; large scar on right leg.
Nancy Queen. 3 Nov. 1837. Born free and raised in AA Co. Age about 50; 5' 1 1/2"; dark complexion; scar on left wrist.
Peter Waters. 7 Nov. 1837. DOM recorded by Amos Black 1 April 1834. Age about 24; 5' 5 1/4"; brown complexion; scar on left thumb; raised in AA Co.
Nan Butler. 23 Nov. 1837. DOM recorded by Margaret Hopkins 20 Aug. 1813. Age about 52; 5' 2"; brown complexion; scar under right eye; raised in AA Co.
Rachel Ridgely. 23 Nov. 1837. DOM recorded by Margaret Hopkins 20 Aug. 1813. Age about 44; 4' 8 1/2"; brown complexion; scar on breast; raised in AA Co.
Kitt Dorsey. 23 Nov. 1837. DOM recorded by Margaret Hopkins 20 Aug. 1813. Age about 36; 5' 1/2"; brown complexion; scar on forefinger of right hand; raised in AA Co.

Nan Gross. 19 Dec. 1837. DOM recorded by Charles Waters 9 June 1812. Age about 40; 5' 2"; dark complexion; scars under left eye and of back of right hand; raised in AA Co.
David Cross. 30 Dec. 1837. Freedom obtained by judgment on the Oct. 1837 term of the AA Co. Circuit Court against William Black. Age about 45; 5' 3"; very light complexion; scar in left corner of mouth; raised in AA Co.
James Randle. 6 Jan. 1838. Born free and raised in AA Co. Age about 23; 5' 6"; yellow complexion; scar on right side of chin.
William Powell. 9 Jan. 1838. Born free and raised in AA Co. Age about 34; 5' 4"; dark complexion; small scars corner of left eye and mouth.
William Barnett. 13 Jan. 1838. Born free and raised in AA Co. Age about 22; 5' 6"; dark complexion; small scar on nose.
Walter Boothe. 16 Jan. 1838. Born free and raised in AA Co. Age about 25; 5' 11 1/2"; brown complexion; two small scars on forehead.
Elijah Rousale. 16 Jan. 1838. DOM recorded by Samuel Givens 20 June 1818. Age about 25; 5' 7"; brown complexion; scar on left wrist; raised in AA Co.
Mary Green. 16 Jan. 1838. DOM recorded by Thomas Cross 25 March 1835. Age about 33; 4' 11"; brown complexion; scar on inside of left wrist and third finger of left hand; raised in AA Co.
Joseph Smith. 28 March 1838. Freedom obtained by judgment against John M. Peacock in the Oct. term of AA Co. Court 1832. Age about 21; 5' 5"; black complexion; scar on right ankle; raised in AA Co.
Richard Joyce. 29 March 1838. Born free and raised in AA Co. Age about 23; 5' 8"; dark complexion; small scar in right eyebrow.
Henry Johnson. 1 April 1838. DOM recorded by Henry Basford 19 Feb. 182_. Age about 36; 5' 4"; dark complexion; no marks or scars; raised in AA Co.
John H—. 16 April 1838. Born free and raised in AA Co. Age about 21; 5' 6 1/2"; black complexion; small scar in left eyebrow.
Elizabeth Simms. 14 May 1838. Born free and raised in AA Co. Age about 21; 5' 4 1/2"; yellow complexion; small scar in corner of left eyebrow.
George W. Lomres. 14 May 1838. Born free and raised in AA Co. Age about 24; 5' 9 1/2"; dark complexion; scar on right

arm.

Mary Ann Jacobs. 31 May 1838. DOM recorded by Joseph Evans 7 March 1804. Age about 22; 5'; yellow complexion; long black hair; no marks or scars; raised in AA Co.

Elizabeth Queen. 4 June 1838. Born free and raised in AA Co. Age about 19; 5' 1"; yellow complexion; two moles on right cheek.

Eliza Ann Queen. 4 June 1838. Born free and raised in AA Co. Age about 16; 4' 3"; dark complexion; small mole on upper lip.

William (son of Lu. say). 14 July 1838. DOM recorded by Elizabeth and Hester Hood 2 Dec. 1822. Age about 21; 5' 1"; yellow complexion; scar on right arm.

Peter (son of Cupy). 14 July 1838. DOM recorded by Elizabeth and Hester Hood 2 Dec. 1822. Age about 21; 5' 7 1/2"; black complexion; small scar on right eyebrow; raised in AA Co.

Eliza Dennis. 21 July 1838. DOM recorded by Sarah Norris 2 Aug. 1824. Age about 24; 5' 3 3/4"; yellow complexion; no marks or scars; raised in AA Co.

Charlotte Dennis. 21 July 1838. DOM recorded by Sarah Norris 2 Aug. 1824. Age about 19; 4' 3 3/4"; yellow complexion; scar on right wrist; raised in AA Co.

Leonard Dennis. 21 July 1838. DOM recorded by Sarah Norris 2 Aug. 1824. Age about 21; 5' 7"; dark complexion; scars on right thumb and back of left hand; raised in AA Co.

Henry Jennings. 21 July 1838. DOM recorded by John Sellman 5 Jan. 1832. Age about 29; 5' 9"; yellow complexion; large scar on breast; raised in AA Co.

Elizabeth Smith. 21 July 1838. Born free and raised in AA Co. Age about 22; 5' 1 3/4"; brown complexion; scar on right side of face.

—Williams. 31 July 1838. Born free and raised in AA Co. Age about 22; 5' 4 1/2"; black complexion; small scar on forehead.

Harry General. 1 Aug. 1838. DOM recorded by Joseph Evans 2 Aug. 1817. Age about 35; 5' 8 1/4"; dark complexion; small scar on back of left hand; raised in AA Co.

Agnes Queen. 4 Aug. 1838. Born free and raised in AA Co. Age about 19; 5' 1/2"; brown complexion; no marks or scars.

Robert Stevens. 7 Aug. 1838. Born free and raised in AA Co. Age about 24; 5' 6"; black complexion; large scar top of left foot; small scar on back of right hand.

Edward Parker. 3 Sept. 1838. Born free and raised in AA Co. Age about 35; 5' 3/4"; light complexion; scar on small finger of left hand.

Elisha Parker. 14 Sept. 1838. Born free and raise in AA Co. Age about 22; 5' 8 1/2"; brown complexion; no marks or scars.

Andrew Parker. 14 Sept. 1838. Born free and raised in AA Co. Age about 23; 5' 4 1/2"; yellow complexion; scar on back of left hand.

Sussanna Parker. 14 Sept. 1838. Born free and raised in AA Co. Age about 19; 5'; yellow complexion; two small scars on back of right hand.

Kate Barret. 22 Sept. 1838. DOM recorded by Lydia Gambrill 7 July 1837. Age about 37; 5' 3 1/2"; yellow complexion; small scar on back of right hand; raised in AA Co.

Louisa Wills. 23 Oct. 1838. DOM recorded by Joseph Hopkins 25 May 1832. Age about 21; 5'; brown complexion; small scar on right arm; raised in AA Co.

Charles Hopkins. 23 Oct. 1838. DOM recorded by Mary Israel 9 Sept. 1816. Age about 26; 5' 9 1/2"; black complexion; deformed fingers on left hand; raised in AA Co.

Nero Dorsey. 23 Oct. 1838. DOM recorded by Samuel Bradford 20 Dec. 1827. Age about 46; 5' 7"; dark complexion; small scar under left eye; raised in AA Co.

John Boston. 12 Nov. 1838. Born free and raised in AA Co. Age about 23; 5' 7"; black complexion; small scar over left eye.

Becky Boston. 13 Nov. 1838. Born free and raised in AA Co. Age about 17; 5' 2"; brown complexion; small scar on left cheek.

Nelly Boston. 13 Nov. 1838. Born free and raised in AA Co. Age about 14; 5' 4"; yellow complexion; small scar on forehead.

Sarah— 20 Nov. 1838. Born free and raised in AA Co. Age about 18; 4' 10 1/2"; brown complexion; no marks or scars.

John Boston. 1 Jan. 1838. Born free and raised in AA Co. Age about 20 5' 2"; yellow complexion.; no marks or scars.

Richard Davis. 2 Jan. 1839. Born free and raised in AA Co. Age about 21; 5' 7"; yellow complexion; scar on nose.

Dinah Scott. 2 Jan. 1839. DOM recorded by Joseph C. 20 Feb. 1807. Age about 23; 5' 3"; yellow complexion; no marks or scars; raised in AA Co.

Hilliary Hawkins. 21 Jan. 1839. DOM recorded by Jerningham Drury 9 Nov. 1805. Age about 25; 5' 7"; brown complexion; has marks on forehead; raised in AA Co.

Ann Maria Pratt. 27 Feb. 1839. Born free and raised in AA Co. Age about 16; 5' 3 3/4"; brown complexion; scar on left side of neck; mole on chin.
John Henry Price. 8 April 1839. Born free and raised in AA Co. Age about 22; 5' 7 1/2"; black complexion; scar on forefinger of left hand and back of right hand.
Henry Rawlings. 16 April 1839. DOM recorded by Dennis H. Battie 1 April 1824. Age about 26; 5' 4 1/2"; black complexion; scar on the left jawbone; raised in AA Co.
John M. Price. 4 May 1839. Born free and raised in AA Co. Age about 20; 5' 6 1/2; light complexion; no marks or scars.
William Brown. 4 May 1839. DOM recorded by Sarah --- 8 May 1830. Age about 44; 5' 5 3/4"; black complexion; raised in AA Co.
George Martin. May 13, 1839. DOM recorded by --- 28 April 1803. Age about 43; 5' 9"; black complexion; no marks or scars; raised in AA Co.
Margaret Griffin. 17 May 1839. Born free and raised in AA Co. Age about 25; 5' 3"; brown complexion; no marks or scars.
Sarah Carroll. 22 May 1839. Born free and raised in AA Co. Age about 19; 5' 3 1/4'; dark complexion; no marks or scars.
George Addison. 25 May 1839. Born free and raised in AA Co. Age about 23; 5' 4 1/2"; dark complexion; scar over left eye.
Sarah Lane. 25 June 1839. DOM recorded by Emory Sandler 25 June 1839. Age about 29; 5' 1"; black complexion; small scar on right arm; raised in AA Co.
John Johnson. 25 June 1839. Born free and raised in AA Co. Age about 35; 5' 9"; black complexion; scars over and around left eye.
John Brashears. 25 June 1839. Born free and raised in AA Co. Age about 20; 5' 5 1/2"; dark complexion; no marks or scars.
Mary Stewart. 16 July 1839. Born free and raised in AA Co. Age about twenty; 5' 1"; black complexion; scars on left side of mouth and near left eye.
Jane Brashears. 18 July 1839. Born free and raised in AA Co. Age about 15; 5' 2"; light complexion; no marks or scars.
Henrietta Brogden. 23 July 1839. Born free and raised in AA Co. Age about 19; 4' 9"; dark complexion; scar on left arm.
Priscilla Jones. 29 July 1839. Born free and raised in AA Co. Age about 17; 5'; brown complexion; two small scars on right arm.
Nancy Thomas. 6 Aug. 1839. Born free and raised in AA Co. Age about 21; 5' 4"; brown complexion; scar on back of neck.

Susan Thomas. 7 Sept. 1839. Born free and raised in AA Co. Age about 17; 5' 1"; yellow complexion; scars on left arm and wrist.
Salisah Mausfield. 10 Sept. 1839. Born free and raised in AA Co. Age about 22; 5' 3"; light complexion; scar over right eye.
Mary Ann Gaither. 10 Sept. 1839. Born free and raised in AA Co. Age about 20; 5' 4"; yellow complexion; long dark hair; small mole on left side of neck.
Washington Gaither. 10 Sept. 1839. Born free and raised in AA Co. Age about 23; 5' 8"; yellow complexion; small scar over left eye.
John C. Gaither. 10 Sept. 1839. Born free and raised in AA Co. Age about 22; 5' 3"; brown complexion; no marks or scars.
Charlotte Hall. 11 Sept. 1839. Born free and raised in AA Co. Age about 18; 5' 1"; brown complexion; small scar on left wrist.
William Allen. 28 Sept. 1839. Born free and raised in AA Co. Age about 25; 5' 5"; brown complexion; scar on left nostril.
Mary Burgess. 1 Oct. 1839. Born free and raised in AA Co. Age about 24; 5' 3"; dark complexion; scars on right arm.
Ally Offer. 29 Oct. 1839. Born free and raised in AA Co. Age about 17; 5' 3 1/4"; yellow complexion; no marks or scars.
Anthony Boston. 29 Oct. 1839. Declared free by act of the Maryland General Assembly in the Dec. 1835 Session, Chapter 236. Age about 27; 5' 9 1/2"; scars on right wrist and nose; raised in AA Co.
Samuel Boston. 1 Nov. 1839. Born free and raised in AA Co. Age about 24; 5; 5 1/2;; brown complexion; small scar over right eye.
William Green. 12 Nov. 1839. Born free and raised in AA Co. Age about 21; 5' 7 1/2"; black complexion; small scars on back of right hand and wrist.
Thomas Tyler. 21 Nov. 1839. Born free and raised in AA Co. Age about 21; 5' 3'; brown complexion; scar on left wrist.
James Spencer. 26 Nov. 1839. Born free and raised in AA Co. Age about 22; 5' 4"; black complexion; scars over left eye and on left cheek.
Henry Ursolton. 30 Nov. 1839. Born free and raised in AA Co. Age about 22; 5" 6 1/2"; dark complexion; small scar on back of right thumb.
William Creek. 30 Nov. 1839. Born free and raised in AA Co. Age about 21; 5' 4"; dark complexion; no marks or scars.
Issac Johnson. 2 Dec. 1839. Born free and

raised in AA Co. Age about 22; 5' --"; dark complexion; no marks or scars.
Sarah Price. 10 Dec. 1839. Born free and raised in AA Co. Age about 17; 5' 11 1/2"; light complexion; scar near corner of left eye.
James Jordon. 16 Dec. 1839. DOM recorded by Thomas Cross 21 March 1835. Age about 28; 5' 7"; black complexion; small scar on left cheek; raised in AA Co.
James Boothe. 18 Dec. 1839. DOM recorded by William Weems 17 Jan. 1814. Age about 38; 5' 11"; dark complexion; no marks or scars; raised in AA Co.
Thomas Boothe. 18 Dec. 1839. DOM recorded by William Weems 17 Jan. 1814. Age about 30; 5' 8"; dark complexion; small scar near corner of right eye; raised in AA Co.
Lewis Boothe. 18 Dec. 1839. Born free and raised in AA Co. Age about 21; 5' 8 1/2"; dark complexion; small scar on back of left hand.
Harriet Ann Ennis. 20 Dec. 1839. DOM recorded by Samuel Muth 10 July 1827. Age about 17; 5' 1"; light complexion; small mole on right cheek; raised in AA Co.
William S. Smith. 29 Jan. 1840. Born free and raised in AA Co. Age about 20; 5' 7 3/4"; yellow complexion; no marks or scars.
John Matthews. 13 Feb. 1840. DOM recorded by Henry Matthews 26 June 1829. Age about 26' 5' 8"; bright complexion; small scar on forefinger of right hand; raised in AA Co.
Greenbury Johnson. 3 March 1840. Born free and raised in AA Co. Age about 21; 5' 6"; dark complexion; small scar on right jaw.
Catherine Johnson. 3 March 1840. Born free and raised in AA Co. Age about 18; 5"; dark complexion; no marks or scars.
Eliza —. 4 April 1840. DOM recorded by Priscilla Buchanan 1 Dec. 1825. Age about 76; 5' 1"; dark complexion; scar on left side of jaw; raised in AA Co.
Eliza Boston. 18 April 1840. DOM recorded by William Pritchard 29 Sept. 1822. Age about 28; 5' 4"; dark complexion; no marks or scars; raised in AA Co.
David Boston. 20 April 1840. Declared free by act of the Maryland General Assembly Dec. 1825, Chapter 266. Age about 21; 5' 8 1/2"; black complexion; raised in AA Co.
Nelly Johnson. 20 April 1840. DOM recorded by Samuel Jones 11 Jan. 1819. Age about 36; 5'; yellow complexion; scar near corner of right eye; raised in AA Co.
Harriet Sparrow. 21 April 1840. DOM recorded by John Mercer 21 April 1840. Age about 33; 5' --"; dark complexion; no marks or scars; raised in AA Co.
Charlotte Dorsey. 28 April 1840. DOM recorded by John Chew Thomas 3 Feb. 1810; to be free at the age of 25. Age 27; 5' 1 3/4"; dark complexion; small scar near corner of right eye; raised in AA Co.
Harry Dorsey. 28 April 1840. DOM recorded by John Mercer 21 April 1840. Age about 21; 5' 10"; dark complexion; large scar on breasts; raised in AA Co.
Peter Dorsey. 28 April 1840. Born free and raised in AA Co. Age about 18; 5' 11 1/2"; black complexion; small scar near left eye.
Eliza Ann Bo—. 29 April 1840. DOM recorded by George Howard 7 Aug. 1821. Age about 21; 5' 1 3/4" dark complexion; no marks or scars; raised in AA Co.
Margaret Phillips. 29 April 1840. Born free and raised in AA Co. Age about 31; 5' 1 1/2"; dark complexion; scar on forehead.
— Matthews. 10 May 1840. DOM recorded by John Rideout 23 April 1840. Age about 27; 5' 4 1/2"; dark complexion; no marks or scars; raised in AA Co.
Dick Gibson. 16 May 1840. DOM recorded by William Brown 9 May 1820. Age about 21; 5'; brown complexion; no marks or scars; raised in AA Co.
Eliza Gibson. 26 May 1840. DOM recorded by G--- H. L--- 2 Sept. 1826. Age about 28; 5' 5 1/2"; yellow complexion; scars over left lip and on right arm: raised in AA Co.
Polly Matthews. 2 June 1840. DOM recorded by John Rideout 3 April 1840. Age about 50; 4' 11 1/2"; brown complexion; small scar on left thumb; raised in AA Co.
William Matthews. 2 June 1840. DOM recorded by John Rideout 3 April 1840. Age about 28; 5' 6 3/4" brown complexion; scars on forehead and upper lip; raised in AA Co.
Richard Pinkney. 6 June 1840. DOM recorded by H--- 15 July 18 ---. Age about 39; 5' 8"; brown complexion; raised in AA Co.
Jacob Prout. 11 July 1840. DOM recorded by Eliza Hood ---, 1823. Age about 22; 5' 4"; brown complexion; scar on ... of right ... . Raised in AA Co.
Sarah Lyle. 13 July 1840. DOM recorded by Job --- 8 Jan. 1840. Age about 40; 5' 4"; dark complexion; scar on left temple; raised in AA Co.
Benjamin Queen. 23 July 1840. DOM re-

corded by David Weems 22 April 1809. Age about 27; 5' 6"; black complexion; scars on left arm and leg; raised in AA Co.
Charles Luthers. 24 July 1840. Born free and raised in AA Co. Age about 21; 5' 6 1/2"; brown complexion; small scar on left arm.
Fanny Hall. 4 Aug. 1840. DOM recorded by John Chase Hammond 12 Feb. 1812. Age about 45; 5' 7"; dark complexion; scars on forefinger of tight hand and under left eye; raised in AA Co.
Elisha Hall. 6 Aug. 1840. DOM recorded by Margaret Hopkins 21 Aug. 1813. Age about 37; 5' 8"; yellow complexion; large scar on left hand; raised in AA Co.
Henry Jackson. 8 Aug. 1840. Born free and raised in AA Co. Age about 24; 5' 6"; yellow complexion; scar on left arm.
John Thomas. 12 Aug. 1840. Born free and raised on AA Co. Age about 18; 5' 3"; brown complexion; no marks or scars; raised in AA Co.
Benjamin N—. 31 Aug. 1840. DOM recorded by Thomas Owings 8 June 1819. Age about 28; 5' 4 1/2"; yellow complexion; raised in AA Co.
Nancy Queen. 10 Sept. 1840. Born free and raised in AA Co. Age about 16; 5' 1 1/2" yellow complexion; small scar under left eye another between thumb and forefinger of left hand.
Parry More Duppins. 22 Sept. 1840. DOM recorded by Henry C. Drury of Charles 22 Feb. 1822. Age about 46; 5' 9 1/4"; dark complexion; small scar on left thumb; raised in AA Co.
John Franklin. 22 Sept. 1840. DOM recorded by Henry C. Drury of Charles 22 Feb. 1822. Age about 38; 5' 6"; dark complexion; scar on left shin; raised in AA Co.
Thomas Sullivan. 22 Sept. 1840. DOM recorded by Henry C. Drury of Charles 22 Feb. 1822. Age about 33; 5' 7"; brown complexion large scar on forehead; raised in AA Co.
Peter Freelan. 22 Sept. 1840. DOM recorded by Henry C. Drury of Charles. 22 Feb. 1822. Age about 29; 5' 8 1/2"; dark complexion; scar on left elbow; raised in AA Co.
Richard Young. 22 Sept. 1840. DOM recorded by Henry C. Drury of Charles 22 Feb. 1822. Age about 25; 5' 8 3/4"; dark complexion; no marks or scars; raised in AA Co.
Hannah Leherd. 22 Sept. 1840. DOM recorded by Henry C. Drury of Charles 22 Feb. 1822. Age about 24; 5' 5 1/4"; dark complexion; scar on breast; raised in AA Co.
Phoebe Bugg. 22 Sept. 1840. DOM recorded by Henry C. Drury of Charles 22 Feb. 1822. Age about 27; 5' 1/2"; dark complexion; no marks or scars; raised in AA Co.
Rachel Pratt. 22 Sept. 1840. DOM recorded by Henry C. Drury of Charles 22 Feb. 1822. Age about 37; 5' 1/4"; light complexion; scar on right arm; raised in AA Co.
Rose Young. 22 Sept. 1840. DOM recorded by Henry C. Drury of Charles 22 Feb. 1822. Age about 42; 5' 3 1/2"; dark complexion; large scar on left arm; raised in AA Co.
Clarissa Green. 22 Sept. 1840. Born free and raised in AA Co. Age about 19; 4' 11"; dark complexion; no marks or scars.
Susan Young. 22 Sept. 1840. Born free and raised in AA Co. Age about 19; 5' 5 3/4"; dark complexion; one finger of left hand injured.
Jacob Owings. 28 Sept. 1840. Born free and raised in AA Co. Age about 21; 5' 8"; black complexion; small scar on right cheek; crooked little finger on left hand.
Caroline Parker. 28 Sept. 1840 Born free and raised in AA Co. Age about 20; 5' 1/4"; brown complexion; small mole on right cheek.
Phillis Boston. 29 Sept. 1840. DOM recorded by William Pritchard 29 Sept. 1835. Age about 25; 5' 4 1/2"; dark complexion;scar on right hand; raised in AA Co.
John Green. 6 Oct. 1840. Born free and raised in AA Co. Age about 53; 5' 6"; brown complexion; heavily scarred face.
Joshua Dennis. 10 Oct. 1840. DOM recorded by Sarah Norris 2 Aug. 1824. Age about 26; 5' 9"; yellow complexion; no marks or scars; raised in AA Co.
Kitty Crawford. 13 Oct. 1840. Born free and raised in AA Co. Age about 30; 5' 3"; brown complexion; small scar over left eye.
Maria Green. 19 Oct. 1840. Born free and raised in AA Co. Age about 17; 4' 3"; light complexion.
Samuel Hardy. 28 Oct. 1840. DOM recorded by Richard H Batter 14 March 1826. Age about 50; 5' 6"; yellow complexion; no marks or scars; raised in AA Co.
Sophia Hardy. 28 Oct. 1840. DOM recorded by Richard H. Batter 14 March 1826. Age about 50; 5"; black complexion; no marks or scars; raised in AA Co.
Maria Maynard. 2 Nov. 1840. DOM recorded by John Maynard 2 Nov. 1840. Age

about 25; 5' 6"; yellow complexion; small scar on right arm; raised in AA Co.
Catherine Green. 4 Nov. 1840. Born free and raised in AA Co. Age about 19; 5' 3"; brown complexion; small scar on left wrist.
Elizabeth Ann Williams. 11 Nov. 1840. Born free and raised in AA Co. Age about 14; 4' 10 1/2"; yellow complexion; both little fingers are crooked.
Ellen Toogood. 13 Nov. 1840. Born free and raised in AA Co. Age about 19; 4' 11 1/2"; brown complexion; small scar on left hand.
Edith Brogden. 13 Nov. 1840. Born free and raised in AA Co. Age about 17; 5' 2 1/2"; dark complexion;scar on forehead over left eye; another on right corner of mouth.
Mary Williams. 15 Dec. 1840. Born free and raised in AA Co. Age about 20; 5' 4"; yellow complexion; scar on right side of face.
John B—ley. 4 Jan. 1841. Born free and raised in AA Co. Age about 24; 5' 11"; light complexion; straight hair.
Daniel L. Shorter. 4 Jan. 1841. Born free and raised in AA Co. Age about 22; 5' 5"; bright complexion; small scar over left eye.
Thomas Simmons. 2 Feb. 1841. DOM recorded by Nicholas Watkins 19 July 1816. Age about 25; 5' 3"; dark complexion; small scar on forehead; raised in AA Co.
L— Ennis. 10 Feb. 1841. Born free and raised in AA Co. Age about 27; 5' 9"; brown complexion; has a natural mark on calf of right leg 1 small scar on breast.
Dovey Hawkins. 18 Feb. 1841. Born free and raised in AA Co. Age about 21; 5' 1/2"; dark complexion; small scar near left eye.
Eliza Ann James. 18 Feb. 1841. Born free and raised in AA Co. Age about 20; 5' 3"; bright complexion; no marks or scars.
George G—. 8 Feb. 1841. Born free and raised in AA Co. Age about 21; 5' 8"; small scar on middle finger of left hand.
Jerry G—. 18 Feb. 1841. Born free and raised in AA Co. Age about 24; 5' 8 1/2"; dark complexion; no marks or scars.
Charles G—. 18 Feb. 1841. Born free and raised in AA Co. Age about 21; 5' 7"; dark complexion; several small lumps on nose.
Jim Gibson. 11 March 1841. 17; 4' 8"; dark complexion; scar on left hand; small mole left side of ...? .
John C—. 16 March 1841. DOM recorded by Benjamin Thomas 18 May 1822. Age about 32; 5' 7"; black complexion; scar near corner of left eye; raised in AA Co.
John Searkins. 20 March 1841. DOM recorded by Aaron Welch 7 June 1822. Age about 26; 5' 4 1/2"; yellow complexion; no marks or scars; raised in AA Co.
William Smith Price. 30 March 1841. Born free and raised in AA Co. Age about 13; 4' 6"; light complexion; small mole on upper lip.
Charles —. 31 March 1841. Age 16; 5' 2"; brown complexion; scar on upper lip.
Frank Sims. 19 April 1841. Born free and raised in AA Co. Age about 22; 5' 4 1/4"; dark complexion; scar on back of right hand.
Patty Gibson. 19 April 1841. DOM recorded by William Brewer 7 April 1824. Age about 49; 5' 4 1/2"; dark complexion; no marks or scars; raised in AA Co.
Sally Gibson. 19 April 1841 Born free and raised in AA Co. Age about 15; 5' 1/2"; dark complexion; no marks or scars.
Hester Snowden. 4 May 1841. Born free and raised in AA Co. Age about 21; 5' 9 1/2"; dark complexion; scar on back of left arm.
Charlotte Snowden. 4 May 1841. Born free and raised in AA Co. Age about 17; 4' 11 1/2"; dark complexion; scar on right shoulder.
Elizabeth Johnson. 4 May 1841. DOM recorded by Elizabeth Linthicum 7 July 1831. Age about 21; 5' 4 1/2"; black complexion; small scar on forehead; raised in AA Co.
John Johnson. 4 May 1841. DOM recorded by Elizabeth Linthicum 7 July 1831. Age about 22; 5' 11"; black complexion; small scar on right cheek; raised in AA Co.
Margaret Greene. 13 May 1841. Born free and raised in AA Co. Age about 25; 5' 1"; brown complexion.
Mary Ennis. 19 May 1841. DOM recorded by Lewis Neth 30 July 1829. Age about 20; 5' 11 1/4: bright complexion; small mole on left cheekbone; raised in AA Co.
Sarah Matthews. 17 June 1841. Born free and raised in AA Co. Age about 33; 5' 2 1/2"; dark complexion; small scar over right eye.
Nelly Parker. 12 July 1861. DOM recorded by Hester and Elizabeth Hood the second day of Dec. 1822. Age about 2_; 5' 2"; dark complexion; no marks or scars; raised in AA Co.
Sally Parker. 12 July 1861. DOM recorded by Hester and Elizabeth Hood the second day of Dec. 1822. Age about 19; 5' 1/2";

black complexion; raised in AA Co.
Kitty Prout. 2 Aug. 1841. DOM recorded by Elizabeth Hood 19 March 1823. Age about 50; 5' 1 1/2"; black complexion; small scars on forehead and back of right hand; raised in AA Co.
June Prout. 2 Aug. 1841. Born free and raised in AA Co. Age about 15; 5' 1/2"; brown complexion; no marks or scars.
Abraham Brogden. 16 Aug. 1841. Born free and raised in AA Co. Age about 21; 5' 8 1/2"; dark complexion; scar on inside of left wrist.
Rebecca Matthews. 19 Aug. 1841. Born free and raised in AA Co. Age about 18; 5' 1"; black complexion; small scar above right eye.
Clarissa Jennings. 4 Sept. 1841. Born free and raised in AA Co. Age about 18; 5' 3"; dark complexion; small mole on lip.
Stephen Jennings. 4 Sept. 1841. Born free and raised in AA Co. Age about 22; 5' 9"; dark complexion; scars on each hand.
Margaret Johnson. 10 Sept. 1841. DOM recorded by George McChew 24 March 1824. Age about 30; 5' 4"; dark complexion; small scar in left eyebrow; raised in AA Co.
Cato Pr—. 13 Sept. 1841. Born free and raised in AA Co. Age about 21;5' 9"; dark complexion; scars on left cheek and nose.
Arris Queen. 20 Sept. 1841. Born free and raised in AA Co. Age about 18; 4' 11"; dark complexion; small scar in corner of left eye; two small scars on left hand.
Mercy Johnson. 1 Oct. 1841. Born free and raised in AA Co. Age about 29; 5' 2"; light complexion; small scar on left side of neck; small mole on right side of face.
— Johnson. 1 Oct. 1841. Born free and raised in AA Co. Age about 17; 5' 7"; black complexion; small scar on left shoulder.
John Marriott. 19 Oct. 1841. Born free and raised in AA Co. Age about 21; 5' 7 1/2"; light complexion; has straight hair; small scar on left thumb.
Hannah Harris. 21 Oct. 1841. Born free and raised in AA Co. Age about 28; 5' 2"; dark complexion.
Dinah Walls. 21 Oct. 1841. DOM recorded by --- Robison 24 June 1815. Age about 33; 5' 9"; dark complexion; small scar on left wrist; raised in AA Co.
Maria Sadler. 25 Oct. 1841. Born free and raised in AA Co. Age about 17; 4' 7 3/4"; black complexion; injured middle finger of right hand.
John Brown. 1 Nov. 1841. Born free and raised in AA Co. Age about 21; 5' 7 1/2"; brown complexion; scars on left arm and left side of neck.
William Allsop. 17 Nov. 1841. Born free and raised in AA Co. Age about 22; 5' 8 1/2"; light complexion; scar on side of right hand.
James Jackson. 20 Nov. 1841. Born free and raised in AA Co. Age about 21; 5' 5"; light complexion; various tattoos on right arm and left side.
Matilda Sorell. 22 Nov. 1841. DOM recorded by Polly Sassington 18 Dec. 1822. Age about 21; 5' 3"; yellow complexion; scar near corner of right eye; raised in AA Co.
Horace Toogood. 1 Jan. 1842. DOM recorded by Benjamin Sewell 2 Aug. 18--. To be free at the age of 25. Age about 28; 5' 3 1/2"; dark complexion; small scars on forehead and left side of upper lip; raised in AA Co.
Lewis Maynard. 15 Jan. 1842. Born free and raised in AA Co. Age about 21; 5' 8 1/2"; dark complexion; scar on left cheek; large scar on left leg.
Plato B_____. 19 Jan. 1842. DOM recorded by Lucy Harwood 17 March 1823. Age about 27; 5' 6 1/2"; brown complexion; no marks or scars; raised in AA Co. Born free and raised in AA Co.
--- Worthington. 19 Jan. 1842. DOM recorded by --- 4 Jan. 1822. Age about 38; 5' 3 1/2"; dark complexion; scar near right eye; raised in AA Co.
Sasanna Richardson. 20 Jan. 1842. DOM recorded by Aaron Jones 1 March 1830. Age about 29; 4' 11 1/2"; dark complexion; no marks or scars; raised in AA Co.
Nicholas Holland. 11 Feb. 1842 Born free and raised in AA Co. Age about 22; 5' 5 1/2"; dark complexion; small scar near corner of left eye.
Arthur Garrett. 12 Feb. 1842. Born free and raised in AA Co. Age about 24; 5' 7 1/2"; brown complexion.
Edward Garrett. 12 Feb. 1842. Age 23; 5' 5"; yellow complexion; two scars over left eye.
Richard Garrett. 12 Feb. 1842. Born free and raised in AA Co. Age about 21; 5' 9 1/2"; brown complexion; swollen joint of great toe of left foot.
Henry Dodson. 12 Feb. 1842. Born free and raised in AA Co. Age about 22; 5' 5"; dark complexion; scar on left eyebrow; scar on back between shoulders.
Robert Queen. 16 Feb. 1842. Born free and raised in AA Co. Age about 27; 5' 8"; dark complexion; small scar over right

eye.

Nathan —. 23 Feb. 1842. Born free and raised in AA Co. Age about 22; 5' 3"; yellow complexion; small mole on nose between the eyes.

James Larkins. 25 Feb. 1842. Born free and raised in AA Co. Age about 25; 5' 7"; dark complexion; scar in right eyebrow; scar near left eye.

Ellen Young. 26 Feb. 1842. Born free and raised in AA Co. Age about 18; 4' 11 1/2"; yellow complexion; small mole on forehead.

Fanny Young. 26 Feb. 1842. Born free and raised in AA Co. Age about 22; 4' 8 1/2"; dark complexion; small mole on left cheek.

Mary Sanders. 12 March 1842. Born free and raised in AA Co. Age about 19; 5'; black complexion; scar on right cheek.

John Butler. 16 March 1842. Born free and raised in AA Co. Age about 27; 5' 8 1/2"; dark complexion; small scar in right eyebrow.

Charles Gault. 28 March 1842. Born free and raised in AA Co. Age about 22; 5' 4"; dark complexion; small scar near left temple; scar on right leg above the ankle.

Henry Gault. 28 March 1842. Born free and raised in AA Co. Age about 26; 5' 4 1/2"; black complexion; no marks or scars.

— Gault. 28 March 1842. Born free and raised in AA Co. Age about 24; 5' 7 1/2"; black complexion; small scar on right side of face.

Nace Garrett. 29 March 1842. Born free and raised in AA Co. Age about 21; 5' 7 1/2"; dark complexion; small burn on right wrist.

Richard Allsop. 2 April 1842. Born free and raised in AA Co. Age about 33; 5' 7 1/2"; light complexion; scar in left eyebrow; scar on left side of chin.

Betty O' Rouke. 27 April 1842. DOM recorded by Gideon White 19 April 1824. Age about 24; 5' 3 1/4"; bright complexion; small scar on right side of nose; raised in AA Co.

Samuel Walker. 14 May 1842. DOM recorded by Absalom Ridgely 28 Dec. 1816.

Harriet Clarke. 30 May 1842. Born free and raised in AA Co. Age about 17; 5' 2 1/2"; bright complexion; no marks or scars.

Aaron Johnson. 9 June 1842. DOM recorded by James Shaw, James Murray and Henry L. Holland 14 July 1829. 5' 10"; dark complexion; raised in AA Co.

Paul Johnson. 9 June 1842. DOM recorded by James Shaw, James Murray and Henry L. Holland 14 July 1829. Age about 35; 5' 9"; dark complexion; small scars on back of right hand and forehead; raised in AA Co.

Mary Elizabeth Evans. 18 June 1842. Born free and raised in AA Co. Age about 21; 5' 5 1/2'; bright complexion; has a few freckles on face.

Catherine Johnson. 6 July 1842. Born free and raised in AA Co. Age about 21; 5' 1"; dark complexion; no marks or scars.

James Holiday (Heoliday ?). 9 July 1842. DOM recorded by Nicholas Watkins 10 Oct. 1819. Age about 33; 5' 4 1/2' ; brown complexion; small scar beneath right eye; small lump on right eyelid; raised in AA Co.

Henry Thomas. 21 July 1842. DOM recorded by Elizabeth Robinson 13 June 1827. Age about 38; 5' 7"; dark complexion; scar on right arm; raised in AA Co.

Joseph Anderson. 30 Aug. 1842. DOM recorded by Charles Hammond of ___ 18 Feb. 1803. Age about 48; 5' 4 1/2"; dark complexion; raised in AA Co.

Sophia Brown. 1 Sept. 1842. Born free and raised in AA Co. Age about 23; 5' 2 1/2"; light complexion; missing first joint of left thumb.

— Collins. 1 Sept. 1842. Born free and raised in AA Co. Age about 23; 5' 3 1/2"; brown complexion; several small marks on left side of face.

Margaret Parker. 1 Sept. 1842. Born free and raised in AA Co. Age about 19; 5' 9"; dark complexion; large scar on back of right hand.

Harriet Larkins. 27 Sept. 1842. DOM recorded by Mary Ann Warfield 12 Nov. 1831. Age about 21; 5' 6"; bright complexion; raised in AA Co.

Priscilla Prell. 12 Oct. 1842. DOM recorded by Richard P. Snow 24 Nov. 1840. Age about 41; 4' 11 1/2"; black complexion; scar on both sides of face; raised in AA Co.

Zachariah Green. 12 Oct. 1842. DOM recorded by Richard P. Snow 24 Nov. 1840. Age about 37; 5' 4 1/2"; black complexion; scar on right wrist; raised in AA Co.

Betsy —. 13 Oct. 1842. DOM recorded by Richard P. Snow 24 Nov. 1840. Age about 36; 4' 8"; black complexion; no marks or scars; raised in AA Co.

Eugene Waters. 12 Oct. 1842. DOM recorded by Anna Maria Snowden 2 Nov. 1814. Age about 26; 5' 1"; light complexion; small scars on left cheek and breast;

raised in AA Co.
Alice Green. 12 Oct. 1842. Born free and raised in AA Co. Age about 19; 5' 3"; dark complexion; scar on back of right hand.
William Merriken. 12 Oct. 1842. DOM recorded by Richard P. Snowden 24 Nov. 1840. Age about 26; 5' 1"; light complexion; scar on inside of right wrist.
Sampson Gibson. 12 Oct. 1842. DOM recorded by Richard P. Snowden 24 Nov. 1840. Age about 35; 5' 11"; black complexion; small scars on left thumb and on forehead; raised in AA Co.
Asbury Waters. 12 Oct. 1842. DOM recorded by Richard P. Snowden 24 Nov. 1840. Age about 37; 5' 3 1/2"; dark complexion; raised in AA Co.
Nancy Clarke. 12 Oct. 1842. DOM recorded by Richard P. Snowden 24 Nov. 1840. Age about 25; 5'; dark complexion; raised in AA Co.
Polly Briscoe. 12 Oct. 1842. DOM recorded by Richard P. Snowden 24 Nov. 1840. Age about 42; 5' 2 1/2"; light complexion; small scar on third finger of left hand; raised in AA Co.
Priscilla Green. 12 Oct. 1842. DOM recorded by Richard P. Snowden 24 Nov. 1840. Age about 35; 5' 5"; dark complexion; small scar on left corner of mouth; raised in AA Co.
Moses Green. 12 Nov. 1842. DOM recorded 24 Nov. 1840. Age about 27; 5' 3 1/2"; brown complexion; several small scars; raised in AA Co.
John Harrison. 24 Oct. 1842. Born free and raised in AA Co. Age about 26; 5' 5"; black complexion; small scar on right cheek.
Mary Hammond. 21 Oct. 1842. Born free and raised in AA Co. Age about 22; 5' 6"; black complexion.
Sally Hammond. 21 Oct. 1842. Born free and raised in AA Co. Age about 20; 5' 2"; black complexion; no marks or scars.
Frances Dorsey. 23 Dec. 1842. DOM recorded by Mary --- 24 May 1830. Age about 24; 5' 7 1/2' ; brown complexion; small scar on forehead.
Benjamin Thomas. 24 Feb. 1843. DOM recorded by Charles Griffith 9 Sept. 1818 Age about 28; 5' 8 1/2"; dark complexion; small scar over each eye; raised in AA Co.
Frances Roberts. 8 March 1843. Born free and raised in AA Co. Age about 22; 5' 7 1/2"; brown complexion; no marks or scars.
Daniel Roberts. 8 March 1843. Born free and raised in AA Co. Age about 27; 5' 8 1/2"; brown complexion; small scar on back of left hand.
Rachel (Vachel ?) Gibson. 15 March 1843. DOM recorded by Rachel Snowden 6 Jan. 1825. Age about 27; 5' 5 1/2"; black complexion; scar on left side of neck; raised in AA Co.
Philes (Phillis) Williams. 29 March 1843. DOM recorded by William Goldsbourgh 7 Aug. 1842. Age about 27; 5' 1"; brown complexion; small scar on left cheek; raised in AA Co.
Christina R—. 10 April 1843. DOM recorded by Elijah Pennington 25 March 1823. Age about 38; 5' 1/2"; dark complexion; scar on right side of face; raised in AA Co.
Harriet H—ley. 28 April 1843. Born free and raised in AA Co. Age about 18; 5' ; black complexion; small scar on nose.
Henrietta Wil—. 28 April 1843. Born free and raised in AA Co. Age about 17; 5' 2"; yellow complexion; small mole on side of left ear.
Elijah Parker. 2 May 1843. Born free and raised in AA Co. Age about 23; 5' 8 3/4"; dark complexion; no marks or scars.
Nathan Harrison. 20 May 1843. Born free and raised in AA Co. Age about 21; 5' 7 1/2"; black complexion; small scars on upper lip and forehead.
S— Johnson. 29 May 1843,. DOM recorded by Elijah Pennington 25 March 1825. Age about 42; 5' 3"; dark complexion; small scar on forehead; raised in AA Co.
Mary Frances Shorter. 1 June 1843. Born free and raised in AA Co. Age about 17; 5' 1/2"; light complexion; small mole on left ear.
Maria Hias. 10 June 1843. DOM recorded by Benjamin Usilton 17 June 1828. Age about 16; 4' 9 1/4' ; yellow complexion; no marks or scars; raised in AA Co.
Ann Smallwood. 12 June 1843. DOM recorded by Aaron Welch 7 June 1821. Age about 31; 4' 11'; dark complexion; scar over right eye; scar on right cheek; raised in AA Co.
Caroline Robertson. 24 June 1843. DOM recorded by Sarah --- 10 Dec. 1830. Age about 30; 5' 3"; brown complexion; small scar on left cheek; raised in AA Co.
Hannah Walker. 28 June 1843. DOM recorded by Absalom Ridgely 9 Dec. 1816. Age about 53; 5' 1/2"; brown complexion; small scar on left side of neck; raised in AA Co.
James Chew. 5 July 1843. Born free and raised in AA Co. Age about 20; 5' 7"; light complexion; scars on forehead.

Henry —. 8 July 1843. DOM recorded by S--- --- 29 April 1823. Age is ommitted; 5' 3"; dark complexion; raised in AA Co.
Charity (Chastity) B—. 19 July 1843. Subject is identified as the daughter of the Negro Peter who was manumitted by. DOM recorded by Phillip H. Wells (Welks?) 10 Sept. 1808. Age is about 28; 5' 7 1/2"; bright complexion; raised in AA Co.
Rachel —. 21 July 1843. DOM recorded by Lydia Gambrillls 7 July 1837. Age about 37; 5' 2"; dark complexion; raised in AA Co.
— Jackson. 28 July 1843. Born free and raised in AA Co. Age about 18; 5' 8"; light complexion; mole on right cheek.
Richard Richardson. 21 Aug. 1843. Born free and raised in AA Co. Age about 15' 4' 6 1/2"; brown complexion.
Hester Ann Brown. 26 August, 1843. Born free and raised in AA Co. Age about 23; 5' 8 1/2"; yellow complexion; no marks or scars.
Susan Parker. 29 Aug. 1843. Born free and raised in AA Co. Age about 26; 5' 5"; brown complexion; small mole of left side of neck.
John Queen. 29 Aug. 1843 Born free and raised in AA Co. Age about 23; 5' 6"; yellow complexion; mole on upper lip; straight black hair.
Eleanor Parker. 15 Sept. 1843. Born free and raised in AA Co. Age about 17; 5' 3 1/2"; brown complexion; scar on right side of neck.
Benjamin Brown. 16 Sept. 1843. DOM recorded by --- 10 ---, 1815. Age about 32; 5' 4"; brown complexion; raised in AA Co.
Dick Bordley (Bradley ?). 25 Sept. 1843. DOM recorded by Henry Hammond 24 May 1828. Age about 30; 5' 10 1/4"; dark complexion; small scars under left eye and on right wrist; raised in AA Co.
Jack Jones. 24 May 1843. DOM recorded by Eleanor Woodwards 29 May 1832. Age about 15; 5' 2 3/4"; brown complexion; no marks or scars; raised in AA Co.
Bill Bordley (Bradley ?). 31 Oct. 1843. DOM recorded by Henry Hammond 24 May 1828. Age about 31; 6' 1/2"; black complexion; no toes on left foot; raised in AA Co.

CERTIFICATES OF FREEDOM
1845- 1851

Dinah /Dina Green. 18 Feb. 1845. DOM recorded by Richard P. Snowden 24 Nov. 1840. Age 27, 5' 8", yellow complexion,; scar on right wrist; raised in AA Co.
Henny/Henrietta. 18 Feb. 1845. DOM recorded by Richard P. Snowden 24 Nov. 1840 Age about 20, 5' 1/4"; yellow complexion; scar on nose; raised in AA Co.
Sophia. DOM recorded by Richard P. Snowden 24 Nov. 1842. Age about 46; 5' 1 1/2"; scars over eyes in middle of forehead; raised in AA Co.
Charles. 7 March 1845. Manumitted by Richard P. Snowden.
Richard Peterson. 25 Feb. 1845. Freeborn and raised in AA Co.
Thomas Boston. 4 March 1845. Freeborn and raised in AA Co. Age about 21, 5' 8", dark complexion, scar on left arm.
John Scott. 24 March 1845. Freeborn and raised in AA Co. 5' 5 1/2", light complexion.
Mary Ennis. Freeborn and raised in AA Co. Age about 25; 5' 1/12"; light complexion; small scar on back of each hand.
Nancy Ann Ausborn. 3 April 1845. Freeborn and raised in AA Co. Age about 21; 5' 4 1/2"; light complexion; mark on right side of face.
William Parker. DOM recorded by George Barker 10 Jan. 1833; Age about 45; 5' 9"; dark complexion; no marks or scars; raised in AA Co.
Charles Collins. 21 April 1845. Freeborn and raised in AA Co. Age about 22; 5' 8 1/2; dark brown complexion; scar on left side of forehead.
Jane Shorter. 8 May 1845. DOM recorded by Peter Shorter 20 July 1822 (Liber C. Folio 245) Age about 27; light complexion.
Augustine Winale. 10 May 1845. Freeborn and raised in AA Co. Nearly straight hair; scars on forehead.
Jacob Adams. 12 May 1845. DOM recorded by Samuel Norman 23 Dec. 1828. 5' 8"; scar on right ear.
Charles Anderson. 12 May 1845. 5' 6 1/2; indentation on right and small scar on left temple.
Louisa Ann Benson. Freeborn and raised

in AA Co.; 5' 5"; dark complexion; scar in middle of forehead.
Mary Jane Hammond. 12 May 1845. Age about 18; 5' 6 1/2"; raised in AA Co.
Charles Young. 12 May 1845. DOM recorded by Henry Drury of Charles 27 Feb. 1822; 5' 9" scar in middle of forehead.
George Neale. 13 May 1845. DOM recorded by John Rideout of Samuel; 5' 9 1/4: raised in AA Co.
Washington Parker. 22 May 1845. Freeborn and raised in AA Co.; 5' 9 1/4"; dark complexion.
Nick Johnson. 22 May 1845. DOM recorded by Stephen Beard 9 Jan. 1820; 5' 7"; dark complexion; raised in AA Co.
Jim Johnson. Freeborn and raised in AA Co. 5' 6 1/4: scar on right eye.
Elizabeth Jones. 14 June 1845. Freeborn and raised in AA Co.; age about 25; 5' 9'; dark complexion; scar on right shoulder.
Amos Matthews. 17 June 1845. DOM recorded by Nicholas Swann 22 Oct. 1810, age about 32; 5' 7 1/4"; dark complexion; scars above eye, near right ear, and on upper lip.
Maynard Cooke. 25 June 1845. Freeborn and raised in AA Co.; age about 19; 4' 11"; dark complexion; two scars on forehead.
John Beans. 7 July 1845. Freeborn and raised in AA Co.; age about 26; 5' 8'; light complexion.
Richard Harris. 24 July 1845. Freeborn and raised in AA Co.; 5' 3"; light complexion.
Sally Allen. 29 July 1845. Freeborn and raised in AA Co. Age about 20; 5' 3/4"; brown complexion; scar on right side of face.
Lydia West. 2 Aug. 1845. Freeborn and raised in AA Co.; age about 23; 5' 3 1/2"; light complexion.
Elizabeth C— Williams. 5 Aug. 1845. DOM recorded by Stephen Boone Jan. 1819; age about 29; 5' 1 1/2"; brown complexion; scar on right arm; raised in AA Co.
Mary Ann Green. 19 Aug. 1845. DOM recorded by William Brown, age about 34; 5' 4"; light complexion; no marks; raised in AA Co.
Richard Grey. 23 Aug. 1845. DOM recorded by Jerningham Drury; age about 26; 5' 1/2"; dark complexion; two scars on left foot; raised in AA Co.
Thomas Grey. 23 Aug. 1845. DOM recorded by Jerningham Drury; age about 25; 5' 7 1/2"; dark complexion; raised in AA Co.
Henrietta Queen, Sally Queen. 5 Sept. 1845. Freeborn and raised in AA Co. Age about 18; 5' 10 1/2: brown complexion.
Priss Matthews. 9 Sept. 1845. Freeborn and raised in AA Co.; age about 16; 5' 7"; brown complexion.
Ann Queen. 15 Sept. 1845. Freeborn and raised in AA Co.; age about 30; 5' 1 1/2"; light complexion.
John Wright. 18 Sept. 1845. Freeborn and raised in AA Co.; age about 22; 5' 7"; scar on right eye and forehead.
Henry Benson. 23 Sept. 1845. DOM recorded by Nathanial Stinchcomb, Liber C., p. 482, age about 17; 5' 5"; light complexion; raised in AA Co.
Nace Hutton. 27 Sept. 1845. DOM recorded by Harriet Selby 5 July 1834; age about 32; 5' 6 1/4"; large scar on right arm; raised in AA Co.
Mary Beans. 27 Sept. 1845. Freeborn and raised in AA Co. Age about 19; 5' 2 1/2"; light complexion.
John Dodson. 27 Sept. 1845. Freeborn and raised in AA Co.; age about 22; 5' 6 3/4"; dark complexion; scar over left eye.
Rachael Johnson. 2 Oct. 1845. Freeborn and raised in AA Co.; age about 21; 5' 3 3/4"; light complexion.
Sophia Harrison. 14 Oct. 1845. Freeborn and raised in AA Co.; age about 18; 5' 3"; brown complexion.
Joseph Harrison. 14 Oct. 1845. Freeborn and raised in AA Co.; age about 24; 5' 9"; brown complexion; scar on left cheek.
Wesley Simms. 14 Oct. 1845. Freeborn and raised in AA Co.; age about 27; 5' 5 /2"; dark complexion; scar on left forehead.
Thomas Lomas. 6 Nov. 1845. DOM recorded by Dr. Richard Weems 31 Oct. 1845; age about 25; 5' 7"; light complexion; raised in AA Co.
Eliza Davis. 13 Nov. 1845. Freeborn and raised in AA Co.; age about 28; 5' 3"; light complexion.
Perry Wright. 14 Nov. 1845. Freeborn and raised in AA Co.; age about 22; 5' 1/2"; dark complexion.
Richard Lloyd. 18 Nov. 1845. Freeborn and raised in AA Co.; age about 22; 5' 9 3/4"; brown complexion.
— Carroll. 20 Dec. 1845. Freeborn and raised in AA Co.; age about 23; 5' 9 1/2", dark complexion.
Angeline Simms. 24 Dec. 1845. Freeborn and raised in AA Co.; age about 18; 5' 3"; light complexion.
Benjamin Boston. 2 Jan. 1846. Freeborn and raised in AA Co.; Age about 22; 5; 8 1/4"; brown complexion.

Richard Walker. 13 Jan. 1846. DOM recorded by Rezin Snowden 10 Dec. 1845. Age about 34, 5' 8", dark complexion, raised in AA Co.
Henry Lane. DOM recorded by Rezin Snowden 10 Dec. 1845. Age about 32, 5' 10", light complexion, raised in AA Co.
James Butler. 13 Jan. 1846. DOM recorded by Rezin Snowden 10 Dec. 1845. Age about 37, 5' 7 1/2", light complexion, raised in AA Co.
William Lomack. 6 Feb. 1846. DOM recorded by John Childs 28 Aug. 1829. 5' 10 1/4", light complexion, raised in AA Co.
Joshua Toogood. 17 March 1846. DOM recorded by Rezin Snowden 10 Dec. 1845. Age about 40, 5' 7 1/4", dark complexion, raised in AA Co.
Israel Wright. 17 March 1846. DOM recorded by Rezin Snowden 10 Dec. 1845. Age about 35, 5' 6", brown complexion, raised in AA Co.
Henry Hall. 23 March 1846. Freeborn and raised in AA Co. Age about 31; 5' 11", dark complexion.
Meliara Hall. 23 March 1846. Freeborn and raised in AA Co. Age about 28, 5' 3", dark complexion.
Daniel Boston. 24 March 1846. Freeborn and raised in AA Co. Age about 25, 5' 9 3/4", light complexion.
Hester Lane. 24 March 1846. DOM recorded by Rezin Snowden 13 Feb. 1846. Age about 30, 5' 4", light complexion, raised in AA Co.
Ruth Lane. 24 March 1846. DOM recorded by Rezin Snowden 13 Feb. 1846. Age about 28, 5' 3 1/2", light complexion, raised in AA Co.
Fanny Lane. 24 March 1846. DOM recorded by Rezin Snowden 13 Feb. 1846. Age about 26, 5' 4", light complexion, raised in AA Co.
Mary Lane. 24 March 1846. DOM recorded by Rezin Snowden 13 Feb. 1846. Age about 24, 5' 3", light complexion, raised in AA Co.
Sarah Lane. 24 March 1846. DOM recorded by Rezin Snowden 13 Feb. 1846. Age about 16, 5' 2 1/2", dark complexion, raised in AA Co.
Nathan Johnson. 25 March 1846. DOM recorded by Elizabeth Linthicum 27 July 1830. Age about 22, 5' 8 1/2", dark complexion, raised in AA Co.
Mary Ellen Calbert. 31 March 1846. Freeborn and raised in AA Co. Age about 21, 5' 1/4", dark complexion.
Sam Calbert. 31 March 1846. Freeborn and raised in AA Co. Age about 23, 5' 11 1/2", dark complexion.
William Mitchell. 31 March 1846. Freeborn and raised in AA Co. Age about 27, 5' 1", light complexion.
Kitty Brogden. April 1846. Freeborn and raised in AA Co. Age about 22, 5' 9", dark complexion.
Louisa Queen. 2 April 1846. Freeborn and raised in AA Co. Age about 21, 5', dark complexion.
Margaret Ches—. 2 April 1846. Freeborn and raised in AA Co. Age about 24, 5' 8", black complexion.
Susan Queen. 2 April 1846. Freeborn and raised in AA Co. Age about 17, 5' 4", dark complexion, scar on right arm.
Emmeline Brogden. April 1846. Freeborn and raised in AA Co. Age about 25, 5' 4', dark complexion.
Mary Thomas. 2 April 1846. Freeborn and raised in AA Co. Age about ..., 5' 6 1/2", light complexion.
Rachel A. Waters. 2 April 1846. Freeborn and raised in AA Co. Age about ..., 5' 6", dark complexion.
Sally Parker. 7 April 1846. Freeborn and raised in AA Co. Age about 22, 5' 1", dark complexion.
Richard Waters. 7 April 1846. Freeborn and raised in AA Co. Age about 25, 5' 9", light complexion, has six fingers on each hand.
William Waters. 7 April 1846. Freeborn and raised in AA Co. Age about 21, 5' 10", dark complexion, small scar corner of left eye.
Samuel Rowles. 7 April 1846. Freeborn and raised in AA Co. Age about 23, 5' 7", brown complexion, scar in corner of left eye.
Charity Brach—s. 7 April 1846. DOM recorded by Rose Thomas 10 Jan. 1830. Age about 36, 5' 6", yellow complexion, raised in AA Co.
Michael Wallace. 13 April 1846. Freeborn and raised in AA Co. Age about 24, 5' 5 1/2", dark complexion.
Jane Stewart. 13 April 1846. Freeborn and raised in AA Co. Age about 19, 5' 10 1/2", brown complexion.
Betsy Stewart. 13 April 1846. Freeborn and raised in AA Co. Age about 23, 5' 1", brown complexion.
Rachel Stewart. 13 April 1846. Freeborn and raised in AA Co. Age about 21, 5' 11", brown complexion.
Tom Powell. 13 April 1846. Freeborn and raised in AA Co. Age about 23, 5' 1",

brown complexion.
Henry Wallace. 13 April 1846. Freeborn and raised in AA Co. Age about 21, 5' 4 1/2", dark complexion.
Thomas Ennesse. 13 April 1846. Freeborn and raised in AA Co. Age about 21, 5' 4 1/8", black complexion.
Daniel Johnson. 22 April 1846. Freeborn and raised in AA Co. Age about 21, 5' 2", black complexion.
Flora Bordley. 22 April 1846. DOM recorded by Henry Hammond 28 May 1828, Age about 38, 5' 5", black complexion.
John M. Diggs. 23 April 1846. Freeborn and raised in AA Co. Age about 23, 5' 3", light complexion.
Fanny A. Diggs. 23 April 1846. Freeborn and raised in AA Co. Age about 20, 5' 2", black complexion.
Susan Sparrow. 28 April 1846. Freeborn and raised in AA Co. Age about 30, 5' 2", very dark complexion.
Greenbury Gray. 12 May 1846. Freeborn and raised in AA Co. Age about 27, dark complexion, scar on left eye.
Henry Jones. 14 May 1846. Freeborn and raised in AA Co. Age about 21, 5' 8", light complexion.
Lucy Gray. 18 May 1846. DOM recorded by Charles Waters 9 June 1812. Age about 50, 5' 6 1/4", dark complexion, raised in AA Co.
Basil Johnson. 18 May 1846. DOM recorded by Charles Waters 9 June 1812. Age about 49, 5' 7 3/4", dark complexion, raised in AA Co.
Rachel Johnson. 18 May 1846. DOM recorded by Charles Waters 9 June 1812. Age about 47, 5' 5", dark complexion.
Kisiah Brown. 18 April 1846. DOM executed by Stephen Boone 17 March 1815. Age about 40, 5' 5", brown complexion, raised in AA Co.
Eliza Ann Stewart. 20 May 1846. Freeborn and raised in AA Co. Age about 25, 5' 2", light complexion.
Sarah Jane Mitchell. 22 May 1846. Freeborn and raised in AA Co. 5", yellow complexion.
Flora Boardly. 22 May 1846. DOM recorded by Henry Hammond 28 May 1828. Age about 38, black complexion.
Mayard Gross. 23 May 1846. Born free and raised in AA Co. Age about 19, 5' 4 1/2", dark complexion, raised in AA Co.
David Gross. undated. Born free and raised in AA Co. Age about 16, 4' 9", dark complexion, raised in AA Co.
Henry Matthews. 25 May 1846. DOM recorded by John Rideout 25 May 1846. Age about 25, 5' 5", brown complexion, raised in AA Co.
Emanuel Emerson. 2 June 1846. Born free and raised in AA Co. Age about 21, 5' 5", dark complexion.
Eliza Scoggins. 6 June 1846. DOM recorded by Mary Wilson 11 March 1813. Age about 38, 5' 11", dark complexion.
Margaret Denkins. 20 July 1846. Born free and raised in AA Co. Age about 22, 5' 3", yellow complexion.
Wile Toogood. 25 July 1846. DOM recorded by Charles Waters 9 June 1812. Age about 51, 5' 10" dark complexion.
Charlotte Hyams. 25 July 1846. DOM recorded by Charles Waters 9 June 1812. Age about 45, 5' 1", raised in AA Co.
Jacob Johnson. 25 July 1846. DOM recorded by Charles Waters 9 June 1812. Age about 40, 5' 5", dark complexion, raised in AA Co.
Andrew Franklin. 25 July 1846. DOM recorded by Charles Waters 9 June 1812. Age about 35, 5' 3", dark complexion, raised in AA Co.
George Gray. 27 July 1846. Born free and raised in AA Co. Age about 22, 5' 3", brown complexion.
Wesley Offer. 31 July 1846. Born free and raised in AA Co. Age about 22, 5' 6", dark complexion, scar on upper lip.
Dinah Gaither. Born free and raised in AA Co. Age about 22, 5' 9", dark complexion.
James Gaither. Born free and raised in AA Co. Age about 21, 5' 8", light complexion.
Edward Matthews. 8 Aug. 1846. Born free and raised in AA Co. Age about 23, 5", dark complexion.
Maria Beall. 8 Aug. 1846. Born free and raised in AA Co. Age about 22, 5' 3 1/4", brown complexion.
James Larkin. 8 Aug. 1846. Born free and raised in AA Co.
Samuel Talbott. 15 Aug. 1846. Born free and raised in AA Co. Age about 30, 5' 5", yellow.
Jane Johnson. 7 Oct. 1846. Born free and raised in AA Co. Age about 18, 5' 1", black complexion, scars on left elbow, right elbow, and left foot.
Robert Hall. DOM recorded by Charles Waters. Age about 38, 5' 10", dark complexion, raised in AA Co.
Ann Janetta Maynard. 22 Sept. 1846. Born free and raised in AA Co. Age about 22, 5', light complexion, scar on chin.
Jane Stewart. 27 Oct. 1846. Born free and raised in AA Co. Age about 26, 5' 2 1/4",

dark complexion.
Kitty Stewart. 27 Oct. 1846. Born free and raised in AA Co. Age about 24, 5' 4 1/4", dark complexion.
Phillip Stewart. Born free and raised in AA Co. Age about 28, 5' 9 1/4", dark complexion.
Alice Walker. 6 Oct. 1846. Born free and raised in AA Co. 5' 1 1/2.".
Harriett Ann Miller. 13 Nov. 1846. Born free and raised in AA Co.
Jane Green. Born free and raised in AA Co. 4' 9".
Ephriam Green. 16 Nov. 1846. Born free and raised in AA Co. 4' 8 3/4".
Garrison Green. 16 Nov. 1846. Born free and raised in AA Co.
Ann Harris. 17 Nov. 1846. DOM recorded by John Childs 7 Feb. 1831. Age about 30, 5' 1", scar on back of right hand, raised in AA Co.
James Thomas. 17 Nov. 1846. DOM recorded by John Childs 7 Feb. 1831. Age about 34, 5' 9 1/4", scar on finger of left hand, raised in AA Co.
Lewis Hall. 17 Nov. 1846. DOM recorded by John Childs 7 Feb. 1831. Age about 23, 5' 11 1/2", scar over right eye, scars on both legs, dark complexion, raised in AA Co.
Sarah Hodge. 17 Nov. 1846. DOM recorded by John Childs 7 Feb. 1831. Age about 26, 5', missing first joint of little finger on left hand, raised in AA Co.
William Brashiers. 18 Nov. 1846. Born free and raised in AA Co. Age about 28, 5' 7", small scar over left eye, small scar on left side of face.
Catherine. 18 Nov. 1846. DOM recorded by Elizabeth Robinson. 5' 4", dark complexion.
Anne Williams. 18 Nov. 1846. Born free and raised in AA Co. Dark complexion, 5' 7".
Levi Johnson. 16 Nov. 1846. Born free and raised in AA Co. Dark complexion, 5' 7".
Abigail. 20 Nov. 1846. DOM recorded by N. J. Watkins 6 Dec. 1819. Raised in AA Co.
Chevis H. Johnson. 24 Nov. 1846. Born free and raised in AA Co. 5' 6 1/4".
Hannah Gray. 20 Feb. 1847. Born free and raised in AA Co. Age about 21, 5' 5".
Charles Crowner. 24 Feb. 1847. Born free and raised in AA Co. Age about 25, 5' 6", dark complexion.
Daniel Estep. 24 Feb. 1847. Born free and raised in AA Co. Age about 27, 5' 8 3/4", yellow complexion.
Jason Hall. 9 March 1847. Born free and raised in AA Co. Age about 27, 5' 8", dark complexion, scars on left arm and over left eye.
William Hall. 9 March 1847. Born free and raised in AA Co. Age about 25, 5' 8 1/2".
John L—. 15 March 1847. 9 March 1847. Born free and raised in AA Co. Age about 25, 5' 6", scar on forehead.
Jessie Gray. 16 March 1847. 9 March 1847. Born free and raised in AA Co. Age about 21, 5' 8", scar over right eye.
Rachael Ann Gray. 16 March 1847. 9 March 1847. Born free and raised in AA Co. Age about 18, 5' 4", brown complexion, scar on left wrist.
Mary Ann Gray. 16 March 1847. 9 March 1847. Born free and raised in AA Co. Age about 15, 5' 3", black complexion, scar on left wrist.
Mary Jane Morris. 16 March 1847. 16 March 1847. Born free and raised in AA Co. Age about 23, 5' 3".
Henry Green. 11 Aug. 1847. Born free and raised in AA Co. Age about 25, 5' 8", light complexion.
William Phelps. Undated entry. Born free and raised in AA Co. Age about 21. 5' 7 1/2", light complexion.
Daniel Watkins. 1 Jan. 1847. Born free and raised in AA Co. Age about 25, 5' 6", dark complexion.
John H. Tydings. 25 March 1847. Born free and raised in AA Co. Age about 26, 5' 8", light complexion, scar on left foot.
Emily Adrian King. 12 April 1847. DOM recorded by Lewis Neth 30 July 1829, Raised in AA Co.
Robert Miller. 20 April 1847. Born free and raised in AA Co.
Hester Richardson. 26 April 1847. Born free and raised in AA Co.
Freeborn G. Edwards. 26 April 1847. Born free and raised in AA Co.
Richard Titus. 29 April 1847. Born free and raised in AA Co.
Sarah Titus. 29 April 1847. Born free and raised in AA Co.
Jinny Williams. 1 May 1847. DOM recorded by John Gibson 9 March 1819.
Richard Ausborn. 4 May 1847. Born free and raised in AA Co. Age about 25, 5' 1/2", dark complexion.
Solomon Edwards. 4 May 1847. Born free and raised in AA Co.
Harriett Lee. DOM recorded by Mary Merriken 12 Jan. 1821. 5' 3 1/4", light complexion. Raised in AA Co.
Alfred Scott. 6 May 1847. Born free and raised in AA Co. 5' 9", dark complexion.

Milly Scott. 6 May 1847. Born free and raised in AA Co. 5' 4 1/2", yellow complexion.
Henry Holland. 6 May 1847. Born free and raised in AA Co. 5' 3 3/4", brown complexion.
James Turner. 6 May 1847. Born free and raised in AA Co. 5' 4 1/4", dark complexion.
Elizabeth Pall. 6 May 1847. Born free and raised in AA Co. 5', light complexion.
Harriett Calvert. 7 May 1847. DOM recorded by Mary Merriken 12 Jan. 1821. Age about 30, 5' 5", brown complexion.
Horace Walker. 8 May 1847. DOM recorded by David Robinson 7 March 1818. Age about 32, 6' 1", brown complexion, raised in AA Co.
John Hunt. 11 May 1847. Born free and raised in AA Co. Age about 23, 5' 10 1/2", dark complexion.
Nancy Ann Hunt. 11 May 1847. Born free and raised in AA Co. Age about 19, 5' 4", dark complexion.
Lewis Edward Wilson. 14 May 1847. Born free and raised in AA Co. 5' 7", light brown complexion.
Richard Hindsman. 15 May 1847. Born free and raised in AA Co. Age about 29, 5' 2", brown complexion.
Samuel Green. 18 May 1847. Born free and raised in AA Co. Age about 23, 5' 5", dark complexion.
Henry Ridgely. 18 May 1847. DOM recorded by Rezin H. Snowden 10 Dec. 1845. Age about 33, 5' 2", dark complexion, raised in AA Co.
Julia Ann. 21 May 1847. Born free and raised in AA Co. Age about 21, 5' 2", brown complexion.
Margaret Baldwin. 24 May 1847. Born free and raised in AA Co. Age about 18, 4' 9", light complexion.
Charles Ward. 27 May 1847. DOM recorded by Lucy Harwood 10 March 1823. Age about 26, 5' 7", light complexion, raised in AA Co.
Mary Ann Stewart. 28 May 1847. DOM recorded by Louis G--- 24 June 1822. Age about 25, 5' 2", light complexion, raised in AA Co.
Dinah Smith. 29 May 1847. Born free and raised in AA Co. Age about 24, 5' 11", brown complexion.
Susan Harris. 4 June 1847. Born free and raised in AA Co. Age about 24, 5' 1", light complexion, mole on upper lip.
Harriett Ennis. 4 June 1847. Born free and raised in AA Co. Age about 30, 5' 1", dark complexion.
James Bowser. 8 June 1847. Born free and raised in AA Co. 5' 6 3/4".
John Green. 12 June 1847. Born free and raised in AA Co. Age about 25, light complexion, 5' 10".
Henry. 18 June 1847. DOM recorded by Samuel Wood 24 July 1824. Age about 21, 5' 5", raised in AA Co.
John Hawkins. 22 June 1847. Born free and raised in AA Co. Age about 24, 5' 4".
Sophia Johnson. DOM recorded by J. Nevitt Steele and Mary E. Murray 11 Nov. 1846. Age about 38, 5' 3", brown complexion, raised in AA Co.
William Cane. 6 July 1847. Born free and raised in AA Co. Age about 21, 5' 7", light complexion.
John Offer. 8 July 1847. Born free and raised in AA Co. Age about 22, 5' 8", dark complexion.
Hester Cager. 12 July 1847. Born free and raised in AA Co. 5' 5", light complexion.
Ann Brown. 15 July 1847. Born free and raised in AA Co. Age about 31, 5' 1 1/2", dark complexion.
Arminta Grant. 15 July 1847. Born free and raised in AA Co. Age about 21, 5' 5 1/2", dark complexion.
Elizabeth Smith. 16 July 1847. DOM recorded by Emanuel Dodds 16 July 1827. Age about 29, 5' 5 1/2", brown complexion, raised in AA Co.
Henry Green. 10 Aug. 1847. Born free and raised in AA Co. Age about 25, 5" 8 1/2", light complexion.
Susan Richardson. 25 Aug. 1847. Born free and raised in AA Co. Age about 22, 5' 4", dark complexion.
Harriett A. Richardson. 25 Aug. 1847. Born free and raised in AA Co. Age about 20, 5' 4 1/2", dark complexion.
Richard Boston. 30 Aug. 1847. Born free and raised in AA Co. Age about 21, 5' 10".
Jane Hawkins. 31 Aug. 1847. Born free and raised in AA Co. Age about 19, 5".
Charles Johnson. 3 Sept. 1847. Born free and raised in AA Co.
Margaret. 31 Oct. 1847. DOM recorded 21 June 1829. Age about 33, 5' 5 1/4", light complexion.
Ellen Hawmind. 10 Sept. 1847. Born free and raised in AA Co. 5' 4 1/4", light complexion.
Harriett Pearce. 11 Sept. 1848. Born free and raised in AA Co. Age about 25, 5' 3 1/2", light complexion.
Richard Queen. 16 Sept. 1847. Born free and raised in AA Co. Age about 23, 5' 5

1/4", dark complexion.
Issac Barnett. 16 Sept. 1847. Born free and raised in AA Co. Age about 26, 5' 9", light complexion.
Solomon Barnett. 16 Sept. 1847. Born free and raised in AA Co. Age about 28, 5' 8", light complexion.
John Henry Barnett. 16 Sept. 1847. Born free and raised in AA Co. Age about 24, 5' 9", light complexion.
Susan Brown. 16 Sept. 1847. Born free and raised in AA Co. Age about 30, 5' 4 3/4", light complexion.
Anne Queen. 27 July 1847. Born free and raised in AA Co. Age about 25, 5", brown complexion.
Charity. Undated. DOM recorded by Jacob Williams 22 April 1820. 5' 2", dark complexion.
John Holland. 17 Nov. 1847. Born free and raised in AA Co. Age about 21, 5' 10 1/2".
Mary Lokerman. 29 Nov. 1847. Born free and raised in AA Co.
Laura Williams. 29 Nov. 1847. Born free and raised in AA Co.
James Turner. 9 Dec. 1847. Born free and raised in AA Co.
Mary Johnson. 9 Dec. 1847. Born free and raised in AA Co.
Lewis Adams. DOM recorded by Nicholas Watkins 6 Dec. 1819. Age about 20, 5' 1", dark complexion, raised in AA Co.
William Phelps. 24 Dec. 1847. DOM recorded by William Brewer 23 Feb. 1847. Age about 32, 5' 5 1/2", brown complexion, raised in AA Co.
Peter Johnson. DOM recorded by Stephen Beard 6 Jan. 1820. Age about 32, 5' 8", dark complexion, raised in AA Co.[JMH1].
Charles Johnson. DOM recorded by Stephen Beard 6 Jan. 1820. Age about 32, 5' 9", dark complexion, raised in AA Co.
Calvert Harrison. 29 Jan. 1848. DOM recorded by Stephen Beard 6 Jan. 1820. Age about 30, 5' 5", dark complexion, raised in AA Co.
Gabriel Queen. 1 Feb. 1848. Born free and raised in AA Co. Age about 20, 5' 7".
John Harris. 29 Feb. 1848. Born free and raised in AA Co. 5' 3/4", dark complexion.
James Titus. 21 March 1848. Born free and raised in AA Co. Age 33, 5' 5".
Sophia Dinkins. Born free and raised in AA Co. Age about 25, 5' 3", brown complexion.
Thomas Jennings. 3 April 1848. Born free and raised in AA Co. Age about 21, 5' 9", dark complexion.
Jim Smothers. 5 April 1848. DOM recorded by James F. Wood 5 Feb. 1818.
Mary Jane Greenwood. 10 April 1848. Born free and raised in AA Co. Age about 20, 5' 6", dark complexion.
Elijah Parker. 10 April 1848. DOM recorded by Henry Maynadier 10 April 1848. Age about 17, 5' 8", dark complexion.
Joseph Parker. 10 April 1848. DOM recorded by Henry Maynadier 10 April 1848. Age about 19, 5' 8", dark complexion.
Elizabeth Briston. 12 April 1848. Born free and raised in AA Co. Age about 20, 5' 3", light complexion.
William Ross. 18 April 1848. Born free and raised in AA Co. 5' 8", brown complexion.
Thomas Ross. 18 April 1848. Born free and raised in AA Co. 5' 8", brown complexion.
Eliza Booth. 18 April 1848. Born free and raised in AA Co. Age 31, 5' 8", dark complexion.
Thomas Young. 21 April 1848. Born free and raised in AA Co. Age about 24, 5' 10", dark complexion.
Harriet Ennis. 25 April 1848. DOM recorded by Daniel C. Boston 25 April 1848. Age about 24, 5' 3', light complexion, raised in AA Co.
Edward Queen. 1 May 1848. Born free and raised in AA Co. Age about 21, 5' 9", dark complexion.
George Cager. 6 July 1848. Born free and raised in AA Co. 5' 9 1/2" dark complexion.
John Cager. 6 July 1848. Born free and raised in AA Co. 5' 6", dark complexion.
Amelia Cann. 13 July 1848. Born free and raised in AA Co. Age about 24, 5', scar on back of left hand, missing upper front teeth, dark complexion.
William West. 14 July 1848. Born free and raised in AA Co. 5' 2 1/4", dark complexion, scar on right arm.
Ann Brown. 28 July 1848. Born free and raised in AA Co. Age 22, 5' 10 1/2", dark complexion.
Rebecca Brown. 28 July 1848. Born free and raised in AA Co. Age about 20, 5' dark complexion.
Mary Turner. 18 Aug. 1848. Born free and raised in AA Co. Age about 18, 5' 5", light complexion.
Rosetta Toogood. 30 Aug. 1848. Born free and raised in AA Co. Age 22, 5' 5", chestnut complexion.
Issac Queen. 12 Sept. 1848. Born free and raised in AA Co. Age about 22, 5' 4 1/2", dark complexion.
Alice Chase. Born free and raised in AA

Co. Age about 30, 5' 2", dark complexion.
Priscilla Chase. 16 Sept. 1848. Born free and raised in AA Co. Age about 24, 4' 11", dark complexion.
Jane Toogood. 16 Sept. 1848. Born free and raised in AA Co. Age about 20, 5' 9 1/2", dark complexion.
Susan Boston. 4 Oct. 1848. Born free and raised in AA Co. Age about 24, 5' 3 1/2", chestnut complexion.
Mary Robinson. DOM recorded by Stephen Boone 17 Nov. 1815. Age about 37, 5' chestnut complexion, raised in AA Co.
Sarah Johnson. 28 June 1848. Born free and raised in AA Co. Affidavit of Samuel Gover. Age about 23, 5' 2", dark complexion.
Alexander Randall. 8 Feb. 1851. Born free and raised in AA Co. Age about 37, 5' 3 3/4", dark complexion.
Henry —. 12 Oct. 1847. Affidavit of Jacob Tolson. Born free and raised in AA Co. Age 28, 5' 3 1/2", dark complexion.
Thomas Jennings. 3 April 1848. Born free and raised in AA Co. Affidavit of Joseph Nicholson. Age 21, 5' 9".
James Smothers. 5 Jan. 1848. DOM from James T. Wood.
Mary Jane Greenwood. Born free and raised in AA Co. Affidavit of William Earle. Age about 22, 5' 6", dark complexion; certificate issued 15 April 1848.
Julia Queen. 10 Oct. 1848. Born free and raised in AA Co. Affidavit of Gerard R. Hopkins. Age 22, light complexion, 5' 3 1/2".
Mary Brown. 11 Oct. 1848. DOM recorded by Henry Basford 14 Dec. 1847. Age 32, chestnut complexion, 5' 3"; certificate issued on affidavit of Darnell Hyde.
John Matthews. 14 Oct. 1848. Born free and raised in AA Co. Age 21, light complexion, 5' 1"; certificate issued on affidavit of Richard J. Crabb.
Robert Brown. 25 Oct. 1848. Born free and raised in AA Co. Certificate issued on affidavit of Plummer I. Drury.
William Giles. 28 Oct. 1848. Born free and raised in AA Co. Certificate issued on affidavit of Samuel White.
Samuel Bell. 28 Oct. 1848. DOM recorded by Richard P. Snowden 24 Nov. 1840. 5' 8 1/4", light complexion, age 27.
Benjamin Hall. 9 Dec. 1848. Born free and raised in AA Co. Certificate issued by affidavit of Levi Hitchcock. Age 23, 5' 3 1/4, chestnut complexion.
Amelia Stewart. 18 Nov. 1848. DOM recorded by James Legg 18 Nov. 1848.

Walter Ward. 29 Nov. 1848. DOM by James Chester 29 Nov. 1848.
Julia Larkins. 19 Dec. 1848. Born free and raised in AA Co. Certificate issued upon affidavit of William Fell Clande.
Rebecca Mack. 21 Dec. 1848. Born free and raised in AA Co. Certificate issued 21 Dec. 1848 on affidavit of John Parrott.
Harriett Joice. 5 March 1849. Born free and raised in AA Co. Certificate issued 5 March 1849 on affidavit of William Brewer.
John William Wooten. 30 March 1849. Born free and raised in AA Co. Certificate issued 30 March 1849.
Charles Edward Wooten. 30 March 1849. Born free and raised in AA Co. Certificate issued 30 March 1849.
Elizabeth Jennings. 3 May 1849. Born free and raised in AA Co. Certificate issued upon affidavit of Charles A. Waters.
Walter Queen. 19 May 1849. Born free and raised in AA Co. Certificate issued upon affidavit of Dennis Wells.
Mary Matthews. 19 May 1849. Born free and raised in AA Co. Certificate issued upon affidavit of Richard J. Crabb. 4' 3", chestnut complexion, age 7.
Sarah Matthews. 19 May 1849. Born free and raised in AA Co. Certificate issued upon affidavit of Richard J. Crabb. 4' 9 1/4", very light complexion, age 12.
George Smithers. 28 June 1849. DOM recorded by Richard Brown 3 Jan. 1832. Age 35, 5' 5 1/2", dark complexion. Certificate issued on affidavit of Nicholas J. Watkins.
Nackey Brown. 6 July 1849. Born free and raised in AA Co. Certificate issued upon affidavit of Jonathon Weedon. Age about 50, 5' 2 1/2".
Jacob Semmes. 10 July 1849. Born free and raised in AA Co. Certificate issued upon affidavit of William T. Crandall. Age 23, dark complexion, 5' 8 3/4".
William Offer. 11 July 1849. Born free and raised in AA Co. Certificate issued upon affidavit of Nathaniel Chew. Age about 21, 5' 6", dark chestnut complexion, scar on left side of neck.
Susan Bulley AKA "Sook." 31 July 1849. DOM recorded by Rezin H. Snowden 16 March 1847. Certificate issued upon affidavit of John Beard. Age about 40, chestnut complexion, 4' 11".
Charlotte Gordon AKA "Charlotte." 31 July 1849. DOM recorded by Rezin H. Snowden 16 March 1847. Certificate issued upon affidavit of John Beard. Age about

40, dark complexion, 5' 1".
James Carroll. 2 Aug. 1849. Born free and raised in AA Co. Certificate issued upon affidavit of Samuel S. Hopkins. Age 23, 5' 8", black complexion.
Henry Carroll. 2 Aug. 1849. Born free and raised in AA Co. Certificate issued upon affidavit of Samuel S. Hopkins. Age 21, black complexion, 5' 6".
Thomas Perry. 7 Aug. 1849. Born free and raised in AA Co. Certificate issued upon affidavit of Joseph Cole. Age about 25, 5' 4 1/2", dark complexion.
James Henry Smothers. 10 August, 1849. DOM recorded by Emanuel Dadds 14 July 1827. James is son of Rebecca Smothers. Certificate issued upon affidavit of Thomas J. Brice. Age 21, 5' 9 1/2", chestnut complexion.
Ann Ennis. 29 August, 1849. DOM recorded by Samuel Gover. Age about 29, 5' 5 1/2".
David Queen. 21 Aug. 1849. Born free and raised in AA Co. Certificate issued upon affidavit of James C. Cromwell. Age 42, 5' 6", dark complexion.
Sarah Fleetwood. Born free and raised in AA Co. Certificate issued upon affidavit of Edwin W. Duvall. Age about 18, 5' 5 1/2" dark complexion.
Suck. 4 Sept. 1849. DOM recorded by William P. Hardesty 18 Aug. 1828. Certificate issued upon affidavit of Sarah A. Ward. Age about 37, dark complexion, 4' 11".
Hannibal Cooper. 12 Sept. 1849. DOM recorded by William Goldbourgh 7 Aug. 1832. Certificate issued upon affidavit of William Goldbourgh. Age 36, dark complexion, 6' 1".
Thomas Queen. 18 Sept. 1849. Born free and raised in AA Co. Certificate issued upon affidavit of Gerard R. Hopkins. Age 31, 5' 7 1/2, dark complexion.
William Jones. 18 Sept. 1849. Born free and raised in AA Co. Certificate issued upon affidavit of Gerard s. Hopkins. Age 30, 5' 7", light mulatto, scar on left hand.
George Holland. 23 Sept. 1849. Born free and raised in AA Co. Certificate issued upon affidavit of Louis Carr. Age 21, dark complexion, 5' 6.".
Henry Cooper. 2 Oct. 1849. DOM recorded by William T. Goldsborough 17 Jan. 1831. Certificate issued upon affidavit of Andrew Sliver. Age 33, 5' 2 1/2", dark complexion.
Thomas Matthews. DOM recorded by William Matthews 10 March 1825. Certificate issued upon affidavit of William Rawlings. 5' 11", black complexion.
George Williams. 15 Oct. 1849. Born free and raised in AA Co. Certificate issued upon affidavit of Frederick Rawlings. Age 25. 5' 8", light complexion.
Louis Hawkins. 23 Oct. 1849. Born free and raised in AA Co. Certificate issued upon affidavit of Larkin Shipley. 5' 1 1/2", light complexion.
Richard Seems. 23 Oct. 1849. Born free and raised in AA Co. Certificate issued upon affidavit of William T. Crandell. 5' 5", dark complexion.
Maria Boardley. 7 Nov. 1849. Born free and raised in AA Co. Certificate issued upon affidavit of William B. Conaway. Age 26, 5' 2", chestnut complexion.
Lucy Johnson. 7 Nov. 1849. Born free and raised in AA Co. Certificate issued upon affidavit of William B. Conaway. Age 24, 5' 5", light complexion, scar on left hand.
Nancy Butler. 13 Nov. 1849. DOM recorded by Rezin H. Snowden. Certificate issued upon affidavit of Rezin H. Snowden. Age 46, 5' 4", dark complexion.
William H. Butler. DOM recorded by Rezin H. Snowden. Certificate issued upon affidavit of Rezin H. Snowden. Age 7, 3' 10 1/2", light complexion.
Robert Carter. 24 Nov. 1849. Born free and raised in AA Co. Certificate issued upon affidavit of Samuel E. Duvall. Age 21, 5' 2 3/4", dark complexion.
Thomas Anderson. 26 Nov. 1849. DOM recorded by late Foster Maynard of Talbot County 31 Oct. 1818. Subject is identified in the deed as "Tom"; was bequeathed to the granddaughter of the testator TBF at age of 25. Age 35, 5' 8", dark complexion, scars on left arm and over right eye.
Rebecca Boston. 5 Jan. 1850. Born free and raised in AA Co. 5' 7", age 18, chestnut complexion.
Johnanna Boston. 12 Jan. 1850. Born free and raised in AA Co. 4' 7", bright mulatto.
Elias Queen. 30 Jan. 1851. Born free and raised in AA Co. 5' 11", dark complexion, age 21.
Lewis Parker. 30 Jan. 1850. DOM recorded by James Cheston and John Arminger 24 Jan. 1850. 5' 6", mulatto, age 40.
William Lane. 5 Feb. 1850. DOM recorded by Benjamin Sherbet 3 March 1849. 5' 5", mulatto, age 24.
Nicholas Bishop. 12 Jan. 1850. Born free and raised in AA Co. 5' 6 1/4", mulatto, age 22.

Jane Young. 22 Feb. 1850. Born free and raised in AA Co. 5' 1", age 23, dark complexion.
Peter Dervis. 9 March 1850. Born free and raised in AA Co. 5' 4 1/2", dark complexion, age 23.
Lucinda. Manumitted, no other information given. 5' 2", age 23, chestnut complexion.
Stephen Boston. 16 March 1850. Born free and raised in AA Co. 5' 5 1/2", age 21, dark complexion.
William Cromwell. 8 April 1850. DOM recorded by Thomas Robinson 11 March 1839. 5' 5 1/4", dark complexion. Age 41.
Thomas Simms. 16 April 1850. Born free and raised in AA Co. 5' 6 1/2", age 22, light complexion.
Phillip Ijams. 16 April 1850. DOM recorded by Martha Robinson 24 June 1815. 5' 5", dark complexion, age 25.
Margaret Brown. 29 April 1850. Born free and raised in AA Co. Age 18, 5' 1", dark complexion.
Henry Mias. 10 May 1850. Born free and raised in AA Co. Age 23, 6', bright mulatto.
Phillip Crowner. 21 May 1850. Born free and raised in AA Co. Age 25, 5' 7", scars on left wrist and upper arm, dark chestnut complexion.
William Ross Addison. 30 May 1850. DOM recorded by Walter Cross 9 May 1845. 5' 9 1/2", dark complexion, age 25.
Malvina Cager. 5 June 1850. Born free and raised in AA Co. 5' 3", chestnut complexion, age 16.
John Simms. 8 June 1850. Born free and raised in AA Co. 5' 8", chestnut complexion, age 21.
John Wesley Johnson. 8 June 1850. Born free and raised in AA Co. 5' 11", dark complexion, age 21.
William Harrison. 1 July 1850. Born free and raised in AA Co. 5' 9", dark complexion, age 22, scar on left wrist.
John Sisco. 29 June 1850. Born free and raised in AA Co. Age 21, dark complexion, 5' 7", scar on little finger left hand.
John Andrew Jackson Smothers. 13 July 1850. DOM recorded by Emmanuel Dadds 14 July 1827. Age 21, dark complexion, 5' 5".
Jane Parker. 20 July 1850. Born free and raised in AA Co. 5' 3 1/4", light complexion, age 22, scars on left wrist and right arm.
Lybia Ann Watkins. 26 July 1850. Born free and raised in AA Co. Age 22, black complexion, 5' 2", scar on forehead.

Adeline Queen. 30 July 1850. Born free and raised in AA Co. Age 17, 5' 1 1/4", bright mulatto, scar under left eye.
John Duckett. 6 Aug. 1850. DOM recorded by William Brewer 21 June 1820. Age 41, 5' 7", dark complexion, small scar on right ear.
Evan Bacon. 12 Aug. 1850. DOM recorded by Rezin Snowden 22 July 1850. 5' 10 1/2", dark complexion, age 43.
Marion Matthews. 12 Aug. 1850. Born free and raised in AA Co. 5' 8 1/2", dark complexion, age 22.
Thomas Queen. 19 Aug. 1850. DOM recorded by John Redmiles 19 Aug. 1850. Age 37, 6' dark complexion, blind in right eye, scar on right arm.
Mary Boston. 25 Aug. 1847. Born free and raised in AA Co. Age 22, dark complexion.
John Stewart. 26 Aug. 1850. Born free and raised in AA Co. 5' 6", dark complexion, age 23.
Harrietta Roles. 29 Aug. 1850. Born free and raised in AA Co. 5' 5", dark complexion, age 22, scar on right arm.
William Brown. 5 Sept. 1850. Born free and raised in AA Co. 5' 5 1/4", dark complexion, age 21.
Rebecca Allen. 5 Sept. 1850. Born free and raised in AA Co. 5' 2 3/4", age 28, dark complexion.
Thomas H. Barnett. 17 Dec. 1850. Born free and raised in AA Co. Age 25, 5' 7 3/4", light complexion, scar over left eye.
James Parker. 1 Oct. 1850. Born free and raised in AA Co. 5' 3 1/4", age 23, dark complexion.
James J. Hawkins. 4 Oct. 1850. Born free and raised in AA Co. 5' 8 1/4", age 21, dark complexion.
George T. Gibson. 4 Oct. 1850. Born free and raised in AA Co. 5' 4 1/4", age 21, bright mulatto, scars on thumb and nose.
Catherine Butler. 8 Oct. 1850. Born free and raised in AA Co. Age about 19, 5' 1 3/4", light complexion.
Milly Hawkins. DOM recorded by Rezin H. Snowden 16 March 1847. Age 35, complexion is dark, 5'. Certificate issued 21 Jan. 1851.
Edward Brown. DOM recorded by Sarah E. Murray 30 Dec. 1830. Age 22, dark complexion, 5' 7 1/2". Certificate issued 23 Aug. 1851.
Mary Cain. DOM recorded by Thomas Franklin 4 June 1851. Age 34, chestnut complexion, 4' 11".
Cornelia Tydings. DOM recorded by Henry Tydings 23 Feb. 1848. Age 21, light com-

plexion, 5' 6".
Andrew Johnson. DOM recorded by Mary Merriken 12 Jan. 1821. Age 31, 5' 8 3/4", brown complexion, scar on right arm, raised in AA Co. Certificate issued 30 Dec. 1851.
Allen Green. DOM recorded by George Whipps 22 March 1807. Age about 40, 5' 7", yellow complexion, lost left eye. Certificate issued 16 Jan. 1852.
Ellen Smith. Born free and raised in AA Co. Age about 32, 5' 5 3/4", brown complexion.
Caroline Leager. Born free and raised in AA Co. Age about 32, 5' 3 3/4", brown complexion. Certificate issued 9 March 1852.
Jacob Hinsman. Born free and raised in AA Co. Age 29, 5' 3 3/4" yellow complexion, small scar on back of right hand.
Matilda Hinsman. Born free and raised in AA Co. Age about 29, 5' 1 3/4", brown complexion. Certificate issued 13 March 1852.
Edith Merchant. DOM recorded by C. H, Stubling 15 March 1852. Age about 60, 5' 1 1/2", brown complexion, raised in AA Co.
Jim Sifton. DOM recorded by Arnelia Pinkney 15 April 1852. Age about 34, 5' 5 3/4", brown complexion, raised in AA Co.
Brice Brown. Born free and raised in AA Co. Age about 22, 5' 5 3/4", dark complexion. Certificate issued 19 April 1852.
James Davis. Born free and raised in AA Co. Age about 21, 5' 4 1/4", yellow complexion. Raised in AA Co.
Issac Burns. DOM recorded by --- Harriman, 10 April 1818. Age about 34, 5' 4 1/2", dark complexion, raised in AA Co.
William Hutton. Born free and raised in AA Co. Age about 32, 5' 4 1/2", brown complexion, small scar on forehead, raised in AA Co. Certificate issued 22 July 1852.
William Diggs. Born free and raised in AA Co. Age about 23, 5' 7", dark complexion, small scar near left corner of mouth. Certificate issued 31 Aug. 1852.
Maria Boure. Maria is the daughter of Lucretia Boure who received her freedom by decree of the Anne Arundel County Court 7 April 7, 1850. Maria is therefore free. Certificate issued 17 Sept. 1852. Age 18, 5' 2 3/4", dark complexion.
James Dixon. Born free and raised in AA Co. Age 28, 5' 8 1/2", black complexion, scar on back of right hand.
Sussanna Brown. Born free and raised in AA Co. Age about 16, 5' 3/4", black complexion, raised in AA Co.
Elias Gardner. Born free and raised in AA Co. Age about 21, 4' 8 1/2", light complexion, scar on left hand.
Priscilla General. DOM recorded by Henry General 19 Oct. 1850. Age about 42, 5' 5", dark complexion, raised in AA Co.
Daniel General. DOM recorded by Henry General 19 Oct. 1850. Age about 23, 5' 7" 1/4, black complexion, raised in AA Co. Certificate issued 16 Nov. 1832.
Charles Adams. DOM recorded by Samuel Wood 24 July 1824. Age about 24, 5' 3 3/4", dark complexion, small scar on left hand. Certificate issued 29 Nov. 1852.
John Toogood. Born free and raised in AA Co. Age about 24, 5' 5", black complexion. Certificate issued 20 Nov. 1852.
Thomas Bryan. Born free and raised in AA Co. Age about 29, 5' 3", brown complexion, scar near right eye. Certificate issued 3 Jan. 1853.
Benjamin Brown. Benjamin is the son of Henny Johnson who was freed by DOM from Henry Basford 12 Feb. 1821. He therefore, is free. Age about 26, 5' 8", dark complexion. Certificate issued 11 Jan. 1853.
Jerry Wilson. DOM recorded by Samuel Chestor 10 Dec. 1844. Age about 24, 5' 7 1/2", yellow complexion.
Benjamin Heanis. DOM recorded by George Backer 10 Jan. 1833. Age about 30, 5' 7 1/2", dark complexion raised in AA Co.
Mary Burry. DOM recorded by Lydia Garubull 15 Aug. 1835. Age about 35, 4' 7 1/2", yellow complexion, raised in AA Co. Certificate issued 7 March 1853.
Thomas Collins. Born free and raised in AA Co. Age about 25, 5' 9", yellow complexion. Certificate issued 24 March 1853.
Washington Brown. Born free and raised in AA Co. Age about 21, 5' 7 1/2", black complexion, small scar over right eye. Certificate issued 26 March 1853.
Robert Johnson. DOM recorded by Dorsey Jacob 29 Jan. 1853. Age about 34, 5' 8 3/4", black complexion, raised in AA Co. Certificate issued 29 March 1853.
Charles Lucas. Born free and raised in AA Co. Age about 23, 5' 3 3/4", dark complexion. Certificate issued 30 March 1853.
Susan Miles. Born free and raised in AA Co. Age about 18, 5' 3 3/4", dark complexion. Certificate issued 30 March 1853.
William Allen. Born free and raised in AA Co. Age about 23, 5' 7 1/4", black complexion. Certificate issued 5 April 1853.

Harry Barnes. Born free and raised in AA Co. Age about 21, 5' 4 1/2", yellow complexion. Certificate issued 16 April 1853.

Rachel Suggs. Born free and raised in AA Co. Age about 24, 4' 10 1/4, black complexion. Scar on top of right foot. Certificate issued 20 April 1853.

Dinah Sophia Diggs. Born free and raised in AA Co. Age about 19, 5' 2 1/2", dark complexion, small scar on forehead. Certificate issued 20 April 1853.

Samuel Green. Age about 23, 5' 2", dark complexion, raised in AA Co. Certificate issued 21 April 1853.

Sarah Stewart. Born free and raised in AA Co. Age about 37, 5' 2 1/4", black complexion. Small scar on back of left hand. Certificate issued 26 April 1853.

Ann Young. Born free and raised in AA Co. Age about 25, 4' 10 1/4", yellow complexion. Certificate issued 27 May 1853.

Ann Handy. DOM recorded by George W--- 27 May 1853. Age about 27, 5' 1", brown complexion, raised in AA Co. Certificate issued 27 May 1853.

James W. Pointes. DOM recorded by William Brewer and William Rawlings 4 June 1853. Age about 37, 5' 8 1/2", yellow complexion, scar on back of left hand. Certificate issued 7 June 1853.

Ann Reunardo. DOM recorded by Thomas Franklin, trustee of Mary Shaw 14 May 1852. 5' 4", yellow complexion, raised in AA Co.

Sophia Newsen. DOM recorded by Nicholas Brewer 18 Oct. 1831. Age about 37, 5' 2", dark complexion. Certificate issued 29 June 1853.

James Brody. Born free and raised in AA Co. Age about 23, 5' 4", dark complexion, small scar on back of left hand. Certificate issued 28 June 1853.

Susan Owens. Born free and raised in AA Co. Age about 19, 5' 1 1/4", bright complexion. Certificate issued 19 July 1853.

Daniel Collins. Born free and raised in AA Co. Age about 22, 5' 7 1/4", yellow complexion, scar on left forearm. Certificate issued 23 July 1853.

Catherine Collins. Born free and raised in AA Co. Age about 19, 5' 3 1/4", yellow complexion, small scar on left eyebrow. Certificate issued 23 July 1853.

Hager Smith. DOM recorded by Daniel Smith 6 July 1831. Age about 26, 5' 1 1/4", yellow complexion, small scar on left side of nose, raised in AA Co. Certificate issued 23 July 1853.

Samuel Parker. Born free and raised in AA Co. Age about 25, 5' 6", light complexion, large scar on right wrist. certificate issued 1 Aug. 1853.

Harriett Wilson. DOM recorded by Daniel Smith 6 July 1831. Age about 24, 5' 2 1/2", brown complexion. Certificate issued 6 Aug. 1853.

Joseph Queen. Born free and raised in AA Co. Age about 23, 5' 3", yellow complexion, small scar on right thumb, raised in AA Co. Certificate issued 9 August 1853.

Thomas Queen. Born free and raised in AA Co. Age about 22, 5' 1 1/4", yellow complexion, raised in AA Co. Certificate issued 9 Aug. 1853.

Ellen Brown. Born free and raised in AA Co. Age about 24, 5' 4", dark complexion. certificate issued 17 Aug. 1853.

Jane Parker. Born free and raised in AA Co. Age about 20, 5' 1", bright complexion, scar on inside of left hand. Certificate issued 30 August, 1853.

Priscilla Hobbs. Born free and raised in AA Co. Age about 19, 5' 1", brown complexion, raised in AA Co. Certificate issued 5 Sept. 1853.

Ariaima Murray. Born free and raised in AA Co. Age about 20, 5' 3 1/2." Certificate issued 16 Sept. 1853.

Rachel Young. Rachel is the daughter of Priscilla, named in DOM recorded by David Robinson 7 March 1818. Age about 33, 5' 2 1/2", black complexion, raised in AA Co. Certificate issued 27 Sept. 1853.

Mary Ann Wilkens. Born free and raised in AA Co. Age about 20, 5' 4", brown complexion, small scar on back of right hand. Certificate issued 30 Sept. 1853.

Margaret Owens. Born free and raised in AA Co. Age about 24, 5' 1 3/4", yellow complexion, small mark on upper lip. Certificate issued 13 Oct. 1853.

Eliza Ann Owens. Born free and raised in AA Co. Age about 18, 4' 10", brown complexion. Certificate issued 11 Nov. 1853.

Allen Semmes. Born free and raised in AA Co. Age about 23, 5' 10", brown complexion. Certificate issued 20 Dec. 1853.

Thomas Pinkney. Born free and raised in AA Co. Age about 22, 5' 7", black complexion, small scar on left hand. Certificate issued 20 Dec. 1853.

Robert Williams. Born free and raised in AA Co. Age about 25, 5' 2", brown complexion. Certificate issued 22 Dec. 1853.

Ellen Smith. DOM recorded by Thomas Bailey 3 March 1854. Age about 35, 5', yellow complexion, raised in AA Co.

Nicholas Jacobs. Born free and raised in

AA Co. Age about 21, 5' 5", black complexion, small scar on right wrist. Certificate issued 4 March 1854.

Mary Davis. Born free and raised in AA Co. Age about 21, 5' 1 1/2", yellow complexion. Certificate issued 3 April 1854.

Lemuel Davis. Born free and raised in AA Co. Age about 23, 5' 4", dark complexion. Certificate issued 5 April 1854.

Mary Johnson. Born free and raised in AA Co. Age about 18, 5' 1/2", black complexion. Certificate issued 11 April 1854.

George Brown. DOM recorded by John Rideout 21 Nov. 1853. Age 50, 5' 4", brown complexion, raised in AA Co.

Anna Maria Barnett. DOM recorded by Thomas Whittington 10 Feb. 1820. Age about 37, 5' 1 1/4, brown complexion, raised in AA Co. Certificate issued 17 April 1854.

Neeury Barnett. DOM recorded by Thomas Whittington 10 Feb. 1820. Age about 38, 5' 5 1/2", black complexion, raised in AA Co.

Henry Thomas. Born free and raised in AA Co. Age about 22, 5' 9 1/4", light complexion, large burn on back of right hand. Certificate issued 18 April 1854.

Edmund Franklin. Born free and raised in AA Co. Age about 24, 5' 2 3/4", dark complexion, small scar on right hand, raised in AA Co. Certificate issued 21 April 1854.

Robert Curry. Born free and raised in AA Co. Age about 26, 5' 4 1/2", dark complexion, small scar above upper lip. Certificate issued 21 April 1854.

Anna Maria Wallace. Born free and raised in AA Co. Age about 21, 5' 1 1/2", black complexion, small scar on left hand. Certificate issued 21 April 1854.

George Washington Wallace. Born free and raised in AA Co. Age about 26, 5' 8 1/2", dark complexion. Certificate issued 21 April 1854.

Edward Johnson. Born free and raised in AA Co. Age about 23, 5' 6", light complexion. Certificate issued 8 May 1854.

Lucy Barton. DOM recorded by Samuel Jones 11 May 1819. Age about 30, 5' 1 3/4", yellow complexion. Set free at age 21, raised in AA Co. Certificate issued 9 May 1854.

Rachel Ray. DOM recorded by Samuel Jones 11 May 1819. Age about 22, 5' 2 1/2", black complexion, small scar near left eye, raised in AA Co. Certificate issued 9 May 1854.

William Queen. Born free and raised in AA Co. Age about 39, 5' 7 3/4", brown complexion, small scar on upper lip. Certificate issued 19 May 1854.

Mary Queen. Born free and raised in AA Co. Age about 28, 5' 1/4", brown complexion, small scar under left jaw. Certificate issued 19 May 1854.

Mary Ann Parker. Born free and raised in AA Co. Age about 21, 5' 1 1/2, Black complexion, scar under right cheek. Certificate issued 20 May 1854.

Cecelia Parker. Born free and raised in AA Co. Age about 16, 4' 11 1/4", light black complexion, scar on right forearm. Certificate issued 20 May 1854.

Ellen Waters. Born free and raised in AA Co. Age about 21, 5' 6 3/4, black complexion. Certificate issued 23 May 1854.

Hester Waters. Born free and raised in AA Co. Age about 22, 5' 6 3/4." Certificate issued 23 May 1854.

Elizabeth Waters. Born free and raised in AA Co. Age about 28, 5' 5 1/2", brown complexion. Certificate issued 23 May 1854.

Harriett Ogle. DOM recorded by Thomas Davidson 1 Jan. 1849. Age about 43, 5' 3 1/2", dark complexion, raised in AA Co. Certificate issued 3 June 1854.

Mary Purdy. DOM recorded by Henry Hammond 11 April 1818. Age about 31, 5' 6 1/2", black complexion, scars on left breast and hand. Freedom commenced at age 30. Certificate issued 6 June 1854.

Jesse Garner. Born free and raised in AA Co. Age about 21, 5' 6", black complexion, small scar on forehead.

James Keussard. DOM recorded by Anne Gill 26 June 1850. Age about 33, 5' 9", yellow complexion, small scar on right hand, raised in AA Co. Certificate issued 29 June 1854.

Henry Williams. Born free and raised in AA Co. Age about 23, 5' 4", black complexion, scars on right forearm and corner of left eye. Certificate issued 5 July 1854.

John Henry Green. Born free and raised in AA Co. Age about 22, 5' 8 1/4", black complexion, certificate issued 8 July 1854.

Henry Warner. Born free and raised in AA Co. Age about 28, 5' 1/4", black complexion, certificate issued 17 July 1854.

William Warner. Born free and raised in AA Co. Age about 24, 5' 2 3/4", black complexion, certificate issued 17 July 1854.

Nathan Jackson. Born free and raised in AA Co. Age about 23, 5' 7 1/4", black complexion. Certificate issued 17 July

1854.
Mary Shaff_. Born free and raised in AA Co. Age about 24, 5' 2", yellow complexion. Certificate issued 17 July 1854.
Margaret Shaaff. Born free and raised in AA Co. Age about 20, 5' 3", yellow complexion. Certificate issued 17 July 1854.
Rebecca Crowner. Born free and raised in AA Co. Age about 23 5' 1", brown complexion, small scar on right forearm. Certificate issued 17 July 1854.
Lavili Louisa Maum. Born free and raised in AA Co. Age about 22, 5' 2 1/4", black complexion. Certificate issued 17 July 1854.
Hester Ann Johnson. Born free and raised in AA Co. Age about 17, 5' 1/2", brown complexion. Certificate issued 17 July 1854.
Lavale Ann Cvoiore. Born free and raised in AA Co. Age about 24, 5' 2 1/2", brown complexion, has lost sight in right eye.
William Jennings. Born free and raised in AA Co. Age about 30, 5' 6 1/2", black complexion. Certificate issued 29 July 1854.
Daniel Clarke. Born free and raised in AA Co. Age about 21, 5' 8", yellow complexion, scar under chin. Certificate issued 29 July 1854.
Hannah Ann Johnson. Freeborn and raised in AA Co. Age about 22, 5' 3 1/4", yellow complexion, small scar on each wrist. Certificate issued 29 July 1854.
Caroline Ray. Freeborn and raised in AA Co. Age about 21, 5' 5", dark complexion, face is marked by smallpox, scar on right wrist. Certificate issued 8 Aug. 1854.
Wesley Jackson. DOM recorded by William Jacobs 16 Dec. 1820. Freedom commenced at age 30. Age about 30, 5' 7 1/4", brown complexion, scars on forehead and left cheek. Is the son of Hager. Certificate issued 30 Aug. 1854.
Ann Catherine Thomas. Freeborn and raised in AA Co. Age about 19, 5' 2 1/2", brown complexion, scars on forehead and right arm. Certificate issued 6 Sept. 1854.
Priscilla Adams. Freeborn and raised in AA Co. Age about 18, 5' 3", brown complexion, scar on side of face. Certificate issued 8 Sept. 1854.
Ellen Adams. Freeborn and raised in AA Co. Age about 21, 5' 2 3/4" brown complexion, scar near corner of right eye. Certificate issued 8 Sept. 1854.
Ann Adams. Freeborn and raised in AA Co. Age about 21, 5', brown complexion, scars on right side of face and between the eyes. Certificate issued 8 Sept. 1854.
George Harden. Freeborn and raised in AA Co. Age about 25, 5' 11 1/4", brown complexion. Certificate issued 9 Sept. 1854.
Thomas Harden. Freeborn and raised in AA Co. Age about 28, 5' 9 1/4", brown complexion, small scar on forehead.
Margaret Matthews. Freeborn and raised in AA Co. Age about 29, 5' 5 1/2", brown complexion, small scar on breast. Certificate issued 9 Sept. 1854.
George Alfred Hammond. Freeborn and raised in AA Co. Age about 21, 5' 7 1/2", yellow complexion, scar in right eyebrow. Certificate issued 13 Sept. 1854.
Caroline Franklin. DOM recorded by Andrew Franklin 10 Sept. 1854. Age about 42, 5' 2 3/4", brown complexion, small scar on right corner of mouth. Certificate issued 13 Sept. 1854.
Richard Henry Parker. Freeborn and raised in AA Co. Age about 23, 4' 8 1/4", yellow complexion. Certificate issued 19 Sept. 1854.
Elizabeth Prout. Freeborn and raised in AA Co. Age about 18, 5' 5 1/4" brown complexion. Certificate issued 19 Sept. 1854.
William Green. Freeborn and raised in AA Co. Age about 21, 5' 11", black complexion. Certificate issued 21 Sept. 1854.
Betsy Wright. Freeborn and raised in AA Co. Age about 21, 4' 11", brown complexion, scar on neck. Certificate issued 22 Sept. 1854.
Caroline Jones. DOM recorded by William Disney Sr. 21 Aug. 1854. Age about 30, 5' 8 1/2, dark complexion. Raised in AA Co. Certificate issued 26 Sept. 1854.
Mary Harrwood. DOM recorded by William Brewer 28 Jan. 1854. Age about 27, 5' 1 3/4, brown complexion. Raised in AA Co. Certificate issued 11 Oct. 1854.
Matthew Turner. DOM recorded by Thomas Roberison 11 March 1839. Age about 42, 5' 6 1/4", dark complexion, scar on left hand, raised in AA Co. Certificate issued 24 Oct. 1854.
Alexander Harwood. Freeborn and raised in AA Co. Age about 24, 5' 5 1/2", brown complexion, Certificate issued 26 Oct. 1854.
Elizabeth Guy. Freeborn and raised in AA Co. Age about 18, 5' 5 1/2", small scar on left thumb, brown complexion. Certificate issued 1 Nov. 1854.
Charles Gibson. DOM recorded by Thomas Benson 4 Oct. 1854. Age about 36, 5' 5 3/4", black complexion, scar over right

eye, raised in AA Co.
Thomas Leager. Freeborn and raised in AA Co. Age about 27, 5' 7 3/4", brown complexion, two small scars on forehead. Certificate issued 7 Nov. 1854.
Charles Matthews. Freeborn and raised in AA Co. Age about 22, 5' 8 3/4", brown complexion, scar on first finger right hand. Certificate issued 8 Nov. 1854.
John Johnson. Freeborn and raised in AA Co. Age about 25, 5' 6", brown complexion, scar on right side of face.
Eliza Jackson. DOM recorded by William Shipley 9 Nov. 1854. Age about 26, 4' 11 3/4", black complexion, raised in AA Co. Certificate issued 9 Nov. 1854.
Jane Bulter (Butler ?). Freeborn and raised in AA Co. Age about 19, 5' 2 1/4", yellow complexion. Certificate issued 21 Nov. 1854.
Sally Woodward. Freeborn and raised in AA Co. Age about 35, 5' 4", light complexion, Certificate issued 12 Dec. 1854.
Margaret Ann Woodward. Freeborn and raised in AA Co. Age about 29, 5' 4 1/4", light complexion. Certificate issued 12, Dec. 1854.
Jacob Brown. Freedom granted by AA Co. Court during April term 1850. Jacob is the son of Lucretia Bowie, Age 21, 5' 4 1/2", black complexion. Raised in AA Co. Certificate issued 24 Dec. 1854.
Caroline Bowie. Freedom granted by AA Co. Court during April term 1850. Caroline is the daughter of Lucretia Bowie. Age about 16, 5' 3 1/2", dark complexion. Raised in AA Co. Certificate issued 27 Dec. 1854.
Christopher Grinage. DOM recorded by Jesse Grinage 2 Jan. 1854. Age about 24, 5' 8 1/4", black complexion scar on left breast. Certificate issued 2 Jan. 1855.
Rebecca Gassaway. Freeborn and raised in AA Co. Age about 20, 4' 11", brown complexion, small scar under each eye. Certificate issued 11 Jan. 1855.
Moses Gassaway. Freeborn and raised in AA Co. Age about 28, 5' 5 3/4", brown complexion. Certificate issued 11 Jan. 1855.
London Gassaway. Freeborn and raised in AA Co. Age about 22, 5' 9 1/4", black complexion, small scar on nose.
Perry Gassaway. Freeborn and raised in AA Co. Age about 20, 5' 5 1/2", brown complexion. Certificate issued 12 Jan. 1855.
Mary Gassaway. Freeborn and raised in AA Co. Age about 18, 5' 3 1/2" brown complexion. Certificate issued 15 Jan. 1855.
Mary Eliza Parker. Freeborn and raised in AA Co. Age about 46, 5' 4", brown complexion, small scar on right wrist. Certificate issued 17 Jan. 1855.
Thomas Ogle. DOM recorded by Amelia Linthicum 13 Nov. 1854. Age about 43, 5' 8 1/2", black complexion, scar on right hand, raised in AA Co. Certificate issued 17 Jan. 1855.
Mary Jane Brice. DOM recorded by Richard C. MacKubin 18 Jan. 1855. Age about 37, 5' 2 1/2", yellow complexion, raised in AA Co. Certificate issued 19 Jan. 1855.
Eliza Lomax. Freedom received by petition to AA Co. Circuit Court Feb. 1854. Age about 28, 5' 3", yellow complexion, scars on back of right hand and middle finger of left hand, raised in AA Co. Certificate issued 23 Jan. 1855.
James Queen. Born free and raised in AA Co. Age about 21, 5' 7", yellow complexion, long straight hair. Certificate issued 28 Feb. 1855.
William Lane. DOM recorded by Benjamin Sherbet 20 March 1849. Former certificate issued 5 Feb. 1850. Age about 29, 5' 5", yellow complexion, raised in AA Co.
Charles Wright. Freeborn and raised in AA Co. Age about 28, 5' 10 3/4", yellow complexion, scar on right arm. Certificate issued 17 April 1855.
Frank Wallace. Freeborn and raised in AA Co. Age about 23, 5' 8 3/4", dark complexion, small scar near right eye. Certificate issued 17 April 1855.
Richard Gibson. Freeborn and raised in AA Co. Age about 27, 5' 6 1/2", dark complexion, scar over left eye. Certificate issued 18 April 1855.
William Henry Gardner. Freeborn and raised in AA Co. Age about 22, 5' 8 1/2", light complexion, small scar on left arm. Certificate issued 18 April 1855.
Thomas Robinson. Freeborn and raised in AA Co. Age 22, 5' 7 1/2", bright black complexion, small scar on forehead. certificate issued 20 April 1855.
Sophia Hall. DOM recorded by Washington G. Luell 2 April 1811. Age about 43, 5' 2 1/2", dark complexion, small scar on right arm, raised in AA Co. Certificate issued 9 May 1855.
Susan Brown. Born free and raised in AA Co. Certificate issued 22 May 1855. Age about 18, 4' 10 1/2", black complexion.
Stephen Gray. Born free and raised in AA Co. Certificate issued 28 May 1855. Age

about 27, 5' 7 3/4", black complexion.
Samuel Hammond. Born free and raised in AA Co. Certificate issued 17 June 1855. Age about 21, 5' 5", yellow complexion, small scar on left thumb, mole on left eyebrow.
Elizabeth Ellen Matthews. Born free and raised in AA Co. Certificate issued 13 July 1855. Age about 18, 5' 3 1/4", light complexion, small scar under right eye, raised in AA Co.
Ellen Matthews. Born free and raised in AA Co. Certificate issued 13 July 1855. Age about 43, 5' 5 1/2", light complexion, small scars across the nose and on the right arm.
Martha Eliza Jacobs. Born free and raised in AA Co. Certificate issued 10 Aug. 1855. Age about 21, 5', brown complexion, scar on left arm.
Alexander Dennis. Born free and raised in AA Co. Certificate issued 18 Aug. 1855. Age about 22, 5' 1/4" yellow complexion, small scar on back of right hand.
Richard Holland. Born free and raised in AA Co. Certificate issued 18 Aug. 1855. Age about 24, 5' 8 1/4", black complexion, raised in AA Co. Has small scar on forefinger of left hand.
Daniel Brown. Born free and raised in AA Co. Certificate issued 27 Aug. 1855. Age about 23, 5' 6 1/4", brown complexion, small scar on forefinger of left hand.
— Phelps. DOM filed by Nicholas J--- 3 Sept. 1855. Age about 39, 5' 3 1/2", yellow complexion, raised in AA Co. Certificate issued 5 Sept. 1855.
Soleri Burlie. DOM recorded by Eleanor Cowley 17 Sept. 1829. Deed provoded for freedom at age 21. Age is 21, 5' 7", light complexion, small scar under tight eye, raised in AA Co. Certificate issued 22 Oct. 1855.
Elias Williams. Born free and raised in AA Co. Certificate issued 17 Nov. 1855. Age about 22, 5' 7", black complexion. Certificate issued 17 Nov. 1855.
M— Alsop. DOM recorded by William Lomax 22 Dec. 1855. Certificate issued 22 Dec. 1855. Age about 25, 5' 3/4", yellow complexion, small mole on upper lip, raised in AA Co.
Richard Chambers. Born free and raised in AA Co. Certificate issued 13 Jan. 1856. Age about 23, 5' 4 3/4", dark complexion, has a deformed leg.
George W. Matthews. Born free and raised in AA Co. Certificate issued 3 March 1856. Age 21, 5' 10", brown complexion, scar on right leg below the knee.
Maria Smothers. Born free and raised in AA Co. Certificate issued 3 April 1856. Age about 19, 5' 3", brown complexion, small scar on lower lip.
Eliza Jane Gross. DOM recorded by Stephen Beard 10 May 1856. Certificate issued 22 April 1856. Age about 33, 4' 11", dark complexion, raised in AA Co.
Mary Eliza Snowden. Born free and raised in AA Co. Certificate issued 23 April 1856. Age about 19, 5' 4 1/4", brown complexion, scar under right eye.
William Fleetwood. Born free and raised in AA Co. Certificate issued 25 April 1856. Age about 22, 5' 7 1/4", black complexion.
Elizabeth S—. DOM recorded by Thomas Burley 3 March 1854. Age about 18, 4' 2", bright complexion, raised in AA Co.
— Stepney. Child of negro Charity, who (Charity) was manumitted by Stephen Boone 17 Nov. 1815. DOM provided that issue of Charity would be free at age 35. Age is 44, 5' 4 1/4" black complexion. Raised in AA Co. Certificate issued 19 May 1856.
Robert Stepney. Child of negro Charity, who (Charity) was manumitted by Stephen Boone 17 Nov. 1815. DOM provided that issue of Charity would be free at age 35. Age 41, 5' 11", black complexion, scar on left side of face.
Eliza Ann Stepney. Child of negro Charity, who (Charity) was manumitted by Stephen Boone 17 Nov. 1815. DOM provided that issue of Charity would be free at age 35. Age about 39, 4' 11 1/4", black complexion, scar on chin. Certificate issued 19 May 1856.
William Stepney. Child of negro Charity, who (Charity) was manumitted by Stephen Boone 17 Nov. 1815. DOM provided that issue of Charity would be free at age 35. Age about 37, 5' 7", black complexion, scar on forehead, raised in AA Co. Certificate issued 19 May 1856.
Hillery Calvert. Born free and raised in AA Co. Certificate issued 20 May 1856. Age 24, 5' 2", dark complexion, scar on left corner of mouth.
Isiah Lee. Born free and raised in AA Co. Certificate issued 20 May 1856. Age about 23, 5' 3", black complexion, scar on left side of neck.
Priscilla Boone. Born free and raised in AA Co. Certificate issued 29 May 1856. Age about 21, 5' 3/4", brown complexion, large burn scar on right arm.
Margaret Johnson. Born free and raised in

AA Co. Certificate issued 27 May 1856. Age about 24, 5' 11", yellow complexion, small scar on back of left hand.
James Stewart. Born free and raised in AA Co. Certificate issued 31 May 1856. Age about 22, 5' 6 1/2", black complexion.
Sidney S—. Born free and raised in AA Co. Certificate issued 14 June 1856. Age about 20, 5' 1", brown complexion, scar on right arm.
Harriett Stepney. DOM recorded by Sophia W. Brice 29 May 1856. Certificate issued 29 May 1856. Age about 33, 5" 1 1/2", black complexion, scar on right arm, raised in AA Co.
Julia Hammond. Born free and raised in AA Co. Certificate issued 21 June 1856. Age about 23, 5' 4 1/2", yellow complexion, scar on left wrist.
Richard Weston. Freeborn and raised in AA Co. Certificate issued 12 July 1856. Age about 23, 5' 8", black complexion, scars on left and right hands.
Sarah Ann Rutland. Freeborn and raised in AA Co. Age about 18, 4' 10", dark complexion. Certificate issued 16 July 1856.
Benjamin Parker. Freeborn and raised in AA Co. Age about 23, 5' 4 1/2", small scar on forehead. Certificate issued 19 July 1856. Original certificate granted 11 Nov. 1840. This issue replaces lost original.
Levi Johnson. Freeborn and raised in AA Co. Age 25, 5' 8", brown complexion. Certificate issued 5 Aug. 1856.
Nathan James. Freeborn and raised in AA Co. Age about 34, 5' 4", dark complexion, scar on forehead. Certificate issued 12 Aug. 1856.
Margaret Ann James. Freeborn and raised in AA Co. Certificate issued 12 Aug. 1856. Age about 19, 5' 1", black complexion.
Emmaline James. Freeborn and raised in AA Co. Age about 17, 4' 11", brown complexion, small scar on forehead. Certificate issued 12 Aug. 1856.
Rachel Thompson. DOM recorded by Amelia M. Disney 21 May 1850. Raised in AA Co. Age about 42, 5' 9", brown complexion. Certificate issude 12 Aug. 1856.
Stephen Queen. Freeborn and raised in AA Co. Age about 43, 5' 5 1/4", brown complexion, small scar on right forefinger. Certificate issued 2 Sept. 1856.
Mary Jane Queen. Freeborn and raised in AA Co. Certificate issued 2 Sept. 1856. Age about 30, 5' 4 1/2", brown complexion.
Susan Queen. Freeborn and raised in AA Co. Certificate issued 2 Sept. 1856. Age about 32, 4' 11", brown complexion, small scar on right side of face.
Celena Sanders. Freeborn and raised in AA Co. Age about 31, 5' 2 1/4", yellow complexion. Certificate issued 4 Sept. 1856.
Issac Clarke. Freeborn and raised in AA Co. Certificate issued 8 Sept. 1856. Age about 22, 5' 4 1/4", black complexion, small scar on right arm.
Lucinda Clarke. Freeborn and raised in AA Co. Certificate issued 8 Sept. 1856. Age about 17, 5' 1 3/4", black complexion, scar on left thumb.
Benjamin Snowden. Freeborn and raised in AA Co. Certificate issued 8 Sept. 1856. Age about 21, 5' 5", brown complexion, large scar on right arm and hand (burn).
Elizabeth West. Freeborn and raised in AA Co. Certificate issued 12 Sept. 1856. Age about 28, 5' 1/2", black complexion, small scar on neck.
Isiaah Hammond. Freeborn and raised in AA Co. Certificate issued 18 Oct. 1856. Age about 21, 5' 4 3/4", black complexion, burn scar on left wrist.
Richard P. Bell. DOM recorded by Richard P. Snowden 24 Nov. 1840. Raised in AA Co. Age about 30, 5' 7", yellow complexion. Certificate issued 14 Oct. 1856.
Cyrus Bell. DOM recorded by Richard P. Snowden 24 Nov. 1840. Raised in AA Co. Age about 28, 5' 7", brown complexion, small scar on forehead. Certificate issued 24 Oct. 1856.
George W. Bell. DOM recorded by Richard P. Snowden 24 Nov. 1840. Raised in AA Co. Certificate issued 24 Oct. 1856. Age about 32, 5' 7 1/4", brown complexion, deformed little finger on left hand.
Mary Ann Bell. DOM recorded by Richard P. Snowden 24 Nov. 1840. Raised in AA Co. Age about 23, 5' 1", brown complexion, scar on forehead. Certificate issued 24 Oct. 1856.
Molly Ann Ennis. Freeborn and raised in AA Co. Certificate issued 1 Nov. 1856. Age about 21, 5' 1 1/4", dark complexion.
Mary Ann Dorsey. Freeborn and raised in AA Co. Certificate issued 8 Nov. 1856. Age about 33, 5' 11", brown complexion.
Charles Howard. Freeborn and raised in AA Co. Certificate issued 8 Nov. 1856. Age about 31, 5' 5 1/2", brown complexion.
William Henry Howard. Freeborn and raised in AA Co. Certificate issued 8 Nov. 1856. Age about 27, 5' 7 1/4".
Peter Howard. Freeborn and raised in AA

Co. Certificate issued 8 Nov. 1856. Age about 24, 5' 3 1/4", brown complexion.
Eliza Paul. DOM recorded by A. Randall 27 Dec. 1854. Raised in AA Co. Age about 29, 5' 4 1/2", yellow complexion. Certificate issued 13 Nov. 1856.
Memca Queen. Freeborn and raised in AA Co. Certificate issued 27 Nov. 1856. Age about 42, 5' 12", yellow complexion.
Maria Boston. DOM recorded by Charles Munroe 9 Oct. 1829. Certificate issued 1 Dec. 1856. Raised in AA Co. Age about 31, 5', yellow complexion, small scar on nose.
Stephen Court. DOM recorded by Eleanor Corby 17 Sept. 1829. Certificate issued Dec. 1856. Raised in AA Co. Age about 22, 5' 7 1/2", yellow complexion, mark of right side of neck. Stephen is one of the issue of "Marr" who was manumitted by Corby.
Henry Anderson. Freeborn and raised in AA Co. Certificate issued 22 Dec. 1856. Age about 27, 5' 4 1/2", black complexion.
Phoebe Ann Spencer. DOM recorded by John Maynard 5 Feb. 1857. Certificate issued 5 Feb. 1857. Age about 25, 5' 2", yellow complexion, raised in AA Co.
John Nicholas Hart. Freeborn and raised in AA Co. Certificate issued 20 Feb. 1857. Age about 23, 5' 11 1/2", yellow complexion, small scars on chin and back of left hand.
Cerissy Neale. Freeborn and raised in AA Co. Certificate issued 21 Feb. 1857. Age about 37, 5' 5." yellow complexion, several small marks on face.
Eleanor Ann Kersey. DOM recorded by Joseph McClean 17 March 1857. Certificate issued 28 March 1857. Age about 30, 4' 11", yellow complexion, raised in AA Co.
Margaret Ann Downs. Daughter of Hannah,, the latter being manumitted by Henry C. Drury. DOM 22 Feb. 1822. The deed provided that the issue of Hannah were to be free at age of 18. Age about 24, 5' 5 3/4", dark complexion, small scar near right wrist. Certificate issued 22 April 1857.
Mary Jane Cleen. Daughter of Hannah, the latter being manumitted by Henry C. Drury. DOM 22 Feb. 1822. The deed provided that the issue of Hannah were to be free at age of 18. Age about 22, 5' 5 3/4", brown complexion, small scar on right wrist, Certificate issued 22 April 1857.
Samuel Turner. Freeborn and raised in AA Co. Certificate issued 29 April 1857. Age about 25, 5' 4 1/2", dark complexion. Certificate issued 29 April 1857.
Thomas Warfield. DOM recorded by Thomas Burley 3 March 1854. Certificate issued 9 May 1857. Age about 22, 5' 4", yellow complexion, small scar on back of right hand.
Thomas H. Ward. Freeborn and raised in AA Co. Certificate issued 13 May 1857. Age about 26, 5' 9 1/2", yellow complexion, raised in AA Co.
William Brashear. DOM recorded by William Brashear 16 Aug. 1856. Certificate issued 14 May 1857. Age about 27, 5' 2 3/4", black complexion, raised in AA Co.
Augusta Tyler. Freeborn and raised in AA Co. Certificate issued 2 June 1857. Age about 21, 5' 8", yellow complexion.
Thomas William Henry Johnson. DOM recorded by John --- Philip 13 June 1857. Age about 2_, 5' 6 1/2", brown complexion, scars on right cheek and back of left hand, raised in AA Co.
Junas Davis. DOM recorded by Thomas Robinson 11 March 1857. Age about 42, 5' 3 1/2", brown complexion, raised in AA Co.
Elizabeth Shorter. Freeborn and raised in AA Co. Certificate issued 7 July 1857. Age about 27, 5' 1/2", yellow complexion.
Lucy Williams. Freeborn and raised in AA Co. Certificate issued 1 Aug. 1857. Age about 30, 4' 10 1/2", brown complexion, small scar on back of left hand.
Henrietta Welch. Freeborn and raised in AA Co. Certificate issued 1 Aug. 1857. Age about 37, 5' 1 1/2", brown complexion, scar on left arm.
Julia Johnson. DOM recorded by Lucy Harwood 17 March 1827. Certificate issued 24 Aug. 1857. Age about 38, 5', brown complexion, small scar on back of left hand.
Nack Edwards. DOM executed by Lydia Gambrill 15 Aug. 1835. Certificate issued 24 Aug., 1857. Age about 37, 5' 3 1/2", brown complexion, scar on chin, raised in AA Co.
Dennis Rawlings. DOM recorded by Ann Stewart 2 March 1808 to Nelly. Subject is issue of Nelly. Age about 32, 5' 1 3/4", black complexion lump on left side of forehead, raised in AA Co. Certificate issued 11 Sept. 1857.
William Rawlings. DOM recorded by Ann Stewart 2 March 1808 to Nelly. Subject is issue of Nelly. Age about 30, 5' 7 1/2", black complexion, small scar on forehead,

raised in AA Co. Certificate issued 11 Sept. 1857.
Eleanora Green. Freeborn and raised in AA Co. Certificate issued 16 Sept. 1857. Age about 19, 5' 1 1/4", yellow complexion, small scar on left eyebrow, raised in AA Co.
Catherine Richardson. Freeborn and raised in AA Co. Certificate issued 23 Sept. 1857. Age about 16, 4' 9 1/2", yellow complexion, scarred knuckle on middle finger of right hand.
Mary Jane Garrett. Freeborn and raised in AA Co. Certificate issued 24 Sept. 1857. Age about 28, 5' 3 1/2", brown complexion, small scar on left wrist, raised in AA Co.
Nicholas Johnson. Freeborn and raised in AA Co. Certificate issued 7 Oct. 1857. Age about 21, 5' 7 1/2", dark brown complexion.
Lavinia Brashears. Freeborn and raised in AA Co. Certificate issued 9 Oct. 1857. Age about 20, light complexion.
John Addison. Freeborn and raised in AA Co. Certificate issued 9 Oct. 1857. Age about 22, 5' 7 1/2", brown complexion.
Franklin Buchanan. Freeborn and raised in AA Co. Certificate issued 12 Oct. 1857. Age about 21, 5' 4 1/2", dark complexion, small mole near corner of mouth.
Juner Simmes. Freeborn and raised in AA Co. Certificate issued 13 Oct. 1857. Age about 25, 5' 7", black complexion.
Ellen Simmes (Semins ?). Freeborn and raised in AA Co. Certificate issued 13 Oct. 1857. Age about 20, 5' 2 1/2", brown complexion.
John Henry Hammond. Freeborn and raised in AA Co. Certificate issued 13 Oct. 1857, Age about 19, 5' 7 1/2", dark complexion.
Maria Wings. Freeborn and raised in AA Co. Certificate issued 13 Oct. 1857. Age about 20, 5' 4", brown complexion.
Nachel Gaskins. Freeborn and raised in AA Co. Certificate issued 20 Oct. 1857. Age about 24, 5', yellow complexion.
Hester Ann Brown. Freeborn and raised in AA Co. Certificate issued 24 Oct. 1857. Age about 24, 4' brown complexion, raised in AA Co.
Letty Brown. Freeborn and raised in AA Co. Certificate issued 27 Oct. 1857. Age about 26, 5' 3 1/4", brown complexion, scar on right cheek, raised in AA Co.
Samuel Calvert. Freeborn and raised in AA Co. Certificate issued 27 Oct. 1857. Age about 23, 5' 6 1/4", dark complexion, small scars left of lip and over left eye.
Samuel Williams. Freeborn and raised in AA Co. Certificate issued 27 Oct. 1857. Age about 21, 5' 3 1/2", black complexion.
Eliza Toogood. DOM recorded by Lydia Gambrill 7 July 1837. Certificate issued 31 Oct. 1857. Age about 35, 5' 2", yellow complexion, small scar on little finger of left hand, raised in AA Co.
Kelson Cammel. DOM recorded by Amelia Goit 14 Oct. 1857. Age about 38, 5' 7 1/4", dark complexion, raised in AA Co. Certificate issued 7 Nov. 1857.
Eliza Peterson. Freeborn and raised in AA Co. Certificate issued 10 Nov. 1857. Age about 46, 5' 1 1/4", dark complexion.
— Loury. DOM recorded by Charles Waters 21 March 1842. Certificate issued 24 Nov. 1857. Age about 40, 5' 1 3/4", dark complexion, raised in AA Co.
Elizabeth Pinkney. Freeborn and raised in AA Co. Certificate issued 8 Dec. 1857. Age about 23, 5' 2", brown complexion, scar on right side of face.
Catherine Pinkney. Freeborn and raised in AA Co. Certificate issued 8 Dec. 1857. Age about 20, 5' 4", brown complexion.
Margaret Pinkney. Freeborn and raised in AA Co. Certificate issued 8 Dec. 1857. Age about 18, 5' 3 1/2", brown complexion, small scar on back of right hand.
John S. Pinkney. Freeborn and raised in AA Co. Certificate issued 15 Dec. 1857. Age about 21, 4' 5", brown complexion.
Linden Pinkney. Freeborn and raised in AA Co. Certificate issued 23 Dec. 1857. Age about 22, 5' 6 1/2", dark complexion.
Richard Pearman. Freeborn and raised in AA Co. Certificate issued 12 Jan. 1858. Age about 21, 5' 6 1/2", dark complexion.
Isabella Harris. Freeborn and raised in AA Co. Certificate issued 13 Jan. 1858. Age about 26, 5' 2 1/2", brown complexion.
Catherine Turner. Freeborn and raised in AA Co. Certificate issued 13 Jan. 1858. Age about 20, 5' 1 1/2", yellow complexion.
Levinia Smothers. Freeborn and raised in AA Co. Certificate issued 13 Jan. 1858. Age about 19, 5' 4", black complexion.
Robert Washington. Freeborn and raised in AA Co. Certificate issued 13 Jan. 1858. Age about 38, 5' 7 1/2", brown complexion.
Thomas Crowner. Freeborn and raised in AA Co. Certificate issued 28 Jan. 1858. Age about 22, 5' 4 1/2", black complexion.
William Williams. Freeborn and raised in AA Co. Certificate issued 23 Feb. 1858.

Age about 34, 5' 9 3/4", yellow complexion.
Millie Calvert. DOM recorded by Jemima Seavall 26 Nov. 1830. Certificate issued 23 Feb. 1858. Age about 32, 5' 3", yellow complexion, small scar over right eyebrow, raised in AA Co.
Cesar Hindman. Freeborn and raised in AA Co. Certificate issued 23 Feb. 1858. Age about 25, 5' 5", yellow complexion, scar on left cheek.
Hester Wright. Freeborn and raised in AA Co. Certificate issued 23 Feb. 1858. Age about 32, 5', brown complexion.
Ellen Barnes. Freeborn and raised in AA Co. Certificate issued 23 Feb. 1858. Age about 22, 5' 1", black complexion.
Lewis Maynard. Freeborn and raised in AA Co. Certificate issued 23 Feb. 1858. Age about 25, 5' 3", brown complexion.
Benjamin Fleetwood. Son of Jenny, manumitted by Jimina Duvall 13 Jan. 1857. DOM provided that issue would be free at age 31. Benjamins age is 33, 5' 9", black complexion, raised in AA Co. Certificate issued 1 March 1858.
Elizabeth Butler. Freeborn and raised in AA Co. Certificate issued 2 March 1858. Age about 20, 5' 3/4", yellow complexion.
Sally Queen. Freeborn and raised in AA Co. Certificate issued 2 March 1858. Age about 19, 5' 11", brown complexion.
Elizabeth Wright. Freeborn and raised in AA Co. Certificate issued 4 March 1858. Age age about 22, 4' 11", brown complexion.
Rachel Wright. Freeborn and raised in AA Co. Certificate issued 4 March 1858. Age about 20, 5', brown complexion.
Robert Acquar. Freeborn and raised in AA Co. Certificate issued 4 March 1858. Age about 24, 5' 11", black complexion.
John Acquar. Freeborn and raised in AA Co. Certificate issued 4 March 1858. Age about 18, 5' 9 1/4", brown complexion, scar on left cheek.
Cinderella Ann Jennings. Freeborn and raised in AA Co. Certificate issued 6 March 1858. Age about 21, 5' 8 3/4", dark complexion.
John Henry Jennings. Freeborn and raised in AA Co. Certificate issued 6 March 1858. Age about 21, 5' 8 3/4", dark complexion.
George Garrett. Freeborn and raised in AA Co. Certificate issued 16 March 1858. Age about 21, 5' 4 1/2", brown complexion, large scar on forehead.
Eb Hawkins. Freeborn and raised in AA Co. Certificate issued 27 March 1858. Age about 21, 5' 9 3/4", black complexion.
Charlotte Gaither. Freeborn and raised in AA Co. Certificate issued 27 March 1858. Age about 26, 5' 1 3/4", brown complexion.
Ann Hawkins. Freeborn and raised in AA Co. Certificate issued 27 March 1858. Age anout 24, 5' 4 3/4", brown complexion.
Maria Hawkins. Freeborn and raised in AA Co. Certificate issued 27 March 1858. Age about 19, 5' 4 1/2", brown complexion.
Charity Queen. Freeborn and raised in AA Co. Certificate issued 27 March 1858. Age about 23, 5' 6", yellow complexion.
William G—. Freeborn and raised in AA Co. Certificate issued 5 April 1858. Age about 22, 5' 7", light complexion small scar on chin.
Sarah Ann Lee. Freeborn and raised in AA Co. Certificate issued 7 April 1858. Age about 20, 4' 11 1/2", dark complexion, small scar on each hand.
Charity Scott. DOM recorded by Stephen Beard 5 June 1833. Certificate issued 15 April 1858. Age about 35, 5' 2 1/4", brown complexion, raised in AA Co.
Solomon Hall. DOM recorded by Stephen Beard 26 Jan. 1820. Certificate issued 15 April 1858. Age about 30, 5' 9 1/4", black complexion, scar over right eye, scar on first finger left hand, raised in AA Co. Solomon Hall is issue of Judy, the subject of the. DOM.
Nellie Hall. Issue of Judy, who was manumitted by. DOM recorded by Stephen Beard 26 Jan. 1820. Certificate issued 15 April 1858. Age about 30, 5' 3 1/4", brown complexion, small scar on back of left wrist, raised in AA Co.
Jane Kelly. Freeborn and raised in AA Co. Age about 22, 5' 1/4", dark complexion, deformed left ear. Certificate issued 26 May 1858.
Henrietta Kelly. Freeborn and raised in AA Co. Certificate issued 26 May 1858. Age about 18, 5' 2 3/4", dark complexion.
Abby Kelly. Freeborn and raised in AA Co. Certificate issued 26 May 1858. Age about 20, 5' 1/2", dark complexion.
Sarah Ann Kelly. Freeborn and raised in AA Co. Certificate issued 26 May 1858. Age about 15, 5' 2", dark complexion.
Edward Ringold. Freeborn and raised in AA Co. Certificate issued 27 May 1858. Age about 21, 5' 8 1/4", dark complexion, missing first finger of left hand, large mark on left side of face.
Emily Ringold. Freeborn and raised in AA

Co. Certificate issued 27 May 1858. Age about 24, 5' 1/4", brown complexion, scar on back of right hand.
Frana Ann Franklin. DOM recorded by --- Ridgely 6 April 1836. Certificate issued 12 July 1858. Age about 33, 5' 5", dark complexion.
Eliza Ann Suggs. Freeborn and raised in AA Co. Certificate issued 5 Aug. 1858. Age 28, 5' 3 1/2", brown complexion.
Emeline Diggs. Freeborn and raised in AA Co. Certificate issued 5 Aug. 1858. Age about 29, 5' 3", brown complexion, scar on left side of neck.
Debra Ann Diggs. Freeborn and raised in AA Co. Certificate issued 5 April 1858. Age about 19, 4' 11", brown complexion.
John Henry Diggs. Freeborn and raised in AA Co. Certificate issued 5 Aug. 1858. Age about 24, 5' 6", brown complexion, little finger on left hand is deformed.
Margaret Isabelle Diggs. Freeborn and raised in AA Co. Certificate issued 5 Aug. 1858. Age about 17, 5' 1/4", brown complexion.
Sarah Rose. Freeborn and raised in AA Co. Certificate issued 21 Aug. 1858. Age about 25, 5' 1 3/4", brown complexion, two scars on left side of face.
Mary Jane Boston. Freeborn and raised in AA Co. Certificate issued 21 Aug. 1858. Age about 23, 4' 11", yellow complexion.
Robert Hearnwood. DOM recorded by Wm. G. Lorton 30 Aug., 1858. Certificate issued 30 Aug. 1858. Age about 28, 5' 5", dark complexion, raised in AA Co.
Rebecca Edwards. Freeborn and raised in AA Co. Certificate issued 31 Aug. 1858. Age about 28, 5' 3/4", dark complexion.
John Hawkins. Freeborn and raised in AA Co. Certificate issued 4 Sept. 1858. Age about 21, 4' 1", brown complexion, small scar on back of right hand.
Nicholas Butler. Freeborn and raised in AA Co. Certificate issued 4 Sept. 1858. Age about 39, 5' 7 3/4", brown complexion, small scar on right wrist.
Gabriel Sewell. Freeborn and raised in AA Co. Certificate issued 4 Sept. 1858. Age about 22, 5' 9", yellow complexion.
Jane Snowden. Freeborn and raised in AA Co. Certificate issued 4 Sept. 1858. Age about 27, 5' 5 1/4", black complexion.
Elias Queen. Freeborn and raised in AA Co. Certificate issued 7 Sept. 1858. Age about 21, 5' 7", yellow complexion, small scar near right eyebrow.
Mary Rebecca Gassaway. Freeborn and raised in AA Co. Certificate issued 21

Sept., 1858. Age about 25, 5' 1 1/4", yellow complexion.
Mary Ann Richardson. Freeborn and raised in AA Co. Certificate issued 4 Oct. 1858. Age about 25, 5' 3", black complexion, small scar on back of right hand.
Francis Ann Kelly. Freeborn and raised in AA Co. Certificate issued 4 Oct. 1858. Age about 25, 5' 1 1/2", brown complexion.
Sarah Ann Gray. Freeborn and raised in AA Co. Certificate issued 4 Oct. 1858. Age about 19, 4' 11", brown complexion, scar on right arm, small mole on face.
Emily Smothers. Freeborn and raised in AA Co. Certificate issued 5 Oct. 1858. Age about 20, 5' 3", brown complexion, small scar on left thumb.
James Henry Lee. Freeborn and raised in AA Co. Certificate issued 7 Oct. 1858. Age about 22, 5' 3 1/2", brown complexion.
Rezin Ijams. DOM recorded by Martha Roboson 24 June 1815 to Hannah of whom Rezin is issue. Certificate issued 25 Oct. 1858. Age about 25, 5' 3 1/2", black complexion, scars across right eyebrow and on right wrist, raised in AA Co.
Louis W. Estep. Freeborn and raised in AA Co. Certificate issued 27 Oct. 1858. Age about 26, 6' 3", black complexion.
Caroline Ijams. Freeborn and raised in AA Co. Certificate issued 28 Oct. 1858. Age about 23, 4' 10", black complexion, scar on right temple and forehead.
George Kent. DOM recorded by William Pinkney 8 Nov. 1858. Certificate issued 9 Nov. 1858. Age about 35, 5' 6 1/4", yellow complexion, small scar across nose.
William Dodson. Freeborn and raised in AA Co. Certificate issued 9 Nov. 1858. Age about 22, black complexion.
John Stewart. Freeborn and raised in AA Co. Certificate issued 10 Nov. 1858. Age about 25, 5' 8", brown complexion, small scar on right thumb.
Rebecca Garrett. Freeborn and raised in AA Co. Certificate issued 16 Nov. 1858. Age about 18, 5' 1/2", brown complexion, small scar on face.
Henry Hearnwood. DOM recorded by William Brewer 10 Nov. 1858. Certificate issued 16 Nov. 1858. Age about 35, 5' 4", brown complexion, small scar on left side of face, raised in AA Co.
Joshua Matthews. DOM recorded by George Wells 24 Nov. 1858. Certificate issued 24 Nov. 1858. Age about 38, 5' 3 1/4", brown complexion, raised in AA Co.
Brister Matthews. DOM recorded by George Wells 24 Nov. 1858. Certificate

issued 24 Nov. 1858. Age about 36, 5' 4", brown complexion, raised in AA Co.
Henry Ennis. Freeborn and raised in AA Co. Certificate issued 29 Dec. 1858. Age about 23, 5' 6 1/4", dark complexion.
Charles Stewart. Freeborn and raised in AA Co. Certificate issued 7 Jan. 1859. Age about 23, 5' 2 1/4", dark complexion, scar on back of left hand.
Thomas Queen. Freeborn and raised in AA Co. Certificate issued 18 Jan. 1859. Age about 32, 5' 10 1/4", brown complexion, scar on back of left hand.
John Queen. Freeborn and raised in AA Co. Certificate issued 18 Jan. 1859. Age about 26, 5' 4 1/2", brown complexion.
James Parker. Freeborn and raised in AA Co. Certificate issued 18 Jan. 1859. Age about 23, 5' 7 1/4", brown complexion.
Benjamin. DOM recorded by Rezin H. Snowden 16 March 1847. Age about 25, 5' 10 1/4", black complexion, raised in AA Co.
Edward Smothers. Freeborn and raised in AA Co. Certificate issued 31 Jan. 1859. Age about 21, 5' 5", brown complexion.
John Anderson. Freeborn and raised in AA Co. Certificate issued 3 Feb. 1859. Age about 22, 5' 5", yellow complexion, small scar on right hand.
Joshua Taylor. Freeborn and raised in AA Co. Certificate issued 17 Feb. 1859. Age about 25, 5' 7 1/2", brown complexion.
George Hammond. Son of Rachel, manumitted by John Lovell 15 Aug. 1808, to be free at age 25. Age 35, 5' 2 3/4, dark complexion, raised in AA Co. Certificate issued 22 Feb. 1859.
John Johnson. Freeborn and raised in AA Co. Certificate issued 26 Feb. 1859. Age about 25, 5' 4", dark complexion.
James Galloway. Freeborn and raised in AA Co. Certificate issued 26 Feb. 1859. Age about 22, 5' 3", black complexion.
Sarah Jane Allen. DOM recorded by Joseph Harrison 4 Oct. 1844. Certificate issued 1 March 1859. Age about 32, 5' 4 1/2", brown complexion, raised in AA Co.
Thomas Randall. Freeborn and raised in AA Co. Certificate issued 2 March 1859. Age about 26, 5' 8 1/2", brown complexion, small scar on back of right hand.
John Randall. Freeborn and raised in AA Co. Certificate issued 2 March 1859. Age about 22, 5", black complexion, large scar on left side of head.
Margaret Batson. Freeborn and raised in AA Co. Certificate issued 8 March 1859. Age about 29, 5' 4", brown complexion.

Sallie Barr. Freeborn and raised in AA Co. Certificate issued 8 March 1859. Age about 27, 5' 3", brown complexion, large scar on right forearm.
Sarah Ann Elliott. Freeborn and raised in AA Co. Certificate issued 15 March 1859. Age about 30, 5' 2", yellow complexion, small scar on right hand.
Betty Norwood. Freeborn and raised in AA Co. Certificate issued 15 March 1859. Age about 22, 5' 9 3/4" small scar on forehead, brown complexion.
Jessie Gaither. Freeborn and raised in AA Co. Certificate issued 15 March 1859. Age about 21, 5' 7 3/4", bright complexion, straight hair.
George Bradford. Freeborn and raised in AA Co. Certificate issued 24 March 1859. Age about 28, 5' 7 3/4", yellow complexion.
— Johnson. Freeborn and raised in AA Co. Certificate issued 24 March 1859. Age about 30, 5' 5", black complexion, small scar on left arm.
Martha Parker. Freeborn and raised in AA Co. Certificate issued 24 March 1859. Age about 29, 5' 1", yellow complexion.
Elizabeth Parker. Freeborn and raised in AA Co. Certificate issued 24 March 1859. Age about 18, 5' 3 1/2", yellow complexion.
Mary Parker. Freeborn and raised in AA Co. Certificate issued 24 March 1859. Age about 29, 5' 1", yellow complexion.
Janee Bradford. Freeborn and raised in AA Co. Certificate issued 24 March 1859. Age about 25, 5' 5 1/4", brown complexion.
Elizabeth Bradford. Freeborn and raised in AA Co. Certificate issued 24 March 1859. Age about 23, 5' 3 1/4", yellow complexion.
Mary Bradford. Freeborn and raised in AA Co. Certificate issued 24 March 1859. Age about 24, 5' 1", brown complexion.
Emily Bradford. Freeborn and raised in AA Co. Certificate issued 24 March 1859. Age about 20, 5' 4", yellow complexion, small scar on forehead.
William Leavis. Freeborn and raised in AA Co. Certificate issued 28 March 1859. Age about 21, 5' 5 3/4", dark complexion.
James Peterson. Freeborn and raised in AA Co. Certificate issued 29 March 1859. Age about 22, 5' 8 3/4", black complexion.
William Coates. DOM recorded by Elizabeth Hubbley 24 Oct. 1859. Age about 35, 5' 5 1/2", black complexion, small scar on each side of face.
James Henry Mack. Freeborn and raised

in AA Co. Certificate issued 7 April 1859. Age 23, 6', scar on forehead.

Charity Scott. DOM recorded by Stephen Beard 5 June 1823. Age about 35, 5' 2 1/4", raised in AA Co.

Solomon Hall. DOM recorded by Stephen Beard 20 Jan. 1820. TBF at age 30. Certificate issued 15 April 1859. Age 30, 5' 9 1/4." Child of slave Judy, subject of original DOM.

Nelly Hall. DOM recorded by Stephen Beard 20 Jan. 1820. TBF at age 30. Certificate issued 15 April 1859. Age 30, 5' 9 1/4." Child of slave Judy, subject of original. DOM.

Charlotte Ann Shavis. Freeborn and raised in AA Co. Certificate issued 28 April 1859. Age about 18, 5' 2", black complexion.

Maria Jacobs. Freeborn and raised in AA Co. Certificate issued 30 April 1859. Age about 24, 5' 3 1/2", dark complexion.

Nancy Harwood. DOM recorded by William Brewer 16 May 1859. Certificate issued 16 May 1859. Age about 22, 5' 1", brown complexion, large scar on neck.

Charles Newson. Freeborn and raised in AA Co. Certificate issued 24 May 1859. Age about 34, 5' 6", brown complexion, small scar in corner of right eyebrow.

Eliza Stepney. Freeborn and raised in AA Co. Certificate issued 24 May 1859. Age about 35, 5' 2", dark complexion.

Rachel Ann Crawford. DOM recorded by Martha Robinson 24 June 1855. Certificate issued 24 May 1859. Age about 55, 5' 5", dark complexion, raised in AA Co.

William Henry Mullen. Freeborn and raised in AA Co. Certificate issued 24 May 1859. Age about 21, 5' 9", yellow complexion, scar on hand.

Jacob Ross. Son of Nelly who was manumitted by Stephen Beard. DOM recorded 26 Jan. 1820. TBF at age 30. Age about 31, 5' 2 1/2", brown complexion. Certificate issued 31 May 1859.

Anna Maria Blackiston. Freeborn and raised in AA Co. Certificate issued 7 June 1859. Age about 18, 5' 1", yellow complexion.

Lindy Smothers. Freeborn and raised in AA Co. Certificate issued 14 June 1859. Age about 23, 5' 1/2", brown complexion.

Mary Jane Baynard. Freeborn and raised in AA Co. Certificate issued 14 June 1859. Age about 21, 4' 11", brown complexion.

Wesley Anderson. Freeborn and raised in AA Co. Certificate issued 15 June 1859. Age about 29, 5' 8 1/2', black complexion, small scar on back of left hand.

Locenso Lane (Lorenzo ?). Freeborn and raised in AA Co. Certificate issued 25 July 1859. No age given, 4' 10".

Elizabeth Ann Carroll. Freeborn and raised in AA Co. Certificate issued 25 July 1859. Age about 23, 5' 2", yellow complexion, small mole on right side of face.

Mary Ellen Ridgely. Freeborn and raised in AA Co. Certificate issued 25 July 1859. Age about 23, 5' 2", yellow complexion.

Sarah Jane Couitly (Costley ?). Freeborn and raised in AA Co. Certificate issued 25 July 1859. Age about 19, 5' 5 1/4", yellow complexion.

Lavinia Pinkney. Freeborn and raised in AA Co. Certificate issued 7 Aug. 1859. Age about 19, 4' 11 1/4", dark complexion, scar on right arm.

John Simms. Freeborn and raised in AA Co. Certificate issued 11 Aug. 1859. Age about 21, 5' 4", dark complexion.

Henrietta Wallace. Freeborn and raised in AA Co. Certificate issued 31 Aug. 1859. 5', brown complexion, scar on left ear and neck.

Sarah Garrett. Freeborn and raised in AA Co. Certificate issued 31 Aug. 1859. Age about 24, 5' 3", dark complexion.

Samuel Jones. DOM recorded by Ellen Stockett 27 Aug. 1859. Certificate issued 2 Sept. 1859. Age about 44, 5' 5", black complexion, raised in AA Co.

Ben Berdley. DOM recorded by John G. Hammond 30 Sept. 1859. Certificate issued 30 Sept. 1859. Age about 25, 5' 7 1/4", yellow complexion, raised in AA Co.

Henny Stewart. Freeborn and raised in AA Co. Certificate issued 5 Oct. 1859. Age about 21, 5' 2", brown complexion, small scars on right arm and left wrist.

Henry Lee. Freeborn and raised in AA Co. Certificate issued 10 Oct. 1859. Age about 29, 5' 4", yellow complexion.

Mary Ann Stewart. DOM recorded by --- Gassaway 24 June 1822. Certificate issued 19 Oct. 1859. Age about 37, 5' 2", yellow complexion. Original certificate granted 28 May 1847.

Charles Calvert. Freeborn and raised in AA Co. Certificate issued 25 Oct. 1859. Age about 21, 5' 4 1/2", brown complexion.

Nancy Queen. Freeborn and raised in AA Co. Certificate issued 26 Oct. 1859. Age about 33, 4' 10 1/2", brown complexion, large scar on right arm.

Ellen Parker. Freeborn and raised in AA Co. Certificate issued 26 Oct. 1859. Age

about 23, 5' 2", dark complexion.
Mary Ann Parker. Freeborn and raised in AA Co. Certificate issued 26 Oct. 1859. Age about 22, 5', yellow complexion, small scar on left eye.
Alexander Hall. Son of Rachel manumitted by. DOM recorded by Henry Drury 22 Feb. 1822. DOM providing that issue of Rachel TBF at age 22. Age 30, 5' 11", brown complexion. Certificate issued 26 Oct. 1859.
Mary Jane Estep. Freeborn and raised in AA Co. Certificate issued 26 Oct. 1859 Age about 24, 5' 3/4", brown complexion, scar on right arm.
David Hall. Son of Rachel manumitted by. DOM recorded by Henry Drury 22 Feb. 1822. DOM providing that issue of Rachel TBF at age 22. Age 27, 5' 5 3/4", brown complexion. Certrificate issued 27 Oct. 1859.
Teresa Pratt. Freeborn and raised in AA Co. Certificate issued 27 Oct. 1859. Age 23, 5' 6", yellow complexion.
Jane Brice. Freeborn and raised in AA Co. Certificate issued 27 Oct. 1859. Age about 37, 5' 5 3/4", brown complexion, small scar left side of face.
Kinsey Baldwin Freeborn and raised in AA Co. Certificate issued 27 Oct. 1859. Age about 22, 5' 9", brown complexion, mole on under lip.
Kussa Neall. Freedom received by judgement of Anne Arundel Circuit Court April 1856 against --- Long. Certificate issued 28 Oct. 1859. Age about 40, 5' 4 3/4", black complexion.
Cesar Johnson. DOM recorded by Jacob Winchester 16 Nov. 1859. Certificate issued 16 Nov. 1859. Age about 40, 5' 10 1/4", yellow complexion, scar on back of neck.
Lemuel Stewart. Freeborn and raised in AA Co. Certificate issued 26 Nov. 1859. Age about 35, 5' 5 1/4", yellow complexion, scar on back of left hand.
Jane Thompson. Freeborn and raised in AA Co. Certificate issued 29 Nov. 1859. Age about 19, 5' 1", brown complexion.
Allen Bugg. Freeborn and raised in AA Co. Certificate issued 12 Dec. 1859. Age about 21, 5' 4 1/2", black complexion, scar on back of left hand.
Susan Brown. Freedom received by Judgement of AA Co. Circuit Court Oct. 1859 against John Collison. Certificate issued 13 Dec. 1859. Age about 48, 5' 3", dark complexion, raised in AA Co.
Harriett Ann Brown. Freedom received by Judgement of AA Co. Circuit Court Oct. 1859 against John Collinson. Certificate issued 13 Dec. 1859. Age about 17, 4' 10 1/2", brown complexion, raised in AA Co.
Charles Brown. Freedom received by Judgement of AA Co. Circuit Court Oct. 1859 against John Collinson. Certificate issued 13 Dec. 1859. Age about 21, 5' 4 3/4", black complexion.
Nancy Brown. Freedom received by Judgement of AA Co. Circuit Court Oct. 1859 against John Collinson. Certificate issued 13 Dec. 1859. Age about 19, 5', dark complexion.
Henry Brown. Freedom received by Judgement of AA Co. Circuit Court Oct. 1859 against John Collison. Certificate issued 13 Dec. 1859. Age about 18, 5' 1/2", dark complexion, small scar on forehead.
William Ennis. Freeborn and raised in AA Co. Certificate issued 26 Dec. 1859. Age about 32, 5' 5", dark complexion.
Wm. Ennis. Freeborn and raised in AA Co. Certificate issued 26 Dec. 1859. Age about 25, 5', dark complexion.
Adeline Allen. DOM recorded by Hazel Hanes 27 Dec. 1859. Age about 27, 4' 11 1/2", brown complexion, burn scar on neck, raised in AA Co.
Samuel Collins Jr. Freeborn and raised in AA Co. Certificate issued 4 Jan. 1860. Age about 24, 5' 11", scar on right hand.
John Butler. Freeborn and raised in AA Co. Certificate issued 10 Jan. 1860. Age about 24, 5' 4 1/4", black complexion.
George Davis. DOM recorded by Susan Gambrill 23 Sept. 1820. Certificate issued 10 Jan. 1860. Age about 39, 5' 7 1/2", yellow complexion, raised in AA Co.
George Scott. Freeborn and raised in AA Co. Age about 26, 5' 6 1/2", yellow complexion.
Ellen Scott. Freeborn and raised in AA Co. Certificate issued 10 Jan. 1860. Age about 20, 5' 4 1/2", yellow complexion, scar on right side of face.
John Trout. Freeborn and raised in AA Co. Certificate issued 19 Jan. 1860. Age about 21, 5' 5 1/4", black complexion.
Louisa Garrison. Freeborn and raised in AA Co. Certificate issued 29 Jan. 1860. Age about 18, 5' 1 1/2", black complexion.
Sarah J. Stewart. Freeborn and raised in AA Co. Age about 22, 5' 5 3/4." Certificate issued 14 Feb. 1860.
Catherine Stewart. Freeborn and raised in AA Co. Age about 23, 5' 4", brown complexion, small scar over right eye. Certificate issued 16 Feb. 1860.

Julia Ann Dorsey. Freeborn and raised in AA Co. Certificate issued 21 Feb. 1860. Age about 18, 5' yellow complexion, small scar on back of left hand.
Rachel Marie Issacs. Freeborn and raised in AA Co. Certificate issued 22 Feb. 1860. Age about 24, 5' 3", brown complexion, deformed right thumb.
Zena Jennings. Freeborn and raised in AA Co. Certificate issued 28 Feb. 1860. Age about 18, 5' 1", brown complexion, small scar on right eyebrow.
James Jennings. Freeborn and raised in AA Co. Certificate issued 28 Feb. 1860. Age about 21, 6", brown complexion.
Daniel Myers. Freeborn and raised in AA Co. Certificate issued 28 Feb. 1860. Age about 23, 5', black compexion, small scar over right eye, left leg has been broken.
— Smith. DOM recorded by Thomas Barby 3 March 1854. Certificate issued 28 Feb. 1860. Age about 19, 5' bright complexion, raised in AA Co.
Mary Ellen Smith. DOM recorded by Thomas Barby 3 March 1854. Certificate issued 28 Feb. 1860. Age about 18, 5' 1 1/4", bright complexion, raised in AA Co.
Charlotte Lee. Daughter of negro Charity manumitted by J. Williams 22 April 1820. Charity's female issue TBF at age 25. Certificate issued 29 Feb. 1860 Age is 26, 5' 4 3/4", brown complexion, raised in AA Co.
Phillip Gray. Freeborn and raised in AA Co. Certificate issued 29 Feb. 1860. Age about 26, 5' 2 1/2", dark complexion.
Sally Wells. Freeborn and raised in AA Co. Certificate issued 6 March 1860. Age about 24, 4' 11 1/2", brown complexion.
Louisa Smothers. Freeborn and raised in AA Co. Certificate issued 6 March 1860. Age about 21, 5' 3 1/4", yellow complexion.
William Queen. Freeborn and raised in AA Co. Certificate issued 6 March 1860 Age about 30, 5' 6 1/2", dark complexion, scar on forehead.
Henry Brogden. Freeborn and raised in AA Co. Certificate issued 13 March 1860. Age about 35, 5' 9 1/4", dark complexion, scar on right hand.
Frank Brogden. Freeborn and raised in AA Co. Certificate issued 13 March 1860. Age about 22, 5' 9", black compexion, small scar on right wrist.
Matilda Brown. Freeborn and raised in AA Co. Certificate issued 13 March 1860. Age about 24, 5' 1 1/2", yellow complexion, small scar on right side of face.
Maria Brown. Freeborn and raised in AA Co. Certificate issued 13 March 1860. Age about 28, 5' 4 1/2", brown complexion.
Thomas Toogood. Freeborn and raised in AA Co. Certificate issued 14 March 1860. Age about 23, 5' 4 1/2", brown complexion.
Sarah Ann Hobbs. Freeborn and raised in AA Co. Certificate issued 16 March 1860. Age about 18, 5' 1 3/4", brown complexion, scars on right wrist and arm.
Nancy Lee. Freeborn and raised in AA Co. Certificate issued 24 March 1860. Age about 33, 5' yellow complexion.
Charles Hynsman. Freeborn and raised in AA Co. Certificate issued 24 March 1860. Age about 24, 5' 5", dark complexion.
Sally Queen. Freeborn and raised in AA Co. Certificate issued 3 April 1860. Age about 18, 5' 2", brown complexion, pitted by smallpox.
Barbara Queen. Freeborn and raised in AA Co. Certificate issued 3 April 1860. Age about 28, 5', dark complexion.
Susan Queen. Freeborn and raised in AA Co. Certificate issued 3 April 1860. Age about 17, 4' 9", brown complexion.
Hannah Queen. Freeborn and raised in AA Co. Certificate issued 3 April 1860. Age about 19, 5' 2", brown complexion.
Mary Queen. Freeborn and raised in AA Co. Certificate issued 3 April 1860. Age about 22, 5' dark complexion, scar on right wrist.
Elizabeth Brogden. Freeborn and raised in AA Co. Certificate issued 3 April 1860. Age about 26, 5' 2", black complexion, scar on right arm.
June Robinson. Freeborn and raised in AA Co. Certificate issued 11 April 1860. Age about 25, 4' 11", brown complexion. Daughter of Suck, manumitted by William Hardesty 18 Aug. 1828. Issue manumitted at age 16.
Richard Lane. Freeborn and raised in AA Co. Certificate issued 11 April 1860. Age about 29, 5' 6 1/4", brown complexion. Son of Suck, manumitted by William Hardesty 18 Aug. 1828. Issue manumitted at age 16.
John Henry Lane. Freeborn and raised in AA Co. Certificate issued 11 April 1860. Age about 25, 4' 11", brown complexion. Son of Suck, manumitted by William Hardesty 18 Aug. 1828. Issue manumitted at age 16.
Thomas Bailey. Freeborn and raised in AA Co. Certificate issued 11 April 1860. Age about 24, 5' 6", bright complexion, small

scar in corner of right eye.
Sophia Jennings. Freeborn and raised in AA Co. Certificate issued 14 April 1860. Age about 27, 5' 4 1/4", brown complexion, small scar between the eyes.
Amelia Jacobs. Freeborn and raised in AA Co. Certificate issued 24 April 1860. Age about 20, 5' 10 3/4, freckles on face, small scars in left eyebrow.
William Tilghman. Freeborn and raised in AA Co. Certificate issued 24 April 1860. Age about 24, 5' 11 1/2", yellow complexion, face pitted with smallpox.
Joseph Wright. Freeborn and raised in AA Co. Certificate issued 24 April 1860. Age about 21, 5' 5", brown complexion.
Elizabeth Boone. Freeborn and raised in AA Co. Certificate issued 24 April 1860. Age about 18, 5' 1", brown complexion.
Mary Ann Toogood. Freeborn and raised in AA Co. Certificate issued 24 April 1860. Age about 17, 5' 2", yellow complexion, scar on upper lip.
Elizabeth M. Wells. Freeborn and raised in AA Co. Certificate issued 24 April 1860. Age about 20, 5' 3 3/4", yellow complexion.
Martha Savoy. Freeborn and raised in AA Co. Certificate issued 1 May 1860. Age about 18, 5' 1/2", brown complexion, scar on left arm.
— Turner. Freeborn and raised in AA Co. Certificate issued 8 May 1860. Age about 24, 5' 3 1/2", brown complexion, scar on side of face (left), right eye injured.
Ellen Turner. Freeborn and raised in AA Co. Certificate issued 8 May 1860. Age about 22, 5', brown complexion, middle finger on right hand is deformed.
Issac Pratt. Freeborn and raised in AA Co. Certificate issued 10 May 1860. Age about 21, 4' 11 1/2", dark complexion.
John Jerry Ross. Freeborn and raised in AA Co. Certificate issued 15 May 1860. Age about 28, 5' 6 1/2", bright complexion.
Thomas Short. Freeborn and raised in AA Co. Certificate issued 21 May 1860. Age about 22, 5 1 1/2", yellow complexion, small mark on left little finger.
William Short. Freeborn and raised in AA Co. Certificate issued 21 May 1860. Age about 21, 5' 11 1/4", black complexion.
Cortes Baker. DOM recorded by R. P. Snowden 4 March 1841. Raised in AA Co. Age about 28, 5' 9 1/2". Certificate issued 22 May 1860.
Wesley Nepburn. DOM recorded by R. P. Snowden 4 March 1841. Raised in AA Co. Age about 30, 5' 4 1/2", brown complexion, scar on left jaw.
Sussanna Edwards. Freeborn and raised in AA Co. Certificate issued 26 May 1860. Age about 24, 5' 1/2", dark complexion.
Elizabeth Edwards. Freeborn and raised in AA Co. Certificate issued 26 May 1860. Age about 23, 5' 4", dark complexion, scar near corner of left eyebrow.
Lavinia Edwards. Freeborn and raised in AA Co. Certificate issued 26 May 1860. Age about 22, 5' 1 1/2", brown complexion, small scar on index finger of right hand.
Nelson Garner. Freeborn and raised in AA Co. Certificate issued 30 May 1860. Age about 25, 5' 5 3/4", brown complexion, scar on breast.
Wesley Jones. Freeborn and raised in AA Co. Certificate issued 2 June 1860. Age about 45, 5' 6 1/2", brown complexion.
Elizabeth Butler. Freeborn and raised in AA Co. Certificate issued 2 June 1860. Age about 34, 5' 2 1/4", yellow complexion.
Basil Jones. Freeborn and raised in AA Co. Certificate issued 2 June 1860. Age about 25, 5' 3 1/2", black complexion.
Emily Hawkins. Freeborn and raised in AA Co. Certificate issued 2 June 1860. Age about 32, 4' 9 1/4", brown complexion, scar on back of right hand.
Mahala Merriken. Freeborn and raised in AA Co. Certificate issued 5 June 1860. Age about 25, 5' 6 1/2", black complexion.
Henry Merriken. Freeborn and raised in AA Co. Certificate issued 5 June 1860. Age not clear, 5' 7 1/4", black complexion.
William Merriken. Freeborn and raised in AA Co. Certificate issued 5 June 1860. Age about 30, 5' 10 1/2", black complexion, scars on left hand and left side of face.
Elizabeth Tyler. Freeborn and raised in AA Co. Certificate issued 11 June 1860. Age about 25, 4' 11 1/2", yellow complexion, scar on back of left hand.
Susan Nepburn. Freeborn and raised in AA Co. Certificate issued 12 June 1860. Age about 17, 5' 2", black complexion, scar on left wrist.
Joseph Owens. Freeborn and raised in AA Co. Certificate issued 19 June 1860. Age about 27, 5' 1 1/4", small scar on forehead, light complexion.
Jane Wallace. Freeborn and raised in AA Co. Certificate issued 19 June 1860. Age about 29, 4' 11", brown complexion.
Charyly Shorter. DOM recorded by Jacob Fowler 19 Nov. 1815. Certificate issued 15

June 1860. Age about 62, 4' 10 3/4", yellow complexion, mole on left side of face.
Mary Turner. Freeborn and raised in AA Co. Certificate issued 21 June 1860. Age about 17, 5' 2 1/2", yellow complexion.
Eliza Tydings. Freeborn and raised in AA Co. Certificate issued 21 June 1860. Age about 17, 5' 2 1/2", yellow complexion.
Nelly Mack. Freeborn and raised in AA Co. Certificate issued 21 June 1860. Age about 28, 5' 2", brown complexion, scar on left cheek, large scar on left side of head (burns).
Ann Smothers. Freeborn and raised in AA Co. Certificate issued 21 June 1860. Age about 15, 5' 1 1/2", dark complexion.
Jemima Holland. Freeborn and raised in AA Co. Certificate issued 21 June 1860. Age about 20, 5' 4", dark complexion, small scar on left hand.
James Walker. Freeborn and raised in AA Co. Certificate issued 22 June 1860. Age about 24, 5' 4 1/2", black complexion, small scars on forehead and back of left hand.
John Powell. Freeborn and raised in AA Co. Certificate issued 25 June 1860. Age about 26 5' 4 1/2", black complexion.
Emeline Powell. Freeborn and raised in AA Co. Certificate issued 25 June 1860. Age about 24, 5', dark complexion, small mole on left wrist.
Nancy Ann Lee. Freeborn and raised in AA Co. Certificate issued 28 June 1860. Age 22, 5' 5", yellow complexion, small scar on nose.
Angelina Johnson. Freeborn and raised in AA Co. Certificate issued 28 June 1860. Age about 19, 5' 4 1/4", brown complexion.
Eliza Johnson. Freeborn and raised in AA Co. Certificate issued 28 June 1860. Age about 30, 5' 5", yellow complexion, small scar on left arm.
Margaret Jane Johnson. Freeborn and raised in AA Co. Certificate issued 28 June 1860. Age about 20, 5' 1", yellow complexion.
James Green. Freeborn and raised in AA Co. Certificate issued 28 June 1860. Age 21, 5' 4 1/2", yellow complexion, small scar on forehead.
Benjamin Green. Freeborn and raised in AA Co. Certificate issued 28 June 1860. Age about 20, 5' 4 3/4", black complexion.
Sam Gordon. DOM recorded by Rezin H. Snowden 16 March 1847. Age about 29, 5' 10 1/4", black complexion, scars on right eyebrow and left hand, raised in AA Co.

Sally Johnson. Freeborn and raised in AA Co. Certificate issued 28 June 1860. Age about 28, 5' 6", black complexion.
William Briggs. Freeborn and raised in AA Co. Certificate issued 29 June 1860. Age about 25, 5' 9", black complexion, blind in left and has multiple little fingers on each hand.
Benjamin Bailey. Freeborn and raised in AA Co. Certificate issued 29 June 1860. Age about 29, 5' 3 1/4", brown complexion, lage scar on left wrist, scar under left eye.
Betsy Bond. Freeborn and raised in AA Co. Certificate issued 10 July 1860. Age about 35, 5' 2 1/2", dark complexion, small scar on right arm.
Andrew Queen. Freeborn and raised in AA Co. Certificate issued 10 July 1860. Age about 25, 5' 4 1/2", black complexion, scar on forehead.
Issac Queen. Freeborn and raised in AA Co. Certificate issued 10 July 1860. Age about 23, 5' 9", black complexion, small scar over left eye.
Charles Tally. Son of Sary manumitted by Stephen Boone, 11 July 1918. Certificate issued 10 July 1860. Age about 35, 5', brown complexion, small scar on forehead.
John Turner Lane. Freeborn and raised in AA Co. Certificate issued 10 July 1860. Age about 31, 5' 5 1/2", brown complexion.
Nace Adams. Son of Abigal manumitted by N. J. Watkins, 6 Dec. 1819. Age about 34, 4' 11", black complexion. Certificate issued 10 July 1860.
Henry Offer. Freeborn and raised in AA Co. Certificate issued 17 July 1860. Age about 23, 5' 6 3/4", yellow complexion, scar on little finger of left hand.
Vachel Williams. Freeborn and raised in AA Co. Certificate issued 24 July 1860. Age about 37, 5' 9", black complexion, small scar on back of left hand.
Alexander Williams. Freeborn and raised in AA Co. Certificate issued 24 July 1860. Age about 23, 5' 4 3/4", brown complexion, scar near corner of left lip.
Phillip Williams. Freeborn and raised in AA Co. Certificate issued 24 July 1860. Age about 23, 5' 7 3/4", yellow complexion, injured thumb on left hand.
Emeline Williams. Freeborn and raised in AA Co. Certificate issued 24 July 1860. Age about 27, 5' 3 1/2", brown complexion, scar on back of right hand.
Mary Jane Williams. Freeborn and raised in AA Co. Certificate issued 24 July 1860.

Age about 19, 5 1 3/4", small scar on right arm.
Martha Bailey. Freeborn and raised in AA Co. Certificate issued 27 July 1860. Age about 28, 5' 3 1/4", black complexion.
Katherine Bailey. Freeborn and raised in AA Co. Certificate issued 27 July 1860. Age about 19, 5' 2 1/2", light compexion, straight hair.
Mary Calvert. Freeborn and raised in AA Co. Certificate issued 27 July 1860. Age about 23, 5' 5 1/4", light complexion, small scar on forehead, straight hair.
Henry Calvert. Freeborn and raised in AA Co. Certificate issued 27 July 1860. Age about 18, 5' 2 1/4", light complexion, straight hair.
Elizabeth Queen. Freeborn and raised in AA Co. Certificate issued 31 July 1860. Age about 25, 5' 1 1/2", yellow complexion.
Thomas. DOM recorded by Rezin S. Snowden 16 March 1847. Age about 33, 5' 5", black compexion, raised in AA Co. Certificate issued 30 July 1860.
Caesar Neall. DOM recorded by John Rawlings 28 May 1860. Age about 44, 5' 8 1/2", dark complexion, scar between the eyes. Certificate issued 1 Aug. 1860.
Clara Seappin. Freeborn and raised in AA Co. Certificate issued 7 Aug. 1860. 4' 10 1/2", dark complexion, scar on forehead.
Ann Butler. Freeborn and raised in AA Co. Certificate issued 7 Aug. 1860. Age about 18, 5' 1/4", light complexion.
Caleb Stewart. Freeborn and raised in AA Co. Certificate issued 7 Aug. 1860. Age about 26, 5' 8 1/4", light complexion, scar on right hand.
Jane Davis. Freeborn and raised in AA Co. Certificate issued 7 Aug. 1860. Age about 47, 5' 8", dark complexion.
Catherine Wells. Freeborn and raised in AA Co. Certificate issued 7 Aug. 1860. Age about 19, 5' 3/4", dark complexion, scar under right eye.
Priscilla Wells. Freeborn and raised in AA Co. Certificate issued 7 August, 1860. Age about 18, 5' 3 1/4", dark compexion, scar under right eye.
William Bradford. Freeborn and raised in AA Co. Certificate issued 10 Aug. 1860. Age about 35, 5' 7", yellow complexion, scart on forehead.
Dorcas Blunt. Freeborn and raised in AA Co. Certificate issued 16 Aug. 1860. Age about 40, 5' 2 1/2", yellow complexion, scar on left wrist.
Serena Offer. Freeborn and raised in AA Co. Certificate issued 16 Aug. 1860. Age about 22, 5' 1", yellow complexion.
Eliza Bennett. Freeborn and raised in AA Co. Certificate issued 16 Aug. 1860. Age about 28, 5' 3 1/2", brown complexion, small scar on back of right hand.
Martha Scrivener. Freeborn and raised in AA Co. Certificate issued 16 Aug. 1860. Age about 18, 5' 4 1/2", yellow complexion.
Betty S. Freeborn and raised in AA Co. Certificate issued 16 August, 1860. Age about 16, 5' 5 1/2", yellow complexion.
Jane Holland. Freeborn and raised in AA Co. Certificate issued 16 Aug. 1860. Age about 23, 5' 2", yellow complexion.
Maria Holland. Freeborn and raised in AA Co. Certificate issued 16 Aug. 1860. Age about 26, 4' 11 1/2", yellow complexion.
Jane Mitchell. Freeborn and raised in AA Co. Certificate issued 16 Aug. 1860. Age about 20, 4' 8 1/2", brown complexion.
Virginia Blunt. Freeborn and raised in AA Co. Certificate issued 16 Aug. 1860. Age about 17, 5' 2", yellow complexion.
Thomas Offer. Freeborn and raised in AA Co. Certificate issued 16 Aug. 1860. Age about 29, 5' 8 1/2", small scar on right hand.
Peter Offer. Freeborn and raised in AA Co. Certificate issued 16 Aug. 1860. Age about 21, 5' 10 1/4", black complexion, scar on left thumb.
Thomas Scott. Freeborn and raised in AA Co. Certificate issued 16 Aug. 1860. Age about 28, 5' 6 1/2", yellow complexion, scars in eyebrows and on idex finger of right hand.
Elizabeth Blunt. Freeborn and raised in AA Co. Certificate issued 16 Aug. 1860. Age about 23, 5' 2 3/4", dark complexion.
William Mack. Freeborn and raised in AA Co. Certificate issued 16 Aug. 1860. Age about 22, 5' 7 1/2", brown complexion, small scar under right eye.
Harriett Gross. Freeborn and raised in AA Co. Certificate issued 16 Aug. 1860. Age about 24, 5' 7 1/4", yellow complexion, small scar near corner of left eye.
Charlotte Sampson. Freeborn and raised in AA Co. Certificate issued 16 Aug. 1860. Age about 21, 5' 3 1/4", brown complexion, small scar on left side of face.
Jane Johnson. Freeborn and raised in AA Co. Certificate issued 16 Aug. 1860. Age about 23, 5' 2", yellow complexion.
Benjamin Rawlings. Freeborn and raised in AA Co. Certificate issued 21 Aug. 1860. Age about 35, 5' 4 1/4", brown complexion,

scar near right eye.

Sally Ann Bailey. Freeborn and raised in AA Co. Certificate issued 22 Aug. 1860. Age about 20, 5", brown complexion, large scar on side of neck.

Linda Thomas. Freeborn and raised in AA Co. Certificate issued 28 Aug. 1860. Age about 22, 5' 2 3/4", dark complexion, scars on right arm and forehead.

Alsey Neall. Freeborn and raised in AA Co. Certificate issued 28 Aug. 1860. Age about 31, 4' 10 1/2", dark complexion, small scar on forehead.

Sarah Smith. Freeborn and raised in AA Co. Certificate issued 28 Aug. 1860. Age about 35, 5' 1 1/2", dark complexion.

Letty Foster. Freeborn and raised in AA Co. Certificate issued 28 Aug. 1860. Age about 54, 4' 11 3/4", dark complexion.

Adeline Baldwin. DOM recorded by Edward and Mary A. Simpson 26 Jan. 1813. Raised in AA Co. Age about 22, 4' 11 1/2", dark complexion, scar over left eye.

Mary Blackestone. DOM recorded by John Rideout 8 Sept. 1853. Certificate issued 1 Sept. 1860. Raised in AA Co. Age about 26, 5' 3 1/2", brown complexion.

Sophia Brown. Freeborn and raised in AA Co. Certificate issued 3 Sept. 1860. Age about 25, 5' 1/4", yellow complexion.

Sally Butler. Freeborn and raised in AA Co. Certificate issued 3 Sept. 1860. Age about 21, 5' 3 3/4", yellow complexion.

John Ennis. Freeborn and raised in AA Co. Certificate issued 4 Sept. 1860. Age about 24, 5' 3 1/4", black complexion.

Mary Queen. Freeborn and raised in AA Co. Certificate issued 5 Sept. 1860. Age about 25, 5' 1/2", brown complexion, small scar on back of right hand.

John Colbert. Freeborn and raised in AA Co. Certificate issued 5 Sept. 1860. Age about 32, 5' 10 3/4", yellow complexion.

Elizabeth Calvert. Freeborn and raised in AA Co. Certificate issued 5 Sept. 1860. Age about 21, 5' 3/4", black complexion.

Ann Newbury. Freeborn and raised in AA Co. Certificate issued 12 Sept. 1860. Age about 17, 4' 9 3/4", dark complexion.

William Crothers. Freeborn and raised in AA Co. Certificate issued 17 Sept. 1860. Age about 23, 5' 10 1/2", yellow complexion, large scar on left side of neck.

Eliza Tydings. Freeborn and raised in AA Co. Certificate issued 17 Sept. 1860. 5' 1/2", yellow complexion.

Margaret Ann Watkins. Freeborn and raised in AA Co. Certificate issued 20 Sept. 1860. Age about 35, 5' 4 1/2", brown complexion.

Ellen Ann Boston. Freeborn and raised in AA Co. Certificate issued 20 Sept. 1860. Age about 21, 4' 9 3/4", brown complexion, small scar on lower lip.

James New Dorsey. Freeborn and raised in AA Co. Certificate issued 26 Sept. 1860. Age about 24, 5' 11 1/2", yellow complexion.

Ellen Offer. DOM recorded by Lydia Gambrills 19 Sept. 1849. Age about 35, 4' 10", brown complexion, scar on left arm.

Mary Jane Richardson. Freeborn and raised in AA Co. Certificate issued 28 Sept. 1860. Age about 22, 5' 3 1/4", dark complexion, small scar on left eyebrow.

Ellen Barber. Freeborn and raised in AA Co. Certificate issued 2 Oct. 1860. Age about 30, 5' 7 1/4", black complexion, small scar on left wrist.

George Boston. Freeborn and raised in AA Co. Certificate issued 2 Oct. 1860. Age about 22, 5' 2 1/2", brown complexion, small scar on left wrist and on forehead.

Eliza. Daughter of Charity, who was manumitted by Jacob Williams 22 April 1820. Deed providing for freedom of all issue at age of 25. Certificate issued 4 Oct. 1860. Age 33, 4' 11 1/2", dark complexion.

John Hanson Harwood (Hearnwood ?). Freeborn and raised in AA Co. Certificate issued 16 Oct. 1860. Age about 22, 5', brown complexion, small scar under right eye.

Washington Garrett. DOM recorded by Elizabeth and Hester Wood 20 Oct. 1821. Certificate issued 16 Oct. 1860. Raised in AA Co. Age about 49, 5' 10", black complexion. Certificate issued 16 Oct. 1860.

Basil Garrett. DOM recorded by Elizabeth and Hester Wood 20 Oct. 1821. Certificate issued 16 Oct. 1860. Raised in AA Co. Age about 44 5' 8 1/2", black complexion, scar on left thumb.

Richard Garrett. DOM recorded by Elizabeth Hester Wood 20 Oct. 1821. Certificate issued 16 Oct. 1860. Raised in AA Co. Age about 42, 5' 9 1/4", brown complexion, small scar between the eyes.

Harriett Garrett. DOM recorded by Elizabeth Hester Wood 20 Oct. 1821. Certificate issued 16 Oct. 1860. Raised in AA Co. Age about 40, 4' 11 3/4", black complexion.

Susan Butler. Freeborn and raised in AA Co. Certificate issued 17 Oct. 1860. Age about 39, 5' 1 1/4", yellow complexion, scar on right wrist.

Henry Chew. Freeborn and raised in AA

Co. Certificate issued 24 Oct. 1860. Age about 20, 5' 8 1/4", dark complexion.
Lewis Henry Powell. Freeborn and raised in AA Co. Certificate issued 24 Oct. 1860. Age about 26, 5' 9", black complexion.
Richard Powell. Freeborn and raised in AA Co. Certificate issued 24 Oct. 1860. Age about 21, 5' 1 1/2", brown complexion.
Sarah Ann Semmes. Freeborn and raised in AA Co. Certificate issued 29 Oct. 1860. Age about 28, 4' 10 1/2", black complexion.
Louisa Young. Freeborn and raised in AA Co. Certificate issued 29 Oct. 1860. Age about 22, 5' 1/4", brown complexion.
Peter Hepburn. Freeborn and raised in AA Co. Certificate issued 1 Nov. 1860. Age about 35, 5' 5", black complexion, no little finger on right hand.
Hester Burley. DOM recorded by Richard Snowden 4 Nov. 1840. Raised in AA Co. Age about 34, 4' 8", yellow complexion.
Samuel Hepburn. Freeborn and raised in AA Co. Certificate issued 5 Nov. 1860. Age about 26, 5' 4 3/4", black complexion.
Sarah Ann Laws. Freeborn and raised in AA Co. Certificate issued 6 Nov. 1860. Age about 23, 5' 2 3/4", yellow complexion.
Nancy Brashears. Freeborn and raised in AA Co. Certificate issued 11 Nov. 1860. Age about 21, 5' 2 1/2", brown complexion.
John Ward. Freeborn and raised in AA Co. Certificate issued 12 Nov. 1860. Age about 26, 5' 6 3/4", yellow complexion, small scar on right hand.
Sophia Watkins. Freeborn and raised in AA Co. Certificate issued 14 Nov. 1860. Age about 39, 5' 1/2", dark complexion, small scar near left ear, small lump on left wrist.
Louisa Dutton. Freeborn and raised in AA Co. Certificate issued 15 Nov. 1860. Age about 35, 5' 5 1/2", yellow complexion.
James Stephens. DOM recorded by Richard P. Snowden 24 March 1849. Certificate issued 20 Nov. 1860. Raised in AA Co. Age about 26, 5' 5 1/2", dark complexion.
Elizabeth Stephens. Freeborn and raised in AA Co. Certificate issued 20 Nov. 1860. Age about 18, 5' 1 1/2", scar on left wrist, light complexion.
Catherine Ellen Shephard. Freeborn and raised in AA Co. Certificate issued 20 Nov. 1860. Age about 19, 4' 11 1/2.".
Dennis Wings. Freeborn and raised in AA Co. Certificate issued 21 Nov. 1860. Age about 21, 5' 8 1/4", dark complexion.
Joseph Burgess. Freeborn and raised in AA Co. Certificate issued 14 Nov. 1860. Age about 24, 5' 7 1/4", black complexion.
Fanny Bargen. Freeborn and raised in AA Co. Certificate issued 14 Nov. 1860. Age about 23, 5' 2 1/2", black complexion.
Martha Ellen Young. Freeborn and raised in AA Co. Certificate issued 12 Dec. 1860. Age about 19, 5' 2", brown complexion, scar on right wrist.
Edward Brooks. Freeborn and raised in AA Co. Certificate issued 24 Dec. 1860. Age about 23, 5' 6 1/2", black complexion.
Maria Collins. Freeborn and raised in AA Co. Certificate issued 24 Dec. 1860. Age about 22, 5' 4", brown complexion.
John Thomas. Freeborn and raised in AA Co. Certificate issued 24 Dec. 1860. Age about 23, 5' 5 1/4", black complexion.
Richard Holland. Freeborn and raised in AA Co. Certificate issued 27 Dec. 1860. Age about 20, 5' 7", black complexion.
Samuel Simms. DOM recorded by Samuel Cheston 28 May 1860. Certificate issued 27 Dec. 1860. Age about 25, 5' 7 3/4", raised in AA Co.
Joseph Collins. Freeborn and raised in AA Co. Certificate issued 28 Dec. 1860. Age about 21, 5' 8 1/4", yellow complexion.
Issac Johnson. Freeborn and raised in AA Co. Certificate issued 24 Dec. 1860. Age about 23, 5' 10 1/2", brown complexion.
John Fortee. Freeborn and raised in AA Co. Certificate issued 1 Jan. 1861. Age about 22, 5' 7", dark complexion.
Lewis Williams. Freeborn and raised in AA Co. Certificate issued 7 Jan. 1861. Age about 26, 5' 7", dark complexion.
Jane Scott. Freeborn and raised in AA Co. Certificate issued 9 Jan. 1861. Age about 18, 5' 1/2", light complexion.
Thomas Weston. Freeborn and raised in AA Co. Certificate issued 21 Jan. 1861. Age about 25, 5' 11 1/2", dark complexion, scar behind the left ear, scar on right side of face.
Frank Jenkins. DOM recorded by william Bateman 13 June 1860. Raised in AA Co. TBF at age of 31. Age 32, 5' 11", black complexion. Certificate issued 11 Feb. 1861.
Janie Bryan. Freeborn and raised in AA Co. Certificate issued 19 Feb. 1861. Age about 21, 5' 9 3/4", yellow complexion, freckles on face.
William Johnson. Freeborn and raised in AA Co. Certificate issued 17 April 1861. Age about 32, 5' 11", brown complexion,

Age about 32, 5' 11", brown complexion, missing index finger of right hand.
Thomas Williams. Freeborn and raised in AA Co. Certificate issued 23 April 1861. Age about 22, 5' 9 3/4", dark complexion, scar on back of left hand.
William Gantt. Freeborn and raised in AA Co. Certificate issued 17 April 1861. Age about 23, 5' 10 1/2", light complexion.
John Evans. Freeborn and raised in AA Co. Certificate issued 17 April 1861. Age about 30, 5' 7 3/4", light complexion, scar on left side of face, missing one front tooth.
Mary Ann Johnson. Freeborn and raised in AA Co. Certificate issued 21 May 1861. Age about 28, 4' 10 1/2", yellow complexion.
Harriett K. Brown. Freeborn and raised in AA Co. Certificate issued 21 May 1861. Age about 20, 5' 2 1/4", brown complexion, scar on the neck.
John Blackeston. DOM recorded by John Rideout 23 April 1844. Age about 25, 5' 5", black complexion, raised in AA Co. Certificate issued 5 Aug. 1861.
Kitty Wilson (formerly Kitty Neale). DOM recorded by J. Cheston 27 March 1844. Certificate issued 23 Aug. 1861. Age about 40, 5' 2", brown complexion, scar on left wrist, raised in AA Co.
Henry Nearris (Morris ?). Freeborn and raised in AA Co. Certificate issued 3 Sept. 1861. Age about 18, 5' 4 3/4", black complexion, scar on right wrist.
Henry Smith. DOM recorded by Daniel Smith 6 July 1831. Certificate issued 17 Sept. 1861. Age about 31, 5' 9 1/2", brown complexion. DOM identifies him as "Henry".
Henry Lee. Freeborn and raised in AA Co. Certificate issued 2 Oct. 1861. Age about 21, 5' 7 3/4", yellow complexion.
Mary Kent. Freeborn and raised in AA Co. Certificate issued 2 Oct. 1861. Age about 15, 5' 1 1/2", brown complexion.
John Gassoway. Freeborn and raised in AA Co. Certificate issued 6 Dec. 1861. Age about 18, 5' 6", brown complexion, scar on left side of neck.
Elijah Boston. Freeborn and raised in AA Co. Certificate issued 19 Dec. 1861. Age about 21, 5' 5 1/4", brown complexion, scar on left cheek.
Nicholas Gibson. DOM recorded by Nicholas Snowden 21 Nov. 1840. Certificate issued 27 Jan. 1862. Age about 25, 5' 6 1/2", brown complexion, raised in AA Co.
— **Merriken.** DOM recorded by Nicholas Snowden 21 Nov. 1840. Certificate issued 27 Jan. 1862. Age about 25, 5' 8 1/4", yellow complexion, small scar on lower lip.
Maria. DOM recorded by Thomas Robinson 11 March 1839. Age about 43, 5' 2 1/4", dark complexion, scar on right arm. Certificate issued 31 Jan. 1862.
Sally Mitchell. Freeborn and raised in AA Co. Certificate issued 12 Feb. 1862. Age not given, 4' 9", brown complexion, small scar under right eye.
Sarah Henry. Freeborn and raised in AA Co. Certificate issued 19 Feb. 1862. Age not given, 5' 2 3/4", brown complexion, small scar under right eye.
Bill Queen. DOM recorded by Lydia Gambrill 7 July 1837. Raised in AA Co. Certificate issued 1 April 1862. Age about 36, 5' 4 3/4", brown complexion.
Charles Davis. Freeborn and raised in AA Co. Certificate issued 28 April 1862. Age about 22, 5' 7 1/2", brown complexion, small scar on left wrist.
John Hammond. Freeborn and raised in AA Co. Certificate issued 29 April 1862. Age about 26, 5' 10 3/4", brown complexion, scar on left thumb.
Neawiel Green (Noel ??). Freeborn and raised in AA Co. Certificate issued 30 April 1862. Age about 22, 4' 7", dark complexion, small scar on back of neck.
Harriett Lee. Daughter of negro Charity who is the subject of. DOM recorded by Jacob Williams 22 April 1820. Age about 26, 4' 10", black complexion, raised in AA Co..
Elizabeth Steward. Freeborn and raised in AA Co. Certificate issued 24 May 1862. Age about 19, 5' 4 1/4", brown complexion, several small moles on face, small scar on right wrist.
Cecelia Taylor. Freeborn and raised in AA Co. Certificate issued 28 June 1862. Age about 35, 5' 2", yellow complexion, small scar on the wrist.
J. Blakestone. DOM recorded by John Rideout 8 Sept. 1853. Age about 31, 5' 3 3/4", black complexion. Certificate issued 31 June 1862.
William Henry Warren. Freeborn and raised in AA Co. Certificate issued 1 July 1862. Age about 25, 5' 6 ", black complexion.
Thomas Allen Warren. Freeborn and raised in AA Co. Certificate issued 1 July 1862. Age about 23, 5' 6 1/2", black complexion.
Elizabeth Diggs. Freeborn and raised in AA Co. Certificate issued 1 July 1862.

ion.

Henrietta Warren. Freeborn and raised in AA Co. Certificate issued 1 July 1862. Age about 21, 4' 7 1/2", yellow complexion, burn on righty arm.

Anthony Harrison. Freeborn and raised in AA Co. Certificate issued 5 July 1862. Age about 30, 6', dark complexion, small scar under left eye.

Jim Thompson. Freeborn and raised in AA Co. Certificate issued 8 July 1862. Age about 18, 5' 1 1/2.".

Jacob Freeland. Freeborn and raised in AA Co. Certificate issued 11 July 1862. Age about 30, 5' 9 1/4", black complexion.

William Adam Givens. Freeborn and raised in AA Co. Certificate issued 11 July 1862. Age about 21, 5' 7 1/2", yellow complexion, small scar near right eye.

Charles Henry Sifton. Freeborn and raised in AA Co. Certificate issued 4 Aug. 1862. Age about 21, 5' 5 1/4", yellow complexion.

John Dennis. Freeborn and raised in AA Co. Certificate issued 7 Aug. 1862. Age about 22, 5' 9", yellow complexion, swelling on each side of neck.

Sedonia Dennis. Freeborn and raised in AA Co. Certificate issued 7 Aug. 1862. Age about 25, 5' 1 1/4", yellow complexion.

Margaret Myers. Freeborn and raised in AA Co. Certificate issued 7 Aug. 1862. Age about 32, 5' 6 3/4", yellow complexion.

Rachel Crowner. Freeborn and raised in AA Co. Certificate issued 13 Aug. 1862. Age about 24, 5' 1 1/4", small scar on forehead.

Harriett Mack. Freeborn and raised in AA Co. Certificate issued 13 Aug. 1862. Age about 19, 5' 1 3/4", yellow complexion, straight black hair.

Solomon Butler. Son of Nelly manumitted by Samuel Jones 11 Jan. 1819, TBF at age 25. Age 27, 5' 8 1/4", brown complexion, scars on thumb and index finger of left hand, raised in AA Co.

George Brown. DOM recorded by Editha Williams 15 Nov. 1837. Age about 35, 5' 7", yellow complexion, raised in AA Co.

Thomas Sellman. Freeborn and raised in AA Co. Certificate issued 22 Dec. 1862. Freeborn and raised in AA Co. Certificate issued 22 Dec. 1862. Age about 45, 5' 9 1/2", yellow complexion, small scar on right cheek.

Margaret Ann Sellman. Freeborn and raised in AA Co. Certificate issued 22 Dec. 1862. Age about 20, 5' 5 1/2", yellow complexion, small scar on left side of face.

Sarah Bond. Freeborn and raised in AA Co. Certificate issued 4 Sept. 1862. Age about 29, 5' 2 1/2", dark complexion, scar on right hand.

Jane Holland. Freeborn and raised in AA Co. Certificate issued 14 Jan. 1863. Age about 31, 4' 11 1/2", light complexion, scar under left eye.

Sarah Jane Johnson. Freeborn and raised in AA Co. Certificate issued 14 Jan. 1863. Age about 18, 4' 11", dark complexion, scar under right eye.

Jacob Peters. Freeborn and raised in AA Co. Certificate issued 14 Jan. 1863. Age about 21, 5' 9 1/4", dark complexion, two fingers of right hand are bowed.

Samuel Allen. Son of Mary Ennis manumitted by Samuel Jones 20 June 1818, TBF at age 25. Age about 27, 5' 3", dark complexion, raised in AA Co.

Margaret Booth. DOM recorded by Smauel Jones 20 June 1818. TBF at age 21. Age about 30, 5' 4 3/4",, dark complexion, raised in AA Co.

Elizabeth Williams. Freeborn and raised in AA Co. Certificate issued 28 Feb. 1863. Age about 20, 5' 1 1/2", black complexion.

Elizabeth Gassoway. Freeborn and raised in AA Co. Certificate issued 24 March 1863. Age about 20, 5' 1/2", brown complexion.

Thomas. DOM recorded by Thomas James Stockett 27 Sept. 1827. Raised in AA Co. Certificate issued 4 April 1863. Age about 36, 5' 7", brown complexion.

William Richardson. Freeborn and raised in AA Co. Certificate issued 6 April 1863. Age about 23, 5' 4 1/2", black complexion.

Mary Ann Williams. Freeborn and raised in AA Co. Certificate issued 11 April 1863. Age about 23, 5' 1 1/4", dark brown complexion, small scar on back of left hand.

Harriett Scott. Freeborn and raised in AA Co. Certificate issued 25 April 1863. Age about 25, 5' 8 1/2", yellow complexion, scar on left side of face.

Rachel General. Freeborn and raised in AA Co. Certificate issued 4 May 1863. Age about 22, 5' 3", small scar right side of face.

James Henry Lee. Freeborn and raised in AA Co. Certificate issued 14 May 1863. Age about 20, 5' 6", light complexion, scart on left side of forehead.

Harriett Ann Brashears. Freeborn and raised in AA Co. Certificate issued 14 May 1863. Age about 21, 5' 1 1/2", yellow complexion.

Richard Parker. DOM recorded by Rezin H. Snowden 13 Feb. 1846. Certificate issued 13 Feb. 1846. Age about 23, 5' 9", brown complexion, small scar on right side of face.

—W Sellinan. DOM recorded by Rezin H. Snowden 13 Feb. 1846. Certificate issued 13 Feb. 1846. Age about 23, 5' 8 1/4", yellow complexion.

Martha Nichols. Freeborn and raised in AA Co. Certificate issued 22 May 1863. Age about 28, 5' 2 1/4", brown complexion.

Rebecca Williams. Freeborn and raised in AA Co. Certificate issued 5 July 1863. Age about 23, 5' 1 1/2", black complexion.

Elizabeth Peterson. Freeborn and raised in AA Co. Certificate issued 8 Sept. 1863. Age about 26, 5' 3 3/4", brown complexion, scar above right eye.

John Davis. Freeborn and raised in AA Co. Certificate issued 17 Sept. 1863. Age about 23, 5' 7 1/2", light complexion, scar on forehead.

Sarah Eliza Blackestone. Freeborn and raised in AA Co. Certificate issued 14 Oct. 1863. Age about 21, 5' 3 1/4", yellow complexion.

Julia Irving. DOM recorded by William Brewer 28 ---, 1859. Raised in AA Co. Certificate issued 29 Oct. 1863. Age about 31, 5' 1 1/2", yellow complexion, small scar on right arm.

William Adams. Freeborn and raised in AA Co. Certificate issued 27 Oct. 1863. Age about 25, 5' 8 1/2", black complexion, scar on nose.

Richard Adams. Freeborn and raised in AA Co. Certificate issued 27 Oct. 1863. Age about 24, 5' 7 1/4", dark brown complexion, small scar on left side of chin, another on left side of cheek, another on forehead.

Caroline Adams. Freeborn and raised in AA Co. Certificate issued 27 Oct. 1863. Age about 22, 5' 1 1/2", brown complexion, small scar under left eyebrow.

Margaret Wooton. Freeborn and raised in AA Co. Certificate issued 28 Oct. 1863. Age about 34, 5' 1 1/2", dark complexion.

Sarah Gassoway. Freeborn and raised in AA Co. Certificate issued 11 Nov., 1863. Age about 20, 5' 1", brown complexion, small scar on right side of face.

John Crowner. Freeborn and raised in AA Co. Certificate issued 25 Nov. 1863. Age about 26, 5' 10", light complexion.

John T. Turner. Freeborn and raised in AA Co. Certificate issued 25 Nov. 1863. Age about 36, 5' 9", light complexion.

William Thomas Matthews. Freeborn and raised in AA Co. Certificate issued 25 Nov. 1863. Age about 33, 5' 6 3/4", light complexion.

Henry. DOM recorded by John Solliman 5 Jan. 1832. Age about 34, 5' 5 1/2", dark complexion, scar on back of right hand, raised in AA Co.

Henry Young. Freeborn and raised in AA Co. Certificate issued 2 Dec. 1863. Age about 39, 5' 7 1/2", yellow complexion.

William H. Calvert. Freeborn and raised in AA Co. Certificate issued 8 Dec. 1863. Age about 25, 5' 1 1/4", light brown complexion.

Henry Day Calvert. Freeborn and raised in AA Co. Certificate issued 8 Dec. 1863. Age about 21, 5' 7", dark complexion.

Henry Ray Johnson. Freeborn and raised in AA Co. Certificate issued 12 Dec. 1863, 1863. Age about 21, 5' 6 1/2", yellow complexion.

Henry Queen. DOM recorded by Lydia Gambrill 7 Jan. 1837. Age about 35 5' 6 1/2", brown complexion. Certificate issued 15 Dec. 1863.

Charles Blackestone. DOM recorded by John Rideout 23 April 1840. Raised in AA Co. Certificate issued 22 Dec. 1863. Age about 25, 4' 1 3/4", dark complexion. scar on left arm.

— Brown. Freeborn and raised in AA Co. Certificate issued 23 Dec. 1863. Age about 22, 5' 10 1/2", dark complexion.

Ann Parker. DOM recorded by Edith Williams 15 Nov. 1837. Certificate issued 29 Dec. 1863. Age about 32, 5', brown complexion, raised in AA Co.

Joseph G. Smith. Freeborn and raised in AA Co. Certificate issued 6 Jan. 1864. Age about 35, 5' 7", dark complexion, scar on right ear.

Sophia. Daughter of Sarah who, (Sarah) was manumitted by Jerningham Drury. Age about 30, 5' 1", dark complexion, scar near right elbow. Document is deposition of Charles Hodges, Justice of Peace to AA Co. Circuit Court dated 27 March 1846. Document also bears the following notation Certificate issued to Sophia and Henrietta 25 April 1851. Signature is "Mrs Sarah Drury."

INDEX

Single named persons are included with persons of surnames. The first entries below are persons whose surnames were not given or the compiler was unable to read.

LAST NAMES
UNKNOWN
  Betsy, 70
  Charles, 68
  Elijah, 61
  Eliza, 66
  Elizabeth, 8
  Henry, 26, 72, 79
  John, 26
  Joseph, 63
  Leonard, 12
  Margaret, 58
  Mary, 27, 71
  Nathan, 70
  Nelson, 61
  Rachel, 72
  Sarah, 64, 71
  Susan, 61
  Sussanah, 59
  Thomas, 62
  Virgil, 23
  William, 22

-A-
AARON, 9, 4
ABIGAIL, 12, 15, 18, 76
ABIGAL, 98
ABRAHAM, 1, 2, 3, 19
ACQUAR, John, 91
  Robert, 91
ADAM, 3
ADAMS, Ann, 85
  Caroline, 104
  Charles, 82
  Ellen, 85
  Jack, 62
  Jacob, 72
  Lewis, 78
  Maria, 30
  Nace, 98
  Priscilla, 85
  Richard, 104
  Thomas, 35
  William, 104
ADDISON, George, 65
  John, 4, 90
  Patty Malinda, 12
  Walter, 2
  Walter D., 2
  William Ross, 81
AGGY, 4
AIRRY, 23
ALEEN, Hester, 25

ALEXANDER, 5
  William, 11
ALFRED, Benjamin, 19
ALINTA, 41
ALLEN, 15
  Adeline, 95
  Charles, 36
  George, 51
  Hester, 25
  Jerry, 55
  John, 57
  Mary, 53
  Nancy Ann, 53
  Nathan, 13
  Nathanial, 5
  Patsy, 53
  Rebecca, 81
  Robert, 40
  Sally, 73
  Samuel, 6, 13, 103
  Sarah Jane, 93
  Solomon, 28
  Thomas, 62
  William, 53, 65, 82
ALLISON, James, 29
ALLSOP, Richard, 70
  William, 69
ALSOP, M---, 87
  Nancy, 50
AMOS, 3
ANDERSON, Ann, 39
  Charles, 72
  Henry, 89
  James, 57
  Jerry, 42
  John, 39, 93
  Joseph, 39, 70
  Mary, 31, 39
  Nancy, 41
  Thomas, 42, 80
  Wesley, 94
ANDREW, 1, 2, 4, 28, 29, 31
ANN, 1, 2, 4, 5, 15
ANNA, 1, 31
ANNE, 2, 4, 5, 13, 37
ANNIE, 46
ANTHONY, 3, 4, 20, 27, 46
ANY, 47
ARMINGER, John, 80
  Mary, 18
ARTRIDGE, 1
AUGUSTUS, John, 55

AUSBORN, Nancy Ann, 72
  Richard, 76

-B-
B---, 3
  Charity, 72
  Chastity, 72
  Plato, 69
  William, 31
B---LEY, John, 68
BA---ES, nacy, 33
BACKER, George, 82
BACON, Benjamin, 20
  Evan, 81
  Nace, 56
BADYS, Acksah ---, 29
  Nace, 29
BAILEY, Benjamin, 98
  Katherine, 99
  Martha, 99
  Sally Ann, 100
  Thomas, 83, 96
BAINES, Charles, 13
BAKER, Cortes, 97
BALDWIN, Adeline, 100
  John, 47
  Kinsey, 95
  Margaret, 77
  Nicholas, 9
  Priscilla, 47
BARBER, Ellen, 100
BARBY, Thomas, 96
BARGEN, Fanny, 101
BARKER, George, 72
BARNES, Charlotte, 41
  Dinah, 41
  Ellen, 91
  Harry, 83
  Ruchel, 41
BARNET, James, 49
BARNETT, Anna Maria, 84
  Frances, 53
  Issac, 78
  John Henry, 78
  Nancy, 53
  Neeury, 84
  Samuel B., 49
  Solomon, 53, 78
  Thomas H., 81
  William, 63
BARNETTE, Henrietta, 61
  Mary Ann, 61
BARR, Sallie, 93

BARRET, Kate, 64
BARRETT, Jane, 50
BARRY, George W., 59
BARTON, Lucy, 84
BASFORD, Benjamin, 2
　Henry, 63, 79, 82
BATEMAN, William, 63, 101
BATSON, Margaret, 93
　Sally, 50
　Vachel, 16
BATTEE, Dennis H., 36
BATTER, Richard H., 67
BATTIE, Dennis H., 65
BAYLEY, Nancy, 26
BAYNARD, Mary Jane, 94
BEALE, Lemuel H., 51
　Samuel H., 51
BEALL, Maria, 75
BEAN, Stephen, 61
BEANS, John, 73
　Mary, 73
BEARD, John, 79
　Stephen, 60, 73, 78, 87, 91, 94
BEAS, Elizabeth, 40
BEASLEY, Elizabeth, 25
BECK, 1, 4, 20
BEDHAM, William, 38
BEDLAM, William, 38
BEICLEY, Elizabeth, 25
BELL, 19
　Cyrus, 88
　George W., 88
　Mary Ann, 88
　Richard P., 88
　Samuel, 79
BELLAS, 15
BELT, Joseph S., 3
BEN, 1, 3, 4, 11, 23, 26
BENJAMIN, 1, 3, 6, 25, 93
BENNETT, Darnell, 3, 4
　Eliza, 99
BENSON, Henry, 73
　Louisa Ann, 72
　Thomas, 85
BERBICK, William, 2
BERDLEY, Ben, 94
BERRY, 2
BET, 1, 4, 10, 17
BETSY, 5, 33
BETT, 1, 6
BETTY, 4, 28, 29
BETTY S., 99
BEUBEN, 59
BEVERIDGE, 17
BIAS, Henny, 47
　Jonny, 49
　Rachel, 47

BILL, 1, 2, 4, 24
BISHOP, Charity, 38
　Horace, 37
　Nicholas, 80
　Rebecca, 39
BLACK, Amos, 63
　William, 63
BLACKE, Staphen, 57
BLACKESTON, James, 49
　John, 102
BLACKESTONE, Charles, 104
　Mary, 100
　Sarah Eliza, 104
BLACKISTON, Anna Maria, 94
BLADEN, Margaret, 7
BLAKESTONE, J., 102
BLUNT, Dorcas, 99
　Elizabeth, 99
　Richard, 50
　Titus, 50
　Vitgina, 99
BO---, Eliza Ann, 66
BOARDLEY, Henny, 60
　Maria, 80
　Matilda, 60
BOARDLY, Flora, 75
BOB, 32
BOND, Betsy, 98
　Charlotte, 31
　Edward, 16
　Richard, 13
　Sarah, 103
　Thomas, 4
BOONE, Ann, 33
　Anne, 36
　Elizabeth, 97
　Harriiot, 56
　James, 2
　John, 5, 14, 28
　Josephine, 28
　Matilda, 44
　Priscilla, 87
　Rezin, 34
　Stephen, 15, 31, 49, 75, 87, 98
BOOTH, Eliza, 55, 78
　Margaret, 103
　Romina, 62
BOOTHE, Edward, 13
　Eleanor, 17
　James, 6, 17, 52, 66
　Lewis, 66
　Walter, 63
BORDLEY, Bill, 72
　Dick, 72
　Flora, 75
　John B., 33

BOSTON, Annie, 40
　Anthony, 65
　Aquila, 45
　Becky, 64
　Benjamin, 73
　Caesar, 16
　Catherine, 42
　Charlotte, 38
　Clarissa, 18
　Daniel, 1, 12, 38, 40, 63, 74
　Daniel C., 78
　Darky, 18, 40
　David, 66
　Dorcas, 40
　Elijah, 102
　Eliza, 66
　Ellen Ann, 100
　George, 24, 100
　Harriett, 38
　Henry, 34, 42
　Jacob, 22
　Jane, 62
　John, 49, 64
　Johnanna, 80
　Libby, 40
　Maria, 23, 89
　Mary, 17, 61, 81
　Mary Jane, 92
　May, 17
　Nancy, 45, 52
　Nelly, 64
　Peter, 10, 17
　Phillip, 8, 28, 47
　Phillis, 67
　Polly, 58
　Rachel, 42
　Rebecca, 80
　Richard, 77
　Robert, 9, 45, 46
　Samuel, 65
　Sarah, 17
　Stephen, 81
　Susan, 61, 79
　Thomas, 72
　Violetta, 61
BOTTEE, Dicius H., 38
BOURE, Lucretia, 82
　Maria, 82
BOWIE, Caroline, 86
　Lucretia, 86
BOWIES, Washington, 58
BOWLAS, Ben, 38
BOWMAN, Joseph, 12
BOWSER, James, 28, 77
　William, 60
BR---, George G., 28
BRAAFOOT, Hannah, 33
BRACH---S, Charity, 74

BRADFORD, Elinor, 4
  Elizabeth, 93
  Emily, 93
  George, 93
  Hannah, 33
  Janee, 93
  Mary, 93
  Samuel, 64
  William, 99
BRADLEY, Bill, 72
  Dick, 72
BRADSHAW, Gilbert, 30
BRANFOOT, Mary, 54
BRASHEAR, William, 89
BRASHEARS, Gilbert, 30
  harriett Anna, 103
  Jane, 65
  John, 65
  Lavinia, 90
  Nancy, 101
  Thomas, 23
BRASHEAWS, Gilbert, 30
BRASHEERS, Nancy, 54
BRASHIERS, William, 76
BRAYER, Acksah ---, 29
  Nace, 29
BREENFOOT, Betsy, 8
BREWER, Charles, 5
  Edmond, 26
  George, 37
  John, 3
  Lucy, 5
  Nicholas, 9, 14, 23, 83
  Rachel, 2
  William, 6, 38, 60, 68, 78, 79, 81, 83, 85, 92, 94, 104
BRICE, Jane, 95
  John, 4, 12, 29, 41, 45, 46, 47, 57
  Mary Ann, 61
  Mary Jane, 86
  Sophia W., 88
BRIGGS, William, 98
BRISCOE, Polly, 71
BRISTER, Bill, 8
BRISTON, Elizabeth, 78
BRODY, James, 83
BROGDEN, Abraham, 11, 69
  Edith, 68
  Elisha, 20
  Elizabeth, 96
  Emmeline, 74
  Frank, 96
  Henrietta, 65
  Henry, 96
  John, 37
  Kitty, 74
  Samuel, 44

Solomon, 12
BROOKES, Charles, 50
  Fannie, 44
  Kate, 54
  William, 16
BROOKS, Ann, 61
  Cadioallades, 20
  Edward, 101
  Priscilla, 34
BROWER, A., 30
BROWN, 30
  ---, 104
  Adeau, 27
  Andrew, 27
  Ann, 77, 78
  Anna, 43
  Benjamin, 11, 22, 26, 36, 59, 72, 82
  Brice, 82
  Charity, 26
  Charles, 95
  Daniel, 87
  David, 17, 39
  Dinah, 21, 57
  Edward, 51, 81
  Eliza, 25
  Ellen, 83
  Ezekiel, 58
  George, 17, 84, 103
  Harriett Ann, 95
  Harriett K., 102
  Henry, 37, 61, 95
  Hester Ann, 72, 90
  Jacob, 86
  James, 60
  John, 3, 5, 7, 31, 38, 42, 69
  John G., 40
  Julia Ann, 63
  Kisiah, 75
  Letty, 90
  Lucretia, 44
  Margaret, 15, 81
  Maria, 96
  Mary, 19, 45, 55, 79
  Matilda, 96
  Nace, 35
  Nackey, 79
  Nancy, 31, 50, 95
  Peter, 56
  Polly, 56
  Rachel, 15, 23
  Rebecca, 78
  Richard, 35, 79
  Robert, 25, 79
  Rosetta, 62
  Sarah, 15, 31
  Selana, 31
  Sophia, 70, 100

Susan, 38, 55, 56, 78, 86, 95
  Sussanna, 82
  Thomas, 21
  Thomas E., 31
  Washington, 82
  Will---, 29
  William, 5, 40, 61, 65, 66, 73, 81
BROWNE, Richard, 59
BRUCE, Louther, 2
  Lucretia, 51
BRUMMER, Benjamin, 5
  James, 5
BRUNFOOT, Henry, 40
  John, 40
BRYAN, Charles, 1
  Janie, 101
  Thomas, 82
BUCHANAN, Franklin, 90
  Priscilla, 66
BUCHER, George, 17
  John, 17
BUCKINGHAM, Phillip, 44
BUGG, Allen, 95
  Phoebe, 67
BULGER, Margaret, 5
BULL, Louisa, 53
  Mary, 53
  Nancy, 53
  Patsy, 53
BULLEY, Susan, 79
BULTER, Jane, 86
BURGESS, John, 51
  Joseph, 101
  Joshua, 34
  Maria, 59
  Mary, 65
  Polly, 62
BURKE, Joliet., 62
BURLEY, Dick, 6
  Eleanor, 44
  Hester, 101
  Thomas, 87, 89
BURLIE, Soleri, 87
BURLY, Thomas, 9
BURNESTON, Joseph, 13
BURNS, Issac, 82
BURRY, Mary, 82
BUSH, William, 4
BUTLER, Ann, 99
  Bill, 2
  Catherine, 81
  Elizabeth, 91, 97
  James, 74
  Jane, 86
  John, 70, 95
  Nan, 63
  Nancy, 80

Nicholas, 92
Patty, 2
Sally, 100
Sarah, 27
Solomon, 103
Susan, 59, 100
William H., 80
BYAS, Rachel, 54

-C-
C---, Elizabeth, 29
John, 68
C., Joseph, 64
CAESAR, 2, 3, 5
CAGER, George, 78
 Hester, 77
 John, 40, 78
 Malvina, 81
 Priscilla, 44
 Rosannah, 40
 Sally, 44
CAGIS, James, 30
CAIN, James, 21, 59
 John, 35
 Mary, 81
 Richard H., 39
CAINE, James, 11
 Thomas, 10
CALBERT, Mary Ellen, 74
 Sam, 74
 Samuel, 90
CALDER, Harriet, 7
CALE, 23
CALEB, 3, 11, 23
CALLAHAN, Margaret, 14, 17, 36
 Mary, 3, 27, 37, 39
CALVER, Millie, 91
CALVERT, Charles, 25, 94
 Elizabeth, 100
 Harriett, 77
 Henry, 99
 Henry Day, 104
 Hillery, 87
 Mary, 99
 Suddy, 44
 Tom, 44
 William, 44
 William H., 104
CAMMEL, Kelson, 90
CAMPBELL, Sussanna, 20
CANE, William, 77
CANN, Amelia, 78
CAPHNE, 8
CAROLINE, 23
CARR, Louis, 80
CARROLL, ---, 73
 Anne, 35
 Charles, 3, 4, 5, 25, 30

Elizabeth Ann, 94
Henry, 80
James, 80
John, 49
Rachel, 42
Sarah, 65
CARROT, Joseph, 62
CARTER, Bill, 23
 Harriott, 19
 James, 2
 Robert, 80
 William, 23
CASSA, 1
CASSANDRA, 5
CASSY, 11, 14
CASTLE, Polly, 8
 William, 29
CATE, 4, 16, 23, 24
CATHERINE, 7, 76
CATO, 4
CEZAR, 1
CHAGER, George, 18
CHAMBERS, Richard, 87
 Thomas, 18
 William, 13
CHANCE, 5
CHANCY, Joseph, 33
CHANEY, Joseph, 33
 Richard, 4
CHARETY, 4
CHARITY, 4, 20, 25, 78, 87, 96, 100, 102
CHARLES, 1, 2, 3, 4, 5, 6, 8, 11, 16, 17, 19, 22, 24, 35, 72, 3
 Jane, 25
 Peter, 25
CHARLOTTE, 4, 27, 29, 37, 79
CHASE, Alice, 78
 Jeremiah, 1
 Jeremiah P., 2
 Priscilla, 79
 Richard M., 49
CHEERS, Samuel, 25
CHENEY, Richard, 6, 7
CHERI, Nelly, 35
CHERRY, Nelly, 35
CHES---, Margaret, 74
CHESTER, James, 79
CHESTON, Harriet, 2
 James, 80
 Samuel, 101
 Sarah, 2
CHESTOR, Samuel, 82
CHEW, Arminta, 23
 Henny, 49
 Henry, 101
 James, 71

John, 15
Nathanial, 4, 25
Nathaniel, 79
Richard, 52
CHILDS, John, 62, 74, 76
 Martha P., 28, 29
CHLOE, 2
CHRISTMAS, Nicholas, 37
CILLE, 4
CLANDE, William Fell, 79
CLARK, Amos, 59
 Iannetta, 38
CLARKE, Daniel, 85
 Deborah, 22
 Eleanor, 22
 Harriet, 70
 Issac, 88
 Lucinda, 88
 Nancy, 71
 Sarah, 52
CLARRIDGE, Solomon, 37
CLAUDE, Abram, 13
 Dennis, 13, 27
 John, 13, 27
CLAYTON, Phillip, 62
CLEEN, Mary Jane, 89
CLOE, 29
CLOSY, 15
COATES, William, 93
COE, William, 2
COLBERT, John, 100
COLE, Joseph, 80
COLLINS, ---, 70
 Catherine, 83
 Charles, 72
 Daniel, 83
 Joseph, 101
 Maria, 101
 Samuel, 95
 Thomas, 82
 William, 2, 60
COLLINSON, John, 95
CONAWAY, William B., 80
CONNER, Richard, 24, 55, 23
COOK, Hager, 17
 Phillip, 55
 Thomas, 7
COOKE, John, 22
 John Henry, 34
 Maynard, 73
COOPER, Hannibal, 80
 Henry, 80
 Rachel, 56
CORBY, Eleanor, 89
CORD, John, 6
CORDELIA, 23
CORNELIA, 12
CORNELIOUS, 3

CORSEY, Charles, 4, 18
COSTLEY, Sarah Jane, 94
COUITLY, Sarah Jane, 94
COUNT, Joseph, 24, 34
COUNTEE, George, 51
  Polly, 51
COUNTS, Charles, 57
  John, 50
COURT, Joseph, 3, 5
  Stephen, 89
COWIMAN, John, 12, 13
COWLEY, Eleanor, 87
COWMAN, Joseph, 9, 59
  William, 14
CRABB, Richard J., 79
CRANDALL, William T., 79
CRANDELL, William T., 80
CRAWFORD, Kitty, 67
  Rachel Ann, 94
CREEK, Priscilla, 55
  William, 52, 65
CROMWELL, Abigail, 37
  Charlotte, 51
  Frances, 16
  Francis, 10, 24
  Hestor, 62
  James C., 80
  John, 24
  Oneal, 15
  Richard, 30
  Samuel, 37
  Susan, 37
  William, 81
CROSS, David, 63
  N---, 32
  Thomas, 58, 59, 63, 66
CROTHERS, William, 100
CROWNER, Charles, 76
  Henry, 33
  John, 45, 104
  Louisa, 44
  Luther, 43
  Odessa, 46
  Phillip, 81
  Rachel, 103
  Rebecca, 85
  Thomas, 90
CRURY, Charles, 24
  Jerningham, 46
CULDESS, Benjamin J., 61
CUMMINGS, Arminta, 2
CUPY, 64
CURRY, Robert, 84
CVOIORE, Lavale Ann, 85
CYRUS, 6

-D-
DADDS, Emanuel, 80
DANIEL, 1, 3, 18, 19, 20, 28, 32, 34
DANIELSON, Charles, 6
  Sarah, 6
DAPHNE, 6
DARKINS, Sarah, 31
DARNALL, Bennet, 41
  Bennett, 15
  Phillip, 41
DAVID, 1, 2, 28, 32
DAVIDGE, Peter, 48
DAVIDSON, Eleanor, 3
  Thomas, 84
DAVIDSSON, Rebecca, 4
DAVIS, 11
  Betsy, 55
  Charles, 102
  Eliza, 73
  Fanny, 17
  George, 95
  Henny, 10
  Henry Lyon, 35
  James, 82
  Jane, 99
  John, 36, 46, 104
  Junas, 89
  Kiziah, 41
  Lemuel, 84
  Mary, 84
  Matilda, 27
  Moses, 6
  Nancy, 33
  Polly, 33
  Rebecca, 59
  Richard, 64
  Ruth, 57
  Samuel, 3
  Sarah, 46
  Suck, 37
  Wappen, 53
  Wassen, 53
DEALE, Rachael, 35
DEB, 3
DEBORAH, 15, 34
DEIVIES, James, 32
DELIA, 23
DENKINS, Margaret, 75
DENNIS, 18
  Alexander, 87
  Eliza, 64
  John, 103
  Joshua, 67
  Leonard, 64
  Sedonia, 103
DENNISS, Jacob, 59
DERVIS, Peter, 81
DICK, 4, 5, 10, 11, 13, 22

DIGGES, Dennis, 49
  Willy, 51
DIGGS, Debra Ann, 92
  Dinah, 59
  Dinah Sophia, 83
  Elizabeth, 102
  Emeline, 92
  Fanny A., 75
  John Henry, 92
  John M., 75
  Margaret Isabelle, 92
  Willliam, 82
DINAH, 1, 2, 4, 5, 6, 7, 9, 15, 19, 31
DINKINS, Sophia, 78
DINNAH, 4
DISNEY, Amelia M., 88
  William, 85
DIXON, James, 82
DOCKER, William, 16
DOCKIER, Benjamin, 11
DODDS, Emanuel, 59, 77
DODSON, Henry, 48, 69
  John, 73
  Mary, 57
DOLL, 3
DOMAN, George, 3
DONALDSON, John, 6
DORKAS, 2
DOROTHY, 3
DORSEY, Charles, 60
  Charles M., 18
  Charlotte, 66
  Davey, 60
  Elizabeth, 1
  Frances, 71
  George, 18, 42, 55
  Gustava, 37
  Harry, 66
  Henry Hall, 1, 6
  James New, 100
  John, 3
  Julia Ann, 33, 42, 96
  Kitt, 63
  Lucy, 2
  Mary Ann, 88
  Michael, 60
  Ned, 42
  Nero, 64
  Peter, 42, 66
  Rachael, 9
  Rose, 10
  Stephen, 60
  William, 38
DOSON, William, 92
DOUGLASS, Samuel, 33
DOVE, Adam, 47
DOWELL, Edward, 63
DOWNS, Margaret Ann,

89
Robert, 14
DRUMMER, Jenny, 5
Kinoe, 5
Rosetta, 5
DRURY, Charles, 1, 16, 58
Henry, 95
Henry C., 89
Henry C. of Charles, 67
Henry of Charles, 73
Jerningham, 1, 4, 19, 40, 59, 64, 73, 104
Plummer I., 79
Sarah, 104
DUCKETT, John, 81
DUFFIN, Nicholas, 8
DULANY, Elizabeth, 57
Sarah Ann, 57
Walter, 3
DUNKINS, Betsy, 57
DUPPIN, Charles, 51
DUPPINS, Parry More, 67
DUTTON, Louisa, 101
DUVALE, John W., 33
DUVALL, Edwin W., 80
Henry, 6, 16, 26
Howard, 4
Jimina, 91
Lewis, 34
Samuel E., 80
Zachariah, 8, 9, 12, 13, 14, 45, 56

-E-
E---, Nancy, 62
EARLE, William, 79
EASTER, 1, 2, 5
EASTON, John, 14
William, 51
EDMUND, 3
EDWARD, 37
EDWARDS, Aquila, 47
Basil, 45
Charity, 47
Dennis, 36
Elizabeth, 97
Freeborn G., 76
John, 36
Lavinia, 97
Louisa, 45
Mary, 45
Nack, 89
Phoda, 47
Rebecca, 92
Sarah, 5, 6
Solomon, 76
Susanna, 97
ELDER, Charles, 1
ELEANOR, 5, 9, 32

ELINOR, 4
ELIZA, 3, 100
ELIZABETH, 1, l, 15, 17, 5
ELLEN, 2
ELLIOTT, Richard, 29
Sarah Ann, 93
ELMS, Thomas, 6
ELSON, Mary, 29
ELVIRA, 23
ELY, 3, 22
EMANUEL, 1
EMERSON, Cornelious, 55
Emanuel, 75
John, 55
ENNESSE, Thomas, 75
ENNIS, Ann, 80
Benjamin, 17
David, 54
Edward, 36
Harriet, 78
Harriet Ann, 66
Harriett, 17, 77
Henry, 57, 59, 93
John, 100
Joshua, 50
L---, 68
Mary, 68, 72, 103
Molly Ann, 88
Richard, 50
Sarah, 50, 54
William, 95
EPHRIAM, 3
ESTEP, Daniel, 76
Louis W., 92
Mary Jane, 95
ESTHER, 4, 19
EUICES, John, 14
EVANS, John, 102
Joseph, 4, 20, 25, 33, 64
Mary Elizabeth, 70

-F-
FAN, 3
FANNIE, 11
FANNY, 1, 4, 6, 13, 18, 21, 25, 30, 35
FILL, Anne, 84
FISHER, James, 11, 12
Stephen, 30
Thomas, 7, 12
William, 13, 50, 53
FLAVA, 46
FLEETWOOD, Benjamin, 91
Sarah, 80
Willilam, 87
FLIVA, 19
FLORA, 2, 27, 29, 60
FOGGETT, Richard, 38

FOLKS, Charity, 1, 7
Henry, 10
Mary, 7
Peggy, 10
Thomas, 4
FOOTE, Henry, 6
FORD, Charlotte, 46
Edward, 46
FORTEE, John, 101
FORTY, Harriett, 32
Jacob, 1, 32, 59
John, 59
Mary, 32
Sarah, 32
FOSSAT, Richard, 1
FOSTER, Letty, 100
FOWLER, J---, 27
Jacob, 31, 97
FR---, Henny, 29
Louisa, 22
FRANCES, 1, 12
FRANK, 4
FRANKLIN, Abraham, 39, 44
Andrew, 75, 85
Ann, 58
Caroline, 85
Edmund, 84
Eleanor, 2
Frana Ann, 92
Henry, 44
Jacob, 2
John, 22, 23, 67
Joseph, 17
Susan, 37
Thomas, 81, 83
William, 2, 11
FRAZIER, Anna, 43
Cassandra, 24
Samson, 22
FREDERICK, 4
FREELAN, Peter, 67
FREELAND, Jacob, 103
London, 2
Susan, 59
Thomas, 30
FROST, Henrietta, 59
Rebecca, 41
Will, 4

-G-
G---, Charles, 68
George, 68
Jerry, 68
Louis, 77
Richard, 32
William, 91
GAANA, Hannah, 56
GAITHER, Abraham, 4

Benjamin, 34
Dinah, 75
Elizabeth, 38
James, 38, 75
Jeremiah, 21, 38
Jessie, 93
John C., 65
Lucy, 4
Mary, 38
Mary Ann, 65
Samuel, 38
Sarah, 38
Washington, 65
GAITHERS, Charlotte, 91
  Eleanor, 33
  Rachael, 33
  Richard, 33
GALE, Harriet, 26
GALLOWAY, James, 93
  Ned, 15
  Sarah, 23
GAMBRILL, Augustine, 4
  Lydia, 62, 64, 89, 90, 102
  Samuel, 57
  Susan, 95
GAMBRILLS, Lydia, 72, 100
GANTT, Flora, 54
  Richard, 61
  William, 102
GARDNER, Elias, 82
  M's, 1
  Nelly, 54
  Sarah, 1
  William Henry, 86
GARNER, Jesse, 84
  Nelson, 97
GARRETT, Alexander, 46
  Amos, 60
  Arthur, 69
  Basil, 100
  Edward, 69
  George, 91
  Harriett, 60, 100
  John, 28
  Maria, 61
  Mary Jane, 90
  Nace, 70
  Peggy, 18
  Rebecca, 92
  Richard, 39, 54, 69, 100
  Richard Savoy, 18
  Samuel, 16
  Sarah, 94
  Thomas, 28, 46
  Washington, 100
GARRISON, Louisa, 95
GARUBULL, Lydia, 82
GASKINS, Nachel, 90

GASSAWAY, ---, 94
  London, 86
  Mary, 86
  Mary Rebecca, 92
  Moses, 86
  Perry, 86
  Rebecca, 86
  Watt, 38
GASSOWAY, Eilza, 4
  Elizabeth, 8, 103
  John, 102
  Louis, 21
  Sarah, 104
GAULT, ---, 70
  Charles, 70
  Henry, 70
GENERAL, Daniel, 82
  Harry, 64
  Henry, 82
  Prisciolla, 82
  Rachel, 103
GEORGE, 2, 3, 4, 5, 13, 14, 19, 20, 26, 31, 41
GIBSON, Charles, 85
  Dick, 66
  Eliza, 66
  George T., 81
  Henry, 34
  Hercules, 34
  Hercules L., 48
  Horatio, 14
  Jim, 68
  John, 3, 76
  Nicholas, 102
  Patty, 68
  Rachel, 71
  Richard, 86
  Sally, 68
  Sampson, 71
  Vachel, 71
  William, 29
GIDEON, 11
GILES, William, 79
GINGES, William, 13
GIVENS, Samuel, 63
  William ADam, 103
GLOVER, Mary, 28
  William, 28
GOIT, Amelia, 90
GOLD, Amelia, 15
  Jane, 3
  John, 3
GOLDBOURGH, William, 80
GOLDEN, Archibald, 5
GOLDSBOROUGH, William T., 80
GOLDSBOURGH, Robert, 3

William, 71
GOODIN, Kitty, 36
GOOLD, Peter, 11
GORDON, Benjamin, 98
  Charlotte, 79
  Sam, 98
GOUGH, Lloyd, 63
GOVER, Samuel, 80
  William, 33
GRACE, 1, 4, 8, 11
GRANT, Arminta, 77
GRAY, Beck, 56
  Elijah, 3, 34, 47
  Eliza, 5
  George, 75
  Greenbury, 75
  Hannah, 76
  James, 55
  Jessie, 76
  Kitty, 5
  Leonard, 4
  Letty, 5
  Levi, 54
  Lucy, 75
  Margaret, 56
  Martin, 5
  Mary Ann, 76
  Otho, 54
  Phillip, 96
  Rachael Ann, 76
  Sarah Ann, 92
  Stephen, 86
  Washington, 60
GREEN, Africa, 29
  Africa A., 3
  Alice, 71
  Allen, 82
  Benjamin, 98
  Betty, 6, 57
  Catherine, 68
  Clarissa, 67
  Darius, 36
  Davies, 33
  Dina, 72
  Dinah, 72
  Eleanora, 90
  Elizabeth, 35
  Ephriam, 76
  Frederick, 17
  Garrison, 76
  Hannah, 35
  Harriett, 60
  Harriot, 55
  Henry, 76, 77
  James, 21, 98
  Jane, 76
  Jenny, 47
  John, 6, 33, 38, 57, 67, 77
  John Henry, 84

Kitty, 3, 29
Maria, 67
Mary, 63
Mary Ann, 73
Moses, 71
Nancy, 33, 55
Neawiel, 102
Nicholas, 59
Noel, 102
Owen, 60
Pheles, 63
Priscilla, 71
Rachael Ann, 35
Sacou, 60
Samuel, 37, 50, 77, 83
Sarah, 3, 57
Saul, 45
Susan, 60
William, 65, 85
Zachariah, 70
GREENE, Margaret, 68
GREENWELL, Lydia, 60
GREENWOOD, Mary
 Jane, 78, 79
GREY, Richard, 73
 Thomas, 73
GRIFFIN, Kinsey, 29
 Margaret, 65
GRIFFITH, Charles, 31, 71
 Charles Greenbury, 31
GRINAGE, Christopher, 86
 Jesse, 86
GROOVES, Solomon, 34
GROSS, David, 75
 Eliza Jane, 87
 Harriett, 99
 Mary, 48
 Mayard, 75
 Nan, 63
GUSTAVIES, 32
GUSTAVUS, 26
GUY, 10
 Elizabeth, 85
GUYNN, Allen, 2
GWINN, John, 1

-H-
H---, John, 38, 63
 Sarah Ann, 33
H---LEY, Harriet, 71
HACKETT, ---, 46
HACKMAN, Amelia, 26
 Samuel, 24
HACKNEY, Catherine, 21
 George, 27
 Margaret, 18
HAGAR, 45, 52
HAGER, 1, 3
HAGNER, Peter, 5

HAINES, Dick, 17
HALL, Alexander, 95
 Benjamin, 79
 Charlotte, 65
 David, 95
 Dinah, 23
 Edward, 6, 62
 Eleanor, 1, 7, 11
 Elisha, 67
 Fanny, 67
 Henry, 74
 Jacon, 76
 James, 4
 Jerry, 36
 John, 19
 Lewis, 76
 Mary, 56
 Meliara, 74
 Mordica, 6
 Nellie, 91
 Nelly, 94
 Richard, 62
 Robert, 75, 16
 Sam, 36
 Solomon, 91, 94
 Sophia, 86
 Thomas, 2, 62
 Tom, 6
 William, 58, 62, 76
HALTON, Richard G., 10
HAMIAL, 32
HAMMENS, Grace, 5
HAMMOND, Catherine, 60
 Charles, 3, 25, 53, 70
 Charles of Charles, 22
 Eliza, 22
 George, 93
 George Alfred, 85
 Greenbury, 1
 Henry, 24, 47, 62, 72, 75,
  84
 Isiaah, 88
 John, 102
 John Chase, 67
 John Henry, 90
 Julia, 88
 Mary, 53, 71
 Mary Jane, 73
 Nace, 53
 Phillip, 5, 23, 44
 Rachael, 36
 Rachel, 51
 Rezin, 4
 Richard, 11, 53
 Sally, 71
 Samuel, 87
 William, 3, 56
HAMY, 5
HANCOCK, Francis, 4, 23,

 47
HANDY, Ann, 83
HANES, Hazel, 95
HANNAH, 2, 5, 24, 27, 30,
 31, 47, 89
HANSON, Henry, 54
 Ignacious, 18
 John, 38, 56
 Mary, 60
 Nace, 18
 Sukey, 3
 Thomas, 3
 William, 61
HARDEN, George, 85
 Thomas, 85
HARDESTY, William, 96
 William P., 80
HARDY, Agnes, 42
 Rachel, 55
 Samuel, 67
 Sophia, 67
HARICOT, 25
HARIOTT, 5
HARRIA, Isabella, 90
HARRIETT, 2, 5, 13
HARRIMAN, ---, 82
 John, 18
HARRIOT, 1
HARRIOTT, 45, 8
HARRIS, Ann, 76
 David, 5
 Elizabeth, 61
 Hannah, 69
 John, 50, 78
 Joseph, 56
 Rachael, 5, 10
 Rachel, 58
 Richard, 43, 73
 Sarah, 53
 Susan, 77
 Thomas, 3, 35
HARRISON, ---, 21
 Anthony, 103
 Arminta, 36
 Benjamin, 2
 Bennett, 11, 17
 Betsy, 53
 Calvert, 78
 Edward, 14
 Eleanor, 2
 Elisha, 5
 Elizabeth, 48
 Harriett, 58
 Issac, 5
 James, 48
 John, 38, 71
 Joseph, 73
 Mary, 2
 Nathan, 71

Norry, 24
Richard, 11, 48
Samuel, 2, 58
Sarah, 5
Sophia, 73
Thomas, 14
Walter, 4
William, 34, 81
HARROD, Isaac, 52
HARRWOOD, Mary, 85
HARRY, 2, 3, 4, 12, 14, 19, 28, 59
HART, John Nicholas, 89
HARWOOD, Alexander, 85
John Hanson, 100
Joseph, 46
Julia Ann, 42
Lucy, 30, 35, 38, 42, 58, 59, 69, 77, 89
Nancy, 94
Richard, 5, 11
Thomas, 11
HAWK, Davis, 39
HAWKINS, Augustine, 56
Ann, 91
Archibald, 9
Dovey, 68
Eb, 91
Eliza, 47
Emily, 97
Flava, 46
Hannah, 47
Hilliary, 64
Isaac, 45
James J., 81
Jane, 77
John, 77, 92
Levy, 16
Lewis, 30
Louis, 80
Margaret, 47
Maria, 91
Matilda, 46
Milly, 81
Noah, 36
Peter, 2
Priscilla, 47
Rachael, 4
Samuel, 6, 16
Susan, 46
Susanna, 4
William, 40
HAWMIND, Ellen, 77
HAYES, Bennett, 49
Betsy, 50
Charles, 49
HAYNES, Hazel, 53
HAYWOOD, Bill, 25, 26
Samuel, 4

Tom, 25, 26
HEANIS, Benjamin, 82
HEARNWOOD, henry, 92
John Hanson, 100
Robert, 92
HECTOR, 10
HEMMINGS, Nince, 21
HENNY, 4, 5, 27, 72
HENRIETTA, 1, 72
HENRY, 1, 2, 3, 4, 5, 37, 77, 104
James, 62
Sarah, 102
HENSON, James, 28
Polly, 53
HEOLIDAY, James, 70
HEPBURN, Peter, 101
Samuel, 101
HEPSELIUS, John, 4
HERBERT, Sam, 53
HESS, 36
HEWITT, Thomas, 3
HEY, Henny, 35
HIAS, Maria, 71
HICKS, Mary, 1
William, 26, 27
HIGGINS, Richard, 5
HILL, Abe, 1
Abel, 14
Delilah, 51
Ned, 1
Sarah, 47
HILLIARY, 1, 6
HILLS, Abel, 6
HINDMAN, Cesar, 91
HINDSMAN, Richard, 77
Rosetta, 61
HINSMAN, Jacob, 82
Matilda, 82
Rachael, 27
HITCHCOCK, Levi, 79
HOBB, Ephraim, 37
HOBBS, ---, 34
Beowulf, 63
Charles, 51
Gerard, 40
Henry, 40
Priscilla, 83
Sarah Ann, 96
HODGE, Charles, 36
Sarah, 76
HODGES, Charles, 104
HOLIDAY, James, 70
HOLLAND, George, 80
Henry, 77
Henry L., 70
Jane, 99, 103
Jemima, 98
John, 78

Maria, 99
nancy, 50
Nicholas, 69
Richard, 87, 101
HOLLIDAY, Isaac, 46
HONOR, 5
HOOD, Eliza, 35, 66
Elizabeth, 24, 25, 29, 54, 62, 64, 68, 69
Elizabeth Glester, 55
Hester, 22, 24, 25, 62, 64, 68
Hestor, 54
HOOL, Elizabeth, 59
Hester, 59
HOOPER, Ezekiel, 40
Harry, 26
Henry, 26, 40
John, 22
HOPKI8NS, Joseph R., 53
HOPKINS, Charles, 64
Erasmus, 43
Gerard R., 79, 80
Johns, 10
Joseph, 52, 64
Joseph R., 20
Margaret, 20, 30, 32, 43, 63, 67
Phillip H., 27
Phillip Hammond, 30
Richard, 2, 43
Richard of Gerard, 13
Samuel, 4, 26, 62
Samuel S., 80
Sarah, 8
HOWARD, Amey, 37
Amy, 58
Ann, 3
Charles, 88
Frank, 23
George, 40, 66
John Eager, 5
Lucy, 52
Mary, 52, 55
Mary Anne, 23
Peter, 88
Phillip, 23
Rachel, 56
Ruth, 23
Samuel, 63
Thomas Worthington, 5
William Henry, 88
HOWELL, Gilbert, 52
HUBBLEY, Elizabeth, 93
HUGHES, Jeremiah, 10
HULL, Eliza, 37
Henry, 56
HUNT, John, 77
Michael, 45

Nancy Ann, 77
HUNTER, James, 57
HURST, John, 2
HUTTON, Catherine, 41
   Charlotte, 62
   Nace, 73
   Richard, 18
   Richard G., 41
   William, 82
HYAMS, Charlotte, 75
HYDE, Darnell, 79
HYNSMAN, Charles, 96

-I-

IJAMS, Caroline, 92
   Hannah, 49
   Phillip, 81
   Rezin, 92
   Washington, 48
IRVING, Julia, 104
ISAAC, 1, 3, 16
ISAACS, Caroline, 52
   Eliza, 52
   Julia Ann, 43
   Susan Ann, 43
ISABELLA, 8
ISRAEL, Mary, 18, 62, 64
ISSAC, 1, 8, 11, 12, 18, 19, 32
   Shaddrach, 21
   William, 24
ISSACS, Rachel Marie, 96

-J-

J---, Thomas, 31
JACK, 2, 3, 4, 5, 6
JACKSON, ---, 72
   Ann, 33
   Cate, 58
   Dianh, 52
   Eliza, 86
   Henry, 67
   James, 6, 69
   Linda, 11
   mary Ann, 58
   Milly, 42
   Nathan, 84
   Sarah, 45
   Stacey, 57
   Sussanna, 58
   Wesley, 85
   William, 61
JACOB, 1, 3, 4, 8, 11, 27, 34
   Dorsey, 82
JACOBS, Amelia, 97
   Harriet, 60
   Harriott, 50
   Maria, 94
   Martha Eliza, 87
   Mary Ann, 64
   Nicholas, 83
   Phillip, 34
   Sarah, 60
   William, 85
JACON, 4
JAMES, 2, 3, 5, 6, 7, 9, 14, 41
   Eliza Ann, 68
   Emmaline, 88
   Lillie, 41
   Margaret Ann, 88
   Nathan, 88
   Thomas, 60
JAMINA, 9
JANE, 2, 4, 6, 19
JANNIE, 1
JANSON, Ephraim, 42
JEM, 2
JENIFER, Ann, 25
   Daniel of Saint Thomas, 5
   Joseph, 5, 25
JENKINS, Frank, 101
   Jasper, 22
   Milly, 57
JENN, 1
JENNIFER, Ann, 20, 22, 25
   Anne, 19
   Daniel of St. Thomas, 7, 8, 19
JENNINGS, Cinderella Ann, 91
   Clarissa, 69
   Elizabeth, 79
   Henry, 64
   James, 96
   John Henry, 91
   Sophia, 97
   Stephen, 69
   Thomas, 1, 78, 79
   Viney, 28
   William, 85
   Zena, 96
JENNY, 2, 3, 4, 6, 10, 32, 47
JEREMIAH, 1, 2, 31
JERRY, 1, 10
JIAMS, Judy, 9
JIM, 1, 3, 21, 24
JOAN, 5
JOCKY, 1, 6
JOE, 1, 2, 3, 7
JOHN, 1, 2, 3, 4, 5, 9, 13, 15, 21, 26, 29, 37
JOHNSON, ---, 69, 93
   Aaron, 70
   Andrew, 82
   Angelina, 98
   Ann, 54
   Artridge, 44
   Basil, 75
   Betsy, 44
   Catherine, 66, 70
   Cesar, 95
   Charles, 77, 78
   Chevis H., 76
   Cyrus, 42
   Daniel, 75
   David, 39
   Delilah, 43
   Dick, 52
   Dinah, 59
   Edward, 34, 84
   Eliza, 98
   Elizabeth, 68
   George, 22
   Greenbury, 66
   Hannah Ann, 85
   Henry, 4, 63, 82
   Henry Ray, 104
   hester Ann, 85
   Issac, 39, 65, 101
   Jacob, 32, 61, 75
   James, 16, 22, 29
   Jane, 54, 75, 99
   Janet, 51
   Jenny, 63
   Jim, 73
   John, 24, 51, 65, 68, 86, 93
   John Wesley, 81
   Julia, 89
   Levi, 76, 88
   Lucy, 51, 80
   Margaret, 69, 87
   Margaret jane, 98
   Maria, 59
   Mary, 78, 84
   Mary Ann, 102
   Mercy, 69
   Nathan, 74
   Nelly, 66
   Nicholas, 90
   Nick, 73
   Paul, 70
   Peter, 78
   Rachael, 38, 73
   Rachel, 75
   Richard, 39
   Robert, 10, 82
   S---, 71
   Sally, 98
   Samuel, 18
   Sarah, 24, 45, 47, 79
   Sarah Jane, 103
   Sophia, 47, 77

Stephen, 35, 51
Thomas, 51
Thomas William Henry, 89
William, 21, 30, 101
JOICE, Harriett, 79
Kitty, 26
Thomas, 34
JONATHAN, 4
JONES, Aaron, 36, 58
Abraham, 35
Basil, 97
Betsy, 3, 55
Caroline, 85
Elizabeth, 73
Flavilly, 47
Francis, 58
Henry, 75
Jack, 72
Jeremiah, 61
John, 5
John O. L., 23, 28, 36
John of, 5
Julia Anne, 43
Maria, 31
O. L., 10
Priscilla, 65
Rachel, 55
Samuel, 103, 47, 66, 84, 94, 103
Sarah, 54
Welsy, 97
William, 8, 36, 51, 80
JORDON, James, 66
JOSEPH, 1, 25, 30
JOSHUA, 13
JOYCE, John, 3
Richard, 62, 63
JUBA, 13
JUDA, 6
JUDE, 6
JUDY, 1, 91
JULIA, 46
JULIA ANN, 77
JULIET, 41

-K-
K., Issac, 17
KASS, 14
KATIE, 2
KELLY, Abby, 91
Annie, 27
Catherine, 30
Francis Ann, 92
Henrietta, 91
Jane, 91
Laphea, 24
Sarah Ann, 91
KENT, Ann, 38

George, 92
Mary, 102
Rosetta, 31
KERSEY, Eleanor Ann, 89
KESIAH, 1
KESSY, 20
KEUSSARD, James, 84
KEY, Ann, 49
Mary, 52
Thomas, 52
KILTY, William, 3, 41
KING, Emily Adrian, 76
William, 36
KITTY, 4, 26, 29, 33, 51, 52
KUNTI, 5
KYER, Richard, 7

-L-
L---, Augustine, 44
Benjamin, 59
Cassy, 33
Daniel, 22
John, 76
Nicholas, 23
LA LANDELLE, Francis Maria, 3
Maria Emily Sainte Mayon, 3
LAMER, 16
LANDY, 32
LANE, 3
Benjamin, 2
Fanny, 74
Henry, 74
Hester, 74
John Henry, 96
John Turner, 98
Locenso, 94
Lorenzo, 94
Mary, 74
Richard, 96
Ruth, 74
Sarah, 65, 74
Susanna, 6, 8, 9, 10
Sussanna, 22
William, 80, 86
LARKIN, James, 75
LARKINS, Harriet, 70
James, 70
Julia, 79
LATIMER, Randolph B., 1, 4
LAUGHLIN, Jonathan, 55
LAVINA, 52
LAWS, Sarah Ann, 101
LAWTON, Sarah, 15
LEAGER, Caroline, 82
Thomas, 86

LEAVIS, William, 93
LEE, Betty, 48
Charlotte, 96
Harriett, 76, 102
Henry, 48, 102, 94
Isiah, 87
James Henry, 92, 103
Kitty, 17
Lewis, 48
Martha, 48
Nancy, 48, 96
Nancy Ann, 98
Rachel, 21
Sarah Ann, 91
Stephen, 38
LEGG, Elias P., 59
James, 79
LEHERD, Hannah, 67
LEIGH, Benjamin, 9
LEMUEL, 2, 32
LETTY, 19
LEVI, 1, 5
LEWIS, 6
Ellen, 37
Ginny, 37
Thomas, 5
LIB, 5
LIBB, 1
LIBBY, 6
LIELY, 2
LILE, 4
LILEY, 18
LILI, 10
LILVEY, 11
LINTHICUM, Amelia, 86
Elizabeth, 68, 74
Wesley, 24
LITTLE JAMES, 41
LITTLE JANE, 19
LLOYD, Richard, 73
LOCKETT, Richard, 32
LOKERMAN, Mary, 78
LOMACK, William, 74
LOMAS, Thomas, 73
LOMAX, Eliza, 86
William, 62, 87
LOMRES, George W., 63
LONEY, 14
LONG, ---, 95
LONSDALE, John W., 31
LORTON, William G., 92
LOUDON, 12
LOUGHLIN, Jonathan, 27
Jonathan N., 26
LOURY, ---, 90
LOVE, Nelson, 57
LOVELL, John, 93
LOWRY, Fanny, 57
LUCAS, Charles, 82

116

Eliza, 62
Lucy, 57
Nacina, 39
Sarah, 9
LUCE, 4, 10
LUCINDA, 81
LUCY, 2, 3, 5, 6, 20
LUELL, Washington G., 86
LULE, 25
LUNKS, John, 43
Sarah, 43
LUTHERS, Charles, 67
LUTHIA---, Charles G., 58
LYDIA, 1, 6
LYLE, Sarah, 66
LYLES, Joe, 43
Tom, 43
LYNN, Jim, 58

-M-
MCCEOIRE, Handy, 11
MCCHEW, George, 69
MCCLEAN, Joseph, 89
MACCUBBIN, Charles, 5
Eleanor, 34
John S., 33
Samuel, 17, 26
MCCUBBIN, Samuel, 28
MACCUBIN, Samuel, 11
Susan, 16
MCCULLOCH, James, 19
MCCURRY, Joseph, 25
MCHENRY, James, 4
MACK, harriett, 103
James Henry, 93
Nelly, 98
Rebecca, 79
William, 99
MACKBEE, Thomas, 3
MACKUBIN, Elizabeth, 2
John, 15
Richard C., 86
MACUBIN, Elizabeth, 58
MADISON, William, 11
MAGRUDER, Alexander, 37
Henry, 59
MAHAND, Nancy, 25
Nanny, 25
MAHONEY, Ann, 14
Annie, 5
Charles, 5, 14
Nancy, 5
MAJOR, 5
MALLONEE, Leonard, 23
MALONY, Leonard, 23
MARGARET, 1, 3, 77
MARIA, 4, 17, 23, 26, 31, 48, 102

MARRIOTT, John, 69
MARSHALL, Mary, 5
Sarah, 5
MARTIN, George, 11, 17, 65
Harry, 17
MARY, 1, 2, 4, 5, 6, 1, 27, 45
MASON, Archibald, 56
MATHIAS, 2
MATILDA, 3, 45
MATTHEW, 1, 24
MATTHEWS, ---, 66
Amos, 73
Anna, 40
Barbara, 52
Bill, 21
Brister, 92
Charles, 21, 86
Daniel, 43
Dick, 30
Edward, 75
Eliza, 43
Elizabeth Ellen, 87
Ellen, 87
Frank, 8
George W., 87
Hannah, 30
Henry, 32, 55, 58, 62, 66, 75, 51
Jacob, 53
James, 26, 61
Joe, 20
John, 40, 66, 79
Joshua, 92
Kitty, 30, 54
Lydia, 43
Margaret, 85
Marion, 81
Mary, 52, 59, 79
Matilda, 59
Milly, 40
Nelly, 30
Nicholas, 4, 6, 53
Polly, 30, 66
Priss, 73
Rachael, 42
Rachel, 30
Rebecca, 42, 69
Sally, 56
Samuel, 55
Sarah, 68, 79, 56
Stephen, 4
Thomas, 43, 80
Vachel, 30
William, 40, 66, 80
William Thomas, 104
MATTHIAS, 18
MAUN, Lavili Louisa, 85

MAUSFIELD, Salisah, 65
MAY, Johnson, 13
MAYERS, George, 23
MAYNADIER, Henry, 2, 78
MAYNARD, Ann Janetta, 75
Foster, 80
John, 39, 67, 89
Lewis, 69, 91
Maria, 67
William, 45
MAZEY, 5
MERCER, Harry, 7
John, 66
Margaret, 43
MERCHANT, Edith, 82
MEREDITH, James, 11
MERREET, Kitty, 34
MERRIKEN, ---, 102
Cassy, 52
Elizabeth, 2, 4
Henry, 97
John, 6, 9, 14, 50, 52, 58, 61
Mahala, 97
Mary, 18, 77, 82, 767
Richard, 2, 6, 12
William, 71, 97
MERRIKIN, Henry, 39
John, 39
MERRIWEATHER, Marry, 27
Mary, 42
Nicholas, 4, 6, 24, 42, 56
Sarah, 22, 24, 28
MERRIWETHER,
Nicholas, 55
MEYERS, George, 23
MIAS, Henry, 81
MILES, Levi, 28
Susan, 82
MILLER, Adam, 57
Harriett Ann, 76
John, 57
Robert, 76
MILLY, 1, 2, 3, 5, 15, 16, 19
MINOR, William, 31
MINT, 10
MINTA, 22, 23, 52
MISTA, 22
MITCHELL, Elizabeth, 12
Jane, 99
Polly, 43
Sally, 102
Sarah Hane, 75
Thomas, 61
William, 74
MOLLY, 27

MONROE, Thomas, 6
MONTGOMERY, Peter, 46
MOORE, Benjamin, 50
Elijah, 57
Frank, 50
Tolly, 50
MORMAN, Nicholas, 11
MORRIS, Henry, 102
Mary Jane, 76
Sarah, 32
MORRISON, Ann, 18
Patience, 42
MORTON, Thomas, 6, 16
MOSES, 2, 4, 24
MUELLIN, Hager, 56
Richard, 56
MULLEN, Dick, 11
Elizabeth, 50
Priscilla, 50
Richard, 50
Thomas, 17
William Henry, 94
MUNDY, Sarah, 46
MUNROE, Charles, 89
MURDOCK, Tye, 59
MURRAY, Ariaima, 83
James, 70
Sarah E., 46, 81
William, 3, 6
MURREA, 2
MURRER, 9
MUTH, Samuel, 66
MYERS, Charlotte, 53
Daniel, 96
Louisa, 51
Margaret, 103

-N-
N---, Benjamin, 67
Betty, 33
NACE, 3, 5
NACH, James, 51
NACHEY, 32
NACIE, 2, 5
NACK, 23
NACKY, 20
NACY, 16, 6
NAN, 3, 5, 20
NANCE, 23
NANCY, 1, 5, 19, 26, 41, 52
NANNY, 3, 5, 16, 33
NATHAN, 28
NEAD, 4
NEALE, Cerissy, 89
David, 58
Francis, 8, 16
George, 73
Kitty, 102

NEALL, Alsey, 100
Caesar, 99
Kussa, 95
NEARRIS, Henry, 102
NECESSITIES, Aaron, 55
NED, 2, 3, 4, 20, 33
NEEDON, Ruth, 37
NEGRO PETER, 72
NELE, 5
NELL, 1, 2, 10
NELLIE, 2
NELLY, 3, 6, 7, 1, 89, 94, 103
NELSON, Benjamin, 28
Nathan, 34
NEPBURN, Susan, 97
Wesley, 97
NETH, Lewis, 54, 59, 68, 76
NEWBURY, Ann, 100
NEWSEN, Sophia, 83
NEWSON, Charles, 94
James, 28
NICECHULL, John, 33
NICHOLAS, 1, 2, 35, 61
NICHOLS, Anthony, 2
Eliza Ann, 55
John, 33
Martha, 104
NICHOLSON, Nelly, 34
NICK, 2, 3
John, 4
NINA, 14
NORMAN, Samuel, 72
Thomas, 3, 8, 11
NORRIS, Eleanor, 34
Elsinore, 34
Mary, 2, 19
Sarah, 19, 32, 59, 64, 67
Thomas, 19
NORWOOD, Betty, 93
John, 4, 13, 26, 51
NYVILLE, Susanna, 35

-O-
OFFER, Ally, 65
Ellen, 100
Henry, 60, 98
John, 77
Peter, 99
Serena, 99
Thomas, 99
Wesley, 75
William, 79
OGLE, Anne, 3
Harriett, 84
Thomas, 86
OLIVER, A---, 55
Elizabeth, 6, 14

Frances, 55
Issac, 6
Jacob, 6, 14
Lucy, 6
Rachael, 6
ORANGE, 27
ORGAN, Henry, 8, 16
ORGANS, Sarah, 9
O'ROUKE, Betty, 70
OSBORN, Bob, 61
Christopher, 3
Fannie, 3
OSGOOD, William, 27
OSS---, Philis, 33
OWENS, Eliza Ann, 83
Henry, 52
Joseph, 97
Margaret, 83
Nicholas, 57
Susan, 83
OWINGS, Delial, 14
Jacob, 67
James, 14
Thomas, 67

-P-
P---, Issac, 23
Nicey, 23
Nicholas, 46
P---SLY, 15
PACA, John P., 2
PACK, Levi, 61
Susan, 62
PACKER, John, 14
PALL, Elizabeth, 77
PARK, Susan, 62
PARKEL, 2
PARKER, 29
Alfred, 57
Andrew, 29, 64
Ann, 9, 12, 104
Benjamin, 31, 88
Betsy, 54
Caroline, 54, 67
Cecelia, 84
Charity, 24, 62
Charles, 8, 12, 22
Daniel, 31
Edward, 25, 64
Eleanor, 72
Elijah, 71, 78
Elisha, 13, 64
Eliza, 41
Elizabeth, 93
Ellen, 12, 94
Emanuel, 60
Frederick, 27
Harriett, 54
Harry, 14

Henrietta, 38
Henry, 18, 30
Herring, 54
Issac, 61, 36
Jacob, 28
James, 12, 35, 81, 93
Jane, 81, 83
John, 9
Joseph, 35, 78
Kitty Ann, 54
Lewis, 80
Lloyd, 30
Louisa, 25
Lydia, 54
Margaret, 12, 54, 70
Martha, 93
Mary, 29, 30, 93
Mary Ann, 41, 84, 95
Mary Eliza, 86
Milly, 22
Molly, 50
Nancy, 41, 54
Ned, 13
Nelly, 68, 39
Nicholas, 28
Peggy, 27
Peter, 20
Richard, 104
Richard Henry, 85
Sally, 68, 74
Samuel, 83
Sarah, 18
Susan, 12, 19, 41, 72
Susane, 41
Susanna, 18
Susannah, 10, 20
Sussanna, 64
Thomas, 19, 34
Washington, 12, 73
William, 19, 54, 72
PARKES, Alfred, 57
PARROTT, John, 79
PARSONS, William, 57
PATIENCE, 1, 10
PATRICK, 1
PATTY, 14
PAUL, Eliza, 89
PEA, Priscilla, 45
PEACO, Samuel, 1, 10, 14
PEACOCK, John M., 63
PEARCE, harriett, 77
PEARMAN, Richard, 90
PEARSON, Mary, 16, 51, 55
  Samuel, 51
PEERER, 1, 14
PEGG, 10
PEGGY, 4
PEMBROKE, Andrew, 2

PEMBROOKE, Towerhill, 2
PENDER, 5
PENN, Joseph, 6
  Joshua, 6
  Mary, 6
  Rachel, 6
PENNINGTON, Elijah, 21, 71
PEPPER, Jerry, 7
PERRY, 3
  Thomas, 80
PETER, 4, 6, 7, 21, 22, 25, 30, 64
PETERS, Jacob, 103
PETERSON, Eliza, 90
  Elizabeth, 104
  James, 93
  Richard, 72
PETTIBONE, 5
  Charles, 6, 11, 13, 26, 28, 37, 43, 51, 61
PHELPS, ---, 87
  Joseph, 56
  Sarah, 27
  William, 78
PHILIP, John, 89
PHILIPS, Issac, 34
  Nancy, 57
PHILIS, 7
PHILL, 16
PHILLIP, 2, 3, 4, 15
PHILLIPS, Charles, 26
  Chloe, 58
  John, 1
  Margaret, 66
  Sarah, 27
  Thomas, 35
PHILPS, Thomas, 23
  William, 76
PINKNEY, Arnelia, 82
  Catherine, 90
  Elizabeth, 90
  John S., 90
  Jonathan, 1
  Jonathon, 17
  Lavinia, 94
  Linden, 90
  Margaret, 90
  N., 8
  Niman, 4
  Richard, 66
  Thomas, 83
  Vivian, 2
  William, 92
PITTS, Edmond, 47
  John, 8, 55
PLINA, 7
PLUMME, Jerome, 4

PLUMMER, A. H., 26
  Ann H., 27
  Gerald, 1
POETT, Joseph S., 3
POINTES, James W., 83
POL, 4
POLL, 1, 4, 5, 13, 14
POLLY, 2, 7, 16, 21
POMPEY, 2
POMPHREY, Aquila, 6
POWELL, Emeline, 98
  George, 45
  Jack, 52
  John, 98
  Lewis Henry, 101
  Mahaila, 50
  Minty, 34
  Rachel, 50
  Richard, 101
  Tom, 74
  William, 63
PR---, Cato, 69
PRATT, Ann Maria, 65
  David, 40
  Issac, 97
  Rachel, 67
  Teresa, 95
PREI, Stephen, 38
PRELL, Priscilla, 70
PRICE, Henrietta, 13
  Henry, 13, 41
  Henry H., 57
  James, 21, 22, 27, 63
  John, 22, 25, 40
  John Henry, 65
  John M., 65
  Judy, 60
  L., 39
  Nancy, 7
  Sarah, 66
  Thomas, 26, 63
  William Smith, 68
PRINCE, 3
PRISCILLA, 7, 27, 83
PRISS, 4, 5, 7, 13, 20
PRITCHARD, Mary, 35
  William, 63, 66, 67
PROUD, Rezin, 27
PROUT, Charity, 22
  Debby, 45
  Edmund, 27
  Edward, 27
  Elizabeth, 85
  Emmanuel, 27
  Frederick, 8
  Harriet, 18
  Isabella, 4
  Jacob, 66
  Joseph, 23

June, 69
Kitty, 19, 24, 69
Lot, 53
Mary, 28, 45
Philip, 14
Polly, 4
Richard, 5
Samuel, 26
William, 4, 5, 34
PRYOR, James, 35
PUMPHREY, Ebenezer, 1, 2, 44
PUR---, Sarah Ann, 49
PURDY, Mary, 84

-Q-
QUEEN, ---, 18
Adeline, 81
Agnes, 64
Andrew, 29, 98
Ann, 42, 61, 73
Anne, 53, 78
Arris, 69
Barbara, 96
Benjamin, 66
Bill, 102
Charity, 91
Chastity, 18
Crissy, 44
Daniel, 56
David, 16, 80
Delia, 44
Dennis, 17
Edward, 48, 78
Eleais, 24
Eleanor, 18
Elias, 80, 92
Eliza, 44, 46, 61
Eliza Ann, 64
Elizabeth, 54, 64, 99
Emanuel, 39
Fanny, 19, 50
Gabriel, 12, 33, 78
Hannah, 96
Harriett, 44, 48
Henrietta, 73
Henry, 104
Issac, 12, 78, 98
Jacob, 49
James, 12, 60, 86
Jane, 57
Joe, 28
John, 15, 18, 22, 32, 35, 48, 49, 53, 72, 93
Joseph, 48, 83
Julia, 79
Julianna, 57
Kizzey, 35
L---, 56

Louisa, 74
Margaret, 39, 60
Mary, 12, 15, 27, 42, 44, 84, 96, 100
Mary Ann, 10, 62
Mary Jane, 88
McCall, 26
Memca, 89
Michael, 49
Milly, 44
Monaco, 44
Nancy, 15, 33, 42, 46, 63, 67, 94
Nellie, 15
Noah, 48
Paul, 17
Rachel, 54
Ragis, 19
Richard, 77
Robert, 15, 48, 69
Sally, 27, 73, 91, 96
Samuel, 32
Sarah, 35, 43, 61
Stephen, 88
Susan, 54, 74, 88, 96
Thomas, 48, 80, 81, 83, 93
Walter, 79
William, 12, 15, 44, 48, 50, 58, 84, 96
Winny, 44
QUEENE, Robert, 63
QUEENS, Matilda, 52

-R-
R---, Christina, 71
RACHAEL, 2, 3, 12, 47
RACHEL, 2, 4, 5, 9, 20, 93, 95
RACKEL, 2
RANDALL, A., 89
Alexander, 79
John, 93
Thomas, 93
RANDLE, James, 63
RAWLINGS, Benjamin, 99
Frederick, 80
Henry, 65
John, 99
Ned, 36
William, 80, 83, 89
RAWLLINGS, Dennis, 89
RAY, Caroline, 85
Rachel, 84
Susan, 61
REBEAH, 3
REBECCA, 1, 2, 12
RECORDS, Mary, 3
REDMILES, John, 81
REECE, John, 31

REUNARDO, Ann, 83
REYNOLDS, William, 5
REZIN, 18, 23, 58
RHODA, 28
RHODE, 1, 16
RHODES, Chloe, 56
John, 56
RICHARD, 10, 24, 25, 28, 33
RICHARDS, Hiriam, 60
Priscilla, 37
RICHARDSON, Catherine, 90
Harriett A., 77
Hester, 76
Jack, 5
James, 6, 38
Mary, 14
Mary Ann, 92
Mary Jane, 100
Richard, 72
Sasanna, 69
Susan, 77
William, 103
RIDEOUT, Horatio, 2, 3, 6, 7
John, 66, 100, 102, 104
John of Samuel, 73
Mary, 1, 5, 6, 7
Mary Ann, 38
Samuel, 1, 2, 3, 4, 6, 7, 8, 56
RIDGELY, Absalom, 71
Charles S., 17
Greenberry, 2
Greenbury, 12, 45
Henry, 77
Mary, 55
Mary Ellen, 94
Nicholas, 55
Philemon D., 34
Rachel, 63
William, 3
RIGGS, Sarah, 10, 23, 24
RINGGOLD, Ann, 60
Polly, 44
RINGOLD, Edward, 91
Emily, 91
ROADS, John, 56
ROBERISON, Thomas, 85
ROBERT, 2, 3, 4, 1
ROBERTS, Daniel, 71
Frances, 71
ROBERTSON, Caroline, 71
Matthew, 1
ROBINSON, Caroline, 32
David, 7, 20, 27, 77, 83
Dow Madison, 33
Elizabeth, 61, 70, 76

Hester, 32
Joseph, 32
June, 96
Martha, 49, 81, 94
Mary, 11, 79
Thomas, 81, 86, 89, 102
ROBISON, ---, 69
ROBOSON, Martha, 92
ROGERS, Arthur, 2
Mary, 9
Nancy, 9
ROLES, Harrietta, 81
ROSE, 10, 17
Sarah, 92
ROSS, Eleanor, 5
Jacob, 94
James, 56
John, 29, 51
John Jerry, 97
Julia, 46
Kitty, 61
Nancy, 37
Robert, 38
Thomas, 78
William, 78
ROUSALE, Elijah, 63
ROUSBY, 5
ROWLES, David, 11
John, 11
Samuel, 74
RUTH, 1, 4, 20
RUTHY, 2
RUTLAND, Harriet, 53
Sally, 53
Sarah Ann, 88

-S-
S---, Elizabeth, 87
Geneva, 29
Sidney, 88
SADLER, Maria, 69
SAL, 5
SALL, 1, 9, 10, 14, 45
SALLIE JOE, 1
SALLY, 14
SAM, 1, 3, 4, 12
SAMPSON, 24
Charlotte, 99
SAMUEL, 2, 4, 5, 6
Frederick, 49
SANDERS, Celena, 88
Dinah, 52
Elizabeth, 52
Mary, 70
SANDLER, Emory, 65
SANDS, Tom, 21
SARAH, 1, 2, 3, 4, 5, 6, 13, 16, 34, 104
SARY, 98

SASSINGTON, Polly, 69
SAUCY, 10
SAUL, 23
SAUNDERS, Rachel, 14
Richard, 53
SAVOY, Ann, 55
Elizabeth, 48
Martha, 97
Moses, 35
Rachel, 7
Richard, 7, 48
Sarah, 8
William, 35
SCOGGINS, Eliza, 75
Samuel, 61
SCOGGLE, Anne, 17
SCOTT, Alfred, 76
Charity, 91, 94
Dinah, 64
Doll, 62
Eliza, 62
Ellen, 95
Frances, 54
George, 44, 95
Gustavious, 39
Harriett, 103
Helen, 1
Jane, 101
John, 72
Leonard, 2, 3, 5, 14, 15, 16, 17, 29
Lucy, 3
Maria, 54
Milly, 77
N., 32
Nicholas, 22
Phillis, 58
Thomas, 99
Upton, 4
SCRIVENER, Martha, 99
William, 48
SCRIVNER, James, 48
SEAPPIN, clara, 99
SEARKINS, John, 68
SEAVALL, Jemima, 91
SEEMS, Richard, 80
SELBY, Elizabeth, 8
Harriet, 73
Joseph, 10, 13, 41, 42
SELLINAN, ---W, 104
SELLMAN, John, 64
Margaret Ann, 103
Thomas, 103
SEMINS, Ellen, 90
SEMMES, Allen, 83
Jacob, 79
Sarah Ann, 101
SEVERNESS, Eliza, 62
Isacc, 62

SEWELL, Benjamin, 63, 69
Gabriel, 92
John, 16, 36
SHAAFF, Charlotte, 37
Margaret, 85
SHAFF, Arthur, 4
John T., 1
Mary, 85
SHALLOP, 2
SHARP, Jim, 62
SHAVIS, Charlotte Ann, 94
SHAW, James, 70
John, 1
Mary, 83
SHEEN, Andrew, 57
SHENER, 15
SHEPHARD, Butch, 62
Catherine Ellen, 101
Henry, 58
SHERBET, Benjamin, 80, 86
SHIPLEY, Catherine, 4
Eleanor, 60
Hannah, 4
Larkin, 80
Mary, 55
Richard, 2
Sam, 4
William, 86
SHORT, Thomas, 97
William, 97
SHORTER, Charles, 32
Charyly, 97
Daniel L., 68
Elizabeth, 89
Jane, 25, 72
Mary Frances, 71
Peter, 25, 32, 72
Sarah, 25
SHUAFF, Ann, 51
SIBBY, 45
SIFTON, Charles Henry, 103
Jim, 82
SIMMES, Ellen, 90
Juner, 90
SIMMONS, Elizabeth, 2
Thomas, 68
Williams, 16
SIMMS, Angeline, 73
Elizabeth, 63
John, 81, 94
Samuel, 101
Thomas, 81
Wesley, 73
SIMON, 31
SIMPSON, Edward, 100
Mary A., 100

SIMS, Frank, 68
SISCO, John, 81
SLATER, Charles, 58
SLIVER, Andrew, 80
SMALLWOOD, Ann, 71
SMITH, ---, 96
  Abram, 21
  Benjamin, 42
  Bessie, 33
  Daniel, 51, 83, 102
  Dinah, 77
  Elizabeth, 64, 77
  Elizabeth Ann, 57
  Ellen, 82, 83
  Harriet, 51
  Hater, 83
  Henry, 102
  John, 6, 10, 25, 38, 62
  Joseph, 63
  Joseph G., 104
  Lucy, 10
  Mary, 17, 31
  Mary Ellen, 96
  Nancy, 31
  Sarah, 100
  Susan, 27
  Sussanna, 6
  William Henry, 60
  William S., 66
SMITHERS, George, 79
SMOTHER, Louisa, 96
SMOTHERS, Ann, 98
  Edward, 93
  Emily, 92
  James, 79
  James Henry, 80
  Jim, 78
  John Andrew Jackson, 81
  Levinia, 90
  Lindy, 94
  Maria, 87
SNOW, Richard P., 70
SNOWDEN, Ann, 62
  Anna Maria, 53, 54, 70
  Bea, 39
  Benjamin, 88
  Charlotte, 68
  Eliza, 47
  G--- H., 34
  Hester, 68
  Jane, 92
  Mary Eliza, 87
  Nace, 5
  Nase, 8
  Nicholas, 102
  Patience, 56
  R. P., 97
  Rachael, 18, 35
  Rachel, 17, 20, 30, 53

Rezin, 55, 74, 81
Rezin H., 104, 22, 77, 79, 80, 81, 93
Rezin S., 99
Richard P., 71, 72, 79, 88, 101
  Sarah, 47
  William, 17
SOLLIMAN, John, 104
SOLOMON, 2, 4, 28
SOOK, 2, 79
SOPHIA, 1, 8, 24, 72, 104
SORELL, Matilda, 69
SOUTH, John, 58
  Mary, 31
SPARROW, Cassandra, 16
  Harriet, 66
  Susan, 75
  Thomas, 10
SPEAKS, Elizabeth, 18
SPENCER, Ann, 47
  James, 65
  Kitty, 43
  Nelly, 58
  Philemon, 3, 7
  Philomon, 2
  Phoebe Ann, 89
SPRIGG, ---, 28
  Margaret, 4, 5
  Richard, 8
SPRIGGS, Jerry, 24
STACEY, 19
STANSBURY, Benjamin, 45
  Joseph, 3, 11, 15
  Rachael, 2, 3
STEELE, Mary, 18
STEP, Charity, 49
STEPHEN, 8, 13
STEPHENS, Elizabeth, 101
  James, 101
STEPHEY, Eliza, 94
STEPNEY, ---, 87
  Charles, 2
  Eliza Ann, 87
  Harriett, 88
  William, 87
STEVENS, Betty, 3
  Elizabeth, 50
  Maria, 37
  Robert, 64
  Sophia, 37
STEWARD, Elizabeth, 102
STEWART, Amelia, 79
  Ann, 34, 89
  Benjamin, 55
  Betsy, 74
  Caleb, 99

Catherine, 95
Charles, 5, 30, 35, 93
Deborah, 41
Eliza Ann, 75
Henny, 94
James, 88
Jane, 74, 75
John, 1, 81, 92
Kitty, 76
Lemuel, 95
Mary, 46, 65
Mary Ann, 77, 94
Mordecai, 9, 10
Phillip, 76
Poll, 46
Rachel, 74
Sarah, 83
Sarah J., 95
Susan, 27
Theodore T., 34
William, 5, 21
STINCHCOMB, A., 27
  Anne, 1
  George, 17, 26
  Nathanial, 73
STOCKETT, Thomas
  James, 103
  William, 5
STONE, John, 3
  John Hoskin, 5
STOVEWALL, Mary, 39
STRINGER, Richard, 22
STUBLING, C. H., 82
STUVELL, Mary, 39
SUBBRO, 5
SUCK, 1, 27, 80, 96
SUGGS, Eliza Ann, 92
  Rachel, 83
SUKEY, 2, 3, 5, 16, 25
SULIVAN, Sophia, 33
SULLIVAN, Thomas, 67
SUNDER, Elizabeth, 47
SUSAN, 13, 15, 17
SUSSANAH, 3, 4
SUSSANNA, 5, 6
SWANN, Henry, 55
  Nicholas, 73
SWEETSER, Seth, 5
SWEETSON, Seth, 11
SWETZER, Seth, 5
SWORMSTEDT, Nicholas, 52
SYLELY, 1
SYLVESTER, James, 40
  Mary, 40

-T-

T---, Thomas, 57
William, 33

TALBOT, Richard, 3
TALBOTT, Murray, 9
  Richard, 11
  Samuel, 75
TALLY, Charles, 98
TANNER, Jeremiah, 46
TANNERT, Jeremiah, 4
  Peggy, 4
TAYLOR, Anne, 24
  Cecelia, 102
  Dilly, 23
  Joshua, 93
  Luce, 57
  Patience, 35
TH---, Robert, 60
THEKELLS, Francis, 6
THOMAS, 1, 2, 6, 8, 10, 99, 103, 5
  Abraham, 40
  Ann Catherine, 85
  Benjamin, 60, 68, 71
  Charles, 41
  Daniel, 56
  Eleanor Yieldhall, 18
  Flora, 56
  George, 52
  Henry, 70, 84
  Jack, 57
  James, 76
  John, 2, 13, 15, 35, 67, 101
  John Chew, 6, 8, 14, 21, 29, 31, 40, 52, 66
  Joseph, 19
  Linda, 100
  Mary, 22, 47, 54, 74
  Nancy, 65
  Phillip I., 33
  Phillip W., 13
  Priscilla, 56
  Rose, 74
  Sarah, 57
  Susan, 65
  Thomas, 36
  Tom, 40
THOMPSON, Jane, 95
  Jim, 103
  Kitty, 34
  Princees, 50
  Rachel, 88
TILGHMAN, Emory, 37
  William, 97
TIM, 1
TIMMINS, Edward, 7
TIMMONS, Williams, 16
TITUS, 1
  James, 9, 78
  Richard, 76
  Sarah, 76

TOBY, 1
TODD, Polly, 46
TOM, 4, 5, 18, 26
TOOGOOD, Ann, 41
  Benjamin, 48
  Bill, 59
  Eliza, 90
  Ellen, 39, 68
  George, 39
  Horace, 69
  Jane, 79
  John, 28, 82
  Joshua, 2, 7, 74
  Mary, 48
  Mary Ann, 97
  Nancy, 43
  Nicholas, 48
  Polly, 43
  Rosetta, 78
  Thomas, 96
  Wile, 75
TOPPIN, Sarah, 29
TROUT, John, 95
TROY, Benjamin, 26
  Daniel, 28
  Henry, 26
TURNER, ---, 97
  Allen, 49
  Catherine, 90
  Charles, 9
  Eleanor, 49
  Ellen, 97
  Harriett, 48
  Henry, 7
  James, 9, 17, 77, 78
  John T., 104
  Mary, 78
  mary, 98
  Matthew, 85
  Milly, 55
  Rebecca, 30, 51
  Richard, 50
  Sally, 18
  Samuel, 89
  Sarah, 50
  Thomas, 49
  Thomas W., 42
  William, 36, 41, 56
TYDINGS, Cornelia, 81
  Eliza, 98, 100
  Henry, 81
  John H., 76
  Sophey, 58
TYLER, Augusta, 89
  Elizabeth, 97
  Thomas, 65

-U-
URGAHART, Bill, 36

Jim, 36
URGUHART, Bob, 36
URQUAHART, Fancy, 55
URSOLTON, Henry, 65
USHER, James, 2
USILTON, Benjamin, 71

-V-
VACHE, 21
VACHEL, 30, 31
VALENTINE, 2, 4
VANHORN, Issac, 63
VERN, 1
VINEY, 13

-W-
W---, George, 83
  Huel, 28
  Sussanah, 19
WALKER, ---, 55
  Alice, 76
  Hannah, 71
  Horace, 77
  James, 98
  Liley, 44
  Mary, 45
  Richard, 74
  Robert, 39
  Samuel, 70
WALLACE, Anna Maria, 84
  Beky, 42
  Charles, 3, 7
  Frank, 86
  George Washington, 84
  Henrietta, 94
  Henry, 75
  Jane, 97
  Mary, 5
  Michael, 74
  Rachel, 9
  Richard, 50
  Robert, 5, 10, 58
  Sam, 36
WALLAS, Ceasar, 47
WALLS, Dinah, 69
  George, 58
WAPPION, 6
WARD, Adeline, 59
  Charles, 77
  Elizabeth, 61
  John, 101
  Lucy, 17
  Sarah A., 80
  Sophia, 61
  Thomas H., 89
  Walter, 79
WARFIELD, Amelia, 17
  Bani, 6

Lancelot, 9
Mary Ann, 37, 70
Nicholas, 3
Polly, 43
Rachel, 6
Robert, 17, 37
Sarah, 59
Thomas, 89
WARNER, Henry, 84
Nancy, 31
William, 84
WARREN, Henrietta, 103
Nancy, 31
Thomas Allen, 102
William Henry, 102
WASHINGTON, 26
Robert, 90
WATERS, Asbury, 71
Charles, 63, 75, 90
Charles A., 79
Elizabeth, 84
Ellen, 84
Eugene, 70
Hester, 84
Lydia, 34
Noah, 39
Peter, 63
Rachel A., 74
Richard, 74
Vachel, 39
William, 74
WATKINS, Charles, 40
Daniel, 76
Henrietta, 46
Jane, 46
John, 29
Kitty, 11
Lybia Ann, 81
Margaret Ann, 100
Maria, 42
N. J., 98
Nicholas, 70, 78
Nicholas J., 13, 16, 79
Rachael, 2
Samuel, 40, 51
Sarah E., 46
Sophia, 42, 101
Stephen, 30
Thomas, 11, 15, 40
William, 9, 12, 13
WATSON, Charlotte, 54
WATTS, George, 9
Phillip H., 9
Richard B., 23
WEB---, Mary L., 28
WEEDON, Jonathon, 79
Richard, 6
WEEM, David, 55
WEEMS, David, 4, 5, 27, 67

James, 13
James N., 10
John, 1, 4
John of Richard, 13
Mason, 2, 8
Richard, 3, 30, 49, 73
William, 1, 2, 4, 5, 6, 7,
15, 47, 55, 66
WELCH, Aaron, 57, 59, 68,
71
Henrietta, 89
John, 4
Robert of Ben, 36, 37, 49
WELKS, Phillip H., 72
WELLS, Catherine, 99
Dennis, 79
Elizabeth M., 97
George, 92
Nanny, 51
Phillip H., 72
Priscilla, 99
Sally, 96
WEST, Elizabeth, 88
Jacob, 15
Julianna, 52
Lydia, 73
William, 78
WESTON, Richard, 88
Thomas, 101
WHARSIE, Eleanor, 2
James, 2
WHEELER, Esther, 6
Jocky, 6
WHI---, George, 60
WHI., George, 60
WHIPPS, George, 55, 82
WHIPS, George, 2
WHITE, Gideon, 5, 9
Samuel, 79
WHITTINGHAM, Thomas,
1
WHITTINGTON, Thomas,
84
WIL---, Henrietta, 71
WILKENS, Anna, 1
Mary Ann, 83
WILKES, William, 41
WILKINS, Peter, 55
William, 7
WILL, 1, 4, 21
WILLIAM, 1, 2, 3, 4, 5, 6,
8, 14, 22, 25, 31, 37, 64
WILLIAMS, ---, 64
Alexander, 98
Anne, 76
Ariana, 58
Betsy, 52
Bryan, l, 14, 31
Caesar, 41

Charles, 48
Charlotte, 42, 51
Darky, 56
Dick, 21
Edith, 104
Editha, 103
Edward, 54
Eleanor, 10
Elias, 87
Elijah, 39, 45
Elizabeth, 58, 103
Elizabeth Ann, 68
Elizabeth C---, 73
Emeline, 98
George, 80
Harriet, 58
Henry, 84
Isaac, 45
J., 96
Jacob, 58, 61, 62, 100,
102
James, 23
Jinny, 76
John, 59
Joseph, 59
Laura, 78
Lewis, 101
Linny, 58
Lucy, 89
Maria, 62
Martha Ann, 38
Mary, 51, 52, 68
Mary Ann, 103
Mary Jane, 98
Matilda, 52
Nace, 22
Nanny, 3
Nathan, 1
Philes, 71
Phillip, 98
Phillis, 71
Ponphrey, 57
Rachel, 6
Rebecca, 6, 104
Richard, 22, 58
Robert, 83
Sally, 59
Samuel, 52, 90
Sarah, 52, 56
Thomas, 102
Vachel, 98
William, 10, 36, 41, 58, 90
WILLILGMAN, Charles
William, 35
WILLILY, 3
WILLKES, John, 4
WILLS, Frederick, 29
George, 22, 36
Louisa, 64

WILLSBY, Benjamin, 63
WILSON, Eleanor, 49
  Eliza A., 49
  Harriett, 83
  Harriott, 49
  Henry, 34
  Hillary, 62
  Jerry, 82
  Julia, 49
  Kitty, 102
  Lewis Edward, 77
  Mary, 75
  Samuel, 12, 46
  Thomas, 1, 6, 17, 34
  William, 49, 53
WINALE, Augustine, 72
WINCHESTER, jacob, 95
WINGS, Dennis, 101
  Maria, 90
WINTERS, James, 16
  William, 13
WOOD, ---, 46
  Elizabeth, 100
  Hester, 100
  John, 35
  Samuel, 77, 82
WOODFIELD, William, 27
WOODWARD, Jane, 13
  Margaret Ann, 86
  Sally, 86
WOODWARDS, Eleanor, 72
WOOTEN, Charles Edward, 79
  James, 8
  John William, 79
WOOTON, Margaret, 104
WOOTTS, Philip H., 60
WORTHINGTON, ---, 69
WRIGHT, ---, 32
  Benjamin, 32
  Betsy, 85
  Charles, 86
  Eleanor, 41
  Elizabeth, 91
  Hester, 91
  Israel, 74
  John, 73
  Joseph, 97
  Perry, 73
  Rachel, 91
  Susan, 46
WY---, Mary, 22
WYORILL, Susannah, 60
WYRELL, Sussanna, 57
-Y-
YALE, Harriet, 26
YELDELL, willilam T., 3
YIELDHALL, Eleanor, 18, 20, 25, 26, 31
YOUNG, Ann, 83
  Charles, 73
  Darkey, 25
  Ellen, 21, 70
  Fanny, 70
  Forrester, 43
  Henry, 104
  Jane, 81
  John, 43
  Louisa, 101
  Martha Ellen, 101
  Mary, 58
  Milly, 43
  Nel, 21
  Rachel, 83
  Richard, 67
  Rose, 67
  Susan, 67
  Thomas, 45, 78

-Z-
ZACK, 3, 22

Heritage Books by Jerry M. Hynson:

Absconders, Runaways and Other Fugitives in the Baltimore City and County Jail

Baltimore [Maryland] City Jail War Docket

Baltimore Life Insurance Company Genealogical Abstracts

District of Columbia Runaway and Fugitive Slave Cases, 1848–1863

Free African-Americans Maryland, 1832: Including Allegany, Anne Arundel, Calvert, Caroline, Cecil, Charles, Dorchester, Frederick, Kent, Montgomery, Queen Anne's, and St. Mary's Counties

Maryland Freedom Papers, Volume 1: Anne Arundel County

Maryland Freedom Papers, Volume 2: Kent County

Maryland Freedom Papers, Volume 3: Maryland Colonization Society Manumission Book, 1832–1860

The African American Collection: Anne Arundel County, Maryland Marriage Licenses, 1865–1888

The African American Collection: Cecil County, Maryland Indentures, 1777–1814

The African American Collection: Kent County, Maryland Marriages, 1865–1888

www.ingramcontent.com/pod-product-compliance
Lightning Source LLC
Chambersburg PA
CBHW070456090426
42735CB00012B/2581